THE MUSHROOM LOVER'S

MUSHROOM COOKBOOK

AND PRIMER

01/17/10

To Jim

Life is short...
find time for fungus!

Amy Farges

THE MUSHROOM LOVER'S

MUSHROOM COOKBOOK

AND PRIMER

BY AMY FARGES

CO-OWNER OF AUX DELICES DES BOIS™
RECIPES WITH CHRISTOPHER STYLER

WORKMAN PUBLISHING · NEW YORK

Library of Congress Cataloging-in-Publication Data
Farges, Amy.
The mushroom lover's mushroom cookbook and primer / Amy Farges.
p. cm.
ISBN 0-7611-2202-8 (hc.)—ISBN 0-7611-0660-X (pbk.)
1. Cookery (Mushrooms) 2. Mushrooms. I. Title
TX804.F37 2000
641.6'58—dc21   00-030670

Cover design by Paul Hanson
Book design by Lisa Hollander with Jeanne Hogle and Susan Macleod

Workman Publishing Company, Inc.
708 Broadway
New York, NY 10003-9555
www.workman.com

Printed in the United States of America
First Printing September 2000
10 9 8 7 6 5 4 3 2 1

For Thierry,
Julien, and Claire
with love

Acknowledgments

Thanks go first to my husband and business partner, Thierry, who not only got me into this larger-than-life book project, but also had a brilliant idea thirteen years ago: "Let's sell wild mushrooms, honey! Nobody's doing it!" Thierry made sure I missed nothing of his mushroom heritage. Each time we visited friends and relatives in France, there were lovingly prepared mushrooms, French mushroom magazines to review, and tours to museums and truffle growers planned for us. Once I was expert enough to write this book, he spent countless Saturdays hauling our children Julien and Claire off to playgrounds and museums, kept quiet at the fifth straight dinner of mushrooms, and shouldered my share of the business as book deadlines neared. I couldn't have chosen a more exquisite partner in life and love.

When I was little, Alma McAllister, my mother, made sure I had a pencil and paper next to my bed to record my random bursts of poetic inspiration. Later, when I graduated from college, my father, Bill McAllister, pushed me into my first typing classes. Then they pitched in when the assignments came through. During this project they babysat our children countless times, left encouraging messages on my answering machine, and would have written the book for me if I'd just asked (darn!). My brothers and sisters pulled through countless times, too, reminding me that big ideas are accomplished in small steps.

Chris Styler was such a natural fit for this project that I danced a jig the day we re-met after a dozen years of being out of touch. There can't be a more good humored, easygoing, creative, and exacting cooking professional in the world. I always giggle when I think about meeting him across subway turnstiles and on crushingly busy street corners to exchange recipe samples and fresh mushrooms. His inquiring mind, enviable patience, and clear thinking come through in the recipes—you will see as you follow the directions that he sees things from a beginner's point of view, reassuringly suggesting what you might encounter en route to finished dish.

I am really grateful to my editor Suzanne Rafer for breaking this huge terrifying project into manageable parts for me. She kept me on track, and even more amazingly, kept her cool when we hit the inevitable glitches, like a featured mushroom rendered obsolete by its producers, on the eve of publication. She also taught me a thing or two about the human aspect of book publishing (not to mention showing me the finer points of mechanical pencils!).

The whole staff at Workman, from Peter Workman on through the troops, were so responsive that it was a pleasure to build this book with them. I thought I'd send the art department around the bend, yet under the direction of Lisa Hollander and Paul Hanson, they wove a stunning tapestry of elegance, practicality, and whimsy to house my recipes. Thanks, also to publicist Jim Eber, and the many others who helped get this book to press and into the bookstore.

All the chefs who dropped their grill tongs and butcher knifes to put their recipes onto paper are the real heroes of the mushroom world. We've grown up with a lot of them—Tom Colicchio, Kerry Heffernan, Mario Batali, Thierry Rautureau, Michael Lomonaco—and feed off their inspiration. The chef who folds a chanterelle into a seafood emulsion or trickles truffle oil over salmon tartare creates an excitement that is too powerful to resist. And so many thanks to the mentors, friends, and customers who contributed recipes, bringing a personal note to this book.

The chefs, suppliers, and world of mushroom people who shared their insights and passion with me will see themselves in the pages that follow. Thank you, everyone!

Amy Farges

Contents

INTRODUCTION:
The Many Fungus Among Us

*I*s there anything more provocative and mysterious than a mushroom? This fungus defies the logic followed by plant and animal. In its various forms, the wild mushroom resembles a chicken's feathers, a head of cauliflower, and a pig's ear. A menu that lists Lobster and Oyster is as likely as not to promise a heady mushroom feast. This little nonconformist can't be planted nor ordered in specific sizes. Yet it holds our palates in thrall and in titillating suspense. Its flavors range from earthy to fruity to seafood-like, with dazzling possibilities for the home cook. It surprises us with sweet succulence, toothsome crunch, and vibrant color. Every wild mushroom tempts us with a chance at gastronomic Russian roulette. Add to that its terribly ephemeral nature, and you'll agree the wild mushroom holds mighty power over us.

It wasn't always this way. Aux Delices des Bois, the wild mushroom and truffle business my husband Thierry Farges and I have nur-tured for thirteen years, has always invested in diversity. In fact, our offerings expanded, so our name changed to Marché aux Delices, with our mushroom and truffle line now bearing the trademark Aux Delices des Bois. But before the company came to be, mushrooms in the marketplace were generic— whitish, plumpish, and often past their prime. Our business was born out of and fed into a targeted need.

We rented half of a restaurant cooler too short to stand erect in, pressed an inherited (and intermit-tently broken-down) Chevette into use, and got up at dawn to deliver shiitake, portobello, cremini, and oyster mushrooms to adventurous American chefs. We didn't know— or care—that we were partaking in the advent of a new food era. Not when a major Oregon mushroom source told us to call back when our company became something. Not when restaurants expected thirty days credit and farmers gave fifteen. And certainly not on tow days (courtesy of NYPD blues), when we made deliveries on the subway and with borrowed supermarket shopping carts.

It all seems so exciting, looking back at our little mushroom business, in the making and in the growth of wild mushrooms as a food category. Eventually, we busted out at the seams and set up a warehouse in a then-sleepy Manhattan neighborhood called Tribeca. Too many yellowfoot, black trumpet, and hedgehog mushrooms in a shipment meant begging cooler space from neighboring restaurants. Then the mail-order business started, first as a fun thing, and ending up so successful we could barely keep up with it. Walk-in customers, sometimes three deep at our makeshift counter, made schmoozing and recipe-trading my second full-time business.

Therein lies the reason for this book. There are so many cooks who didn't get a chance to stop in at our Tribeca warehouse. The always extemporaneous cooler tours (especially popular in August!) ended, but not before we got an idea of what people wanted to know. I hope all the answers lie within these pages.

Each mushroom has its own texture, its own affinities, its own preferred cooking method. Even size is a factor in preparation. Thierry, my partner in business and marriage, and I will never tire of wild mushrooms. We've cooked our way through fifty-two seasons of them. And yet, each season's impending arrivals leave us both nervous and thrilled with anticipation. Will the morels go to worm before we've had our fill? Will black trumpets have a summer season this year? With mushrooms always fruiting somewhere in the world, we're confident we'll never have to do without. We eat them not only because stacks of mushroom-filled wood crates lie tempting us in the cooler but also because there's not an ingredient you can name that doesn't pair up with one mushroom or another. Mushrooms never get old or boring.

The *we* in this book refers sometimes to Thierry and me as a couple, other times to Aux Delices des Bois as a company. But if the truth be known, there never was a difference between the two. As dedicated as we are to the business, we are to each other, and that's what makes the words *À table* the most meaningful ones we can say.

A table, alors!

Mushrooms 101

As a neophyte "foodie" in the early '80s, I moved to the Big City, New York, where foodiness was oozing out of every third storefront. After a day of tasting my way through all the gourmet boutiques, emporiums, and related purveyors I could find, I took refuge in a local bar. In the glow of the Bud sign, red leather stools invited cool anonymity . . . and blissful ignorance. I asked the bartender what kind of wine he poured. "This here's your basic white, and we got red too," came the response. "How nice," I mused, "no choices to make!"

The simple life applied to mushrooms, too. Buttons, whites, supermarket variety—all these names referred to the white-beige, bulbous, cultivated mushroom. Flash forward to the present, and the tremendous variety out there, so many in fact that getting familiar with them can be daunting, but well worth the effort. A good way to understand new types is to just try one at a time. Buy a handful and substitute it for the white mushrooms called for in your favorite recipes.

Here are some guidelines to exotic and wild mushrooms. Specifics are spelled out in the primer, under each mushroom's profile (see pages 287 to 323).

Wild and Cultivated Mushrooms

Before the food category "mushroom" took on a life of its own, our choices were pretty limited to either cultivated white mushrooms or foraged wild mushrooms. Since the cultivation boom hit in the mid-'80s, the line between cultivated and wild mushrooms has blurred. Some cultivated varieties—known as exotic to the USDA (U.S. Department of Agriculture)—are so flavorful that consumers tend to think of them as wild. Shiitakes (a cultivated mushroom) have an earthy pungency, which to my taste is more exciting than a wild oyster mushroom. What really matters is that you like what you're eating. The following introduction to cultivated and wild mushrooms will help you navigate the produce market and plan seasonal menus. For more details, see the Wild Mushroom Calendar (page 288).

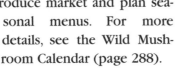

CULTIVATED EXOTIC MUSHROOMS

The first mushrooms to make a big splash in the 1980s were shiitake, cremini, portobello, and oyster. These varieties cost between $8 and $20 a pound and were available only on the shelves of fancy food stores. They were produced by farms and were more readily available than wild mushrooms.

Not all cultivated mushrooms are imitations of varieties that grow in nature. "Browns," the name originally given to cremini, are a more flavorful variation of the common white mushroom. The portobello is an overgrown cremini. Instead of being harvested small, it is allowed to grow about a week longer, which changes its texture—cremini are juicy, portobellos are dry.

Shiitake was first cultivated outdoors on fallen logs in Japan. It went from being a rare, seasonal variety to a commonly used mushroom in a short time span. Farmers not content to reproduce the pearly-gray oyster mushroom, developed it in designer shades: pale blue, ruddy pink, and canary yellow.

Hen of the woods, wine caps, and morels—all wild—are now cultivated. Spawn banks and international cultivation experts now make available such exotic varieties as pompom and honshimeji.

The flavors of exotic mushrooms, though cultivated, are anything but tame. Creamy, spicy, or earthy, they are every bit as exciting as wild varieties. We can use them all year and can generally expect a consistent size, shape, and flavor.

WILD MUSHROOMS

*I*f exotic mushrooms are the safe investment, wild ones are high-risk. Their availability is erratic; sizes and flavors vary; they usually cost more; and they have a shorter shelf life. But the taste payoff is huge. And there's a kind of breathless anticipation associated with wild mushrooms—morels announce that spring has *finally* arrived, and black truffles trumpet the beginning of winter holiday feasts and splurges.

Wild mushrooms are picked in the woods, off riverbanks, in the desert, on lawns, in parking lots. They are organic. Little nibbles mean a deer or other grazer got to the mushroom first; holes mean little critters are paying rent. The roots and caps can be hopelessly matted with dirt, sand, pine needles, and small leaves. They taste *of* the forest and all those damp, leafy, piney aromas we so enjoy on walks in the woods.

Wild mushrooms take flavor nuances from the soil where they grow. Add to that a mixed bag of variables—size, moisture content, and harvest date—and you can pretty much bet a mushroom variety will never taste exactly the same way twice. Porcini from Italy and cèpes from France can taste and look different, but the flavor difference has more to do with the terrain they were plucked from than the country's official borders. So unless your fungus cravings are associated with something like an incredibly romantic fling in Piedmont during the porcini harvest, try to be flexible about the origins of mushrooms you buy.

The nice thing about global marketing is that it extends the mushroom harvesting seasons. When it starts to snow in the Pacific Northwest, we're able to coax chanterelles and hedgehogs out of our compatriots in Spain. Pacific Northwest cèpes (also called porcini) grace our tables in June; France and Italy provide the bulk of our supply in the fall.

There are some surprises, too, made possible by commercial air traffic. Cèpes now travel safely from South Africa to New York. China, too, ranks pretty high on the fungi-tourism circuit; It produces matsutake, chanterelle, Oakwood shiitake, and the Himalayan truffle. Turkey and Mexico harvest tons of morels; eastern Europe ships out cèpe, chanterelle, hedgehog, and yellowfoot. Even Sweden exports its boletus and chanterelle.

But for really fresh wild mushrooms, watch for the word "local" at your produce market. As I write, on a sultry August afternoon, my fridge is stocked with large, fragrantly fruity chanterelles; firm, red lobster mushrooms; pickling-quality lactaire; lace-edged yellowfoot; tiny, hairy hedgehogs; gorgeous, perfectly round cèpes, and spiky antique-white coral. They were all plucked wild in the New York Catskills, and being so fresh, can be held under refrigeration for a week or more.

Selecting Mushrooms

Hold a fresh mushroom close to your nose and inhale its aroma. Cèpes (porcini) give off the aroma of damp, autumn leaves. Chanterelles bring ripe apricots to mind, oyster mushrooms, a whiff of the sea. Aroma is essential to a good-tasting mushroom, so be sure to choose only pleasant-smelling specimens (when cold, a mushroom's aroma will be less pronounced). Look for taut mushrooms that have a dewy moistness, are whole, and are free of small holes. A good way to assure quality is to shop at a reputable, high-traffic store. Quick turnover means more frequent shipments of fresh product.

Pass up mushrooms with wet spots, cracked or shriveled caps, and ammonia odors. Mushrooms can be wrinkled and shrinking, a sign that they dried out. Sometimes they are wet and dark, or develop a whitish mold. Tiny worms can inhabit meatier mushrooms, such as morels and lactaires. Subtler signs of past-their-prime mushrooms include splayed-out caps on usually downturned mushrooms, floppy, cracked gills, and musty odors.

There are always exceptions—the naturally cracked cap of an Oakwood shiitake, the fraying edges of still-aromatic chanterelles that got jostled in transit. Some wild mushrooms, like yellowfoot, can be very wet (the leaf canopy does only so much in a downpour) but still taste delicious. So use your nose as a guide: Imagine tasting what you smell and if it works, go for it.

Storing Mushrooms

Mushrooms make good house-guests if you treat them right. Store them in the refrigerator, spread out in a shallow woven basket loosely covered with paper towels. Keep them on a wire shelf so that air can circulate around them. Vegetable bins and plastic bags intensify the humidity in mushrooms and speed up spoilage. To travel, place mushrooms in a paper wrapper in a cooler, top with newspaper, and lay an ice pack on top. Packed like this, they will even survive overnight shipping.

Cleaning Mushrooms

Wild mushrooms are organic. Often there will be a clump of moss clinging to a chanterelle, sand hitching a ride in the hollow stems of black trumpets, or a worm gorging himself on a meaty cèpe. Cultivated mushrooms sometimes have growing medium—a silty or dry dirt-like substance—stuck on the cap. Naturally, these need to be cleaned off before cooking. And because produce is hard to find in its most perfect state, you'll sometimes have to trim off wet spots, darkened sections, and wilted stems.

When it comes to cleaning mushrooms, each person has his own style. Here are a few ways that I use to rid mushrooms of cling-ons and unwanted guests.

BASIC CLEANING: Use a paring knife to trim off wormholes, gnarled root ends, and blemished sections. Some mushroom stems are edible and should be saved to make broths; others are tough and unpleasant. Check a mushroom's primer entry for stem information.

THE COLANDER SHAKE: This works with most wild mushrooms, which tend to bring the forest home with them. Place them in a colander. Bounce them up and down, then back and forth and around. Leaves, pine needles, and dirt clumps will shake out. If you still have sand or clinging dirt, move on to one of the other methods.

THE DAMP PAPER TOWEL: This gets at the obvious grit. Lightly dampen a paper towel. Gently wipe the cap, stem, and interior of a stem that has been split in half.

THE BRUSH-OFF: Use a mushroom brush or soft toothbrush kept just for cleaning mushrooms and truffles. Gently brush out sand and earth-bits. Used on a firm mushroom, get these brushes into those crevices, stems, and other annoyingly hard-to reach places. For more fragile mushrooms, such as black trumpet, mousseron, and yellowfoot, try using a baby hairbrush.

THE MUSHROOM BATH: Mushrooms are so full of water that one thing they don't need is more of it. But when those pesky bits won't go, water may be your last resort. Put the mushrooms in a colander, and rinse and gently rub them with a spray nozzle just before that magical rendezvous with the sauté pan. I like to—and you may cringe at this—spin them in the salad spinner after this, to rid them of excess water. You could also layer them between sheets of paper towels and pat lightly to remove water. Then, immediately toss them in a hot sauté pan to dry. Cook them at very high heat until excess water has evaporated. The important thing to avoid is steaming the mushrooms. This robs them of their texture and doesn't do anything to enhance their flavor. Once the water has evaporated remove the mushrooms from the saute pan, wipe out the pan, and add the oil or butter called for in the recipe.

Cooking Notes

Earthy, fruity, nutty, licoricey, piney. The flavors of mushrooms are as elusive as the wood nymphs and fairies that dance around them. Some wild mushrooms, such as black trumpet, chanterelle, and hen of the woods, are exhibitionists, sounding notes of garlic or apricot. Others need to be coaxed, such as the oyster with its timid seafood nuances. The flavors wild mushrooms often evoke for me are of fresh-turned earth in an autumn forest.

Every home cook favors certain go-with ingredients. When it comes to mushrooms, I'm partial to corn, peas, and fresh herbs. Chris Styler, who developed many of the recipes in this book, sneaks in scallions and iron-rich spinach wherever possible. He's a kosher-salt guy; I've got a thing for sea salt. We both think eggs, used in moderation, set off a wild mushroom's enticing flavors.

All varieties of mushrooms add flavor, texture, and even color to a dish. Substitute one kind for another, and you may be pleasantly surprised at the results. Even four-star chefs let market freshness rather than inflexible recipes be their menu-planning guide.

So get your mushrooms into the fridge, and peek at them from time to time. They'll whisper enticing recipes to you.

BEST COOKING METHODS FOR ALL TYPES OF MUSHROOMS

MEATY/FIRM: These mushrooms resist pressure when pressed or sliced. Firm mushrooms, whether cultivated, like portobello and pompom, or wild, like lobster and hen of the woods, are delicious grilled and roasted.

MEDIUM: Fairly firm mushrooms, with a juicy yield in the sauté pan, yet succulent enough for roasting. The flesh holds its shape in soups, sautés, and some stews. Examples are cèpe (porcini), hedgehog, chanterelle, and shiitake.

DELICATE: These mushrooms can

be dry (white or black trumpet) or moist (yellowfoot, mousseron). They are light so you get more mushrooms per pound. Sautéing works best, with a little stock added as the liquid evaporates.

Preserving the Harvest

*L*ucky is the cook who ends up with too many mushrooms. However, an abundance of fresh product always calls for a sense of urgency, whether it's tomatoes the night before a frost or morels in the heat of a summer flush. Facing a cooler full of mushroom surpluses, I've spent many a night salvaging mushrooms on the cusp of decay. Here are some ideas on how to keep your bounty.

OVER-THE-HILL MUSHROOMS

*B*roken and water-damaged mushrooms still have something to give. Clean them enough to remove dirt and cling-ons and cook into Basic Duxelles (page 283). Sauté the salvaged parts with shallots, add an assertive meat stock, and call it

soup. Or toss them with wild rice to use as a stuffing for poultry or tiny turnovers.

DRYING

*D*rying mushrooms is an excellent way to keep a good thing going. The ones that dry best are cèpes, morels, mousserons, and shiitakes. Drying concentrates their flavor, which imparts an intense mushroom-ness to a slow-cooked dish.

Morels and mousserons reconstitute to almost the same fork-tender texture as fresh and can be sautéed in the same manner as fresh. Other reconstituted mushrooms can be chewy. Think of them as you would dried herbs or vanilla beans (they give so much flavor to a soaking liquid): dice them fine, then use the liquid to suck every last bit of flavor out of them. The liquid from soaked mushrooms is pure forest-in-a-jar. Take it to its maximum with Mushroom Jus (page 254).

TO DRY MUSHROOMS: Fleshy mushrooms such as chanterelles and cèpes should be sliced thin before drying. Small varieties (mousseron, black trumpet) can be left whole. Dehydrators make the job easy. Lacking a home dryer, you can string the mushrooms like popcorn and hang them in a breezy, sunny window. But if you're like me, you'd rather throw out socks with holes than thread a needle. So here's my lazy man's way. In warm weather, lay the mushrooms on a wire rack out in the sun. Make sure to bring them inside to a dry place at night. Turn from time to time until the mushrooms are brittle. This takes about two days in midsummer.

Or preheat the oven to the lowest possible setting and turn it off. Lay out the mushrooms on the oven rack. Check them every twelve hours or so. Depending on their size, mushrooms should dry in two or three days. Mushrooms are dried when they are brittle and crack. With this indoor method you don't need to worry about squirrels and stiff breezes.

TO SELECT DRIED MUSHROOMS: Look for firm, whole (where appropriate) mushrooms that do not appear to be flaking. They should smell of mushrooms, not must. If they look like they have been languishing in a dust-covered plastic bag on the supermarket shelf, look elsewhere. Even dried mushrooms will eventually fade.

TO STORE DRIED MUSHROOMS: Store dried mushrooms in the freezer in airtight containers such as tightly closed jars or sealed zipper-lock plastic bags. It's best to use several zipper bags one inside another to keep out freezer frost.

TO RECONSTITUTE DRIED MUSHROOMS: Place the dried mushrooms in a small deep bowl. Add hot water (preferably water that has been boiled and rested) to cover. Soak until the mushrooms have softened, usually about 20 minutes. Strain the liquid through cheesecloth placed inside a strainer or through a paper towel or a coffee filter. Reserve the soaking liquid to use in the recipe or refrigerate and save for stock for risotto, soup, or sauce. When reconstituted, dried mushrooms can triple or even quadruple in volume. The yield depends on how long the mushrooms have been dried and how long they were soaked. When purchasing dried mushrooms, it's best to buy extra, just in case. Dried mushrooms will nearly always be a little chewy; to avoid the unpleasant texture, chop them fine before cooking.

INSECTS IN DRIED MUSHROOMS: Sometimes insects will fly out of a package of dried mushrooms. This is due to the fact that insect larvae, or eggs, were already present when the mushrooms were dried. When the mushrooms get warm or come into contact with moisture, the eggs can hatch. That's why I recommend keeping mushrooms in the freezer. Another protection is to buy from a trustworthy source that will refund your purchase if insects are found. By the way, the mushrooms are safe to eat, anyway.

FREEZING MUSHROOMS

What to do with those fleshy mushrooms that we overbought or overpicked? Apart from the obvious orgy, there's no better quick-fix than flash-freezing. Freezing works great for cèpes/porcini, chanterelles, oysters, and hedgehogs. The following method minimizes the risk of freezer burn and clumping.

Wipe clean each mushroom without using water. Trim off the stem ends. Lay the mushrooms on a baking sheet without touching each other and place in the freezer at the coldest temperature possible. When rock-solid, pack the mushrooms together in a sealable plastic zipper-lock freezer bag. Place the bag inside another zipper bag. Frozen mushrooms will last forever, but only the vagaries of your freezer will tell how long they will taste good. Try to use them within three months. Chanterelles, hedgehogs, and oysters freeze well. The cèpes that our Dordogne cousin freezes last for a year and still taste delicious.

We also like to create mixtures of frozen mushrooms. Cut the mushrooms into 1- or 2-inch dice before placing on the baking sheet. Use several varieties, even button mushrooms. Sautéed, they make a wonderful last-minute pasta or pizza topping.

If you want to smell the mushrooms cooking (actually morels, black trumpet, yellowfoot, and lobster mushrooms aren't worth freezing unless cooked first), sauté as usual, cool completely, then spread in a thin layer in a shallow freezer container without clumping. Then pack in doubled sealable zipper-lock plastic freezer bags. Partially thaw—to the point where the ice is crushable—before preparing.

To use frozen mushrooms, do not thaw. Slice or dice with a sharp knife (you'll need some muscle). Place in a roasting pan and roast at 350°F for 45 minutes to 1 hour. Or, cook in a dry, hot sauté pan. Continue cooking until the juices are released, about 5 minutes, then reduce the heat to medium. Add a little garlic or shallot, some Mushroom Jus (page 254), stock, or wine, and salt and pepper to taste. Simmer the mushrooms to a nicely thickened consistency.

PICKLING

Preserving mushrooms is common in eastern Europe. The basic principle of pickling is to retain the mushroom's integrity while preserving it for later consumption. Firm mushrooms with a low water content, such as lactaire, lobster, and bluefoot, benefit most from preserving.

Pickled mushrooms can be used in salads, on an antipasto platter, or in recipes calling for fresh mushrooms. (For a recipe, page 88.)

Pass the Shopping List, Please

*I*n the years that I've been cooking with mushrooms, I've come across certain ingredients—as simple as salt, as elegant as truffle oil—that add an extra flourish or extra flavor layer to a dish. Some of these are pantry items, others are condiments that can be made and stored. Recipes for these homemade items—Mushroom Soy Sauce, Basic Mushroom Duxelles— add a special depth or sparkle to other recipes and I have included recipes for them, as well. Do take the time to prepare them; you'll find yourself adding them to all sorts of dishes.

SALT: I find the crunch and utterly pure, saline flavor of French sea salt irreplaceable. It finds its way into just about every dish I prepare. It heightens the flavor of mushrooms more fully than table salt. Kosher salt is a good Plan B, and, of course, fine table salt will do.

SEASONING SALT: We often toss pinches of this mixture into the sauté pan as soon as mushrooms have released some of their juices. The mixture contains some herbs that are classic mushroom partners—

sage, thyme, and rosemary—and will keep on your shelf for a year or more. (For the recipe, see page 253.)

PEPPER: Freshly ground pepper adds a fuller pepper flavor than preground pepper. Since it's a pain to measure freshly ground pepper, go with two twists of the peppermill to start when seasoning mushrooms.

FAT: If you're planning to cook a lot of mushrooms, you may want to pick up a five-liter tin of olive oil. We always use extra virgin, but lesser qualities do just fine. Because it has a fairly high smoking point, olive oil is ideal for sautéing. If you happen upon a really special, fruity olive oil, keep it for salad dressings and for drizzling. Duck fat gives a hearty, meaty flavor to some dishes, particularly rich meat stews and the like.

VINEGAR: Ordinary red wine vinegar goes well in most of our recipes. However, if you are a flavor-craver like I am, balsamic vinegar will take taste to a sweeter finish in vinaigrettes and marinades. It should not always be used as a substitute for red wine vinegar because it does have a dramatically different flavor and it will darken the color of the sauce.

FRESH HERBS: As a lover of spring and worshipper of summer and all the greenness associated with these seasons, I have become a firm believer in herbs as an edible garnish. The herbal notes of fresh chives, chervil, and parsley make a perfect counterpoint to all the earthiness packed into mushrooms. Even if parsley is all you can find, chopped fine, it provides a raw contrast to cooked mushrooms and certainly adds to a dish's visual appeal.

GARLIC: The perfect mushroom-flavor enhancer, go for fresh garlic only.

NUTS: Since lots of nut trees host mushrooms, it only seems fitting to combine nuts and mushrooms. Hazelnuts warm up to chanterelles, walnuts go well with cèpes, and pine nuts with matsutake. Nuts also provide a crunchy contrast to mushrooms that are cooked to a soft, creamy state.

MUSHROOM JUS: Think *eau de champignon*, and you have the idea of what this essence of mushroom does to enhance just about any kind of food. It is a simple reduced stock made with button mushrooms and mushroom trimmings (you don't think cost-conscious chefs would actually discard all those portobello stems, did you?!), a proven flavor-maker in a jar. Store this reduction in the refrigerator for up to two months, or make ice cubes with it and keep them in a freezer storage bag (for how-to, see page 284, step 3). It's at the ready to splash into any dish that needs a jolt—pan sauces, rice cooking liquid, vinaigrettes, vegetable sautés. (For the recipe, see page 254).

CEPE POWDER: You can make this yourself by finely grinding dried cèpes/porcini or other dried mushroom. It's a handy flavor-maker to have in your pantry. I use it in a myriad of ways—to add flavor to soup or bread, to jump-start sauces, to flavor pasta dough, to coat chicken pieces for panfrying. It's fairy dust with a different kind of magic. (For the recipe, see page 285.)

BLACK TRUFFLE OIL: This incredible oil is infused with black truffle aroma and, accordingly, costs more than standard fruit and nut oils. But it takes just drops to infuse a dish with flavor. In fact, if you overdo it, a dish like risotto could become unpleasantly saturated. Whether scoping out the specialty shelf at your local market or gourmet shop, or ordering by mail (see page 324), make sure the label defines the truffle as *Tuber melanosporum*. Rub it over the skin of a roasting chicken, add it to pan sauces, and use it to enhance marinades. Black truffle oil is best used in a cooked dish, as it takes gentle heat to release its aroma.

WHITE TRUFFLE OIL: Stand back when you open the bottle: This aromatic oil delivers a garlicky wallop derived from the Alba white truffle itself. Use in small quantitites—drops at a time—to flavor vinaigrettes; splash over polenta, risotto, and pasta; and drizzle over cold vegetables and meats. Fill up a spray bottle to spritz over lettuce leaves or

antipasti just before serving. White truffle oil can easily become rancid, so if you do not have a reliably cool place to store it, store it in the refrigerator. It will congeal, but it easily returns to liquid when left out for fifteen minutes or so.

MUSHROOM SOY SAUCE: Since soy sauce adds an extra flavor note to mushrooms, it makes sense to combine soy and mushrooms in one handy condiment. It adds depth to lots of different preparations—not just dishes with a Chinese or Japanese accent. In addition to the recipes that call for Mushroom Soy Sauce, it works well with steamed vegetables, pan roasts, and pouch-cooked fish. Store in a jar in the refrigerator for up to a year. You can buy it or make your own. (For the recipe, see page 255.)

MUSHROOM-INFUSED SHERRY: This is another indispensable, do-ahead pantry item. Splash this perky condiment

into chowders, gravies, and deglazing juices. The longer it sits, the more intense the flavor gets. I always have a jar of it in the fridge, to use in the book's recipes as well as to add a last-minute flavor punch when needed. (For the recipe, see page 255.)

TRUFFLE BUTTER: This recipe is so easy to make—and it stores almost forever in the freezer—that I've included it as a flavor enhancer in lots of recipes. After an initial outlay (one truffle goes a long way, and the butter can be made with trimmings), you'll only have to go as far as the freezer for a lusty hit of truffle. It can be made with black or white truffle. Swirl it into meat sauces to add velvety body and unmistakably elegant flavor. It goes a long way when layered between sliced potatoes for a gratin, and can be spread on little toasts and topped with a parsley leaf for a quick hors d'oeuvre. (For the recipe, see page 256.)

For Saucepans

Savon de Marseille is an all-purpose cleaner. It's a soap from Provence, available in specialty cookware and gourmet shops, that is nicely fatty and formed in sturdy blocks. Use it on a scratchy sponge to scrub those nasty black marks off the outside bottom of saucepans.

A Word on Equipment

I don't know about you, but when I see the gorgeous, perfectly appointed kitchens in cooking and lifestyle magazines, I feel impoverished. It appears to me that every possible piece of equipment has been anticipated, and that each object and work surface is in the precise place where it will be needed. These kitchens may be for the lucky few—perhaps you are one of them—but most of us can pretty much make do with the utensils and space available.

If you're thinking of adding to or replacing your *batterie de cuisine,* consider investing in a good, heavy skillet. I love my 10-inch cast-iron skillet, but would go for 12 inches next time around. (See Seasoning Skillets, this page.) It keeps the mushrooms hopping, since it can withstand the high heat that is needed to sauté mushrooms.

Likewise, a stainless steel saucepan with heft works in myriad ways. Go for one that has a heavy bottom sandwiched with aluminum and alloyed aluminum. It heats quickly and retains heat for long-simmering soups, stews, and reductions.

I used to live for the food processor, but rediscovered the pleasure of hand chopping after willing mine to the business. Hand cutting allows you to control the size and shape of your pieces, and odd-shaped, sometimes slippery, and often tiny mushrooms can be challenging. To do the job, I employ a 15-year-old, 10-inch chef's knife. Its heavy handle and wide blade suit just about any food being cut into any size. If you're in the market for a knife, look for high-carbon stainless steel. But hang onto your quick blades because the thrill of chopping lots of mushrooms by hand fades fast.

I use a spray bottle filled with black truffle oil to spritz roasting birds, composed salads, and pasta and risotto dishes. It makes a little luxury go a long way.

One thing you'll see a lot of in this book is dried mushrooms; they always need to be soaked and drained. To filter the grit and sand out of the soaking liquid, I use a cone-shaped *chinois,* a strainer with extra-tiny mesh holes. But there are other devices that do the job well—a few thicknesses of cheesecloth laid inside an ordinary strainer or a coffee filter.

Seasoning Skillets

Every autumn, I get a primal urge to rake leaves and season my cast-iron skillets. The first takes care of physical yearnings; the second may be the human version of squirrels' nut-hoarding. Anyway, here's how to do the seasoning. Preheat the oven to 200°F. Heat the dry skillet on the burner until very hot. Then pour in about 1 cup of vegetable or seed oil—don't waste your money on olive oil—for a 12-inch skillet (less for smaller skillets). Heat it over medium heat just until the oil begins to smoke. Then place the skillet with the oil in the oven for 2 hours. Carefully remove the skillet from the oven and allow to cool. When cooled, pour out the oil into a clean jar with a lid (this oil can be used to clean the skillet after each use). Wipe out the inside of the skillet with paper towels until just a slight film of oil remains. The skillet is now ready to use.

The best way to clean cast iron after cooking is to loosen the stuck bits by soaking in hot water or scrubbing with a soft sponge. Then wipe the skillet clean with a paper towel dipped in cooking oil. Avoid using soap to clean the skillet, and try not to let it stay submerged in water too long. Dry it by putting it on a heated burner just until the water droplets dry up.

Finger Foods

Many an impromptu party at our house begins with a glass of wine and hors d'oeuvres magically and quickly put together with ingredients on hand. I used to feel too scared to look into the fridge at such moments, wondering what suitable snacks could possibly emerge from the disparate ingredients and leftovers there. Then I discovered that mushrooms can readily save the day. And not just for old tried-and-true dishes like stuffed mushrooms or creamed mushrooms on toast, but for so many other, exciting recipes.

One of our favorites is bruschetta, which requires only Italian bread, olive oil, and a few mushrooms—or just about any moist heapable or spreadable topping. Variations on the sandwich theme—Mushroom Finger Sandwiches and Mini Pitas with Honey Mushrooms, Blue Cheese, and Port—turn a backyard gathering into a garden party. Elegant goes without saying when Ovoli and Fig Crostini arrive or Cocktail Cèpes in Phyllo Nests, bubbly and creamy in their flaky pastry cups.

Whatever the occasion, it's nice to have a variety of finger foods, some hot, some cold, some laid out for picking, and some passed on serving plates. We encourage guests to dunk Shrimp, Shiitake, and Wood Ear Wontons or Cauliflower Mushroom Fritters into a variety of brightly-flavored sauces, to pluck morsels from Curry-Glazed Mushroom Brochettes, and to slather garlicky mayonnaise on crunchy, juicy Wild Rice and Sweet Potato Pancakes with Roasted Cremini.

Many of these recipes can be prepared up to a point and set aside until assembly time, just before serving. Sandwiches can be stacked, covered tightly to prevent air from getting in, and refrigerated. Mushroom brochettes do just fine with an extra day's marinating. Others may be laid out on disposable aluminum foil trays with tops, stacked in the freezer, and forgotten until a college roommate or the in-laws show up at your doorstep. After all, showing off is what hors d'oeuvres are all about—right??

Curry-Glazed Mushroom Brochettes

MAKES 16 BROCHETTES, SERVES 8 AS AN APPETIZER OR 4 AS A MAIN COURSE

This clever way of grilling food on skewers will never get boring. Little morsels of the most heavenly food ever—mushrooms, of course—become earthier, sweeter, and more intense when basted in curry and honey. Try them as an appetizer with a quick yogurt dip, over rice as a main course, or as part of a buffet. For serving ease at a cocktail party, thread just two or three mushrooms onto presoaked wooden toothpicks.

1 medium (about 8 ounces) portobello, cleaned, stemmed and cut into ½-inch cubes

8 medium (about 10 ounces total) shiitakes, cleaned, stemmed, and quartered

6 ounces firm mushrooms, like chicken of the woods or lobster, cut into ½-inch cubes (about 2 cups)

2 tablespoons vegetable oil

1 tablespoon good-quality curry powder

2 tablespoons fresh lime or lemon juice

1 tablespoon honey

1 teaspoon kosher or sea salt

¼ teaspoon freshly ground black pepper

Mushroom Sour Cream or Yogurt (page 258) or plain yogurt

1. Soak twenty 6-inch wooden skewers in cold water to cover for 2 to 3 hours. This will make them less likely to burn during grilling. Any unused soaked skewers can be dried and reused. Drain before using.

2. Put the mushrooms in a bowl. Mix the vegetable oil and curry powder together in a small saucepan or skillet and heat over low heat just until the curry is fragrant, about 1 minute. Remove and cool the curry mixture.

3. Stir in the lime juice, honey, salt, and pepper until the honey is dissolved. Scrape the curry mixture over the mushrooms and toss to coat. Marinate at room temperature for 2 hours. (The brochettes may be prepared to this point up to 2 days in advance. Store them in a heavy, sealed plastic bag in the refrigerator. Rotate the bag occasionally to season the mushrooms evenly.)

4. Preheat a barbecue grill to very hot or heat a grill or heat an indoor grill pan over medium heat for 10 minutes.

5. Thread the mushrooms onto the prepared skewers, alternating pieces of the different kinds and leaving about 2 inches of the non-pointed end of the skewer empty. Reserve any leftover marinade.

6. Grill the brochettes, turning often, until all sides are seared and well browned and the mushrooms are tender, about 6 minutes. Work in batches on the grill pan if necessary to prevent overcrowding. Baste the brochettes occasionally with the reserved marinade. Serve hot or warm, passing the sour cream separately.

Prosciutto-Stuffed Pompoms

Just when stuffed mushrooms began to get boring, along came pompoms with their delicate flavor and velvety texture. We've tucked a slab of prosciutto into a mushroom pocket, then panfried the mushrooms. Spear these round surprise packages with toothpicks or serve them as an accompaniment to a simple roast chicken.

MAKES 12 STUFFED MUSHROOMS, SERVES 6 AS AN APPETIZER, 4 AS A SIDE DISH

5 medium (4 to 5 inches across)
   pompom mushrooms, trimmed
   of any brown spots and wiped
   clean

2 thin slices of prosciutto

Kosher or sea salt

Freshly ground black pepper

All-purpose flour, for coating

3 large eggs

3 tablespoons water

3 tablespoons extra virgin olive oil

2 tablespoons dry white wine

½ cup Light Chicken Stock (page 280)
   or canned low-sodium
   chicken broth

2 tablespoons chopped fresh flat-leaf
   parsley

1 tablespoon unsalted butter

2 teaspoons drained nonpareil
   capers

¼ cup freshly grated
   Parmesan cheese

1. Cut each mushroom into 1½- to 2-inch pieces. You should get 2 or 3 pieces from each mushroom, depending on the size. The shape isn't important, as long as each piece is no more than 2 inches across at its widest point. Starting from the top side, make a cut down the center of each mushroom piece to within ½ inch from the bottom, leaving the pieces attached along the bottom. Make sure not to cut all the way through.

2. Cut or tear the pieces of prosciutto into pieces large enough to fill the pocket of each mushroom piece with a double thickness of prosciutto. Fold the prosciutto pieces in half and fit them into the pocket. Pinch the mushroom pieces gently so the prosciutto will stay firmly in place during cooking. Sprinkle generously with salt and pepper. Roll them in all-purpose flour until coated and set them on a baking sheet.

3. Heat the oil in a large (at least 12-inch), heavy nonstick or cast-iron skillet over medium heat.

4. Beat the eggs and water in a small bowl until thoroughly blended. Roll the floured mushroom pieces in the egg mixture until coated on all sides. Add them to the hot oil and cook, turning as necessary, until golden brown on all sides, about 4 minutes. Since the mushroom pieces are irregularly shaped, they will need attention to brown them evenly on all sides.

5. Remove the mushroom pieces and drain on paper towels. Pour off any oil from the pan, add the wine to the pan, and return it to the heat. Cook until the wine is almost entirely evaporated, 1 minute. Add the stock, heat to a boil, and boil until the stock is reduced by half, 2 minutes. Add the parsley, butter, and capers and swirl the pan until the butter is dissolved and incorporated into the sauce. Add the mushrooms and toss or stir gently until coated with the sauce. Remove from the heat, sprinkle with cheese, and serve immediately.

Morels with Calvados

*M*orels and apples seem made for each other and in fact they are—the best place to track them down is in abandoned apple orchards. Each spring, I make this recipe with the first morels that come in. The voluptuous flavor of the morels snaps to attention when bathed in apple brandy. Try to ignore the cholesterol factor, for the cream adds a vital, velvety note. You can also serve it as a side dish for chops or a steak, or turn it into a hearty meal tumbled over fresh fettuccine.

2 tablespoons unsalted butter

1 pound morels, trimmed, cleaned, and
    sliced lengthwise in half

Fresh lemon juice

Kosher or sea salt and freshly ground
    black pepper

¼ cup Calvados

½ cup heavy (or whipping) cream

1 teaspoon chopped fresh tarragon

6 slices buttered, toasted
    French bread,
    for serving

1. Melt the butter in a large sauté pan over medium heat. Add the morels and cook, stirring, until the morels give up their liquid, about 6 minutes. Sprinkle with lemon juice and salt and pepper to taste.

2. When just a few drops of liquid remain, remove the pan from the heat. Immediately pour in the Calvados and let it bubble until mostly evaporated. Then add the

Mysterious Morels

*T*he morel has a mystique bordering on cult worship. Mushroom gatherers may divulge the location of a chanterelle hotspot, but the whereabouts of a morel patch is passed on only through bloodlines. Tight-lipped morel stalkers even have pet names for their prey—roon, merkle, morelkie. In fact, Boyne City, Michigan, hosts a now-famous Mother's Day morel hunt, where moms and their kids unearth specimens 10 inches—and more—long! And, in Minnesota, the morel has earned the distinction of State Fungus.

This spongy conehead thrives on misfortune. It inhabits disturbed terrain, such as burn sites and dug-up earth, making cemeteries popular with foragers. It pops up under diseased elms and abandoned apple orchards and flourishes along the banks of swollen trout streams. These persistent little fungi will poke through fire-scorched logs, fields gone to seed, and even the eye sockets of decaying animal skulls.

Out in the Pacific Northwest, news of a forest fire sparks a feverish excitement in morel hunters. The eruption of the Mount Saint Helens volcano produced a bumper crop. Morels are so sure to crop up in fire-ravaged forests that the government auctions off picking rights on state-owned land.

cream, and return to the stove. Boil over medium-high heat until the sauce is of coating consistency, 2 to 3 minutes.

3. Stir in the tarragon and spoon onto individual plates, each garnished with a slice of buttered and toasted French bread.

Sherried Mousseron Tapas

I've borrowed Spanish flavors to suit this light little mushroom. The delicate mousserons are bound by an assertive sauce that's the consistency of a loose pesto. Serve it in a ramekin to scoop onto crisp toasts. Or use it to sauce rice, polenta, or a quick-sautéed fish filet.

¼ cup whole blanched almonds, toasted
(see box, this page)
2 tablespoons chopped fresh flat-leaf parsley
¼ cup Light Chicken Stock (page 280) or
canned low-sodium chicken broth
2 tablespoons dry sherry
1 tablespoon extra virgin olive oil
1½ teaspoons red wine vinegar or sherry
vinegar
2 green olives, either pitted or pimiento
stuffed, finely chopped
1 clove garlic, sliced
8 ounces (about 4 cups) mousserons,
wiped clean

Kosher or sea salt or Seasoning Salt (page
253) and freshly ground black pepper
Toasted thin slices of French bread,
for serving

1. Place the almonds in a food processor and process until coarsely chopped, stopping once or twice to scrape down the sides of the workbowl. Add the parsley and process until the almonds and parsley are finely chopped. Transfer the almond mixture to a small bowl and set aside.

2. Place the broth, sherry, olive oil, vinegar, olives, and garlic in a small bowl and stir to blend. Pour the mixture into a medium-size skillet. Add the mushrooms and heat over medium heat to a boil. Reduce the heat, cover the skillet, and simmer until the mushrooms are tender, about 4 minutes. (The mushrooms may be prepared to this

To Toast Almonds

*P*reheat the oven to 350°F. Spread the almonds out on a baking sheet and place in the oven, stirring occasionally, until golden brown, about 10 minutes. Cool completely.

point up to 1 day in advance. Store in a covered plastic container in the refrigerator. You may have to add a little water when reheating to return it to its original consistency.) Remove the cover, raise the heat, and bring back and reheat to a boil.

Add the almond mixture and cook just until the sauce is boiling. Remove from the heat. Add salt and pepper to taste. Serve hot with crisp toasted bread.

Mushroom Finger Sandwiches

These tea sandwiches might look white-glove, but with their woodsy flavor and chive edges, they'll steal the show. We made them for our child's birthday party and are happy to report that the kids loved them!

MAKES TWENTY 2-INCH TRIANGLES, SERVES 4 TO 6 AS AN APPETIZER

1 recipe Basic Duxelles (page 283), at room temperature
¼ cup freshly grated Parmesan cheese
2 tablespoons chopped fresh flat-leaf parsley
10 slices very thin white bread, with crusts
2 tablespoons unsalted butter, at room temperature
2 tablespoons very thinly sliced chives (optional)

1. Place the duxelles, cheese, and parsley together in a small bowl and beat until blended. Divide the mixture evenly among five of the bread slices. Spread into an even layer that extends all the way to the crusts. Top with the remaining 5 slices of bread and press gently so the sandwiches hold together. Cut off the crusts, making neat little squares. (You can prepare the sandwiches to this point up to 1 day in advance. Wrap them tightly in plastic wrap and refrigerate until you need them.)

2. Spread both sides of each sandwich lightly with butter. Heat a griddle to medium heat and grill the sandwiches or grill them in a large heavy skillet—cast iron works well. (If you have 2 skillets, use both.) Cook until golden brown on both sides, about 6 minutes total. Remove and keep warm for up to 20 minutes on a baking sheet in a 250°F oven, if necessary, while grilling the remaining sandwiches.

3. Cut each sandwich into 4 triangles. Dip the cut edges into the chives, if using. Serve at once.

Mini Pitas with Honey Mushrooms, Blue Cheese, and Port

MAKES 16 HALF MINI PITAS, SERVES 8 AS AN APPETIZER

*N*ot everyone loves blue cheese, but those who do will find the pungent taste of these little sandwiches irresistible. Make sure the bread is fresh; if not, it breaks as you try to cut and stuff it. Other strong-flavored mushrooms, such as wine cap, shiitake, and fried-chicken, work equally well.

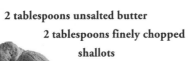

2 tablespoons unsalted butter

2 tablespoons finely chopped shallots

8 ounces honey mushrooms, trimmed, cleaned, and coarsely chopped

¼ cup crumbled blue cheese, at room temperature

2 tablespoons Port

¼ teaspoon freshly ground black pepper

Kosher or sea salt, as needed

⅓ cup finely chopped toasted walnuts (see box, this page)

3 tablespoons finely chopped fresh flat-leaf parsley or chives

8 mini pitas (2 inches across)

To Toast Walnuts

*H*eat a small dry skillet to very hot. Add the unchopped nuts and toast, shaking the pan often, until fragrant and slightly dark, about 2 minutes. Let cool thoroughly. To toast in the oven, spread the walnuts in a single layer on a baking sheet and place them in a preheated 300°F oven. Bake, stirring once or twice, until evenly golden brown, about 12 minutes. Let cool thoroughly. Chop as directed in each recipe.

1. Melt the butter in a large, heavy skillet over medium heat until foaming. Add the shallots and cook, stirring, until wilted, about 2 minutes. Increase the heat to medium-high and stir in the mushrooms. Cook, stirring often, until the mushrooms are lightly browned and softened, about 4 minutes. Transfer the mushroom mixture to a medium-size bowl and cool completely.

2. Add the blue cheese, Port, and pepper to the mushroom mixture and stir gently until mixed. Taste and add salt if needed. Stir the walnuts and chives together in a shallow bowl. Cut the pitas in half crosswise to form two pockets.

3. Divide the mushroom mixture among the pita pockets, spreading it to fill each pocket evenly. Gently dip the edge of the exposed filling into the walnut-chive mixture and arrange the mini pitas, filling side up, on a serving platter.

Ovoli and Fig Crostini

FINGER
FOODS

23

**MAKES 4
CROSTINI,
SERVES 2
TO 4 AS AN
APPETIZER**

An oval shape gives this fragrant, porcini-like mushroom its name; its rarity, if we're to heed food-loving Italians, imbues it with Godlike qualities. If you can't get ovoli from your specialty market, substitute cèpe/porcini. With apologies to all the Italian restaurants that wanted to buy *ovoli* the week we tested this recipe—I really didn't take all that many home!

The thinly shaved Parmesan cheese provides a sharp contrast to the earthy mushrooms. Be sure to serve these crostini warm.

8 ounces ovoli

3 tablespoons best-quality
  extra virgin olive oil

2 teaspoons chopped fresh flat-leaf
  parsley

4 thin slices of rustic, crusty bread

2 tablespoons thinly sliced, dried figs

4 thinly shaved slices of Parmesan
  cheese (see Note)

1. Preheat the broiler.

2. Wipe the ovoli with a paper towel to remove any dirt. Trim off the bottom. Cut ¼-inch slices through the cap and stem.

3. Heat 2 tablespoons of the olive oil in a small sauté pan over medium heat. Add the *ovoli* and sauté, gently turning, until soft and slightly browned, about 4 minutes.

4. Brush the remaining 1 tablespoon olive oil over the bread and broil until lightly browned, 2 minutes. Turn the bread and broil the second side until lightly browned, 1 minute more.

5. Toss the figs into the ovoli, stir, and take the pan off the heat.

My First Memorable Mushroom Encounter

My sister Betsy, two years older than I, dictated everything to me—from "get rid of the bangs" to when to wear go-go boots to which were the right football parties. So when she opened a can of B-in-B mushrooms and tossed them into sizzling butter, I noticed. She cleverly inserted the cooked slices into an about-to-be-grilled cheese sandwich. It certainly elevated my thinking about this funny ingredient. Even though I've moved on to more exotic recipes for mushrooms, I can still get Bossy Betsy to fix me lunch once in a while.

Top the toasts with the mushroom-fig mixture. Lay a slice of cheese on each toast. Serve warm.

Note: For curlicued shavings of Parmesan, use a sharp vegetable peeler. Use one hand to hold the cheese steady on the work surface while you shave downward with the other hand.

Wild Mushroom Bruschetta

Bruschetta (bruschetta is Italian for a little burnt thing) is a crusty slab of grilled or toasted country bread, piled high with robustly flavored toppings. The toasts provide a terrific base for exploring the flavors and textures of new mushroom varieties. Sauté just an ounce or two of a kind you may not know yet—such as the mild yet enticing yellow oyster. Spoon it onto the toast and let the mushroom juices soak in.

12 slices rustic, crusty white, sourdough,
    or whole wheat bread, with
    crust, each ½ inch thick and
    about 6 × 4 inches across
6 tablespoons extra virgin olive
    oil
Kosher or sea salt
Freshly ground black pepper
Topping of your choice (recipes follow)

1. Preheat a charcoal or gas grill to hot.

2. Brush both sides of the bread with olive oil and sprinkle with salt and pepper. Grill them on the cooler part of the grill until golden brown in the center and slightly burnt around the edges. They may not color evenly, but that is fine.

3. Place the bruschetta on serving plates. Divide the topping evenly among them.

Grilled Portobello Bruschetta

Make this bruschetta on a summer evening when the grill is already fired up.

1 recipe Roasted or Grilled Portobello
    Caps (page 193)
3 tablespoons chopped, mixed
    fresh herbs, such as flat-leaf
    parsley, chives, or chervil

Cut the portobello caps into ¼-inch dice. Mix with the herbs, spoon onto the bruschetta, and serve.

Other Bruschetta Ideas

- **White Bean Purée (without the truffle, page 220) with roasted cremini (see page 96, steps 1 and 2) and white truffle oil**

- **Serrano ham, sliced Sicilian olives, and sautéed mousserons**

- **Curried mayonnaise, diced lamb, oyster mushrooms, and cilantro**

- **Raw button mushrooms and Roasted Shiitake Ketchup (page 252)**

Roasted Yellow Oyster Mushrooms and Arugula Bruschetta with Basil Purée

This topping combines mild, soft yellow oysters with salty prosciutto, and the peppery punch of arugula and basil. Yellow oysters are a pretty variety of regular oyster mushrooms.

8 ounces yellow oyster or 12 ounces
    hen of the woods mushrooms, cleaned
2 tablespoons olive oil
Kosher salt
Freshly ground black pepper
1 teaspoon balsamic vinegar
1 bunch (about 2½ cups) tender
    young arugula, stemmed, washed,
    and dried
2 tablespoons Basil Purée (see box)
6 slices (about 4 ounces) of very thinly
    sliced prosciutto, cut in half

1. Preheat the oven to 400°F.

2. Trim the mushrooms, leaving just enough of the central stem attached to hold the mushrooms together. Break or cut the oyster mushrooms into clumps of 2 or 3 mushrooms each. (Cut the hen of the woods mushrooms into 1½-inch-wide strips.) Toss the mushrooms with 1 tablespoon of the olive oil and salt and pepper to taste. Spread in an even layer on a baking sheet. Roast until the mushrooms are lightly browned and tender, about 8 minutes. Keep warm.

3. Stir the remaining 1 tablespoon olive oil, the balsamic vinegar, and salt and pepper to taste in a mixing bowl.

4. If the arugula leaves are longer than 2 inches, cut them into 1-inch strips. Tender baby leaves may be left whole. Add the arugula to the dressing and toss to coat.

5. Spread the bruschettas with the Basil Purée and arrange the

Basil Purée

When you have fresh basil only in the summer months you become obsessive about preserving its herbal, peppery goodness. You can easily prepare this purée to keep a handy supply through the basil-less months.

Choose bunches with very fresh, whole, unblemished leaves. Remove the leaves from the stems. Wash them in cool water to remove all sand and dirt, then dry them very well, preferably in a salad spinner. Loosely fill a food processor with cleaned basil leaves. Drizzle with 1 to 2 tablespoons of olive oil. Process, using on/off pulses, until coarsely chopped. With the motor running, add enough olive oil (not more than ¼ cup) to make a thick but smooth mixture of very finely chopped basil. Pack the purée into small containers and let it stand 1 or 2 minutes. There should be enough oil to form an even layer over the top; if not, drizzle on a little more. Store the basil in the refrigerator up to 1 week or in the freezer for up to 3 months.

prosciutto slices on top. Top with the warm mushrooms and arrange the dressed arugula over the mushrooms. Serve immediately.

Bruschetta with Warm Duxelles and Potato Topping

If you have duxelles already prepared in the freezer, pull it out and combine it with warm potatoes for the rustic appetizer.

3 small new potatoes
1 recipe Basic Duxelles (page 283)
1½ teaspoons extra virgin olive oil,
     if needed
3 teaspoons chopped chives

Boil the potatoes in water to cover until tender but not mushy, about 20 minutes. Peel and finely dice while still warm. Place in a small bowl and gently toss with the duxelles, olive oil (if needed to moisten), and the chives. Spoon onto the bruschetta and serve.

Cocktail Cèpes

MAKES TWELVE
2-INCH PASTRY
CUPS, SERVES 6
AS AN
APPETIZER

The crunchy phyllo pastry with its succulent, creamy filling is equally elegant when passed on a doily-lined tray or presented as a sit-down appetizer. Even though the cèpes are not that easy to find, it's worth tracking them down in their fresh or frozen state. If you can't find any, cremini make an economical substitute.

This recipe makes twelve mini phyllo cups. If your mini muffin pan has twenty-four cups, leave the empty cups empty. There's no need to fill with water. Or if you'd like to make a large amount to freeze, you can easily double or even quadruple the recipe.

12 small (caps about 1 inch across) fresh or
     frozen cèpe mushrooms (see Note)
¼ cup heavy (or whipping) cream
½ teaspoon dried tarragon, crumbled
Kosher or sea salt and freshly ground
     black pepper

2 tablespoons unsalted butter,
     melted
1 sheet phyllo dough,
     thawed
Grated Parmesan cheese
     (optional)

1. Thaw the mushrooms in a bowl if frozen, reserving the liquid that collects in the bottom of the bowl. Separate the caps and stems and drain the caps well on paper towels. Squeeze the liquid from the stems into the bowl. Finely chop the stems and add to the liquid. Place the stems and liquid, cream, and tarragon in a small saucepan. Heat the liquid to a boil over low heat and boil until there is just enough liquid to coat the mushroom stems, about 2 minutes. Season the liquid to taste with salt and pepper. Set aside.

2. Preheat the oven to 400°F. Using some of the melted butter, grease a mini muffin tin, with cups about 1½ inches across the top by ½ inch deep.

3. Arrange the phyllo sheet with one of the long edges facing you. Brush the right half of the phyllo with melted butter. Fold the left side over the buttered side to make a double-thickness. Brush and fold again to make a 4-layer pile of phyllo about 4½ inches wide × 14 inches long. Cut the rectangle cross-wise into 3 equal pieces (each piece will be about a 4½-inch square). Cut each square into 4 even squares. You should have 12 squares altogether. Line the cups of the muffin tins with the phyllo squares. There should be enough dough to completely line the cups, with the points extending over the rim of the cups.

4. Place a mushroom cap, gill side up, in each of the phyllo-lined cups. Spoon the cream mixture over each cap, coating the cap completely. Sprinkle the grated cheese, if using, over the cream mixture.

5. Bake until the phyllo is deep golden brown and crisp and the filling is bubbling and lightly browned, about 10 minutes. Remove and cool for 2 minutes before removing the cups from the muffin tins to serve.

Note: The tiny frozen cèpes I have found are called *bouchon,* literally corks. Some brands label this size "cocktail" or "baby." This category indicates whole mushrooms which measure no more than 2 inches from cap to stem. They are almost always frozen, although in peak season they occasionally appear fresh. This size is a little more costly than the other sizes, but it makes up for price with its juicy goodness.

To Freeze Phyllo Cups

To freeze unfilled phyllo cups, cool them completely to room temperature. Put them on a baking sheet and place them in the freezer until solid. Stack carefully in a plastic container and keep frozen until ready to use, up to 2 months. Reheat the frozen phyllo cups on a baking sheet in a 350°F oven until crisp and heated through, about 12 minutes.

Wild Rice and Sweet Potato Pancakes with Roasted Cremini

MAKES 40
PANCAKES,
SERVES 10 AS
AN APPETIZER,
6 AS A FIRST
COURSE
(SEE BOX,
FACING PAGE)

Sweet potatoes both firm up and sweeten these wild rice pancakes. Crispy and warm and spread with a garlicky mayonnaise, they offer the perfect crunch for toothsome roasted cremini. The leftover mayonnaise made the rounds of other uses in our house—on BLTs, as a crudité dip, and with steamed crab—until there wasn't a drop left.

WILD RICE AND SWEET POTATO PANCAKES

⅔ cup (4 ounces) wild rice

1 pound small (about 2-inch) cremini, bouchons, or button mushrooms, wiped clean

2 tablespoons unsalted butter

1 small rib celery, diced very fine (about ½ cup)

2 shallots, peeled and diced very fine (about ⅓ cup)

¾ cup grated peeled sweet potato (1 medium sweet potato)

2 tablespoons chopped fresh flat-leaf parsley

1 egg

½ cup dry bread crumbs, plus more if necessary

1 teaspoon kosher or sea salt

GARLIC MAYONNAISE

1 tablespoon olive oil

3 cloves garlic, peeled and thinly sliced

Pinch of cayenne pepper

⅓ cup prepared mayonnaise

1 tablespoon fresh lemon juice

1½ teaspoons Dijon mustard

TO FINISH

3 tablespoons olive oil, plus more for cooking the pancakes

1 teaspoon kosher or sea salt

2 teaspoons chopped fresh herb, such as tarragon or thyme

¼ teaspoon freshly ground black pepper

1. To make the pancake mixture, heat 6 cups salted water to a boil in a medium-size saucepan. Stir in the wild rice, reduce the heat to a simmer, and simmer, covered, until tender but still firm, about 30 minutes.

2. Separate the stems from the mushroom caps. Set the caps aside and finely chop the stems. (You should have about ⅔ cup.) Melt the butter in a large, heavy skillet over medium-high heat until foaming. Add the celery, shallots, and mushroom stems. Sauté, stirring, until the vegetables are wilted, about 3 minutes. Stir in the sweet potato and stir constantly until the potato turns bright orange, about 4 minutes. Transfer to a bowl and add the parsley.

3. Drain the rice and spread out on a plate to cool. When it is cool enough to handle but still warm, transfer to a food processor. Using quick on/off motions process the rice just enough to break up the grains. Do not chop the rice fine. Transfer the rice to the bowl containing the sweet potato mixture. Add the egg, ½ cup bread crumbs, and salt and stir until very well blended. Cover and refrigerate until thoroughly chilled, 2 hours. (The wild rice mix can be made up to one day in advance.)

4. To make the garlic mayonnaise, heat 1 tablespoon olive oil in a very small saucepan or skillet over medium heat. Add the garlic and cook just until softened but not brown, about 1 minute. Remove from the heat and add the cayenne. Transfer the garlic mixture into a food processor or blender. Add the mayonnaise, lemon juice, and mustard. Process until smooth. Transfer to a small bowl and set aside. (The mayonnaise can be made up to 3 days in advance and stored, tightly covered, in the refrigerator.)

5. Preheat the oven to 400°F.

6. Toss the reserved mushroom caps with the remaining 3 tablespoons oil, 1 teaspoon salt, the herb, and pepper. Roast them until dark brown, 12 to 15 minutes. (This can be done up to 1 hour in advance.)

7. Form 1½-inch patties using 1 tablespoon of the wild rice mix for each patty. If you have trouble forming firm patties with this mixture, add more bread crumbs, 1 teaspoon at a time, until the patties hold their shape. (This can be done up to 4 hours in advance. Keep in a single layer on a baking sheet, covered with plastic wrap, in the refrigerator.) Fry the patties in a lightly oiled heavy skillet, preferably cast iron, over medium heat, turning them only once, until well browned on both sides, about 5 minutes. Keep warm.

8. To finish, spread each warm pancake with a thin layer of the mayonnaise. Top with a sliced roasted mushroom cap. Serve warm.

Pancakes as a First Course

*F*or a first course version of the Wild Rice and Sweet Potato Pancakes, divide the wild rice mixture into 6 equal patties about 4 inches across and ¾ inch thick. Roast the mushrooms as in step 6. While still hot, toss the mushrooms in a bowl with the mayonnaise and set aside. Fry the wild rice cakes, put each in the center of a serving plate, and top with some of the mushroom mix.

Crèpe Pouches with Shiitakes

New York chef Michael Lomonaco brought good taste to the venerable "21" Club, a former speakeasy with a clubby pedigree and undistinguished menu. He went on to chef at Wild Blue in the World Trade Center and host his own cooking show, "Michael's Place," on the TV Food Network. I was so enthralled by his silky shiitake filling recipe, that we created little crèpe pouches to showcase it.

These little pouches, with their chive tie, make a wonderful, unusual hors d'oeuvre. Also, they can be made entirely in advance. The crèpe batter and the crèpes can be made ahead; the mushroom filling can be made ahead; and the pouches can be formed up to three hours in advance and arranged in the skillet. Then simply put the skillet over heat a few minutes before serving. You can use this technique with many different fillings.

CHIVE CREPES

1¼ cups milk

1 large egg

2 teaspoons sugar

¼ teaspoon kosher or sea salt

1½ cups all-purpose flour

3 tablespoons vegetable oil

¼ cup very thinly sliced chives

SHIITAKE FILLING

2 tablespoons olive oil

½ cup minced onion

2 cloves garlic, minced

½ pound shiitakes, cleaned, stemmed, and cut into ¼-inch dice

Kosher or sea salt

3 tender inner leaves of Napa cabbage, cut lengthwise in half, then thinly shredded crosswise (about 1 cup)

¼ cup dry white wine

½ cup cooked couscous (see box, facing page)

2 tablespoons chopped fresh flat-leaf parsley

Freshly ground black pepper

Vegetable cooking spray

20 whole, thick chives, blanched (see Note)

1. To make the crèpe batter, combine the milk, egg, sugar, and salt in a blender jar and blend at low speed until the egg is completely incorporated. Add the flour and blend at low speed until smooth. Pour the mixture into a bowl and whisk in the vegetable oil and chives. Cover the batter and let rest for 1 hour at room temperature or overnight in the refrigerator.

2. To make the filling, heat the olive oil in a large, heavy skillet over medium heat. Add the onion and garlic and cook, stirring often, until the onion is tender, about 6 minutes. Add the shiitakes and sprinkle lightly with salt. Cook, stirring, until the mushrooms are golden brown, about 8 minutes. Add the cabbage and toss until the cabbage is wilted and bright green, about 2 minutes. Add the white wine and cook, scraping the bottom of the skillet, until the wine is almost completely evaporated, about 2 minutes. Transfer the mushroom mixture to a mixing bowl and stir in the couscous, parsley, and salt and pepper to taste. (The mushroom mixture may be made in advance and stored, covered, in the refrigerator for up to 1 day.)

3. To make the crèpes, spray a 7-inch crepe pan or nonstick pan with vegetable cooking spray and place over medium-low heat. Pour 2 tablespoons of the batter into the pan and immediately tilt the pan to coat the entire bottom of the pan with a thin, even layer of batter. Cook until the underside of the crèpe is a lacy, golden brown, about 1 minute. Flip the crèpe and cook until the second side is golden brown in spots—it will not have the same lacy pattern of the first side. Remove the crèpe to a plate and repeat with the remaining batter, stacking the crèpes on the plate until all are cooked. It will take a few crèpes before you get the knack of making perfect crèpes: The heat should be high enough to brown the first side of the crèpe in a minute or so, but not so high that the batter solidifies before it coats the entire surface of the pan. (The crèpes may be made up to 3 days ahead. Cool, wrap lightly in plastic, and store in the refrigerator.)

4. Place one of the crèpes, lacy side down, on the work surface. Place 2 tablespoons of the mushroom mixture in the center of the crèpe. Gather the edges of the crèpe over the filling, pinching the crèpe together to form a little pouch with a ruffled top. Secure the "neck" of the pouch with a length of blanched chive, tied in a bow. (The pouches may be formed up to 3 hours in advance.)

5. To serve the pouches, spray a large skillet, preferably nonstick, with vegetable cooking spray and place over low heat. Place the

Preparing Couscous

Although the Crèpe Pouches recipe calls for only ½ cup couscous, it's difficult to prepare such a minuscule batch. Best to make at least 1½ cups and serve the rest at another meal. Couscous will keep, tightly covered, in the refrigerator for up to 2 days. Reheat in a covered saucepan with 2 tablespoons water over low heat. Fluff with a fork before serving.

To make couscous, place ¾ cup water, 1 tablespoon unsalted butter, and ½ teaspoon kosher or sea salt in a small saucepan and bring to a boil over high heat. Stir in ½ cup couscous, take the pan off the heat, and cover. Let sit until the water is absorbed, about 3 minutes. Fluff with a fork before measuring; you should have 1½ cups cooked couscous.

pouches ruffled side up in the skillet and cook until the underside is golden brown and crisp, about 5 minutes. Serve immediately. To eat, hold the pouches by the top and bite into the pouch.

Note: To blanch the chives, heat a large skillet of water to a boil. Lay the chives in the water and cook them just until softened, about 5 seconds. Remove with a slotted spoon and drain on paper towels.

Arepas with Shiitakes and Spinach

*A*repas are an ancient and very satisfying bread made of precooked cornmeal and water. In Colombia and Venezuela they are eaten plain or split and filled with any number of hot fillings or stuffed, pita-like, for quick lunches and snacks.

Arepas are easy to make, but there is a catch. Arepas contain no leavening or shortening. A special type of cornmeal—one that has been precooked—is essential for making the dough. If you cannot find this special type of flour, try the filling spooned inside a split loaf of not-too-sweet cornbread or tossed with freshly cooked pasta. The shiitakes, mellowed out with spinach, make a full-flavored filling for either option.

AREPAS DOUGH

1 cup precooked white cornmeal
(see Note)
1 teaspoon kosher or sea salt
1¼ cups warm water
Vegetable oil, as needed

SHIITAKE AND SPINACH FILLING

1 tablespoon olive oil
1 tablespoon unsalted butter
½ cup finely diced red onion
3 cloves garlic, sliced thin
1 pound Oakwood or other shiitake
mushrooms, stems removed, caps
sliced thin
1 pound spinach, stemmed, washed,
and thoroughly dried
¼ cup sour cream
Salt and freshly ground black
pepper

1. To prepare the arepas, place the cornmeal and salt in a medium-size bowl, then slowly pour in the water, mixing as you pour, until the dough is stiff and smooth. Let the dough stand in the bowl 5 minutes. It will become even stiffer as it stands.

2. Divide the dough into 4 equal parts. Shape each into a circle about 2½ inches wide by ½ inch thick. Place the circles on a baking sheet and let stand at room temperature until they feel dry to the touch, about 30 minutes. Turn them over and dry the other side, 30 minutes more.

3. Preheat the oven to 350°F.

4. Use the vegetable oil to lightly grease a heavy, ovenproof griddle or skillet, preferably cast iron, large enough to hold all the arepas. Heat the griddle or skillet over medium heat.

5. Add the arepas to the skillet. Cook them, turning once, until they are crisp and lightly browned in places, about 8 minutes. Place the griddle in the oven and bake the arepas until they feel light when lifted from the griddle, about 20 minutes. The arepas will be quite moist and dense in the center.

6. To prepare the filling, heat the oil and butter in a deep 4-quart pot over medium heat until foaming. Add the onion and cook until wilted, about 3 minutes. Then add the garlic and cook, stirring occasionally, until the onion is tender and lightly browned, about 5 minutes. Add half the mushrooms and cook, stirring, until they begin to wilt. Add the remaining mushrooms and stir until they begin to wilt. Cover the pot and lower the heat to low. Cook until the mushrooms are completely wilted and begin to give up a little of their liquid. If they start to stick before giving up liquid, add 2 to 3 tablespoons water to the pot. Uncover the pot, increase the heat to medium, and cook until the liquid is evaporated and the mushrooms are tender, about 5 minutes. Stir in the spinach, a handful at a time, waiting for each addition to wilt before adding the next. Remove the pot from the heat immediately. Stir

Arepas

I have fond memories of a pre-career job threading tapes in the language lab of an English as a second language school in Boston. Since I was never terribly busy, I hung out in the lunchroom with Yena, a talented belly dancer of Middle Eastern extraction, whose job it was to provide lunch every day. The students—all from foreign countries, of course—liked to get involved in the cooking once in a while. In a basement kitchen the size of refrigerator, the Venezuelan contingent introduced us to arepas. Hot off the skillet, these little buns were crunchy on the outside, oozing with warm cheese on the inside. This comfort food was so evocative that no matter what native language we spoke, we all managed to get the recipe down.

in the sour cream and salt and pepper to taste. You should have about 2 cups of filling.

To Serve Arepas

*A*repas are delicious served piping hot and plain with any zippy mushroom dish, such as Mushroom Chili (page 215) or Mushroom and Ham Gravy (page 258). Split a warm arepa and place it in a shallow bowl before topping with the chili. Or split the arepa in half and fill with roasted cremini (page 28) or Grilled Portobello Caps (page 193). A slice of fresh mozzarella or room temperature Brie and a drizzling of olive oil make an excellent addition.

7. Let the arepas cool for 5 minutes, then split them like English muffins. Place one half on each plate, spoon some of the filling over, and top with the second half.

Note: The special type of cornmeal—precooked white cornmeal—needed to make arepas is available in many Latin markets. One widely available brand, P.A.N., was used to test this recipe.

Double Fun Mushroom Wontons

**MAKES ABOUT
24 WONTONS,
SERVES 6 TO 8**

*G*inger gives wild mushrooms a kick, and wonton wrappers give these a voluptuous shape. The mushrooms may be deep-fried and served with Mushroom Soy Dipping Sauce (page 55) or poached and served in Wontons in Mushroom Broth (page 68)

4 ounces shiitake mushrooms, stemmed and cleaned
4 ounces honshimeji or oyster mushrooms, trimmed
2 tablespoons vegetable oil
2 scallions (white and green parts), trimmed and minced
2 tablespoons minced peeled ginger
1 tablespoon Mushroom Soy Sauce (page 255) or good-quality soy sauce

2 teaspoons sesame oil
1 teaspoon cornstarch
½ teaspoon sugar
20 wonton skins
Vegetable oil, for deep frying (optional)

1. Coarsely chop the shiitake and honshimeji mushrooms, then transfer them to a food processor. Process, using quick on/off pulses, until finely chopped.

2. Heat the vegetable oil in a large skillet over medium heat. Add the scallions and ginger. Cook until the ginger is fragrant, about 30 seconds. Add the mushrooms and cook, stirring constantly, until the liquid is evaporated and the mushrooms are golden brown, about 4 minutes. Transfer the mushrooms to a small bowl and cool completely.

3. Stir the soy sauce, sesame oil, cornstarch, and sugar into the mushrooms until the cornstarch is dissolved.

4. Set the mushroom filling, a small bowl of water, and the wonton wrappers (covered by a clean kitchen towel), side by side on a work surface and form wontons as described on page 36.

5. Once formed, deep-fry the wontons following the directions in steps 4 and 5 on pages 36 and 37 or poach (page 68).

Shrimp, Shiitake, and Wood Ear Wontons

This recipe replaces the usual pork filling of wontons with powerfully flavored shiitakes and springy textured wood ears. Deep-fry the wontons as described below or poach them and serve in broth as described on page 68.

**MAKES ABOUT
36 WONTONS,
SERVES 8 TO 10
AS AN
APPETIZER**

6 small (about 2-inch) dried shiitake
  mushrooms
1 large piece (about ½ ounce) dried wood
  ear mushroom
Hot water, for soaking the mushrooms
½ pound medium (about 16) shrimp, peeled,
  deveined, and cut into 1-inch lengths
2 scallions (white and green parts), trimmed
  and cut into 1-inch lengths
10 slices of canned water chestnuts, coarsely
  chopped (about ¼ cup)
¼ cup fresh cilantro leaves
2 tablespoons Mushroom Soy Sauce (page
  255) or good-quality soy sauce

2 teaspoons Mushroom-Infused Sherry
  (page 255) or good-quality dry sherry
  (optional)
1 tablespoon cold water
1 tablespoon toasted sesame seeds
  (optional; see Notes)
1 teaspoon cornstarch
1 teaspoon sugar
1 teaspoon rice wine vinegar or other mild,
  white vinegar
About 36 wonton wrappers (see Notes)
Vegetable oil, for deep frying
Mushroom Soy Dipping Sauce (page 55),
  for serving

1. Place the dried shiitake and wood ear mushrooms in a heat-proof bowl. Pour in enough hot water to cover them completely. Soak until softened, about 30 minutes. Drain the mushrooms and discard the soaking liquid, which can taste unpleasantly bitter. Remove and discard the stems from the shiitake mushrooms and the hard, central core from the wood ear mushrooms. Coarsely chop all the mushrooms. Combine the mushrooms, shrimp, scallions, water chestnuts, and cilantro in a small bowl. Refrigerate for 20 minutes.

2. Turn the contents of the bowl onto a cutting board. Using a cleaver or large knife, chop all the ingredients with a rocking motion until the scallions and water chestnuts are finely chopped and the shrimp is the consistency of ground beef. Or place half of the chilled shrimp mixture in a food processor and chop, using quick on/off motions, until all the ingredients are finely chopped. Repeat with the remaining shrimp mixture. Return the shrimp mixture to the bowl. Stir in the soy sauce, sherry, water, sesame seeds, cornstarch, sugar, and vinegar until thoroughly mixed.

3. Form the wontons as described in the box.

4. Pour enough vegetable oil into a large (12-inch) deep cast-iron skillet to fill two-thirds full. Heat the oil over medium heat until a deep-fry thermometer inserted into the center of the oil reads 350°F. (If the oil is the right temperature a wonton should float to the top almost immediately after adding it to the oil.) Carefully slip wontons into the oil. Fry only as many wontons as will float freely in the oil at one time. The temperature will drop after adding the wontons. Adjust the heat to maintain the heat as close as possible to 325°F during frying. Fry until the wontons are deep golden brown, about 4 to 5 minutes. Turn

To Form Wontons

Set the filling, a small bowl of water, and the wonton wrappers (covered by a clean kitchen towel), side by side on a work surface. Remove 1 wonton wrapper from under the towel and place it with one of the points toward you. (Keep the remaining wrappers covered.) Dip a finger in the water and moisten all edges of the wrapper. Place 1 level teaspoon of mushroom filling in the center of the wrapper. Fold the bottom half of the wrapper over the filling, to enclose it and make a triangle shape. Press the edges together to seal. Place the tip of your forefinger over the part of the triangle that contains the filling. Fold the left point of the triangle over your finger. Place a dab of water on the right point of the triangle and fold that over your finger so it overlaps the other point. Press firmly to seal the points together. Fold the points back slightly, to give the wonton its distinctive shape. Place the wonton on a kitchen towel–lined baking sheet and repeat with the remaining wrappers and filling.

them as necessary so they cook evenly.

5. Remove the wontons with a slotted spoon or wire skimmer to a plate lined with paper towels to drain. Repeat with the remaining wontons. Keep the cooked wontons warm in a 300°F oven for up to 10 minutes. Serve hot, with Mushroom Soy Dipping Sauce.

Notes: Wonton wrappers can be found in Asian groceries, gourmet markets, and in the frozen food section of supermarkets.

To toast sesame seeds, place the seeds in a large, heavy skillet over medium-low heat. Stir and toss just until the seeds turn golden brown, about 6 minutes.

Openers

There's nothing like the haunting aroma of mushrooms to kick off a dinner in just the right spirit. Piping hot and paired with a selection of complementary ingredients, they entice the diner to dig in—for me, sometimes so beguilingly that I prefer a second helping to the next course. Some of these tidbits, such as the Double Oyster Gratin, and Garlic Flan with Sautéed Bluefoot Mushrooms, seduce the palate with the interaction of woodsy and creamy. Others play with fire, combining mushrooms with spicy, surprising notes such as chili peppers, olives, and poppy seeds.

Often I'll follow a mushroom starter with a hearty winter roast or stew served in small portions, then finish the meal with a salad. In the lighter months of spring and summer, I'll go on to a main-dish salad featuring meat as a minor player or fish roasted with robust ingredients such as tomato and olives or Asian spices.

If it seems I'm tempting the dollars out of your wallet in some recipes, keep in mind that starters are small, teaser portions that are meant to entice and flatter the guests. A splurge on the smaller course makes a good impression and can be followed by economy in the entrée. When it comes to sumptuous dining, first impressions certainly do last!

Porcini Carpaccio on a Bed of Greens

SERVES 4 AS A FIRST COURSE

Beatrice Tosti di Valminiuta is chef/owner of the tiny Il Bagatto on Manhattan's Lower East Side. Her specialty is big-hearted food without the bells and whistles. This salad—a smoky, herbal palate pleaser—calls for the best quality ingredients. Look for the firmest porcini and pull out the vintage balsamic vinegar and boutique olive oil. Smoked scamorza is a firm, piquant cow's milk cheese from Italy. If it's not available at your local cheese or Italian specialty shop, try another firm, smoked cheese, such as gouda or mozzarella.

2 firm, medium porcini, wiped clean
    (about 4 ounces)
3 tablespoons extra virgin olive oil
1 tablespoon fresh lemon juice
Kosher or sea salt and freshly ground
    black pepper

4 cups arugula leaves or mesclun
    salad greens, well cleaned
5 ounces smoked scamorza cheese,
    sliced ⅛ inch thin
4 teaspoons balsamic vinegar

1. Trim off the bottom of the stems of the porcini. Using a very sharp knife, slice the mushrooms through the cap and stem as thin as possible. Place the mushroom slices in a shallow bowl and toss with 2 tablespoons of the olive oil, the lemon juice, a pinch of sea salt, and 2 twists of the peppermill.

2. Toss the arugula in a salad bowl with ½ teaspoon salt, ¼ teaspoon pepper, and the remaining 1 tablespoon olive oil, using just enough olive oil to lightly moisten the leaves.

3. Mound the salad on 4 salad plates. Lay the sliced cheese on top, in concentric circles. Drizzle the vinegar over the cheese. Top with the dressed porcini and serve.

Il Bagatto

Beatrice didn't always have a restaurant; she had knock-'em-dead dinner parties. She'd make the rounds of New York City's widely spread food meccas, ferrying groceries around in an old boat of Cadillac convertible. When Beatrice got to our warehouse in Tribeca, she brought with her a breath of fresh air and a charming Italian accent, as full and round as a porcini. We'd pile up crates of porcini, trays of mâche and melons, and sprigs of rosemary, wistfully wondering if we'd ever get to taste this food born of passion. Luckily, Il Bagatto was begat. Now my husband Thierry and I relish our evenings at the best dinner party in town, feasting on fresh Italian food in the company of grafitti artists and TV newscasters.

Glazed Jade Vegetables with Wood Ears

I think there are people who need crunch in their lives. This vegetable-lover's dream satisfies that need. We make it in the spring, when local asparagus comes on the market. If crisp sugar snap peas show up in your area in spring as well, try them in place of the snow peas. They are thicker, but, like snow peas, only require a quick stir-fry. And the results are sweet and delicious. The wood ear, though not rich in flavor, adds resilient texture and a lovely deep brown color.

SERVES 4 AS A FIRST COURSE OR SIDE DISH

2 large (about 1 ounce) dried
    wood ear mushrooms
Boiling water
10 stalks (about 12 ounces) medium
    asparagus
4 ounces snow peas
2 tablespoons Mushroom Soy Sauce
    (page 255) or good-quality
    soy sauce
2 tablespoons fresh orange juice
1 teaspoon cornstarch
2 tablespoons peanut or vegetable oil
3 tablespoons finely chopped peeled
    hazelnuts or blanched almonds
    (see box, this page)
2 tablespoons minced Black Forest or
    other lean smoked ham

To Peel Hazelnuts

*P*reheat the oven to 300°F. Spread the hazelnuts out on a baking sheet and place in the oven until the skins are loosened, about 6 minutes. Remove from the oven. Place the nuts in a clean kitchen towel and rub off as much of the skin as possible. Cool completely. Chop the nuts.

1. Place the wood ears in a heatproof bowl and pour over enough boiling water to completely cover the mushrooms. Let stand until softened, about 30 minutes. Drain thoroughly. Pinch off or cut out and discard the hard center part of the wood ear. Cut the wood ear into ½-inch strips. Set aside.

2. Cut or break off the tough bottoms from the asparagus stalks. Cut the remainder of the stalks into 2-inch lengths. Trim both ends of the snow peas. Stir the soy sauce, orange juice, and cornstarch in a small bowl until the cornstarch is dissolved. Have all ingredients ready to add to the stir-fry.

3. Pour the oil into a wok or a large, heavy skillet over high heat. When the oil is rippling, add the hazelnuts and ham. Cook until the hazelnuts are golden brown, about 30 seconds. Add the asparagus and stir-fry until bright green, about 1 minute. Add the wood ears and stir-fry to soften, 1 minute. Add the snow peas and stir-fry until crisp-tender, about 1 minute. Stir the soy-cornstarch liquid into the wok and heat until boiling and lightly thickened, about 15 seconds. Remove the wok from the heat and spoon the stir-fry into a serving dish. Serve immediately.

Mexican Puffball Pizza

MAKES ABOUT
8 PIZZAS,
SERVES 8 AS A
FIRST COURSE

This inviting, spiced-up version of pizza comes with a puffball crust. It was invented by Peter Klein, who for years cheffed at El Teddy's, a kooky downtown after-hours hangout for New York's chefs. Puffballs are irregularly shaped, so the number and size of the pizzas you can make will vary from puffball to puffball. As for the end slices, try mini-pizzas or simmer the slices in a clear Japanese-inspired broth. Serve the pizzas as a nibble, vegetarian first course, or side dish for a pork roast.

¼ cup olive oil

1 large clove garlic, sliced

1 large (about ½ pound and 6 inches in diameter), puffball mushroom, cleaned

Kosher or sea salt or Seasoning Salt (page 253) and freshly ground black pepper

1 cup Basic Tomato Sauce (page 284) or other good-quality tomato sauce

1 canned chipotle chili, or less to taste, finely chopped (see Note)

1 tablespoon chopped fresh oregano

1 cup grated Monterey Jack cheese

Few drops of hot chili oil (optional)

1. Preheat a grill to hot or heat a grill pan over medium heat for 10 minutes.

2. Place the olive oil and garlic in a blender. Blend until the garlic is very finely chopped. Cut the puffball into ½-inch-thick slices. Use a long serrated knife with a gentle back and forth motion for best results. (Puffballs that aren't perfectly fresh will tend to crumble.) Brush both sides of the slices with the garlic oil and sprinkle with salt and pepper to taste. Grill the slices until well marked and softened, 2 to 3 minutes on each side. Carefully transfer them to a baking sheet in a single layer.

3. Stir the tomato sauce and chipotle chili together until blended. Spread the sauce in a thin even layer over the puffball slices. Sprinkle with oregano, then cheese. If desired, drizzle with a little chili oil. (The pizzas may be prepared to this point up to 1 day in advance. Cover and refrigerate. Bring to room temperature before continuing.)

4. Place the broiler rack about 3 inches from the heat and preheat the broiler. Broil the pizzas until the sauce is bubbling and the cheese is golden brown, about 2 minutes. Serve hot.

Note: Chipotle chilies are smoked jalapeño chilies, and they are quite fiery. They are sold loose in their dried state or, more often, canned in an *adobo* sauce. If canned chipotle chilies are unavailable, substitute any other hot chili to taste.

Sautéed Foie Gras with Cèpes

In the southwest region of France, some version of this heavenly dish appears on just about every celebration table. This version came to me from Ariane Daguin, co-owner of the specialty food company D'Artagnan. The smooth unctuous—let's just say it—the fat of the foie gras, the woodsy cèpes, and the sweet sauce join together for one purpose: to give pleasure. It's with a special occasion in mind that I recommend this recipe—its cost and pure luxury can be offset with a post-fête week of steamed vegetables and rice. Another way to make the most of it is to put aside just a bit of the main ingredients for Cèpe and Chestnut Soup (page 78).

Fresh foie gras can be confused with foie gras pâté, terrine, and mousse, so be sure to be clear when buying. You want the real unadulterated deal. The key to cooking foie gras is speed. Because it melts on contact with heat, the idea is to cook it just to sear. If you don't use the whole lobe, keep the rest tightly wrapped in plastic wrap in the refrigerator for up to a week, and sneak snacks of seared foie gras on toast for breakfast. Don't worry if it discolors.

SERVES 4 AS A FIRST COURSE

1 lobe (1½ to 2 pounds) grade A fresh
   foie gras (see Note)
Kosher or sea salt and freshly ground
   black pepper
1 cup Demi-Glacé (page 282)
1 cup Port
½ cup balsamic vinegar
2 tablespoons butter or duck fat
   (see page 324), or more if necessary
8 ounces baby new potatoes, such as
   fingerlings, scrubbed and sliced
   ⅛ inch thick
8 ounces fresh cèpes, wiped clean and sliced
   ¼ inch thick through
   cap and stem
2 cloves garlic, finely chopped
1 small shallot, minced
1 cup chopped fresh flat-leaf parsley

1. Cut the foie gras into 8 equal slices. Sprinkle lightly with salt and pepper on both sides.

2. Place the Demi-Glace, Port, and vinegar in a medium-size, heavy, nonreactive saucepan. Boil slowly until reduced to a syrupy consistency, about 15 minutes.

3. Heat a large, dry sauté pan to very hot over high heat. Sauté the foie gras slices for 1 minute on each side. Drain immediately on paper towels. Transfer to a plate, cover with aluminum foil, and keep warm on the back of the stove.

4. Wipe the sauté pan clean. Add the butter and melt it over high heat. Add the potatoes and sauté, stirring rapidly, until both sides have browned, about 4 minutes. Transfer to a plate and keep warm.

5. Add more butter to the pan if it is dry and melt until very hot. Add the cèpes, browning quickly, about 1 minute. Reduce the heat to medium and season with salt and pepper. Cover and cook, stirring frequently, until soft and limp, about 9 minutes. During the last minute, add the garlic, shallot, and parsley. Taste and adjust the seasoning.

6. To serve, place the cèpes in the center of each of 4 serving plates. Top them with a slice of foie gras, sprinkled with sea salt. Surround with the potatoes. Drizzle the sauce over the foie gras.

Note: Fresh foie gras is available year-round (see Mail-Order Sources, page 324).

Cèpes

*T*he stems and caps of cèpes lend themselves to different dishes. If you plan to grill the caps whole or want nice sauté slices, trim off and set aside the stems. Raymonde Monier, our Dordogne cousin, cooks the stems as follows. Using a paring knife and no cutting board, she cubes peeled potatoes and cèpe stems, letting them drop into her apron. She heats up her trusty cast-iron skillet over medium-high heat. In go huge chunks of salted butter and a few spoonfuls of duck fat. As the fat sizzles, Raymonde nonchalantly empties her apronful into the pan. From time to time she gives the skillet a vigorous shake. As the cèpes brown, the heat goes down to low, and in go tiny chopped garlic pieces and a flurry of sea salt. Raymonde covers the top and simmers, shakes, and sniffs for the next half hour, and—in true Périgourdine style—doesn't drop a stitch of conversation the whole time! Of course the results are spectacular.

Candy Cap and Duck Tapas

Candy caps are sweet, ruby-color mushrooms that remind me of the little red hot candies used as buttons on gingerbread men. In this dish, they are tossed with duck, figs, and Port for a topping to spoon or spread. A good substitute mushroom is mousseron, which comes in beige and violet varieties. Preserved duck legs (duck confit) is available in specialty markets and by mail order (see page 324). Roasted turkey legs can be used instead of the preserved duck.

½ cup Port

2 dried juniper berries, crushed

½ teaspoon dried thyme

4 dried figs

2 preserved duck legs or 1 small
    roasted turkey leg

2 tablespoons unsalted butter,
    or more if needed

8 ounces candy cap mushrooms,
    wiped clean

½ onion, thinly sliced

⅓ cup Demi-Glace (page 282)

2 teaspoons fresh lemon juice

Kosher or sea salt and freshly ground
    black pepper

Toasted slices French bread or
    1 recipe Old-World Polenta (page 203)

1. Combine the Port, juniper berries, thyme, and figs in a small bowl. Set aside for 3 hours or cover and leave out overnight.

2. Preheat the oven to 350°F.

3. Place the preserved duck legs in a small, heavy-bottomed baking dish. Bake until the skin crisps, about 20 minutes.

4. Strain the marinade reserving it and the figs. Slice the figs about ⅛ inch thick and return them to the marinade.

5. Remove the duck meat from the bones. Shred it into fine strings with your fingers. You should have about 1½ cups of meat. Set aside.

6. Melt 2 tablespoons butter in a large sauté pan over medium heat until foaming Add the mushrooms and onion and sauté, stirring, until the mushrooms are limp, about 6 minutes. Candy caps do not give up a lot of liquid, so if they stick to the pan, add 1 teaspoon of butter and lower the heat. Stir in the duck meat, the figs with their marinade, the Demi-Glace, and lemon juice. Cook over medium heat, until the sauce is slightly syrupy, 2 minutes. Season with salt and pepper to taste.

7. Serve in a pretty bowl to spoon over crusty toasts, or use as a topping for polenta.

Harry Sasson's Taco Chino

I n the middle of Bogota's humming Zona Rosa is H. Sasson, a spectacularly beautiful restaurant that features the work of local artists, a sit-down saté bar, and Asian-inspired versions of traditional Colombian and other Latin dishes. Harry's Taco Chino (Chinese taco), for example, uses crisp lettuce in place of a tortilla, a mushroom stir-fry for filling, and hoisin sauce in place of the salsa cruda. Harry was kind enough to share this version of his taco chino with us.

Basil Tips à la Barbara

R ight after cooking school in the mid-'80s, I worked as an assistant to Barbara Kafka, the food writer and restaurant consultant. That's where Chris and I met. Chris was in and out of Barbara's home/office too, working with restaurants and recipes. That compact New York townhouse was a whirlwind of high-level food buzz. In the kitchen, grapefruit and couscous were shaped into the nascent spa cuisine. And at the dining room table, a real Italian chef once prepared luncheon with nary a trace of tomato sauce.

On those rare days when the buzz settled to a hum, we got down to basics. Barbara's attention to detail made her food sing. One example is how she handled fragile, fragrant basil. Here are her tips for prepping basil without bruising it.

• Drop the leaves in a basin of cold, still water and press down on the leaves to wash them, without rubbing the leaves too much.

• Dry them gently in a salad spinner or shake out the water in a colander.

• Rip the leaves apart with your hands. Avoid using a carbon steel knife, which will blacken the basil.

About ⅙ of a 12-ounce package Asian rice noodles (2 ounces; long strands pulled apart)

Vegetable oil

1 large head iceberg lettuce

½ cup hoisin sauce

2 teaspoons finely chopped peeled fresh ginger or pickled ginger

1 teaspoon finely chopped garlic

8 ounces honshimeji, oyster, yellow oyster, or shiitake mushrooms, or a mix of any of these, cleaned, trimmed, and coarsely chopped (about 2 cups)

¼ cup finely chopped celery

¼ cup finely chopped carrot

¼ cup finely chopped red onion

¼ cup finely chopped leek, white parts only

2 tablespoons chopped fresh basil

½ cup fresh or frozen corn kernels

2 tablespoons oyster sauce

2 tablespoons Chinese or Japanese dark sesame oil

1. Leave the noodles in the largest pieces possible, pour enough vegetable oil to a depth of about 1 inch into a large (12-inch), deep, heavy skillet, preferably cast iron. Heat the oil over medium heat until a rice noodle placed in the oil puffs and sizzles instantly. Add about half the noodles to the oil. They will instantly expand, turn white, and form a pillow. Insert a long-handled kitchen fork into the center of the pillow and turn it over to cook the other side just until it too expands. The whole process takes about 10 seconds; don't brown the noodles. Remove the noodles from the skillet and drain on paper towels. Repeat with the remaining rice noodles, testing the temperature of the oil with a noodle first to make sure it is hot enough.

2. Pull off any wilted or damaged outer leaves from the lettuce. Carefully remove the large leaves from the lettuce, leaving them intact as much as possible. You will need about 8 large leaves. If they vary in size, that is fine. Cut out and discard the thick part of the central core from each leaf. Wash the leaves in cool water and dry them thoroughly, preferably in a salad spinner. (The tacos may be prepared to this point up to 2 hours in advance. Refrigerate the lettuce leaves and store the noodles, loosely covered, at room temperature until needed.)

3. When ready to serve, place the lettuce leaves and fried noodles in separate bowls and set aside. Place the hoisin sauce in a small bowl, place a small spoon in it, and set aside.

4. Heat 2 tablespoons vegetable oil in a wok over very high heat. Add the ginger and garlic. Fry until lightly browned, about 10 seconds. Watch carefully so they don't burn. Add the mushrooms, celery, carrot, red onion, leek, and basil. Stir-fry 2 tablespoons until the mushrooms are lightly browned, about 4 minutes. Add the corn, oyster sauce, sesame oil, and water. Stir-fry until the sauce is boiling and evenly coats the vegetables. Transfer the mushroom mixture to a serving bowl.

5. To make the tacos, spread a little of the hoisin sauce over the bottom third of a lettuce leaf. Place a small mound of the mushroom filling and noodles on top. Roll the lettuce leaf up from the bottom to cover the filling. Fold in the sides of the leaf over the filling, then continue rolling up the leaf to make a tight taco.

Herb-Crusted Parasols

Each bite of these crusty, juicy parasols must be savored, for they go so quickly! Even though they are delectable on their own, you may want to set out some favorite sauces—garlicky goat cheese, herb-spiked mayonnaise, fresh tomato salsa—for dipping.

SERVES 4 AS A FIRST COURSE

1 pound parasol mushrooms, cleaned
2 large eggs
1 cup all-purpose flour
1 cup fine dry bread crumbs
1 tablespoon finely chopped fresh flat-leaf
    parsley or 1 teaspoon minced tarragon
2 tablespoons grated Parmesan cheese
    (optional)
Vegetable oil, as needed

1. Preheat the oven to its lowest setting.

2. Pull the stems from the caps of the mushrooms, working gently if the caps are cup-shaped and you would like to keep them that way. More mature mushrooms, with opened, flat, or split caps, can be prepared whole or cut in half.

3. Beat the eggs in a shallow bowl with a few drops of water until foamy. Place the flour and the bread crumbs in separate shallow bowls. Stir the parsley and cheese, if using, into the bread crumbs. To bread the mushroom caps, first roll each in flour until completely coated. Then dip into the beaten egg until coated, using your fingers to coat the inside of the cap with egg, if necessary. Let some of the excess egg drip off, then roll the mushrooms in bread crumbs. Press the crumbs gently onto the caps to help them stick. Let stand on a wire rack or baking sheet while coating the others. When all the caps are breaded, reroll them, one by one, in the bread crumbs to make a sturdy coating. Tap off the excess crumbs.

4. Pour enough vegetable oil into a large (10- to 12-inch), deep skillet, preferably cast iron, to fill two-thirds full. Heat over medium heat until a frying thermometer inserted into the center of the oil reads 350°F. (If the oil is the right temperature, a sprinkling of bread crumbs will sizzle immediately after adding it to the oil.)

5. Carefully slip the mushrooms caps into the oil. Add only as many caps as will fit without touching each other. Fry the mushrooms, turning as necessary, until the bread crumbs are evenly golden brown, about 4 minutes. The more cup-shaped the mushroom caps are, the more turning they will need during frying to help them cook evenly. A pair of long chopsticks or a slotted spoon works well for this.

6. Remove the mushrooms with a slotted spoon or wire skimmer to a plate lined with paper towels to drain. Repeat with the remaining mushrooms if necessary. Keep the fried mushrooms warm in the oven for up to 10 minutes. Serve immediately, while hot.

Cauliflower Mushroom Fritters with Indian Dipping Sauce

*C*runchy on the outside, moist and mushroomy inside, these fritters make a good hands-on party dish. Cauliflower mushrooms, with their powerful perfume, are ideal, but hen of the woods are also superb. The lemon-herb dipping sauce can be used in its basic version, but I like to enrich it with yogurt and curry powder. It only gets better as all the flavors are melded together. Chickpea flour is available in Indian groceries, Italian specialty food stores, health food stores, and by mail order (see page 324). The amount of chile pepper used depends upon individual taste. If you do not have a spice mill (I use a well-cleaned coffee grinder), substitute ¾ teaspoon each of ground cumin and coriander for the seeds; leave the fennel seeds whole.

DIPPING SAUCE

¼ cup chopped fresh cilantro

2 tablespoons chopped fresh mint

1 to 2 serrano chilies, stems removed,
    sliced very thin

½ cup fresh lemon juice

1 cup plain yogurt (optional)

1 teaspoon curry powder (optional)

FRITTERS

1 teaspoon whole cumin seed

1 teaspoon whole coriander seed

1 teaspoon whole fennel seed

¾ cup chickpea flour
    (see Mail-Order Sources, page 324)

½ teaspoon baking powder

¼ cup plus 1 tablespoon warm water

3 tablespoons vegetable oil, plus
    more for frying

2 tablespoons finely chopped fresh
    cilantro or flat-leaf parsley

8 ounces cauliflower or hen of the woods
    mushrooms, cleaned and finely chopped

Kosher or sea salt

Canola or vegetable oil, for
    deep-frying

1. To prepare the dipping sauce, stir the cilantro, mint, chilies, and lemon juice together in a small bowl. Use as is or, if desired, stir the mixture into the yogurt. Also stir in the curry powder if desired. The sauce will improve if it stands covered at room temperature for 1 hour or for up to 1 day in the refrigerator.

2. To prepare the fritters, place the cumin, coriander, and fennel seeds in a small dry saucepan or skillet over medium heat and toast until the spices are fragrant and lightly browned, about 3 minutes. Cool the seeds completely. Grind them to a fine powder in a spice grinder.

3. Sift the chickpea flour and baking powder into a mixing bowl. Make a well in the center. Pour in the water and 1 tablespoon of the vegetable oil. Whisk until smooth. Stir in the cilantro. Let stand at room temperature for 30 minutes.

4. Heat the remaining 2 table-spoons vegetable oil in a large skillet over medium heat. Add the mushrooms and stir to coat with oil. Stir in the ground spices and cover the skillet. Cook until the mushrooms begin to give off liquid, about 4 minutes. Uncover the skillet and cook until the mushrooms are tender and lightly browned, about 4 minutes. Cool the mushrooms completely, then stir them into the batter.

5. Preheat the oven to 300°F.

6. Pour enough vegetable oil into a large (12-inch), deep cast-iron skillet to fill two thirds full. Heat the oil over medium heat until a frying thermometer inserted into the center of the oil reads 350°F. (When the oil is the right temperature, a small drop of batter will float to the top almost immediately after adding it to the oil.). Carefully slip rounded teaspoonfuls of the mushroom mixture into the oil. Fry only as many fritters as will float freely in the oil at one time. The temperature will drop after adding the fritters. Adjust the heat to maintain it as close as possible to 325°F during frying. Fry until the fritters are deep golden brown, turning as necessary so they cook evenly, about 4 to 5 minutes.

7. Remove the fritters with a slotted spoon or wire skimmer to a plate lined with paper towels to drain. Sprinkle with salt to taste. Repeat with the remaining batter. Keep the cooked fritters warm in a 300°F oven for up to 10 minutes. Serve the fritters hot, with the dipping sauce on the side.

Mushroom-Stuffed Mini Pumpkins

SERVES 6 AS A FIRST COURSE

The black and orange filling make this a natural for a Halloween centerpiece, but its wild mushroom flavor and creamy goodness make it more than a novelty. Serve it all autumn long, while Jack-Be-Littles are in season. And if you're a fan of pumpkin seeds, see page 52 for instructions on how to toast them.

6 miniature (about 8 ounces and about
    3½ inches in diameter) sugar
    pumpkins, such as Jack-Be-Littles
    or 3 acorn squash, cut in half
3 tablespoons unsalted butter
4 ounces black trumpets, trimmed,
    cleaned, and coarsely chopped
4 ounces yellowfoot mushrooms, trimmed,
    cleaned, and coarsely chopped
¼ cup light cream or part-skim
    ricotta cheese
1 egg yolk
1 teaspoon kosher or sea salt
¼ teaspoon freshly ground black pepper
⅛ teaspoon freshly grated or ground nutmeg
1 teaspoon minced fresh sage
3 tablespoons dry bread crumbs
1 tablespoon grated Parmesan cheese

1. Preheat the oven to 350°F.

2. Place the pumpkins, side by side, in an 11 × 9-inch baking dish, preferably glass or ceramic. Pour in cold water to a depth of about ¾ inch. Cover the dish securely with aluminum foil. Bake the pumpkins until they are easily pierced with a knife but not mushy, about 50 minutes. Remove the pumpkins from the pan and cool completely. (The pumpkins may be refrigerated, whole, after complete cooling for up to 1 day. Store, covered with aluminum foil in the refrigerator.) If you are continuing with the recipe, leave the oven on.

3. Heat 2 tablespoons of the butter in a large skillet over medium heat. Add the black trumpets and sauté, stirring often, until softened, about 3 minutes. Stir in the yellow-foot mushrooms and sauté until all the mushrooms are tender, about 5 minutes. Set aside.

4. When the pumpkins are completely cool, slice off about ½ inch of the top, including the stem. Scrape any flesh from the top and place it in a food processor. Set the tops aside. Working carefully with a teaspoon, scrape away just enough flesh from the center of the pumpkins to reveal the cluster of seeds inside. Remove the seeds and the attached fiber with as little flesh attached as possible. After removing the seeds, scrape the pulp from the pumpkins, leaving about ¼ inch attached to the sides to support the pumpkin shell while baking. Once cooked, the flesh will pull away easily from the shell, especially if the pumpkins have been chilled after baking. Work carefully to avoid tearing the shell. You should have about 1¾ cups of flesh. Place the flesh in a food processor as you work.

5. Process the pumpkin flesh until very smooth. Add the cream, egg yolk, salt, pepper, and nutmeg. Process until the mixture is creamy and light yellow, 1 to 2 minutes. Transfer the mixture to a mixing bowl. Or, pass the flesh through a food mill fitted with the fine disk, then put the purée in a mixing bowl and beat in the cream, egg yolk, salt, pepper, and nutmeg. Fold the sautéed mushrooms into the pumpkin purée.

6. Place the pumpkin shells in an 11 × 9-inch baking pan. Divide the

mushroom filling among them. (The pumpkins may be prepared to this point up to 1 day in advance. Refrigerate them and the tops

separately and bring them to room temperature before continuing.)

7. If you prepared the recipe in advance, preheat the oven to 350°F.

8. Melt the remaining 1 tablespoon butter in a small skillet. Stir in the sage. Cook until the sage is fragrant, about 2 minutes. Stir in the bread crumbs until they absorb all the butter. Cool completely, then stir in the cheese. Sprinkle the seasoned bread crumbs over the pumkins. Bake, uncovered, until the filling is set and the topping is golden brown, about 25 minutes. Serve hot, with the tops partially covering the filling.

To Toast Pumpkin Seeds

Preheat the oven to 350°F. Toss the pumpkin seeds in a colander and rub off the pumpkin flesh under cold running water. Pat the seeds dry with kitchen towels. Spread the seeds out on a baking sheet and bake, checking often after 10 minutes, just until dry and crisp, about 20 minutes. For a little variety, toss with cumin powder before toasting.

Garlic Flan and Sautéed Bluefoot

SERVES 6 AS A FIRST COURSE

Somehow, eggs just seem to cry out for the flavor of wild mushrooms. The velvety texture of this eggy flan reminds me of crème brulée. Any firm mushroom—shiitake or cèpe, for example—can be substituted for the bluefoot.

GARLIC FLAN
Unsalted butter, for greasing the ramekins
1½ cups heavy cream (for whipping)
5 cloves garlic, peeled
¼ cup walnuts, toasted (see box, page 22) and coarsely chopped
4 egg yolks
Kosher or sea salt and freshly ground black pepper
½ teaspoon grated or ground nutmeg
½ teaspoon Cèpe Powder (page 285)

MUSHROOM SAUCE
2 tablespoons unsalted butter
8 ounces fresh bluefoot mushrooms, cleaned and cut into ¾-inch cubes
1 shallot, minced (about 2 tablespoons)
1 cup Light Chicken Stock (page 280) or canned low-sodium chicken broth
2 tablespoons chopped fresh herbs, such as chives, chervil, and/or parsley

1. Preheat the oven to 275°F. Butter the insides of six 3½-inch-wide (4-ounce) ramekins.

2. Heat the cream and garlic in a small, heavy saucepan over low heat. Simmer to reduce to ⅔ cup, about 10 minutes. Do not boil. Place the garlic and a few drops of the cream in a mini food processor or blender and process until the garlic is creamy. Transfer to a medium-size bowl and whisk together the garlic, the remaining warm cream, the egg yolks, ½ teaspoon salt, ¼ teaspoon pepper, nutmeg, and cèpe powder in a shallow bowl until frothy. Divide the mixture among the 6 ramekins.

3. Place the ramekins in a roasting pan large enough to hold them comfortably and place in the oven. Carefully add as much hot water as needed to reach halfway up the sides of the ramekins. Bake until a knife inserted in the center of a custard comes clean, 45 to 50 minutes. Carefully remove the ramekins from the pan and set them on a kitchen towel.

4. To make the mushroom sauce, heat the 2 tablespoons butter over high heat in a large sauté pan. Add the mushrooms and sauté until lightly browned, 1 to 2 minutes. Reduce the heat to medium, add the shallot, and cook until translucent, 1 minute. Add the stock and simmer until it is absorbed by the mushrooms, about 10 minutes. Season to taste with salt and pepper. Stir in the walnuts and herbs.

5. Run a knife around the inside of the ramekins and turn the custards out onto individual salad plates. Spoon the sauce around each custard and serve warm.

Spring Pea Flan with a Mushroom Fricassée

SERVES 4 AS A FIRST COURSE

The color of this flan is beautifully delicate: a dainty mint green set off by chocolate-colored morels. The combination of peas and morels celebrates that most joyous spring moment, the appearance of fresh greens and browns in the produce markets. Kerry Heffernan, the chef at New York's Eleven Madison Park and one of Thierry's fly-fishing buddies, created this flan for a wild mushroom tasting dinner.

SPRING PEA FLAN

1 tablespoon unsalted butter, at room
   temperature
1 cup (1 pound in the shell) fresh peas or
   thawed drained frozen peas
1 cup half-and-half
¼ cup (½ bunch) blanched and
   thoroughly drained fresh spinach
   (about ¼ cup; optional, see Note)
4 sprigs of fresh chervil, tarragon, or flat-
   leaf parsley
Kosher or sea salt and freshly ground
   white pepper
2 large eggs

FRICASSEE

1 cup Light Chicken Stock (page 280) or
   canned low-sodium chicken broth
½ cup fresh peas (½ pound in the shell) or
   thawed, drained frozen peas
8 ounces small fresh morels, cleaned
   and trimmed
2 tablespoons chopped fresh chervil
3 tablespoons unsalted butter, cut into
   6 pieces
Kosher or sea salt and freshly ground
   white pepper

TO FINISH

8 very thin slices of prosciutto
Truffle oil or extra-virgin olive oil
4 sprigs of fresh chervil

1. Preheat the oven to 300°F.
Grease four 3½-inch-wide
(4-ounce) ramekins with the 1
tablespoon butter.

2. To make the flans, if using
fresh peas, cook them in a medium-
size saucepan of boiling salted
water until tender but still bright
green, about 5 minutes. Drain and
rinse the peas under cold running
water. Drain thoroughly. Frozen
peas need no precooking.

3. Combine the peas and half-
and-half in a blender and blend until
completely smooth. Add the
spinach (if using), 4 chervil sprigs,
and salt and pepper to taste. Blend
until very smooth. Add the eggs and
blend just until the eggs are
incorporated, about 10 seconds.
Strain the mixture through a
fine sieve. Divide the
mixture evenly among the
prepared ramekins.

4. Place the ramekins
in a deep baking dish or roasting
pan. Place the baking dish on the
oven rack and pour in enough hot
water to come halfway up the sides
of the ramekins. Bake until the
centers of the flans are set but not
firm to the touch, about 25
minutes. Remove the ramekins from
the baking dish and cool to
lukewarm.

5. While the flans are cooling,
make the fricassee: Heat the stock
to a boil in a medium-size
saucepan. Add the peas, morels,
and chopped chervil and bring
back to a boil. Remove from the
heat and add the butter, swirling
the pan to incorporate the butter
into the liquid. Add salt and pepper
to taste.

6. To serve, run a very thin-bladed paring knife around the edges of the flans to loosen them. Invert the flans onto the center of 4 shallow soup bowls. Divide the fricassee evenly among the bowls, spooning it around the flans. Drape 2 slices of prosciutto over each flan and drizzle the prosciutto with truffle oil. Garnish each plate with a chervil sprig. Serve immediately.

Note: To blanch spinach, first rinse thoroughly. Bring 2 cups of water to a boil over high heat in a medium-size saucepan. Drop in the spinach, leave for 10 seconds, then lift out with a slotted spoon to a colander. Refresh under cold running water, then lay the leaves on paper towels to drain.

Mushroom Tempura with Mushroom-Soy Dipping Sauce

Tempura, the Japanese method of batter-frying, traps the aroma and flavor of bite-size chunks of food—such as exotic mushrooms—inside a crisp, airy coating. It is delicate and delicious. The mushrooms are best right out of the hot oil, with only a brief moment to drain, so it is best to prepare them for just a few friends, gathered informally in the kitchen. Hand each a pair of chopsticks and a small bowl of the dipping sauce and start frying! If you would really like to serve them in a sit-down setting, fry the larger, sturdier mushrooms first and keep them warm in a 300°F oven for no longer than five minutes. Note that the dipping sauce is best prepared two days ahead of serving.

SERVES 6 AS A
FIRST COURSE

MUSHROOM-SOY DIPPING SAUCE

2 scallions (white and green parts),
    trimmed and cut crosswise into
    2-inch lengths
3 slices (⅛ inch thick) unpeeled fresh ginger
½ cup Mushroom Soy Sauce (page 255) or
    good-quality soy sauce
1 tablespoon mirin (see Note)
1 tablespoon sugar

TEMPURA

1 large egg
1 cup beer or water
1 cup all-purpose flour
½ teaspoon paprika
1 teaspoon kosher or sea salt
1 to 1½ pounds assorted wild mushrooms
    (see box, page 56)
About 4 cups vegetable oil, for frying

1. To prepare the dipping sauce, whack the scallions and ginger slices with the side of a cleaver or the bottom of a small, heavy skillet to bruise them. Stir the soy, mirin, and sugar together in a small bowl until the sugar is dissolved. Stir in the scallions and ginger. (The sauce may be prepared to this point up to 3 days in advance. It is best if prepared at least 2 days in advance. Store, covered, in the refrigerator. Bring to room temperature before serving.)

2. To make the tempura batter, combine the egg and beer in a blender. Add the flour, paprika, and salt. Blend at low speed until all the flour is incorporated and the mixture is smooth. Scrape down the sides of the blender jar if necessary during blending. Let the batter stand for at least 30 minutes before using. (The batter may prepared up to 1 day in advance. Cover and refrigerate. Whisk the batter thoroughly and let stand at room temperature for 30 minutes before using.)

3. Prepare the mushrooms as described on this page.

4. Pour enough oil into a large (12-inch), deep cast-iron skillet to fill two thirds of the way full. Heat the oil over medium heat until a frying thermometer inserted into the center of the oil reads 350°F. At the right temperature, a small drop of the batter will race to the top and sizzle steadily almost immediately after adding it to the oil. Work with the firmest mushrooms first. Using a pair of chopsticks or a fork, roll each piece of mushroom in the batter. Let the excess batter drip off the mushroom before carefully

Preparing Mushrooms for Tempura

- **Cauliflower Mushrooms:** Pull the cauliflower into pieces about 2 × ¾ inches thick.

- **Enoki:** Trim off the root tips, leaving enough intact to hold the mushrooms together. Separate the mushrooms into bunches of 4 or 5 mushrooms each.

- **Hen of the Woods:** Remove the central stem. Cut small (less than 2½ inches) mushrooms into ¼ inch slices; cut larger ones in half before slicing.

- **Lobster or Chicken of the Wood:** Trim any very hard parts from the stem end of the mushrooms. Slice the mushrooms about ⅛ inch thick.

- **Oyster Mushrooms:** Separate into individual mushrooms. Leave small (1 inch or less) mushrooms whole, tear larger mushrooms into ¾ to 1-inch strips.

- **Pompoms:** Cut pompoms in half, then into ½-inch wedges.

- **Portobello or Matsutake:** If the portobellos are 4 inches or smaller simply slice the caps ¼ inch thick after removing the stem. For portobellos larger than 4 inches, cut the caps in half then slice them crosswise.

- **Puffballs:** Cut into 3 × ¼ × ¼-inch french-fry shapes.

- **Shiitake:** Remove the stems. Cut large shiitake caps (more than 2 inches) into ¼-inch slices. Cut small caps into quarters.

slipping it into the oil. Fry only as many pieces of mushroom as will float freely in the oil at a time. Fry until golden brown, 1 to 2 minutes. Remove the fried mushrooms with a slotted spoon or wire skimmer to a plate lined with paper towels to drain. Repeat with the remaining mushrooms. Adjust the heat during frying to remain as close to 350°F. as possible. Serve the tempura hot, with dipping sauce on the side.

Note: Mirin, sweet Japanese cooking wine, is available in Asian markets, as well as large supermarkets.

Wild Mushroom Terrine with Goat Cheese

This foolproof recipe was shared with us by the James Beard-award-winning chef Thierry Rautureau, of Rover's in Seattle. He's the kind of guy you'd want at every party, quick-witted and full of the devil. You'd want to make sure, though, that he brought this gutsy terrine along. It works on a buffet (use a fish or crescent mold if you have one), spread on toasts, or as an appetizer with salad. You can cut the slices of terrine into star shapes and top each with little beet cubes. Thierry uses Quillisascut Goat Caillé goat cheese, which you might find, too, if you live near Seattle. However any creamy, assertive goat cheese may be substituted. Other mushrooms can be substituted, as long as you can cut them matchstick thin.

SERVES 12 AS AN APPETIZER, 6 AS A FIRST COURSE

3 tablespoons unsalted butter

6 ounces lobster mushrooms, cut into matchsticks

6 ounces hedgehog mushrooms, cut into matchsticks

6 ounces shiitake mushrooms, cut into matchsticks

6 ounces oyster mushrooms, cut into matchsticks

1 teaspoon Seasoning Salt (page 253)

½ teaspoon freshly ground black pepper

2 tablespoons chopped shallots

1½ teaspoons minced garlic

2 teaspoons black truffle oil, plus more for serving (optional)

2 tablespoons chopped fresh chives

4 ounces soft goat cheese, at room temperature

Salad greens, for serving (optional)

1. Line a decorative terrine or mousse mold with parchment paper. The size and shape of the mold do not affect the texture of the terrine, just the thickness of the serving slices. I use an 11 × 7-inch baking dish, which gives ½-inch-high slices.

2. Melt the butter over medium heat in a large sauté pan. Continue cooking until it turns hazelnut in color, about 3 minutes. Add the lobster mushrooms and cook, stirring, for 1 minute. One by one, add the remaining types of mushrooms, cooking each until it gives up some liquid. Season with the Seasoning Salt and the pepper. When all the

mushrooms have been added, continue cooking until limp and almost dry, about 4 more minutes. Stir in the shallots, garlic, and truffle oil (if using) and cook until the shallots are translucent, about 1 minute. Remove the mushrooms from the heat, taste, and adjust the seasoning. Set aside 1 teaspoon of the chives and stir in the rest.

3. Using a wooden spoon, cream the goat cheese in a medium-size bowl. Thoroughly mix in the mushrooms. Pack the mixture into the mold. Cover with plastic wrap and refrigerate for at least 3 hours and up to 2 days.

4. To unmold, tug on the parchment paper. Lift the cheese out of the mold, then peel off the plastic and the paper. Invert the terrine out onto a serving plate. Or, slice it thin and serve over greens. Drizzle with a drop more of truffle oil (if using) and scatter a few chives on top.

Double Oyster Gratin

**SERVES 4 AS A
FIRST COURSE**

*T*his piping-hot first course, with its briny oysters, creamy sauce, and crunchy topping, satisfies a multitude of cravings in one bite. Oyster mushrooms borrow flavor notes and even their shell shape from the seafood. Wild oyster mushrooms are fleshy and large; the smaller cultivated oyster mushrooms come clustered around a common stem.

Note that you'll need to start a day or two ahead of time to steep the cream.

1 unblemished orange

½ cup light cream

1 piece (1-inch) vanilla bean

16 oysters, shucked, with liquid

½ teaspoon kosher or sea salt or Seasoning
 Salt (page 253)

Freshly ground black pepper

4 ounces small oyster mushrooms

⅓ cup crumbled whole-wheat crackers

2 tablespoons grated Parmesan cheese

1 teaspoon chopped fresh thyme

½ cup coarsely chopped fresh chervil or
 ¼ cup chopped fresh chives or
 flat-leaf parsley

1. Scrub the orange under cool running water and dry it. Use a vegetable peeler to remove the zest, making sure not to take any of the underlying bitter white pith. Combine the cream, vanilla bean, and orange zest in a small small saucepan. Heat over medium heat just until bubbles form around the edges. Cool to room temperature. Transfer the mixture to a small container. Cover and refrigerate for 1 to 2 days.

2. Strain the cream and discard the zest and vanilla bean. Drain the oysters, reserving the liquid. Pass the liquid through a very fine sieve or a sieve lined with a double thickness of cheesecloth. Add the strained oyster liquid, salt, and black pepper to taste to the cream.

3. Cut the individual mushrooms away from the stem. Leave the small mushrooms whole and tear any that are more than 1 inch wide into strips. Add the mushrooms to the cream mixture and let stand, tossing often, until the mushrooms have absorbed some of the cream, about 30 minutes.

4. Arrange the oysters in the bottom of a baking dish in which they fit in a single layer, such as a 9-inch oval dish. Sprinkle generously with black pepper. Arrange the mushrooms in an even layer over the oysters, making sure the oysters are completely covered. Pour the remaining cream mixture over all. (The gratin may be prepared to this point up to 1 day in advance. Cover and refrigerate the dish.)

5. Preheat the oven to 425°F.

6. Stir the cracker crumbs, Parmesan cheese, and thyme together in a small bowl and sprinkle in an even layer over the mushrooms. Bake until bubbling and the top is well browned, about 25 minutes.

7. To serve, bring the baking dish to the table and use a spatula to remove each portion to a plate.

Oyster Tips

It's pretty tricky to pry open oysters without losing the liquid. We open ours over a wide stainless steel bowl to catch the liquor. Get yourself a protective mitt to protect the exposed hand from cuts, a left-hand mitt if you are right-handed, and vice versa. (See Mail-Order Sources, page 324.)

On the Oregon Mushroom Trail

The roads in the heavily mushroomed part of Oregon sometimes appear on maps, other times not. It is suspected that the invisible ones were hit with white-out by local mushroom pickers who have friends in the county engineer's office. Logging companies own and maintain a vast network of forest roads, controlling access to the wild mushrooms that lie within. So it behooves foragers to be nice to the loggers!

Thierry and I managed to find our way to Kathy and Stan's Mushroom Patch in Lyons, Oregon. Here, on the edge of a daunting ravine that ends in a salmon-stocked river, is a typical wild mushroom operation. Long-haired boys with big smiles and dirty fingernails kick a ball around the clearing in front of the family's A-frame. Over near the woods, a shed shelters the walk-in cooler. Stan opens the shed door, and we are mesmerized by the essence of the woods. The swells of decaying leaves, brittle pine needles, and good old earth mingle in the air. Yellowfoot and black trumpet poke through the tiny openings of stacked green plastic baskets. A scale that could hardly be defined as "authorized for commercial use" sits at the ready. Enormous plastic bags bulge with dried morels. As Thierry and Stan talk prices, Kathy shows me her secret mushroom route.

We arrive at a market with a freestanding sign that used to announce the IGA's weekly specials and that now reads "We buy mushrooms." Pickups and old station wagons back into the fifties-style market's parking lot to unload their wares. Crinkled grocery sacks, salvaged grocery cartons, and even windbreakers are emptied of morels, chanterelles, and hedgehogs. Kathy weighs in the goods, chiding one weekend picker for wasting his time on a bagful of mushrooms that rot too fast to be sold commercially. "This batch of boletus is riddled with worms, why did you bother?" she says. She gives an earnest college student a harvesting lesson, swiftly trimming stems to those fancy chefs' specifications: No long stems with dirt clumps, and leave the leaves behind.

Kathy knows her pickers. She comments on their kids' soccer performances, declines messily picked mushrooms from someone who should know her standards better, and counts out $20 bills with quick motions. Morels get packed in five- or six-pound stacking cartons, depending upon their fragility and girth. They get stashed among cartons of Andy Boy broccoli in the market's rattling cooler.

Back at the A-frame, Stan's sweet-talking the Chicago and New York markets, offering airway bill numbers for the day's shipments and preselling tomorrow's harvest. We have to wonder, do they ever stop and fry up a batch for themselves?

Scallops, Fresh Cèpes, and Black Truffles

Scallops still in the shell are sweet, plump, tender, and juicy. In this dish, they provide a stunning presentation. It makes a standout dish for New Years' Eve, a night when splurges are not only encouraged, they're deserved. If scallops in the shell (often called diver scallops) are not available, substitute bottled clam juice for the water and use ½ pound fresh sea scallops. Likewise, the fresh truffle can be replaced by a teaspoon of canned truffle juice. Cèpes offer the best flavor, but you may substitute shiitakes when they are out of season. Serve this as an appetizer or with some risotto or small pasta as a main course.

Kosher or sea salt

12 scallops in the shell

¾ cup bottled clam juice (optional)

1 tablespoon unsalted butter

¼ pound fresh cèpes, sliced ¼-inch thick

1 shallot, finely diced

Freshly ground black pepper

2 tablespoons Demi-Glace (page 282)

½ ounce fresh black winter truffle, thinly
    sliced, or 1 teaspoon black winter
    truffle juice

1 tablespoon chopped fresh herbs, such as
    chervil and chives

1. Place ¼ cup water and a pinch of salt in a medium-size saucepan and bring to a boil over medium heat. Add the scallops, cover, and cook until they open, about 2 minutes. If using scallops out of the shell and bottled clam juice, cook until opaque, 2 minutes. Remove from the heat, cover, and keep warm.

2. Melt the butter in a medium-size sauté pan over medium-high heat. Sauté the cèpes until wilted, about 2 minutes. Reduce the heat and add the shallot, and salt and pepper to taste. Cover and simmer, stirring from time to time, until the mushrooms are browned, about 3 minutes more.

3. Meanwhile, strain the scallop cooking liquid into a small, heavy saucepan. You should have about

Rain, Please

The French look to the magpie for the weather forecast. If the bird makes its nest on top of a tree, it will be a dry, hot summer. If she tucks her nest under the leaves, it will be a rainy one. When it comes to making truffles grow, we prefer to see her under.

½ to 1 cup. Add the Demi-Glace and the truffle or truffle juice. Reduce the sauce over medium heat by half, about 2 minutes.

4. To serve, set the scallops around the edge of the plate, mounding the cèpes in the center. Drizzle the sauce over the mushrooms. Sprinkle the plate liberally with herbs.

Wild Mushroom Tart with a Poppy Seed Crust

MAKES 24
HORS D'OEUVRE
PORTIONS,
SERVES 8 AS A
FIRST COURSE

The allure of this tart begins with its thin, crispy, poppy seed–studded crust. Add to that an aromatic layer of mushroom duxelles, topped with nicely browned mushroom slices. Served warm, its woodsy aroma beckons an invitation to taste. We make it in a rectangular shape for a nice presentation and nicely shaped serving portions.

POPPY SEED CRUST

1½ cups all-purpose flour

3 tablespoons poppy seeds

1 teaspoon kosher or sea salt

6 tablespoons (¾ stick) unsalted butter, chilled, cut into 8 slices

6 to 7 tablespoons ice water

DUXELLES FILLING

½ cup Light Chicken Stock (page 280) or canned low-sodium chicken broth

2 tablespoons unsalted butter

8 ounces small firm mushrooms with tender stems, such as buttons, creminis, or cèpes, sliced ¼ inch thick

1 teaspoon chopped fresh tarragon

1 recipe Basic Duxelles (page 283)

TO FINISH

1 egg, beaten with a few drops of water until smooth

Creme fraîche or sour cream (optional)

1. To make the crust, stir the flour, poppy seeds, and salt in a medium-size mixing bowl until blended. Toss the butter into the flour mixture and quickly rub the butter and flour between your fingertips until the butter is the size and shape of corn flakes. Sprinkle the ice water over the flour mixture a tablespoon at a time, tossing constantly with a fork, to form a dough that holds together when pressed lightly. Turn the dough out onto a lightly floured surface and knead it quickly and lightly just a few times to form an evenly textured dough. Wrap in a clean kitchen towel or plastic wrap and refrigerate for at least 30 minutes or up to 1 day.

2. To make the filling, heat the chicken stock and butter in a medium-size skillet over medium heat. Add the sliced mushrooms. Adjust the heat to a simmer and cook the mushrooms for 3 minutes. Strain the mushrooms, reserving the liquid, and set aside. Return the strained mushroom liquid to the skillet and add the tarragon. Heat to a boil and boil until the liquid is reduced to about 3 tablespoons, 1 minute.

3. Preheat the oven to 375°F.

4. On a lightly floured surface, roll the dough out to 13 × 9-inch rectangle ⅛ to ¼ inch thick. Trim the dough to a neat rectangle, then cut a ½-inch strip from each of the 4 sides, starting with the shorter sides. Transfer the dough rectangle to a baking sheet. Brush the rectangle with the beaten egg. Arrange the strips of dough along the edges of the rectangle, forming a pastry border. (The shorter strips will overlap the longer strips.) Trim off any overhanging dough and brush the pastry strips with the beaten egg.

5. Spoon the duxelles within the pastry border and into an even layer and smooth. Arrange the reserved mushroom slices, side by side in rows, to cover the duxelles. The mushrooms slices may not completely cover the duxelles. Brush the mushroom slices with the reduced cooking liquid.

6. Bake until the pastry border of the crust is golden brown and the mushrooms are browned, about 40 minutes. Remove and cool on the baking sheet for about 15 minutes. Transfer to a cutting board and cut into eight 4 × 3-inch slices for a first-course serving or into 1½-inch squares for hors d'oeuvres. Serve each portion with a dollop of crème fraiche, if desired.

Get That Tart!

When New York magazine proclaimed Jean-Georges Vongerichten's (chef-owner of several restaurants, including Jean Georges) porcini tart one of the culinary wonders of the world, Aux Delices des Bois' porcini department got busy. One call came from Mortimer's, the former staid lunchroom where New York's society ladies organized benefit balls and planned their husbands' social lives over quiche and salad. The owner, the late Glenn Bernbaum, wanted Jean-Georges' recipe badly. Since we supplied mushrooms to Jean-Georges, would we help Mortimer's chef reproduce the tart? "What kind of porcini did Jean-Georges buy?" The next day, "How thin are they sliced?" And then, "What goes between the pastry and the porcini?" We never got answers to all his questions—or a taste of the resulting tart—but we sure did a brisk business in porcini that week!

Wild Mushroom and Sweet Potato Strudel

SERVES 4 AS A FIRST COURSE

This makes a really splendid first course. Thin crunchy sweet potatoes are layered with a tangle of aromatic mushrooms and lightly sauced with diced tomato and sweet cream. Hardly finger food, these napoleons have to be served with a fork: The potato chips will crumble like puff pastry. The napoleons can be prepared a day ahead—and they benefit from at least an hour ahead—and kept in the fridge. Look for sweet potatoes with a regular, straight shape. Peel them if you wish, although we never do. Serve on salad plates, accompanied by a few seemingly random, lightly dressed chicory curls.

FILLING

1 tablespoon olive oil

1¼ pounds wild mushrooms, such as
hen of the woods, chanterelles, black
trumpet, and/or oyster, cleaned,
trimmed, and sliced ¼ inch thick

¼ cup finely chopped shallots
(about 3 large shallots)

Kosher or sea salt and freshly ground
black pepper

2 tablespoons Mushroom-Infused Sherry
(page 255)

1 cup Rich Meat Stock (page 282) or
mushroom soaking liquid

2 tablespoons chopped fresh herbs,
such as parsley, chervil,
and/or chives

STRUDELS

2 sweet potatoes (about ¾ pound total),
scrubbed

1 tablespoon plus 2 teaspoons unsalted
butter, melted

½ teaspoon kosher or sea salt

½ teaspoon freshly ground black pepper

2 teaspoons Cèpe Powder (page 285)

Reserved mushroom cooking liquid from
step 2 (see below)

¼ cup peeled, seeded, and diced tomato

2 tablespoons heavy cream (optional)

1 tablespoon chopped fresh herbs, such as
parsley, chervil, and/or chives

1. Heat olive oil in a large, heavy sauté pan over medium-high heat. Add the wild mushrooms, beginning with the firmest variety, and sauté one kind at a time, leaving them in the pan as you add the next. When each batch releases its liquid, cook another minute before adding the next. Reduce the heat to medium. Add the shallots, and sauté until the mushrooms and shallots are limp, 2 to 3 minutes. Season to taste with salt and pepper.

2. Increase the heat to high and stir in the mushroom sherry. Pour in the stock, reduce the heat, and simmer until ½ cup liquid remains,

10 to 12 minutes. Strain the liquid into a small, heavy saucepan and set aside.

3. Toss the mushrooms with 2 tablespoons of the herbs, in a small bowl; add salt and pepper to taste.

4. Preheat the oven to 350°F.

5. Trim off the sides and ends of the sweet potato, using your sharpest butcher's knife. Trim it to a block about 5 × 2 inches. Slice each sweet potato lengthwise as thinly as possible into 8 rectangular slices (use a mandolin if you have one). Save any irregular slices for another recipe.

6. Very lightly coat a large baking sheet with 1 tablespoon of the melted butter. Sprinkle the sheet with half the salt, pepper, and cèpe powder. Lay the sweet potato slices on top, brush with a teaspoon of the melted butter, and sprinkle with the remaining salt, pepper, and cèpe powder. Bake until a fork slips easily into the potato slices, about 15 minutes. Remove from the oven and cool until easy to handle. Leave the oven on. The potatoes may be prepared to this point up to 2 days in advance. Cool, wrap tightly in plastic wrap, and refrigrate.

7. When the sweet potatoes are cool enough to touch, build the strudels. Grease a heavy, low-sided, 9-inch square baking dish or a 9½-inch oval gratin dish with the remaining 1 teaspoon melted butter. Place 4 slices of sweet potatoes in the baking dish. Top each with about 2 tablespoons of the mushroom mixture. Top the mushrooms with another layer of the sweet potatoes. Continue layering the strudels, ending with a layer of sweet potatoes. Cover the strudels with plastic wrap, place a dish on top of them, then weight it down with heavy cans. Let sit at room temperature for 30 minutes to 1 hour.

8. Remove the cans and top dish, and plastic wrap. Place the strudels in the oven and bake until warmed throughout, uncovered, 5 to 10 minutes.

9. While the strudels heat, to make the sauce: Bring the mushroom cooking liquid to a boil in a small saucepan over high heat. When it boils, reduce the heat to medium and add the tomato. Cook at a lively simmer until slightly thickened, 3 to 5 minutes. Add the cream and continue cooking until the sauce is of coating consistency, about 3 minutes.

10. Place the strudels on individual plates. Spoon some sauce over each, and sprinkle with the herbs.

Soups from the Woods

Every year, the crisp autumn air, the tumble of russet and golden leaves under a bamboo rake, and the aroma of mushrooms rising from the forest floor awaken a desire for—no, an obsession with—wild mushroom soup. So, I gather as many varieties as I can get my hands on, boil up a rich deeply flavored stock, and turn it into a thick mushroom and multigrain soup that is as delicious as it is soul satisfying.

But, in fact, there's no need to wait for autumn. From a clear, truffle-studded broth to that creamy, grain-thickened potage, mushroom soup possibilities are endless. By all means try the recipes here, but don't forget that wonderful soups evolve from forgotten things in the vegetable bin of the refrigerator. Bits of vegetables add depth and color to stock; grains and noodles provide texture and balance. When using pasta, beans, and grains, add them near serving time, because they soak up the liquid. Thicken soups by making a roux, adding potato or cream, or puréeing the soup before serving.

If possible, make a good stock (pages 280 to 282) to enrich your soups. You can freeze it in plastic containers (the 2-cup size works well) to have on hand when the soup mood strikes.

Wontons in Mushroom Broth

SERVES 4

As I write this, snowbound in a city apartment, I feel like kicking myself for not making a double recipe of wontons last time around. They could be waiting in the freezer to be poached in this easy rich mushroom broth. It opens the senses, and makes way for dishes of the same spirit, such as Glazed Jade Vegetables with Wood Ears (page 41) or Many Fragrant Vegetables Fried Rice (page 210). And don't make my mistake—always make a double batch of wontons, keeping one in reserve for a particularly chilly eve.

6 cups Light Chicken Stock (page 280) or canned low-sodium chicken broth

4 ounces shiitakes, stemmed, cleaned, and sliced ¼ inch thick

4 ounces honshimeji, trimmed and halved, or canned straw mushrooms, drained and halved

½ cup thin strips of smoked ham (about 2 ounces)

2 scallions (white and green parts), trimmed and thinly sliced

Mushroom Soy Sauce (page 255) or good-quality soy sauce

1 recipe Double Fun Mushroom Wontons (page 34), prepared through step 4

1. Bring a large pot of water to a boil.

2. Heat the stock and mushrooms to a simmer in a large saucepan and simmer for 4 minutes. Stir in the ham, scallions, and soy sauce to taste. Simmer for 2 minutes.

3. Meanwhile, slip the wontons into the boiling water. Reduce the heat to a lively simmer and cook, stirring gently, just until the wrappers are tender, about 2 minutes. Be careful not to overcook them, or they will fall apart.

4. Drain the wontons well and transfer them with a slotted spoon to the mushroom broth. Serve hot, dividing the wontons among 4 serving bowls and ladling the broth over them.

Honshimeji Udon Broth

One of our favorite stops on a Sunday afternoon is New York's always-bustling Chinatown. We can do marketing for the week here, at a fraction of the cost as elsewhere. However, when we're finished, we don't treat ourselves to a Chinese meal. Instead we squeeze into a little Japanese udon place with our filled-to-bursting pink plastic bags and gorge on meat-and-fish filled soups thick with white noodles and mushrooms. Here is our take on one of those tangy soups, which is served in deep, decorative bowls. If you can't find honshimeji, substitute reconstituted wood ear or bluefoot.

5 cups Rich Meat Stock (page 282) or good-quality canned beef broth

1 teaspoon crushed red pepper

4 ounces roasted pork, cut into 1-inch pieces

4 ounces honshimeji mushrooms, stem ends trimmed off

8 Oakwood shiitake mushroom caps, sliced ¼ inch thick

1 tablespoon fish sauce

1 teaspoon kosher or sea salt

1 teaspoon sugar

4 ounces udon noodles (see Note)

8 medium leaves fresh arugula or spinach, well rinsed

2 scallions (white and green parts) trimmed and sliced on the diagonal ¼ inch thick

3 tablespoons fresh cilantro leaves

1. Bring the stock, red pepper, and pork to a slow boil, in a medium-size saucepan, skimming any foam from the surface. Add the mushrooms, fish sauce, salt, and sugar and simmer until the flavors have melded, about 20 minutes.

2. Bring the soup back to a boil, and add the noodles. Reduce the heat to just under boiling and cook the noodles until firm but no longer crunchy, about 8 minutes. Put the arugula and scallions into the pot and simmer until the arugula wilts.

3. To serve, ladle the soup into 2 bowls and top with cilantro.

Note: Udon noodles are one of the many kinds available at Asian grocers, specialty gourmet stores, and some supermarkets. These are the thick white wheat noodles that slip maddeningly through plastic chopsticks. I use the round kind, but a flat or even the squarish kind work too. Soba noodles, made with buckwheat, do just as well in this recipe.

Matsutake and Seaweed Soup

SERVES 6

The clean, saline taste of the sea mingles with the piney notes of dense forests in this clear soup. Barry Wine, the creator of this recipe, suggests enhancing a rich chicken stock with black truffle and wild mushrooms. You can skip that step and just use one cup of Rich Chicken Stock. If matsutake are not available, make the soup with Oakwood shiitake sliced as thin as possible.

1½ cups Rich Chicken Stock (page 281)

1 ounce black truffle, sliced (optional)

3 ounces yellowfoot and/or honshimeji mushrooms, cleaned (optional)

1 piece of dried kombu (see Note)

2 teaspoons unsalted butter

8 ounces matsutake, cleaned and cut into ¾-inch cubes, or Oakwood shiitake, sliced as thin as possible

3 cloves garlic, chopped

1 small onion, coarsely chopped

Kosher or sea salt and freshly ground black pepper

½ lime

De-Salting the Soup

As liberally as I cook with sea and kosher salt, I sometimes overdose a soup or stew. To remove some of the salt, drop a 2-inch cube of bread into the pot, simmer the soup a few minutes, then remove and discard the bread. The soup should be realigned. If it is still too salty, repeat with a fresh bread cube.

1. If using the truffle and yellowfoot mushrooms, heat the stock in a medium-size saucepan. Add the truffle and yellowfoot, and simmer for 30 minutes. Set aside.

2. Meanwhile, rinse the kombu under running water, shake off the excess, and pat dry with paper towels. Place the kombu in a soup pot with 8 cups of water. Bring to a boil and immediately turn off heat. Let stand for 5 minutes. Remove and discard the kombu.

3. Melt the butter in a medium-size sauté pan over high heat. Add the matsutake, garlic, onion, and ¼ cup of water and cook until softened, 4 minutes. Season to taste with salt and pepper. Add the mushroom mixture and the stock (with or without the truffle and yellowfoot) to the soup pot. Bring to a simmer and simmer for 20 minutes. Season to taste with salt and pepper.

4. To serve, ladle the soup into 6 soup bowls, dividing the mushrooms equally among them. Squeeze a dash of lime juice into each bowl.

Note: Dried kombu is available at Asian markets and health-food stores. The dried sheets are about 3 inches wide and 4½ inches long.

Turkey Broth with Wild Oysters

*A*fter a heavy, sleep-inducing turkey meal, I yearn for something lighter. Richly-flavored clear turkey soup is the answer. The bones are turned into a strong-flavored stock (I make a lot and freeze it) that needs just a few delicate oyster mushrooms to make it a meal.

**SERVES 2 AS A
MAIN COURSE,
OR 4 AS A
FIRST COURSE**

4 cups Rich Chicken Stock (page 281)
    or Rich Turkey Stock
    (see box, this page)
8 ounces wild oyster or cultivated oyster
    mushrooms, cut into 1½ × ½-inch strips
1 carrot, cut into very thin julienne strips
Kosher or sea salt and freshly ground
    black pepper
1 cup broken angel hair pasta
1 bunch chives, cut into ¼-inch
    lengths (about ½ cup)

1. Combine the broth, mushrooms, and carrot in a 3-quart saucepan and heat to a boil over medium heat. Reduce the heat and simmer until the mushrooms are tender, about 3 minutes. Add salt and pepper to taste. (The soup can be prepared to this point up to 1 day in advance. Refrigerate until needed and reheat to a simmer before continuing.)

2. Bring a pot of salted water to a boil. Add the angel hair and cook until al dente, about 2 minutes. Drain thoroughly and add to the soup, then add the chives. Heat for 1 minute and serve in warmed soup bowls.

Rich Turkey Stock

*S*alvage as many bones and pieces of skin as you can from a roast turkey. The browner the better—wings and neck skin are great for this. Break up the bones or whack them with a cleaver, and fit them into a pot just large enough to hold them. Barely cover the bones with cold water and bring to a boil. Let the water boil for 1 minute, then reduce the heat to a simmer. Skim off the foam and fat from the surface. Adjust the heat so 2 or 3 bubbles float to the surface at a time. Gentle cooking will make a clear, richly flavored stock, high in gelatin.

Cook the stock from 6 to 18 hours, depending on the size of the bones. You can do this practically unattended, except for occasionally skimming the surface (more frequently at the start of cooking), and adding water as needed to keep the bones submerged. At the end of cooking, remove some of the larger bones from the stock with a wire skimmer or slotted spoon to make it easier to strain the stock.

Ladle the stock through a sieve lined with cheesecloth or a clean kitchen towel into a bowl large enough to hold it. Cool to room temperature, then refrigerate. Peel off the layer of fat that has solidified on top. The stock is now ready to use.

To store, ladle into storage containers with tight-fitting lids and refrigerate the stock for up to 5 days or freeze for up to 3 months. Heat the stock to boiling before using.

Lamb Broth with Autumn Mushrooms and Pearl Barley

SERVES 6 TO 8

When lamb meets wild mushrooms, as in this subtly flavored, meat-studded broth with barley, the flavors of both sing even louder. This recipe evolved when a huge lamb bone and a handful of wild mushrooms remained after an autumn harvest party. Since our garden had long since stopped giving, we celebrated soft rains, falling leaves, and the eventual hibernation of the bear who regularly cleans out the trash can at our summer house. You can replace the mushrooms called for with what you have on hand.

2 (about 10 ounces each) large lamb shanks
    or 1 bone from a roasted leg of lamb
    (see Note)
1 tablespoon vegetable oil
Kosher or sea salt and freshly ground black
    pepper
¾ cup pearl or medium barley
2 tablespoons unsalted butter
1 medium onion, chopped
1 medium carrot, diced
2 ribs celery, diced
4 ounces hedgehog mushrooms, cleaned,
    trimmed, and thinly sliced
8 ounces black trumpet or yellowfoot
    mushrooms, cleaned, trimmed, and
    coarsely chopped
2 teaspoons chopped fresh sage
1 teaspoon chopped fresh thyme
1 teaspoon chopped fresh rosemary

1. Preheat the oven to 400°F.

2. Rub the lamb shanks or bone with the oil and place in a roasting pan. Roast, turning once, for 45 minutes. The lamb should be well browned. Place the pieces in a heavy 4- to 5-quart pot. Pour in enough cold water to cover by 1 inch. Heat to a boil, boil for 1 minute, then reduce the heat to a simmer. Skim the foam and fat from the surface of the liquid. Simmer, skimming the surface occasionally, for 2 hours. Remove the lamb from the broth and let cool to room temperature. Turn off the heat under the broth.

3. Pull the meat from the bones and trim it of any fat and gristle. Finely dice the meat and set aside. Return the bones to the broth, heat again to a simmer and simmer, uncovered, for 2 hours more.

4. Remove and discard the lamb bones. Strain the broth through a fine sieve. Season with salt and pepper and set aside. You should have about 8 cups. (The broth may be prepared to this point up to 2 days in advance. Refrigerate until needed.)

5. Soak the barley in a large bowl of cold water for about 15 minutes.

6. Melt the butter in a heavy 4-quart pot over medium heat until it foams. Add the onion, carrot, and celery. Cover and cook, stirring occasionally, until the vegetables wilt, about 4 minutes. Reduce the heat if the vegetables begin to brown. Drain the barley and add it to the pot. Add the reserved lamb broth, heat to a boil, and boil for 5 minutes. (The soup can be made to this point up to 2 days in advance. Bring the soup back to a simmer before continuing with the recipe.)

Adjust the heat and simmer the soup for 10 minutes. Stir in the mushrooms and simmer until the barley is tender, about 10 minutes. Add the reserved meat and the sage, thyme, and rosemary, and salt and pepper to taste. Simmer for 5 minutes. Serve the soup hot.

Note: Leave a good amount of meat attached to the bone. It will add greatly to the flavor. If at all possible, cut the leg in two at the knee joint before roasting in step 2.

Wild Mushroom and Multigrain Soup

The steaming succor provided by this naturally thickened potage make it a wonderful cold-weather meal. Just about any exotic mushroom will give the broth a substantial kick. Add whole-grain bread and a plate of cheese to round out the soup. Some or all of the button mushrooms can be replaced with trimmings—such as stems from portobellos or shiitakes—that you've saved from other recipes.

SERVES 8

WILD MUSHROOM STOCK
2 pounds assorted wild mushrooms,
    such as chanterelles, shiitakes,
    mousserons, or oyster mushrooms
2 pounds button mushrooms, cleaned

MULTIGRAIN SOUP
⅓ cup wheat berries, soaked in water
    to cover by 4 inches for 3 hours
⅓ cup red lentils, picked over
⅓ cup quinoa, rinsed

1 cup peanut oil
Wild mushrooms reserved from
    the stock (above)
8 shallots, thinly sliced (about 1 cup)
3 cloves garlic, minced
Kosher or sea salt and freshly ground
    black pepper
½ cup Madeira
6 tablespoons all-purpose flour
½ cup chopped fresh herbs, such as thyme,
    tarragon, chives, dill, and/or parsley

1. To make the stock, clean and trim the wild mushrooms, placing all the trimmings in a large soup pot. Slice the caps ¼ inch thick and set aside. Add the button mushrooms and 8 cups of water to the soup pot. Boil vigorously until the liquid is reduced by half, about 30 minutes. Strain the mushroom stock into a large, heavy saucepan. Push hard on the mushrooms to extract as much stock as possible. Discard the mushrooms.

2. To make the soup, bring a medium-size saucepan of salted water to a boil. Drain the wheat berries, add them to the saucepan and cook for 1 minute. Add the lentils and cook for 1 minute more. Stir in the quinoa and cook until the grains and lentils are tender, about 6 minutes. Drain and transfer to a medium bowl. Set aside.

3. Heat 2 tablespoons of the oil in a large sauté pan over high heat. Sauté the mushrooms until they give up some liquid, 1 minute. Add half the shallots and the garlic and cook over medium heat until the pan is dry, about 6 minutes. Season to taste with salt and pepper. Turn the heat to high, pour the Madeira into the pan, and quickly stir, loosening up any bits that have stuck to the bottom. Reduce the heat and cook over medium heat until the liquid is reduced by half, about 2 minutes.

4. Dredge the remaining shallots in the flour until coated, shaking off the excess. Heat the rest of the peanut oil in a very small saucepan over medium heat until it begins to pop. Add the shallots and fry until crisp and golden brown, about 4 minutes. Remove and drain on paper towels. Set aside.

5. About 30 minutes before serving, combine the reserved grains, the mushrooms, and half the fresh herbs with the mushroom stock. Bring the soup to a boil and boil until slightly reduced, about 3 minutes. If the soup becomes too thick, add water, simmer briefly, and adjust the seasoning.

6. Serve hot, sprinkling the remaining herbs and the fried shallots over the top.

Unflappable Creativity

The recipe for Wild Mushroom and Multigrain Soup comes from a true mushroom devotee, Steven Levine. He has chefed at prominent New York restaurants and followed his star to California to open his own place. Lucky for Californians. Thierry and I were so confident in Steven's creativity that when he was at New York's Soho restaurant, Zoë, we got into the unfair habit of showing up there unexpectedly with a crateful of wild mushrooms and guests who we wanted to wow. In minutes, Steven sent out a dégustation of the most flavor-popping dishes we've ever had, with or without advance planning. His contributions to mushroom cuisine include matsutake and oxtail (see our version of it, page 116); grilled hen of the woods with pear tomatoes and mozzarella; duck broth with duck breast, enoki, and greens; and this earthy but heavenbound soup.

Latin Tomato and Huitlacoche Soup

SERVES 6

Hot, corny, spicy, and thick with beans, this soup satisfies all those south-of-the-border cravings in one lusty dish. Serve it as a main dish with a side of Mushroom Cornmeal Muffins (page 247) and an arugula salad. If you can't find huitlacoche (weet-la-coach-aye), use sautéed portobello mushrooms.

½ cup dried black beans soaked (page 215)
 or 1½ cups drained canned
 black beans
6 cups Light Chicken Stock (page 280) or
 canned low-sodium chicken broth
1 cup shredded cooked chicken meat
1 cup fresh or frozen corn kernels
½ cup fresh or canned tomato purée
4 scallions, trimmed and thinly sliced,
 green and white parts kept
 separate
1 large Anaheim chili, with or without
 seeds, or other chili, stemmed and
 thinly sliced
½ cup (2 ounces) huitlacoche, fresh or
 frozen (see Note) or 3 cups cubed
 portobello caps (about 4 ounces)
1 tablespoon olive oil (as needed)
½ cup (loosely packed) fresh cilantro
 leaves
1 tablespoon fresh lime juice
Kosher or sea salt and freshly ground
 black pepper
1 recipe Tortilla Strips (see box, this page)

1. Place the beans in a small saucepan of simmering water. Cook, uncovered, until tender, about 45 minutes. Add hot water, if necessary,

To Make Tortilla Strips

Preheat the oven to 350°F. Cut four 5-inch corn tortillas in half. Cut the halves crosswise into ¼-inch strips. Transfer the strips to a mixing bowl and drizzle 1 to 2 teaspoons vegetable oil over them. Toss well. Spread the strips out in an even layer on a baking sheet. Bake, stirring and redistributing the strips once or twice, until lightly browned and crisp, about 12 minutes. Cool the strips completely. For simple snacking, sprinkle with sea salt as they come out of the oven. This makes about 1½ cups of strips.

to keep the beans well submerged. Drain the beans.

2. Combine the stock, meat, corn, tomato purée, whites of scallion, chili and beans in a medium-size saucepan over high heat and bring to a boil. Reduce the heat, cover, and simmer for 15 minutes.

3. Stir in the huitlacoche. (If using portobellos, sauté them in 1 tablespoon olive oil over medium heat, until the mushrooms give up their liquid. Remove from the heat and add to the soup.) Add the cilantro, lime juice, and scallion greens and simmer for 2 minutes. Season to taste with salt and pepper.

4. Serve hot, sprinkling some of the tortilla strips over each bowl of soup. Pass the remaining tortilla strips separately.

Note: Huitlacoche, Mexican corn fungus, is available canned, frozen, and occasionally fresh, in different size pieces. Frozen huitlacoche is preferable because it retains a better texture than canned. When chopped, huitlacoche darkens dishes to which it is added; to minimize the darkening of this soup, choose small, peanut-size huitlacoche, which can be added to the soup whole, or slightly larger pieces that will only need to be cut in half before adding them to the soup. Larger pieces, which will have to be chopped or cut several times to make the proper size pieces, will darken the soup more.

White Asparagus Cream with Roasted Cremini and Ramps

The fresh flavor of asparagus, garlicky note of ramps, and earthy punch of mushrooms tie together in this creamy, cool-weather soup. It began as a way to use a bumper crop of white asparagus and has become an annual, very seasonal, favorite. White asparagus are in season only from April to June, and ramps, or wild leeks, appear briefly in May and June. Regular leeks can be used if ramps are not available. Flavorful—and relatively inexpensive—cremini or shiitakes are excellent in their soup, however, slow-roasted morels, sliced in half lengthwise, would be extraordinary.

8 ounces white asparagus

6 ramps, cleaned (see box, facing page), with bottoms trimmed off, or 2 leeks, thoroughly rinsed

1½ cups (1 pound) roasted cremini or morels (page 96, steps 1 and 2)

1 tablespoon olive oil

1 medium onion, coarsely chopped

6 cups Light Chicken Stock (page 280) or canned low-sodium chicken broth

3 fresh sage leaves or ½ teaspoon dried sage

1 sprig of fresh thyme or ½ teaspoon dried thyme

3 peppercorns

Kosher or sea salt or Seasoning Salt (page 253) and freshly ground black pepper

½ cup heavy (or whipping) cream

¼ cup julienned prosciutto

2 tablespoons chopped fresh herbs, such as chives, parsley, and/or chervil

1. Break or cut off the tough ends of the asparagus. Using a vegetable peeler, peel off strips of the tough outer skin all the way to the tip. Discard any dull or limp ramp leaves. Cut the ramps into 2-inch lengths. If using leeks, trim most of the green off, leaving 1 inch. Slice into matchsticks. Thinly slice the cremini and set aside.

2. Heat the olive oil in a medium-size heavy pot over medium heat. Add the onion and cook until translucent, about 3 minutes. Add the asparagus, ramps, stock, sage, thyme, peppercorns, and a pinch of salt. Bring to a boil and skim the foam from the surface. Reduce the heat and simmer, skimming from time to time until the asparagus is very tender, about 1 hour. Using a blender or food processor, purée the soup in batches. Leave a few small chunks for texture.

3. Return the purée to the pot. Season to taste with salt and pepper. (The soup can be made ahead to this point. Cool to room temperature, and, if not serving within 4 hours, refrigerate, covered.)

4. Slowly bring the soup to just under the boiling point. Add the cream and simmer for 15 minutes.

5. To serve, ladle the soup into 4 soup plates, topping each serving with a quarter of the reserved mushrooms, the prosciutto, and herbs.

Note: Leftover sautéed or roasted shiitakes are so popular in our house that double batches are now de rigueur. No velouté is complete without a handful of these mushroom croutons. But they also lend an exotic taste to such ordinary dishes as grilled cheese sandwiches, pasta sauce, and salads. Do keep some on hand. They will keep, well wrapped, in the refrigerator for 1 week.

Ramps

*R**amps, or wild leeks, are a long-awaited spring pleasure. They shoot up along river banks and in swampy areas in May. The leaves look like lily of the valley, but the slender white stems and full green leaves are packed with a garlicky aroma, which tones down a bit during cooking. You can sometimes find them in farmer's markets; if not, substitute leeks in recipes calling for ramps. We cook ramps on the grill or let them mingle with roasting juices.*

Ramps are by nature muddy, so if you find some, stand them up in a container that drains— like a milk crate—and hose them off. Trim off the roots, loose white layers, and leaves and use the bulbs and stems whole or sliced.

Cèpe and Chestnut Soup

SERVES 8

At once hearty and richly elegant, this thick, nutty soup combines the foie gras, chestnuts, and cèpes typical in southwestern France. It comes from Laurent Manrique, who turned the kitchens at the Waldorf Astoria's Peacock Alley, and San Francisco's Campton Place into temples of gastronomy. His Gascon roots come together especially well in this soup with its garnishes. The chanterelles and oyster mushrooms mellow the rich elements of the soup and add luscious volume. It can be made ahead and reheated.

The Supermarket Cèpe Hunt

The robust flavor and texture of the cèpe marks it as a perfect autumnal ingredient, since its growing season peaks before frost. Yet many cooks miss it. When the cèpe pushes up out of the moss, we're still prolonging summer with late-season barbecues and delicate salads. Around the time we're closing the summer house and thinking about mushroom soup, the cèpe campaign is fini.

If you can reprogram your inner food clock, start checking stores for cèpes in late May. The first harvest of cèpes comes mostly from the Pacific Northwest; they pale a bit in comparison to European cèpes. The King Boletus, as some North American cèpes are known, is huge—some single mushrooms weigh in at a pound—the terra cotta-and-plum color European cèpe has a small, firm cap. Its brief season can begin as early as August and be finished by Veteran's Day in November. There have been years, though, that we teased a few cèpes into the sauté pan for Christmas.

2 pounds fresh chestnuts in the
    shell
8 ounces fresh cèpes, trimmed
    and cleaned
2 teaspoons olive oil
2 tablespoons duck fat (see Mail-Order
    Sources, page 324)
    or 1 tablespoon vegetable oil
    and 1 tablespoon unsalted butter
½ small onion, diced
⅓ cup diced leek, white part only
    (about 1 thin leek)
1 tablespoon minced garlic
4 ounces fresh chanterelles, cleaned
    and sliced ¼ inch thick
4 ounces oyster mushrooms, cleaned
    and sliced ¼ inch thick
8 cups Light Chicken Stock (page 280)
    or canned low-sodium chicken
    broth
1 tablespoon Cèpe Powder (page 285)
⅓ cup heavy (or whipping cream) or
    light cream
Kosher or sea salt and freshly ground
    black pepper
⅓ cup (about 2 ounces) diced fresh
    foie gras (optional)
2 tablespoons chopped fresh chives

1. With the tip of a paring knife, mark an X in the flat side of each chestnut. Make the cut large enough to cover the whole flat side but only deep enough to penetrate the shell, not the chestnut itself. Place the chestnuts in a large pot and add enough cold water to cover generously. Bring to a boil over high heat, reduce the heat, and simmer for 20 minutes. Remove a chestnut and while it is still hot try to remove the shell. It should pull off quite easily, along with the thin membrane that coats the nut itself. If not, continue simmering for 5 minutes more, then test again. Peel all the chestnuts, removing them from the hot water a few at a time. Finely dice enough of the chestnuts to measure ⅓ cup. Set the diced and whole chestnuts aside separately.

2. Dice enough of the trimmed cèpe stems to measure about ⅔ cup. Slice the remaining cèpes ¼ inch thick. Heat the olive oil in a small skillet over medium heat. Add the diced cèpe stems and sauté until lightly browned, about 4 minutes. Set aside.

3. Heat the duck fat in a 4- to 5-quart heavy pot over medium heat. Stir in the onion, leek, and garlic and sauté until wilted, about 3 minutes. Add the reserved sliced cèpes, the chanterelles, and the oyster mushrooms. Sauté, stirring, until the mushrooms are wilted and the onion is lightly browned, about 5 minutes. Add the whole chestnuts (save the diced ones for garnish) and stir to coat with fat. Add the stock and cèpe powder and bring to a boil. Reduce the heat and simmer, skimming the fat from the surface occasionally, until the chestnuts are tender, about 30 minutes. Remove from the heat and let stand until lukewarm.

4. Transfer about 2 cups of the soup, including some of the liquid and some of the solids, to a blender. Blend at low speed until very smooth. Continue with the remaining soup. Clean the pot and return the purée to it. Heat the soup over low heat to a simmer. Stir in the cream and salt and pepper to taste.

5. To serve, divide the foie gras (if using), diced chestnuts, and reserved cèpe stems among 8 warm soup bowls. Ladle the soup into the bowls and sprinkle the top with chives. Serve immediately.

To Clean Leeks

*C*ut the root ends from the leeks, then trim the tops down to the white parts or the light green parts only, keeping the parts separate. (Save the dark green leaves for vegetable broth.) Split the leeks lengthwise, then cut them according to the directions in the recipe. Fill a large bowl with cool water, add the cut-up leeks, and swish them around to remove the sand and grit. Let the leeks float, allowing the sand to settle to the bottom. Lift the leeks out to a colander, pour the water out of the bowl, and rinse the bowl. Repeat rinsing and swishing until there is no more sand in the bowl. Spread the drained leeks out on a kitchen towel to dry.

Hedgehog and Buttermilk Soup

SERVES 4

*a*n oversized bowl of this tangy, mushroom-studded soup will do wonders to restore your winter equilibrium. Add a green salad, Porcini-Dust Twists (page 240), and a glass of red wine and you've got a complete supper. If hedgehogs are unavailable, chanterelles may be substituted.

3 leeks (about 1½ pounds), trimmed,
    white and light greens parts only
12 ounces hedgehog mushrooms,
    cleaned
1 small bunch fresh flat-leaf
    parsley
2 tablespoons unsalted butter
2 teaspoons kosher or
    sea salt or less if using
    canned broth
4 cups Light Chicken Stock
    (page 280) or canned
    low-sodium canned
    chicken broth
1 cup buttermilk
2 teaspoons cornstarch
Freshly ground black pepper

1. Cut the leeks into white and light green parts. Cut all parts in half lengthwise, keeping the parts separate, then cut crosswise into ¼-inch-thick strips. Clean the leeks as described on page 79, keeping the whites and greens separate.

2. Cut the stems from the mushrooms and put them with the leek whites. Slice the caps about ½-inch wide and put them with the leek greens. Rinse and dry the parsley. Remove the thick stems and put them with the leek whites. Chop the leaves, measure 2 tablespoons of the chopped parsley, and put with the leek greens.

3. Melt the butter in a heavy 3-quart pot over medium heat. Add the leek whites, mushroom stems, parsley stems, and salt. Reduce the heat to low, cover, and cook for 15 minutes, stirring occasionally. Add the stock, increase the heat to high, and boil, covered, for 5 minutes. Let the mixture cool, then working in batches, transfer to a blender and blend until smooth.

4. Return the purée to the pot, add the leek greens, mushroom caps, and chopped parsley and simmer until the leek greens are tender, about 5 minutes. Stir the buttermilk and cornstarch together in a small bowl until the cornstarch is dissolved. Stir this mixture into the soup and simmer until thickened, about 2 minutes. Add pepper to taste.

5. Serve hot, sprinkling each serving with chopped parsley, if you like.

Fin de Siècle Cream of Mushroom Soup

SERVES 6

*G*one are the days of ornate soup tureens and sixteen-course meals, and with it, heavy, porridge-like cream soups. My version of classic cream of mushroom soup is thickened with potato, and the cream is optional. The mix of mushrooms gives the soup a well-rounded flavor, and the leeks add sweetness and color.

3 leeks (about 1½ pounds), trimmed, white
    and light green parts only
8 ounces shiitakes
8 ounces (about 2 large) portobellos
8 ounces cremini
4 tablespoons (½ stick) unsalted butter
1 large (about 8 ounces) russet potato,
    peeled and cut into 2-inch cubes
1 ounce (about 1 cup) dried porcini
8 cups hot water
2 tablespoons Mushroom-Infused Sherry
    (page 255) or dry sherry
Kosher salt or sea salt and freshly ground
    black pepper
¼ to ⅓ cup heavy (or whipping) cream,
    (optional)
¼ cup chopped fresh chives
Mushroom-Dust Croutons (optional; page 240)

1. Cut the leeks into white and green parts. Cut all parts in half lengthwise, keeping the parts separate, then cut crosswise into ¼-inch-thick strips. Rinse leeks as described, keeping the whites and greens separate.

2. Trim the stems off all the mushrooms and coarsely chop them. Set aside. Cut the portobello caps into quarters and with a paring knife, cut off the black gills on the underside of the cap. Peel and discard the dark outer layer from the portobello caps; it should lift off easily. Slice all the mushroom caps ¼ inch thick.

3. Melt 2 tablespoons of the butter in a heavy 4-quart pot over medium heat. Add the potato, leek whites, and mushroom stems and stir to coat with butter. Cover and reduce the heat to medium-low. Cook, stirring occasionally, until the vegetables are tender, about 20 minutes.

4. Meanwhile place the dried porcini in a medium-size bowl and add 2 cups of hot water. Soak until softened, about 20 minutes. Drain, straining the soaking liquid through a coffee filter or a sieve lined with a double thickness of cheesecloth. Rinse the mushrooms to remove any grit and coarsely chop them.

5. Add the mushroom soaking liquid, 2 cups of hot water, and the chopped dried mushrooms to the pot. Bring to a boil over high heat, reduce the heat, and simmer, covered, for 10 minutes.

6. Working in batches, transfer the contents of the pot to a blender and blend on low speed until smooth. Return each batch to the pot and, when all is blended, add 4 cups of hot water.

7. Melt the remaining 2 tablespoons butter in a large skillet over medium-high heat. Add the leek greens and sliced mushrooms. Cook, tossing the mushrooms so they cook evenly, until they are wilted and begin to release their liquid, about 5 minutes. Increase the heat to high and cook until the liquid is evaporated, about 5 minutes. Add the sherry and boil until evaporated, about 2 minutes. Transfer the contents of the skillet to the soup pot. Heat the soup to a simmer, add salt and pepper to taste, and stir in the cream. Cover and simmer for 10 minutes.

8. Serve the soup hot, sprinkled with chopped chives and croutons, if desired.

Seafood and Lobster Mushroom Chowder

To doll up this hearty, silky chowder, substitute lobster meat for the shrimp and/or scallops. Chicken of the woods and honshimeji as well as lobster mushrooms make a delicious soup. Splash a little Mushroom-Infused Sherry (page 255) into the chowder before serving.

4 ounces medium shrimp

8 ounces firm, skinless fish fillets, such as salmon, halibut, or a mixture of two or more

4 ounces bay scallops, or 4 ounces sea scallops cut into quarters

4 cups Light Chicken Stock (page 280) or canned low-sodium chicken broth

3 tablespoons unsalted butter

1 large onion, diced

2 ribs celery, trimmed and diced

1 pound lobster mushrooms, cleaned and cut into ¼-inch

1 tablespoon fresh thyme leaves

Kosher or sea salt and freshly ground pepper, to taste

2 tablespoons all-purpose flour

4 small (about 12 ounces) red new potatoes, scrubbed and cut into ½-inch cubes

2 cups light cream or half-and-half

3 tablespoons chopped fresh flat-leaf parsley

1. Peel the shrimp, reserving the shells. Devein the shrimp and cut into ½-inch lengths. Cut the fish fillets into ¼-inch pieces. Remove any bones if necessary as you work. Combine the shrimp, fish, and scallops in a small bowl and refrigerate, covered, until needed.

2. Combine the shrimp shells and stock in a small saucepan. Heat to a simmer over medium-low heat and simmer for 5 minutes. Let stand until cool. Strain the broth and discard the shells.

3. Melt the butter in a 4-quart pot over medium heat until foaming. Add the onion and celery and cook until the vegetables are wilted, about 4 minutes. Add the mushrooms and thyme. Cook until the mushrooms are softened, about 5 minutes. Season to taste with salt and pepper.

4. Reheat the stock to a simmer.

5. Increase the heat under the mushroom mixture to medium-high. Stir in the flour and cook until well blended, 3 minutes. Slowly stir in the heated broth. Heat to a simmer, stirring constantly to prevent lumps. Add the potatoes, cover, and cook until the potatoes are tender, about 8 minutes.

(The soup may be prepared to this point up to 1 day in advance and refrigerated. Heat to a simmer before continuing.)

6. Stir in the cream. Heat to a simmer, then stir in the seafood and parsley. Simmer until the seafood is opaque throughout, about 4 minutes. Adjust the seasoning and serve immediately.

Le Chabrol

I will never forget the shock I felt when my portly, well-mannered father-in-law André poured a half-glass of red wine into his empty soup plate, picked it up reverently with two hands, swirled the wine around, eased it down his throat, and smacked his lips, all in one fluid motion. This, as I later discovered, is le chabrol, a custom in which inhabitants of certain regions of France are privileged to partake without suffering any embarrassment whatsoever. Evidently it is the way country folk finish up any soup bits left in the bowl and prepare the palate for the more challenging courses to follow. I have found antique-style postcards in Bergerac, near André's hometown, that show a beefy gentleman with a large napkin tied squarely across his broad shoulders caught in the act. Needless to say, we've adopted the custom in our home, much to everyone's satisfaction.

Mushrooms in Salads

*T*he salads that follow are little vignettes from a decade of lettuce discovery. More than mâche, tatsoi, and radicchio, the salads I love include a tumble of delicious ingredients. A salad can be homey or feisty, warm or cool, delicate or hearty. Soft lettuces make a wonderful backdrop for tender, not-too-chewy seafood and veggies dressed with lemon or red wine vinegar. Tougher, slightly bitter greens can take on a world of ingredients, meeting strongly flavored mushrooms such as hen of the woods on equal ground, and they can handle a chili-pepper vinaigrette.

Not every salad includes greens, as you'll see by some of these tasty varieties. Mushrooms, warm or at room temperature, whether roasted or pickled, add a juicy component to a salad of meat, eggs, or seafood. Recipes such as Pickled Lactaire, Pompom Salad with Bresaola, and Yellow Oyster Mushroom, Lamb, and New Potato Salad are great ways to try a new mushroom. Each of these accentuates the true flavor of mushrooms without distractions.

Mixed Mushrooms à la Grecque

The Mushrooms à la Greque recipe is the most stained page in my copy of *From Julia Child's Kitchen*. Before I stepped into the nether world of wild mushrooms, Julia's recipe for button mushrooms was my favorite bring-along to potluck parties. For this sparkling version of an old favorite, Chris and I added portobellos and shiitakes to the buttons and punched in robust notes of garlic, vinegar, and fennel.

2 bay leaves

2 teaspoons coriander seeds

1 teaspoon black peppercorns

1 teaspoon fennel seeds

½ cup olive oil

¼ cup dry white wine

2 tablespoons red wine vinegar

4 cloves garlic

2 teaspoons kosher or sea salt

1 package (10-ounces) button
   mushrooms, cleaned and
   trimmed

8 ounces (2 medium) portobellos,
   cleaned, stems and gills removed
   (see box, page 189)

4 ounces small shiitakes

¼ cup chopped fresh flat-leaf parsley

12 Boston or red leaf lettuce leaves,
   rinsed and spun dry

1. Tie the bay leaves, coriander seeds, peppercorns, and fennel seeds in a 4-inch square of cheesecloth. Combine 2 cups of water, the olive oil, wine, vinegar, garlic, salt, and cheesecloth-wrapped spice packet in a deep 4-quart pot. Heat to a boil over medium-high heat, then reduce the heat and simmer, covered, for 20 minutes.

2. Cut small (less than 2 inches) button mushrooms into quarters; cut larger buttons into 6 or 8 pieces. Cut the portobello caps into quarters, then cut the quarters into ½-inch wedges. Leave small (less than 1½ inches) shiitake caps whole, cut larger caps in half.

3. Add the mushrooms to the pot. Stir until the mushrooms have wilted enough to be covered by liquid. Cover and simmer until cooked through, about 10 minutes. Cool to room temperature and stir in the parsley.

4. Arrange the lettuce leaves on 6 salad plates. Use slotted spoon to spoon the mushrooms onto the lettuce leaves. Serve chilled or at room temperature.

Love and the Art of the Salad:
A Personal Journey

I have never been a salad head. Iceberg being Option 1, Option 2, and Option 3 in my growing years, I was only too happy to exercise alternative meal choices in the college cafeteria. Later, when I traveled in France, meals were so copious that nobody noticed me refusing the green things at the end of the repast. I continued to develop leaf-avoidance techniques—until deprivation struck. While still in my carefree days, my then-boyfriend Thierry got snared in an immigration dragnet in the Bahamas. I was with him, and our stay involuntarily stretched to about a week. This was a challenge to our twenty-somethings' budgets. Vegetables on the islands were rare, so nary a green passed our lips. After too many nachos and hamburgers, I flew home and tucked right into the hugest, crispest salad I could find. With vinaigrette dripping down my chin, cool and crunchy back in my taste vocabulary, I had one of those culinary epiphanies. It had been so easy to scorn salad when it was plentiful and available. But when the only greens around were on lawns and in window boxes, I discovered that I really did need and love lettuce.

The only thing missing from the ensuing months' toss of greens was the company of a certain beloved Frenchman. When he did return to New York to marry me, I discovered a secret he'd never shared—his special knack for putting together salads.

The act of preparing a simple green salad—which Thierry learned from his mother—is practiced like a ritual every day by millions of French house-wives. Large leaves of soft Boston-style lettuce are rinsed and dried in a salad spinner. These are placed, uncut, in a salad bowl. Next, an unmeasured amount of red wine vinegar is poured into a café-au-lait bowl (a mug works well, too). A paring knife is used to chop a shallot cradled in the hand not holding the knife—French housewives, in the interest of economy, rarely pull out a cutting board. (It would just need to be washed afterwards.) Shallot goes into bowl, followed by a plump dollop of creamy—never grainy—mustard. Finally, the huile de tournesol, or sunflower oil, is added in a slow drizzle, and beaten to blend, using a table fork. A pinch of salt and twist of the pepper mill complete the vinaigrette.

Pickled Lactaire

SERVES 4 TO 6

During the year that the recipes for this book evolved, I kept waiting and hoping for lactaire to appear, for pickled lactaire make a snappy autumn snack. The first autumn brought only a few wormy specimens. I was resigned to turning in the book without lactaire, which I consider the best pickling mushroom around. Then Thierry returned from the airport with a handful of the beauties, just two days before the deadline. Luckily this recipe works well with almost any mushroom. But it really boosts firm mushrooms that have a low water content, such as bluefoot and eryngii. The piquant flavor goes well with sweet ham and dark bread as well as cool rice tossed with pickled ginger. Or use them as a condiment for a cold meat platter or as an hors d'oeuvre (offer toothpicks) with a glass of iced vodka.

¾ pound lactaire mushrooms
4 cups cider vinegar
2 cups water
1 small onion, thinly sliced
1 tablespoon Seasoning Salt (page 253)
1 teaspoon caraway seeds
6 peppercorns
3 bay leaves

1. If you plan to eat the lactaires within a few days, sterilizing isn't necessary. If you will be preserving the mushrooms, sterilize a 1-quart, wide-mouth canning jar, its lid, a slotted spoon, and tongs for 15 minutes in boiling water. Keep them in

Anjey's Lactaires

Anjey Brausch, the artist who illustrated our catalogs for many years, began with Aux Délices as a mushroom packer fresh from the Soviet Union. He barely spoke English, but he was a pleasant fellow with a passion for wild mushrooms. He often displayed bewildering behavior, such as marking restaurant names on the boxes in lettering he thought suited the restaurant's style—Chinese for China Grill, Cyrillic for Russian Tea Room (his amusing creative approach led to his illustrating our catalogs).

Well, the day lactaire came in, he got very excited. Since we were still communicating with gestures and smiles, we were happy to see him take an interest in our products. Anjey came in a few days later, slammed a jar of pickled lactaire and a bottle of vodka down on the desk, and made us understand we were to taste (at 8 A.M.). Gingerly, we followed his example, biting into a vodka-and-juniper-imbued lactaire, then washing it down with a shot of vodka. The first taste sent out taste buds into shock, but later, with ham and sausage as a foil, the mushroom's astringency mellowed pleasantly. I don't recommend it for breakfast, but pickled lactaire makes a good showing on a charcuterie platter!

the water until ready to fill the jar.

2. Trim the lactaire stems flush with the caps. Thoroughly rinse the mushrooms in a basin of water. If they are too large to fit in the jar, cut them in half.

3. Bring the remaining ingredients to a boil in a 4-quart nonreactive saucepan over medium-high heat. Add the mushrooms. Reduce the heat and gently boil for 20 minutes, skimming occasionally.

4. With a slotted spoon (sterilized if preserving), transfer the mushrooms to a 1-quart jar. Pour the pickling liquid over the mushrooms. Let cool. If you are not preserving the mushrooms, store, covered, in the refrigerator for up to 3 days.

5. To preserve the mushrooms, use the tongs to place the sealing lids on the jars when the liquid has cooled. Screw the tops in place. Be careful not to touch the jar or its contents with your hands. Use a clean towel. Place the sealed jar on a rack in a deep pot. Cover the jar with at least 1 inch of water. Bring to a boil and continue boiling for 20 minutes. Remove the jar and set it on a very clean tea towel. After 2 hours, turn the lid to close tightly. Store in a cool, dark place.

Pompom with Bresaola

SERVES 4

Soft yet resilient and sweetly aromatic, the pompom mingles wonderfully with garlic and sage. The bresaola, or air-dried beef, adds texture and is available at specialty food markets and butchers. You could substitute carpaccio from a trusted butcher or slices of thin-cut, rare-roasted beef.

This recipe takes just minutes. It came from Carlo Benevidas, who was the chef at the cozy New York restaurant I Trulli.

8 slices (about 4 ounces) of bresaola

¾ cup olive oil

Juice of ½ lemon

½ teaspoon freshly ground black pepper

3 unpeeled cloves garlic

4 pompoms (about 1 pound),
    sliced ½ inch thick

¼ teaspoon kosher or sea salt

4 leaves fresh sage, sliced thin

4 whole sage leaves, for garnish

1. Fan out the bresaola on a plate in a single layer. Cover it with ¼ cup of the olive oil, the lemon juice and the pepper.

2. Heat the remaining ½ cup of

olive oil in a medium-size sauté pan over medium heat. Sauté the garlic until golden brown, then discard.

3. Increase the heat to high. Quickly sauté the pompoms in the garlic oil for 1 minute, turning once. Reduce the heat to medium and add the salt and sliced sage. Continue cooking until the pompom slices are fairly limp and golden brown, about 3 minutes more.

4. Lift the bresaola from its marinade and arrange 2 slices of it on each of 4 plates. Top with the pompoms and garnish with fresh sage leaves.

Warm Salad of Hen of the Woods with Bitter Greens and Bacon

SERVES 6

This is how we prepared our very first hen of the woods. Although we've stewed, grilled, simmered, and roasted these mushrooms since, a simple green salad always seems so soul-satisfying. Here the traditional French *salade aux frisée et lardons* gets a healthy dose of mushrooms and blue cheese.

8 to 10 cups of greens, such as thinly sliced
    Belgian endive, mesclun, frisée,
    young cress, or a mix
¼ pound slab bacon with or without
    rind 1 piece
Olive oil, if necessary
2 large shallots, chopped
1 pound hen of the woods, cleaned and
    coarsely chopped
2 tablespoons good quality red wine
1 tablespoon red wine vinegar
Kosher or sea salt and freshly ground
    black pepper
1 bunch chervil, large stems removed (about
    1½ cups, lightly packed; optional)
1 bunch chives, cut into 1-inch pieces
    (about ⅓ cup)
4 ounces Roquefort, Danish blue, or
    Stilton cheese, crumbled

1. Swish the salad greens around in a bowl of cool water to remove sand and dirt. Change the water if necessary. Dry the greens, preferably in a salad spinner.

2. Remove the rind from the bacon if necessary and cut the bacon into ¼-inch dice. Place the bacon in a large cold skillet over medium-low heat. Cook, stirring occasionally, until the bacon has rendered its fat and is well browned, about 10 minutes. Remove the bacon with a slotted spoon to a salad bowl.

3. Measure the bacon fat in the pan. If necessary add enough olive oil to make ¼ cup. Place the pan over medium heat and add the shallots. Sauté, stirring, until wilted, about 3 minutes. Add the mushrooms and sauté until tender, about 6 minutes. Add the red wine and vinegar and heat just to a boil. Remove the pan from the heat and add salt and pepper to taste.

4. Place the salad greens, chervil, if using, and chives in the salad bowl. Spoon the contents of the skillet over the salad and toss well to coat. Sprinkle the blue cheese over the salad and serve at once.

Note: Instead of tossing the cheese with the salad, you may prefer to serve it on croutons. Bring the cheese to room temperature and beat it with a few drops of Cognac until smooth. Season the cheese with freshly ground black pepper and spread it on thinly sliced toasted baguette.

Grilled Mushrooms with Preserved Lemon–Chili Vinaigrette

SERVES 6

What a great way to take advantage of the grill's glowing coals! The chili-spiked dressing leaves no doubt as to what a grilled bluefoot suggests to me. Char, hot, bitter; char, hot, bitter goes this delicious toss of greens and mushrooms. You couldn't make this work with chanterelles or black trumpets, but try it with anything in the oyster mushroom family, or with blewit or chicken of the woods mushrooms. We got the recipe from Peter Klein, one of Aux Delices des Bois' first customers. He started a Mexican boom at El Teddy's, the wildly decorated Tribeca eatery where chefs used to hang out after work.

Our Solution for Leftover Salad Greens

If you have leftover greens, shake off excess vinaigrette. In a sauté pan, heat cooked pasta, the greens, and other leftovers such as tomatoes or cubed meat. Moisten with a little soy sauce or some chicken stock, and you've got a quick meal.

PRESERVED LEMON–CHILI VINAIGRETTE

1 small dried ancho chile

Boiling water

¼ Preserved Lemon (recipe follows)

¼ cup cider vinegar

1 serrano chili or ½ jalapeño, seeds
    removed and sliced

1 shallot, sliced

1 teaspoon chopped garlic

1 cup peanut oil, light olive oil,
    canola oil, or a mix

Kosher or sea salt and freshly
    ground black pepper

MUSHROOM SALAD

1 bunch (about 1 pound) of tender young
    dandelion greens or other bitter
    greens, such as arugula, endive,
    radicchio, or frisée, trimmed

4 ounces bluefoot mushrooms, cleaned

Kosher or sea salt and freshly ground
    black pepper

3 tablespoons olive oil, for grilling

4 ounces firm goat cheese, crumbled

1. To make the vinaigrette, stem the ancho chili and tap out the seeds. Soak it in boiling water to cover until soft, 20 minutes. Drain the chili and dry it well. Finely dice the chili. Set aside.

2. Squeeze the juice from the lemon and reserve it. Cut away the pulp from the rind and discard the pulp. Finely chop the rind.

3. Combine the vinegar, serrano, shallot, garlic, chopped lemon rind, and lemon juice in a blender. Blend until well combined. With the motor running on low, pour in the oil very

slowly. Continue blending until the vinaigrette is smooth. Season to taste with salt and pepper and stir in the diced ancho chili.

4. To make the salad, tear or cut the greens into bite-size pieces. Place the greens in a large bowl of cool water and swish around to remove all sand and dirt. Change the water and repeat if necessary. Dry the greens well, preferably in a salad spinner.

5. Preheat a grill pan or outdoor grill until hot.

6. Brush the mushroom pieces with olive oil and sprinkle with salt and pepper. Grill until well marked and softened, about 5 minutes.

7. Toss the greens with the vinaigrette. Divide the dressed salad among 6 serving plates and top with the grilled mushrooms and crumbled goat cheese.

Preserved Lemon

Although preserved lemons are easy to make, they need a month of sitting time before they are ready to use. Therefore, it's a good idea to start making them way before you'll need them. Preserved lemon hails from North Africa, where it adds pungency to native closed-cover stews called tagines. Both juice and rind may be used; the juice as the liquid in a sauce or stew and the rind as a flavor pick-me-up in pasta or grain salads.

6 medium lemons

¼ cup kosher or sea salt, or as needed

8 each coriander seeds (optional) and
cloves, (optional)

About 2 cups fresh lemon juice (8 to 10
medium lemons) as needed

1. Scrub the lemons well and cut off a thin slice from one end so they stand upright on the cutting surface. Cut the lemons into quarters, stopping about ½ inch from the bottom; the lemons should hold together. Gently spread the lemon segments apart and coat the pulp generously with salt, using about 2 tablespoons of the salt.

2. Coat the bottom of a very clean 1-quart canning jar with about 1 tablespoon of the remaining salt and arrange the lemons in the jar, pressing them in tightly to fit as snugly as possibly and to squeeze the juice from them. Sprinkle a light layer of salt between the lemons. When all the lemons are packed into the jar, add as much lemon juice as necessary to cover the lemons.

3. Seal the jar and keep it at warm room temperature for **25 to** 30 days, turning the jar upside down at least every 2 or 3 days.

4. To use, remove and discard the flesh and finely dice the rinds.

Mâche with Cauliflower Mushrooms and Soft-Cooked Egg

There's something about this egg dish that puts it high on my comfort food list. It is a favorite cool weather Sunday supper, which in our family usually involves eggs, mushrooms foraged in breathless hikes that very same afternoon, and meat as a minor player. Eggs pair nicely with just about any mushroom, but do look for cauliflowers in the fall—they are special.

SERVES 4

5 large eggs

1 tablespoon red wine vinegar

5 tablespoons olive oil

Kosher or sea salt and freshly ground
black pepper

2 thick slices pancetta, diced or ⅓ cup
diced slab bacon

8 ounces cauliflower mushrooms, trimmed,
cleaned, and cut into bite-size pieces

2 medium shallots, finely chopped

2 medium cloves garlic, minced

4 cups mâche, washed and dried

1 tablespoon fresh herbs chopped, such as
tarragon, chervil, and chives

1. Put 1 egg in a small saucepan and cover with water. Bring to a boil, then cover and turn off heat. Let stand for 14 minutes. Drain and rinse under cool water.

2. While still warm, cut the egg in half, remove the yolk (it will be firm and pale yellow), and mash it in a small bowl with a fork. Discard the egg white (or sprinkle with salt and eat it out of the shell). Stir the vinegar into the yolk. Drizzle in 4 tablespoons of the olive oil, a little at a time, until emulsified. Season to taste with salt and pepper.

3. Heat the remaining 1 table-spoon olive oil and the pancetta in a large sauté pan over medium heat. Cook, stirring, until the pancetta is crisp, 5 to 6 minutes. Transfer to a paper towel to drain. Turn the heat to medium-high, add the mush-rooms, and cook for 1 minute. Reduce the heat to medium, add the shallots and garlic, and cook until the mushrooms are soft, about 8 minutes. (This can be done up to 2 hours ahead of time and set aside, covered. Reheat over medium-high heat, adding 1 tablespoon of water if the mixture seems dry.)

4. About 10 minutes before serving, soft-boil the remaining 4 eggs. Place them in a medium-size saucepan, cover with water, and bring to a boil. Boil for 3 minutes, then drain, rinse under cool running water for 1 minute, and set aside.

5. Toss the lettuce with the vinaigrette. Divide it among 4 salad plates and top with the mushrooms. Carefully remove the shells of the eggs, disturbing as little of the white as possible. Place an egg on top of each portion of mushrooms and serve. Diners should cut into their egg so that the yolk runs out over the salad (see Note). Sprinkle the pancetta and herbs on top.

Note: If picking away the shell of a soft-boiled egg sounds too difficult, poach the eggs instead. They, too, work well in this salad.

Mushroom and Potato Salad with Toasted Garlic

SERVES 4

Radishes, fresh spinach, and cremini turn potato salad into a dressy affair. This recipe comes from Etienne Merle, a chef/restaurateur we've befriended for his Santa Claus–like twinkle and his enthusiasm for all things food-related. The salad can be made in advance and its components combined just before serving.

1 pound cremini or button mushrooms,
    cleaned and stems cut flush
    with the caps
Sea or kosher salt and freshly ground
    black pepper
10 tablespoons olive oil
1½ pounds large (about 4) red-skinned
    potatoes
1 bunch (1 pound) spinach, tough
    stems removed, rinsed thoroughly,
    dried, and cut into
    ½-inch strips
8 medium red radishes, trimmed and
    sliced very thin
2 tablespoons red wine vinegar
1 tablespoon mirin
1 tablespoon Mushroom Soy Sauce
    (page 255) or good-quality brewed
    soy sauce
1 bunch fresh flat-leaf parsley,
    leaves only, washed, dried,
    and coarsely chopped
3 large cloves garlic, thinly sliced
½ teaspoon sesame seeds
¼ teaspoon green or pink
    peppercorns

1. Preheat the oven to 400°F.

2. Place the mushrooms in a large bowl. Season them generously with salt and pepper and drizzle with 2 tablespoons olive oil. Toss until the mushrooms are lightly coated with oil. Arrange the mushrooms, stem side down, on a baking sheet and roast until deep golden brown and tender, about 15 minutes. Remove and cool the mushrooms.

3. Place the potatoes in a large saucepan of cold water. Add ½ teaspoon of salt and bring to a boil. Cover, reduce the heat, and cook until the potatoes are tender but still firm when tested with a paring knife, about 30 minutes, depending upon their size. Drain and let stand just until cool enough to handle.

4. Cut the mushroom caps into quarters and place in a large bowl. Add the spinach and radishes. Combine 6 tablespoons of the remaining oil, vinegar, mirin, soy sauce, and parsley in a small jar with a tight-fitting lid. Shake vigorously to mix and pour over the spinach mixture. Toss well. Cut the potatoes into ½-inch dice, add to the bowl, and toss well. Cool to room temperature.

5. Heat the remaining 2 tablespoons olive oil in a very small skillet or saucepan over low heat. Add the garlic and cook, shaking the skillet occasionally, until the garlic is golden brown, about 2 minutes. Spoon the garlic and oil over the salad.

6. To serve, place the sesame seeds and peppercorns in a peppermill and grind a generous amount over the salad. Or place the sesame seeds and peppercorns on a flat surface and crush them lightly with the bottom of a small, heavy saucepan, then sprinkle the mixture over the salad. Toss the salad lightly and serve.

Slow-Roasted Cremini with Barley

SERVES 8

Roasting cremini mushrooms intensifies their already deep flavor. Pair them with barley and a tangy, herb-flecked dressing for a simple summer salad. It can be prepared ahead and kept refrigerated. Thierry and I take it picnicking, packed in a zipper-top plastic bag.

ROASTED CREMINI

1 pound cremini mushrooms, cleaned
    with stems trimmed flush with
    the cap

2 tablespoons olive oil

BARLEY SALAD

2 ripe large (about 1¼ pounds) tomatoes,
    cored and cut into ½-inch dice

¼ cup olive oil

¼ cup very finely shredded fresh basil

3 tablespoons fresh orange juice

2 tablespoons chopped fresh oregano or
    marjoram

2 tablespoons chopped fresh flat-leaf
    parsley

1 teaspoon kosher or sea salt

¼ teaspoon freshly ground black pepper

1½ cups (about ¾ pound) pearl barley

1. Preheat the oven to 300°F.

2. Toss the mushrooms in a bowl with 2 tablespoons olive oil and place them, stem side down, on a baking sheet. Roast until very tender and well browned, stirring halfway through, about 35 minutes. Cool completely. Slice the mushrooms and combine them with the juice from the roasting pan. Set aside.

3. To make the salad, toss the tomatoes, ¼ cup olive oil, the basil, orange juice, oregano, parsley, salt, and pepper in a bowl. Set aside. (The salad can be prepared to this point up to 1 day in advance. Refrigerate the mushroom mixture and tomato mixture separately and bring them to room temperature before continuing.)

4. Wash the barley well under cold running water. Stir the barley into a large saucepan of boiling water, reduce the heat, and simmer until tender, about 20 minutes. Drain well and rinse under cold running water just until tepid. Drain well. Transfer the barley to a serving bowl large enough to hold all the ingredients. Add the tomato mixture and the mushrooms and their liquid. Toss well. Let stand for 30 minutes to 1 hour, tossing occasionally, before serving.

Pink Lentils with Shiitakes and Enoki

*T*his colorful salad is served at room temperature, which makes it ideal for a buffet or when the dish must be held. Many other mushrooms, such as bluefoot, wine cap, or honey mushrooms, will do nicely in this recipe.

SERVES 8 AS A FIRST COURSE, 3 TO 4 AS A MAIN COURSE

8 ounces baby spinach or tender flat-leaf spinach, trimmed, washed, and dried

1 log (8 ounces) mild goat cheese

¼ cup toasted chopped walnuts (see box, page 22)

¾ cup pink lentils or ½ cup small brown lentils

1 package (3.5 ounces) enoki mushrooms, trimmed and separated into small clusters

6 tablespoons olive oil

2 cloves garlic, minced

¾ pound shiitake mushrooms, stemmed, cleaned, and caps sliced ½ inch thick

2 tablespoons tamari soy sauce

2 tablespoons white wine vinegar

1. Leave the baby spinach leaves whole or tear the flat-leaf spinach into bite-size pieces. Set aside in the refrigerator.

2. Cut the goat cheese into 8 even rounds. Roll the rounds in the walnuts. Place on a small baking sheet, cover, and refrigerate until needed. (The salad can be prepared to this point up to 1 day in advance.)

3. About 2 hours before serving, boil the pink lentils in salted water just until tender, about 12 minutes.

Drain immediately. Transfer the lentils to a large bowl and cool to room temperature.

4. Preheat the oven to 400°F.

5. When the lentils are cool, sprinkle the spinach and enoki over them. Heat 4 tablespoons of the oil in a large skillet over medium heat. Add the garlic and fry just until you can smell it, about 10 seconds. Add the shiitakes and sauté, stirring almost constantly, until cooked through but still quite firm, about 5 minutes. Remove from the heat, stir in the remaining 2 tablespoons oil, the soy sauce, and the vinegar. Pour the mixture immediately over the spinach and toss quickly to wilt the greens and distribute the ingredients evenly. Let stand at room temperature for 15 minutes, tossing once or twice.

6. Just before serving, uncover the goat cheese and place in the oven. Bake just until warmed through, 2 to 3 minutes. Carefully transfer the cheese to serving plates, keeping them to one side. Toss the salad once more and arrange it in a crescent around the cheese.

Warm White Bean, Ham, and Chanterelle Salad

**SERVES 6 AS A
FIRST COURSE**

*F*ruity nuggets of chanterelles and ham accompanied by almost creamy white beans make a terrific winter salad. If you can find a thick-sliced country ham like jambon de Bayonne with its sweet-salty nip, use it without sautéing. The beans have to be soaked overnight, but they, as well as the leeks and vinaigrette, can be prepared a day in advance and stored, separately, in the fridge.

VINAIGRETTE

1½ teaspoons balsamic vinegar

2 teaspoons fresh lemon juice

½ teaspoon grainy Dijon mustard

¼ teaspoon kosher or sea salt

⅛ teaspoon freshly ground black pepper

2 tablespoons plus 1 teaspoon walnut oil

2 tablespoons vegetable oil

SALAD

1 cup dried small white beans, soaked
   (see box, page 215)

¾ pound leeks, white parts only, cleaned
   (see box, page 79)

1 tablespoon walnut oil

8 ounces chanterelles, cleaned, trimmed,
   and sliced ½ inch thick

¼ teaspoon Seasoning Salt
   (page 253)

1 clove garlic, minced

3 tablespoons coarsely chopped, toasted
   walnuts (see box, page 22)

1 tablespoon unsalted butter

8 ounces smoked ham steak, cut into
   ½-inch × ¼-strips

1 tablespoon Madeira

1 tablespoon chopped fresh chervil leaves

1 tablespoon chopped fresh flat-leaf parsley

1. To make the vinaigrette, whisk together the vinegar, lemon juice, mustard, salt, and pepper in a small, shallow bowl. Whisk in the walnut oil and vegetable oil until incorporated. Adjust the seasoning to taste. (If preparing in advance, transfer to a small jar with a lid and store in the refrigerator. Shake before continuing.)

2. To make the salad, place the beans in a medium, heavy saucepan and add enough water to cover them by 2 inches. Bring to a boil over medium-high heat, skim foam off the surface, and reduce the heat to a simmer. Simmer, replenishing water as it evaporates, until the beans are tender. Depending upon how dry the beans are, this could take 1 to 3 hours. Drain and set aside.

3. Bring a medium-size pan of salted water to a boil over medium-high heat. Cut fine strands of leek, slicing from the root end toward the tip. Drop the leek strands into the water, bring back to a boil, reduce the heat, and simmer until tender, about 8 minutes. Drain and refresh under cold water. Set aside.

4. Heat 1 tablespoon walnut oil in a large, heavy skillet, preferably nonstick, until almost smoking. Add the chanterelles and sprinkle with seasoning salt. Cook over medium heat until limp, about 3 minutes. Add the garlic and cook until the chanterelles are soft. Add the walnuts to the chanterelles, transfer to

above, and keep warm.

5. Melt the butter in the same skillet, over medium heat. Sauté the ham until lightly browned, about 2 minutes on each side. Increase the heat to high, add the Madeira, and scrape up the browned bits of meat.

6. Assemble the salad in a large salad bowl. Toss together the beans, leeks, walnuts and chanterelles, ham, vinaigrette, and herbs. Serve at room temperature.

Maine Lobster Salad

Smoky and sweet, this luxurious lobster and lobster mushroom salad combines some of summer's finest ingredients. The firm red lobster mushroom has a slightly bitter edge. It is best when they are warm off the grill, although room temperature is fine too. If you wish, cook the lobster on the grill as well. This recipe is from Chef John Farnsworth, now the chef at John's Club in Vero Beach, Florida.

SERVES 6

¾ cup canola or grapeseed oil

1 pound lobster mushrooms, wiped clean, stems trimmed flat with cap

Kosher or sea salt and freshly ground black pepper

1 pound ripe tomatoes

1 tablespoon minced shallots

¼ cup fresh lemon juice

1 tablespoon chopped fresh basil

2 tablespoons chopped fresh parsley

1 cooked lobster (1 to 1½ pounds), claw and tail meat diced into 1-inch chunks (see Note)

6 ounces mesclun

1. Preheat a grill to hot.

2. Brush 2 tablespooons of the oil over the lobster mushrooms. Season sparingly with salt and pepper. Set aside.

3. Cut the tomatoes in half through the stem end. Squeeze out the seeds and juice over a bowl. Strain the juice and save to add to vegetable stock or soup. Set a vegetable box grater over a medium-size bowl.

Rub each tomato half over the large holes until all that's left in your hand is the skin. You should have about 1 cup of tomato concassée. Add the remaining canola oil, the shallots, lemon juice, basil, parsley, ¼ teaspoon salt, and ¼ teaspoon pepper to the bowl. Whisk well to incorporate the oil. Set aside for 30 minutes. If you make the sauce more than 2 hours ahead of time, cover and refrigerate it. Bring it to room temperature and whisk well before serving.

4. Grill the lobster mushrooms until tender, 5 to 7 minutes on each side. They will be slightly charred, and a fork will slip in easily when they are done. While still warm, slice the mushroom caps into ¼-inch-thick slices.

5. To serve heap the mesclun in the center of each of 6 salad plates. Set the sliced lobster mushrooms on top of mesclun in a spoke pattern. Top with lobster meat. Spoon the sauce over all.

Note: To cook live lobster, drop it into a large pot of boiling, salted water and cook until the shell turns red, 6 to 8 minutes. Then grill the lobster in the shell for 10 minutes more. It should not sit right over the flames, but off to the side where the smoke can permeate the shell.

Grilled Tuna and Hen of the Woods with Funky Greens

SERVES 2

The very hip love this salad for its exotic ingredients and trendy rare tuna in a truffle-accented sauce. About those funky greens? Go wild to create your own assortment. If you grow lettuce or spinach, you can pick a slew when the leaves are still small. Or scour a farmers' market for shoots and sprouts. If you're using store-bought lettuces, select a variety of colors, textures, and flavors—from soft and herbaceous to chewy and bitter. If hen of the woods are not available, substitute cauliflower or shiitake mushrooms.

½ cup extra virgin olive oil

¼ cup fresh lemon juice

2 tablespoons truffle oil

Kosher or coarse sea salt and freshly
ground black pepper

2 tuna steaks, each about 8 ounces
and 1 inch thick

8 ounces (about 2 large) hen of the woods
mushrooms, cleaned, trimmed, and
sliced ¾ inch thick

6 cups (lightly packed) assorted greens,
such as baby spinach, pepper cress,
baby arugula, tatsoi, mesclun, pea
shoots, and sunflower sprouts, washed
and spun dry in a salad spinner

1 head of Belgian endive, cut in half
lengthwise, cored, and cut lengthwise
into thin strips

1 bunch chives, very thinly sliced
(about ¾ cup)

1 medium-size vine-ripened tomato,
cored and cut into ½-inch dice

1. Beat the olive oil, lemon juice, and truffle oil together in a small bowl until well blended. Add salt and pepper to taste. Beat again to blend and pour off ⅓ cup of the dressing. Set the remaining dressing aside.

2. Pat the tuna steaks dry with paper towels. Sprinkle both sides of each steak generously with salt and pepper. Brush both sides of the tuna steaks and the mushroom slices with the ⅓ cup of dressing. Let stand at room temperature for about 30 minutes.

3. Preheat a grill to hot. Or the tuna and mushrooms can be grilled in a stove-top grill pan. Heat the pan over medium heat until very hot, about 10 minutes.

4. Grill the mushroom slices until lightly browned and tender, about 3 minutes on each side. Set aside. Grill the tuna steaks, turning only once, until medium-rare (still pink and cool in the center), about 5 minutes on each side. For tuna steaks that are cooked through, add about 2 minutes to the cooking time.

5. Toss the greens, endive, chives, tomato, and grilled mushrooms in a large bowl. Beat the dressing well and pour over the greens. Sprinkle the mixture with salt and pepper to taste. Toss well and divide between 2 plates, mounding the salad to 1 side of the plate. Arrange the tuna steaks slightly over the salad and serve immediately.

Sailor's Salad

*I*f you live in Brittany, as do Thierry's old friends Simone and Patrick, mussels are plentiful and cheap. Each time we go to France, a day is reserved for a meal at their house—an entire day, which begins with an

SERVES 4

apéro, then launches into real, robust, and leisurely dining. Between the courses, we stroll through Simone's lettuce garden, check the progress in the pumpkin patch, and clip branches of bay leaf to smuggle back home.

Of all the wonderful dishes Simone has prepared, her mussel salad is my favorite. Once you taste this salad's mushroomy, saline, and herbal notes, you'll probably upgrade it to main-course status. The bluefoot add a subtle seafood flavor, but oyster mushrooms may be used if bluefoot are unavailable. If preparing it ahead, refrigerate all the components separately until serving time.

SALAD

Kosher or sea salt

1 pound mussels, scrubbed clean

1 pound bluefoot, chanterelle, or
    other firm mushroom

1 tablespoon unsalted butter

1 teaspoon fresh lemon juice

¼ teaspoon Seasoning Salt (page 253)

¼ teaspoon freshly ground
    black pepper

8 ounces fresh fava beans, shelled

VINAIGRETTE

1 tablespoon sherry vinegar

1 tablespoon Dijon mustard

⅛ teaspoon sea salt

¼ teaspoon freshly ground black pepper

1 shallot, finely chopped (1 tablespoon)

6 tablespoons extra virgin olive oil

TO FINISH

1 head (about 6 ounces) of frisée or
    endive, cleaned and torn into
    bite-size pieces

3 tablespoons chopped chives

1. Bring a large pot of salted water to a boil. Drop in the mussels, cover, and boil rapidly. As the mussels open, remove, reserving the liquid and set aside. All the mussels should have opened after 6 minutes.

2. Clean and trim the mushrooms. Remove the stems, saving them for stock, and cut the caps into 1-inch wedges.

3. Melt the butter in a medium-size sauté pan, over medium-high heat. Cook the mushrooms until they give up some liquid, about 2 minutes. Reduce the heat to low, add the lemon juice, Seasoning Salt, and pepper. Continue cooking until the mushrooms are wilted, about 15 minutes more. Set aside to cool.

4. Bring the reserved mussel cooking liquid to a boil. Drop in the fava beans. Boil until tender but not mushy, about 8 minutes. Drain under cold water, saving 2 tablespoons of the liquid. Set aside.

5. Slip the fava beans out of their inner shells. Using a shell as a pincher, remove the mussels from their shells.

6. To make the vinaigrette, using a fork, mix the vinegar, mustard, salt, pepper, and shallot in a small, deep bowl. Slowly drizzle in the oil, letting each addition emulsify before adding more. Whisk in the 2 tablespoons mussel liquid. Adjust the seasoning to taste.

7. To finish, or as Simone puts it, *réunissez la salad,* or bring the salad together, place the frisée, mussels, mushrooms, and fava beans in a salad bowl. Drizzle the dressing over all and toss gently. Serve on salad plates garnished with chives.

Grilled Steak and Cèpe Salad with Chipotle Mayonnaise

This hearty, spicy, flavor-packed combination has a punch of chipotle, a dare of charred radicchio, and the no-nonsense intensity of cèpes. If you can't get cèpes, substitute shiitakes or portobellos.

SERVES 6

STEAK AND MARINADE

2 to 3 shell steaks, about 1 inch thick
    (1½ pounds total)
¼ cup dry white wine
1 teaspoon Worcestershire sauce
1 tablespoon Dijon mustard
¼ teaspoon minced canned chipotle
½ teaspoon *adobo* sauce from canned
    chipotle
1 garlic clove, crushed
¼ cup corn or vegetable oil
1 tablespoon tomato paste
¼ teaspoon freshly ground pepper

RADICCHIO AND CEPES

2 tablespoons olive oil, or more if necessary
1 teaspoon kosher or sea salt
Freshly ground black pepper
2 small heads of radicchio
1½ pounds large cèpes or medium shiitakes
    or portobellos, cleaned
1 red onion, peeled

CHIPOTLE MAYONNAISE

½ cup mayonnaise
2 teaspoons minced canned chipotles
1 teaspoon Mushroom-Infused Sherry (page
    255) or regular dry sherry
1 teaspoon balsamic vinegar
6 ounces mesclun

1. Place the steaks in a shallow bowl. Mix together the marinade ingredients in a small bowl. Pour the marinade over and under the meat and refrigerate, covered, for 1 hour or more.

2. Combine the olive oil, salt, and pepper on a large tray. Peel off the outer layers of radicchio. Quarter each head, cutting through the stem end. Separate the cèpe caps from the stems and slice the stems ½ inch thick. (If using shiitakes or

portobellos, discard the stems.)
Slice the onion ¼ inch thick. Roll the
vegetables in the olive oil mixture
to coat, adding more olive oil if
necessary.

3. To prepare the mayonnaise,
mix the mayonnaise, chipotles,
sherry, and vinegar in a small bowl.
Refrigerate until about 1 hour
before serving.

Grilled Vegetables and Mushrooms

*C*ut ½-inch-thick slices of vegetables and mushroom caps; leave small mushrooms whole.
Slather a tray with olive oil, lay down a layer of
mushrooms and vegetables, and sprinkle liberally
with Seasoning Salt (page 253), freshly ground
black pepper, and any dried or fresh herbs on
hand. Let stand at room temperature, turning to
soak up the marinade, for up to 3 hours. Grill the
vegetables over a hot fire until charred and a fork
slips in and out easily.

4. Preheat a grill to hot. Preheat
the oven to the lowest setting.

5. Grill the radicchio and onion
to one side of the flame. Turn as
each side gets crisp and charred.
Grill the cèpes (caps and stems) off
to the side just until grill marks
appear, 1 minute on each side. (Portobellos will take about 5 minutes.)
Remove the vegetables from the
grill, cover with aluminum foil, and
keep warm in the oven.

6. Remove the steaks from the
marinade and grill over the hottest
part of the fire. For rare, it will take
about 3 minutes on each side.

7. Slice the steaks on the
diagonal, ½ inch thick. Fan out
4 to 5 slices on the side of each
plate. Place the mesclun on the
other side. Mound the grilled onion
in the middle and place the
radicchio and cèpes around the
edge. Pour any cooking juices that
have collected over the mesclun
and spoon the mayonnaise over
the steak.

Lamb, New Potato, and Yellow Oyster Mushroom Salad

SERVES 4

*D*elicate yellow oyster mushrooms need to be coddled and grace-
fully presented. And that's what I've done pairing them with
spring lamb, tender new potatoes, and soft lettuce to draw out their

mushroomy notes. This salad would be perfect for a languorous spring evening on the veranda, or a chatty luncheon with the girls. If yellow oysters aren't available, use white oyster, bluefoot, or honshimeji mushrooms. They may need a bit more roasting; cook until a fork inserted in the mushroom slides out easily.

SALAD

4 medium (about 1 pound) red
    new potatoes
4 clusters (about 8 ounces) yellow
    oyster mushrooms
2 teaspoons olive oil
2 loin lamb chops (about 12 ounces)
Kosher or sea salt and freshly
    ground black pepper
½ teaspoon dried rosemary
½ teaspoon dried thyme

VINAIGRETTE

1 tablespoon minced shallots
1 tablespoon Dijon mustard
1 tablespoon red wine vinegar
½ cup plus 2 tablespoons olive oil
Kosher or sea salt and freshly
    ground black pepper

TO FINISH

4 cups soft lettuce, such as mâche,
    Boston, or red leaf
2 ounces pea shoots, stems trimmed
    (optional)

1. Preheat the oven to 350°F.

2. Bring a medium-size pot of water to a boil. Drop in the potatoes and boil until a fork easily pierces the potatoes, about 25 minutes. Let cool slightly. Slice the potatoes ½ inch thick.

3. Gently brush the mushrooms with 1 teaspoon of the olive oil. Place in a shallow ovenproof baking dish and bake until wilted but not browned around the edges, about 8 minutes.

4. Increase the oven temperature to 450°F. Put the lamb chops in a small roasting pan. Drizzle both sides with the remaining 1 teaspoon olive oil. Sprinkle all over with salt, pepper, rosemary, and thyme. Roast the lamb until browned and crusty but still rosy inside, turning once, about 15 minutes.

5. To make the vinaigrette, combine the shallots, mustard, and vinegar in a small, deep bowl and beat with a fork. Add the olive oil in a slow stream, stirring all the while to incorporate. Season to taste with salt and pepper.

6. To serve, toss the lettuce with the vinaigrette. Divide it among 4 salad plates and set a cluster of mushrooms on top of each salad. Thinly slice the lamb. Alternate potato slices, lamb slices, and tufts of pea shoots (if using) around the edge of the plates.

Mushrooms with Meat

eat and mushrooms both like to be the star of the meal, but as you'll see in this chapter, they share the limelight in delicious ways. Often mushrooms such as portobellos, cèpes, and shiitakes are referred to as meaty, both for their rich, forward flavor and their chewy texture. But whether mild or assertive, mushrooms and meat play yin and yang in a delightfully harmonious way.

I am partial to stews, and it probably shows here. When I was little, and steak or chops appeared on the dinner table, I went into a funk. (Of course, being the youngest and not wanting to wield the big scary steak knife might have had something to do with it.) Not so now, but I do love how a simmering stew flavors the apartment with promise. The cowboy

stew, oxtail stew, and even the Neanderthal veal shank included here render the meat spoon-tender and deliver morsels of mushrooms.

For those who enjoy their meat on or under the sauce, instead of in it, there are pan-fried pork chops and lamb roasts, plus sirloin steak with all the richest trimmings, as well as dainty sweetbreads with sweet chanterelles and pecans. Meat sauces generally require last-minute cooking, so I offer some do-ahead steps and unat-tended cooking time wherever possible.

Where do your taste prefer-ences take you? There are some old favorites with new twists in this chapter, as well as some possibly unfamiliar meats—sweetbreads, buffalo, venison—with getting-to-know-you treatments.

Big Fat Sirloin Steak with Red Wine, Marrow, and Wine Cap Mushrooms

SERVES 2

The best way to savor the excellent beef available in this country is with its marrow. It adds a rich texture to red wine sauce, which is further enriched with meaty wine caps (if you can't get them, use morels, shiitakes, or cèpes). If beef marrow is not available, the dish will be a success without it. But if included, what a superb dinner you will have.

Because our Big Fat Sirloin Steak is a rich entrée, surround it with simpler fare. A salad of beefsteak tomato and sweet onion slices to start or one of mixed greens after works well. Alongside, potatoes fried or mashed and steamed spinach with a twist of lemon help showcase the steak. And for dessert, you can't beat the French Country Lemon Tart (page 273). Spectacular!

2 beef marrow bones, poached
(see Note) and chilled
1 tablespoon olive oil
Kosher or sea salt and freshly ground
black pepper
1 center-cut sirloin shell steak
(about 1¼ pounds) 1½ inches
thick, trimmed
¾ cup very good quality red wine
(drink the rest with the meal)
8 ounces wine cap mushrooms or
morels, cleaned and cut in half or
quarters if large
⅓ cup Demi-Glace (see box, page 282) or
2 cups Rich Meat Stock
(page 282)
¼ cup chopped fresh flat-leaf parsley
4 large shallots, sliced ¼-inch thick
(about 1¼ cups)

1. Preheat the oven to 425°F.

2. Cut the marrow into ¼-inch dice. Set aside.

3. Rub the olive oil, 1 teaspoon salt, and ½ teaspoon pepper into both sides of the steak.

4. Place the wine and mushrooms in a large skillet and bring to a boil over medium heat. Cover and cook 10 minutes. Add the Demi-Glace and boil, uncovered, until the liquid is reduced by half, about 5 minutes. Remove from the heat and stir in the parsley.

5. Heat a medium-size, heavy ovenproof skillet, preferably cast-iron, over medium-high heat, until very hot. Add the steak and shallots and cook, stirring the shallots once or twice, until the underside of the steak is seared and dark brown,

about 4 minutes. Turn the steak, stir the shallots once, and place the skillet in the oven. Cook to desired doneness: instant-read thermometer inserted into the thickest part of the steak, from the side, will read 120°F for rare after about 8 minutes. Leave the meat in the pan about 1 minute more to cook to medium-rare (130°F), and another minute more for medium (135°F).

6. Very carefully remove the skillet from the oven to the stove top. Transfer the steak to a cutting board to rest (the internal temperature will climb another 5°F as it rests). Heat the skillet over medium heat. Add the marrow and toss just until the marrow changes color. Add the mushrooms and their liquid. Boil, scraping the bottom of the pan with a wooden spoon, until the liquid is reduced enough to lightly coat the mushrooms, 2 minutes. Season with

Is It Done?

C *ooking red meat is a little different for every-*
body. Several factors can vary: thickness of the
cut, desired doneness, and oven heat. Try to follow
the cooking times, but do adjust them if your oven
or stovetop heat are a bit off the norm. You can
always pull a roast out from a not-quite-finished
sauce, wrap it in aluminum foil, and return it to the
pan/pot in the last few minutes of cooking. At our
house, steak gets sprinkled with coarse sea salt as
it comes off the fire, and sits for 2 to 5 minutes to
reabsorb its juices.

salt and pepper to taste and remove the skillet from the heat.

7. With a thin carving knife, slice the steak about ½ inch thick on an angle. Arrange the slices overlapping on 2 plates and spoon the mushroom sauce over and around the sliced steak.

Note: Blanch the bones in a large saucepan of simmering water for 2 to 3 minutes. Drain the bones and let stand just until cool enough to handle. Push the marrow through the bone with your finger. If it doesn't pop right out, use a small spoon to scoop it out. The marrow may be soft around the edges, but the center should still be quite firm.

Peppery Filets with Ramps and Wild Mushrooms

SERVES 2

The buttery texture of filet mignon takes on a whole new aspect when it is peppered with spices and paired with full-flavored wild mushrooms and ramps. Go for it when only a real steak will do. Garlicky ramps are perfect for this, but when they are not in season use scallions instead. Serve with Truffle Baked Potato (page 234).

DRY RUB AND MEAT

1 teaspoon sesame seeds

¼ teaspoon onion powder

Pinch of crushed red pepper flakes

Pinch of garlic powder

1 teaspoon black sesame or poppy seeds

1 teaspoon pink and/or freeze-dried green peppercorns, or 1½ teaspoons green peppercorns in brine

1 teaspoon kosher or sea salt

½ teaspoon coarsely ground black pepper

2 trimmed center-cut filet mignon (about 8 ounces each), about 1½ inches thick

SAUCE

12 ramps or 4 scallions, cleaned and thinly sliced, green and white parts separate

8 ounces shiitakes, wine caps, or cèpes, trimmed and thinly sliced

1 tablespoon olive oil

⅓ cup dry red wine

½ cup Rich Chicken Stock (page 281) or Rich Meat Stock (page 282)

⅓ cup fresh orange juice

2 tablespoons Demi-Glace (see box, page 282)

1. To prepare the dry rub, stir all the ingredients through the ground pepper together in a small bowl. If using peppercorns in brine, pat them dry first.

2. To prepare the meat, pat the filets dry with paper towels, rub the spice mixture evenly onto the flat sides of both filets. Let stand at room temperature 30 minutes or up to 1 hour.

3. To prepare the sauce, trim the roots and any loose outer layers from the ramps. Cut the white parts from the ramps, leaving enough attached to hold the ramp leaves together. Thinly slice the whites and set aside.

4. Preheat the oven to 450°F.

5. Heat the oil in a heavy, ovenproof skillet, preferably cast-iron, over medium-high heat. Add the filets and cook until the very well browned, about 4 minutes. Turn the filets, sprinkle the sliced ramp whites and the shiitakes around them, and place the pan in the oven. Cook to desired doneness: an instant-read thermometer inserted into the thickest part of the filet, from the side will read 120°F for rare after about 8 minutes. Leave the meat in the pan about 1 minute more to cook to medium-rare (130°F), and another minute more for medium (135°F).

6. Very carefully remove the skillet from the oven to the stovetop. Transfer the filets to a plate to rest and cover with aluminum foil (the internal temperature will climb another 5°F as they rest). Heat the skillet over medium heat. Add the red wine and stir until almost evaporated, about 4 minutes. Add the stock, orange juice, and Demi-Glace. Heat to a boil and lay the ramp or scallion greens in the pan. Boil until the sauce is reduced to about ½ cup and is thick enough to lightly coat a spoon, about 6 minutes. The ramp greens should be tender.

7. Place the filets in the center of the serving plates and surround them with the ramp greens. Check the seasoning of the sauce, then pour the sauce over the ramp greens and serve.

Fondue Sauces

*W*hile meat or poultry is grilling, I often make fondue sauces on the stove. I sauté some thin-sliced onions, over medium heat, then thin-sliced other things—tomato, fennel, red or yellow pepper, leek, mushrooms, garlic, halved string beans. Whatever's around is fodder for a fondue. As the ingredients yield their liquid, I reduce the heat to the barest simmer and let the flavors mingle. If it loses juice, I add a little chicken stock just before serving. Nothing feels as natural as these fresh ingredients, melted together, on sliced beef tenderloin or lamb chops.

Border Follies

*T*hierry and I often traveled together to visit our mushroom suppliers. Sometimes the visits held no surprises; other trips, like one we made to France, offered real insight to the business of mushrooms.

One unbelievably early and slightly chilly September dawn, there we were at a rundown château in the tiny town of Belvès in the Dordogne. My French being more culinary than conversational, I could only vaguely understand the people who ended up in the vast yard with us. Madame and Monsieur Chiron apparently lived in the château, which I longed to enter. Neatly coiffed, petite, and brightly professional, Madame detailed her favorite cèpe recipe in rapturous detail. Her husband's serious demeanor and crowsfeet told me this was a farmer, although I'd been informed they were in the mushroom business.

In typical French fashion, stone outbuildings sprawled over hills and astride pebbled courtyards, roughly connected by hand-built stone walls. Here and there were signs of life, but you really had to guess which buildings harbored carpet-lined offices, and which were home to beasts or bats. As the group chatted, we toured la propriété with its tractors, unbridled horses, and stacked hay. We came to a yard where a container truck sat with its engine running. The side was painted with a huge cèpe and the name, which was something like Cèpe-Bretagne or Agri-Cèpe. The driver, in a gabardine cap and navy turtleneck, pulled on a Gitane through tobacco-stained teeth. After we all shook hands, I began to get the picture. He had driven all night from Brittany, where the cèpe campagne was in full flush. The harvest had been exceptional, and he was here to deliver a truckful of cèpes. The only problem was that the buyer's truck was delayed. Apparently it had broken down during the night, and he was trying to finagle repairs somewhere to the east.

We hoisted ourselves up to the tailgate to check out the cèpes. We were engulfed in a mushroomer's religious moment: inhaling the cool, damp aroma of a fall forest after a soft rain. Perfectly round cèpes peeked out from under green-tinted nets, their chubby caps lined up like bundled babies in a newborn nursery. Brown caps nestled against beige ones, angled in rows across the width of the wooden crates. The final row, just in front, showed off perfect bulbous stems with final clumps of dirt clinging to the roots.

Up the road limped the delayed buyer's truck. Its sides, too, featured an enormous cèpe. But the cap was larger, the stem as full as a matron's bosom. The most revealing part of its logo, however, were the words *Funghi Porcini di Bosco*. Aha! Dawn became day in more ways than one. These cèpes, harvested in France, were soon to be renamed and sold throughout Italy as porcini from Italy!

In the next few hours we learned about the real work of a mushroom exporter. With several hundred three-kilo crates at stake, the Italians weren't about to let the French get away with anything. No simple transfers, quick signatures, or cursory glances. No, the entire shipment had to be offloaded and crates piled onto the cattle scale, and then the haggling began. Mesh nets got ripped off crates, fingers pushed into softening caps, and stems pinched for signs of bugs inside. The Italian driver was relentless, his bleary-eyed fatigue supplanted by a hawklike defense against all these Frenchmen. "Too wet" was countered by "These were firm eight hours ago." Cases were sorted through, recombined, reweighed, and restapled. The barn was a disaster area.

As the day warmed up, a sense of urgency overtook us. The warmer the mushrooms got, the fewer crates would get onto the invoice. The frenetic pace of checking, weighing, and waiting for the approval of Signor Porcini picked up. As the cows chewed in vague curiosity at these invaders, the Italian driver made seemingly haphazard choices of rejects and keepers. Monsieur Chiron firmly stood his ground. International diplomacy was taken to new levels.

With the "takes" and "leaves" scattered over the hay in two vaguely distinguished piles, the Italian pulled out his next weapon— a cellular phone. We didn't even use those in New York! Serious, rapid-fire Italian coursed through the barn, making it known to all that *produzione* and *qualita* were not up to Italian standards. The charade over, out came the dueling calculators. They compromised by using Thierry's. I guess the American element seemed safely neutral. Numbers in French and Italian, acccompanied by red-faced arguments, filled the humid barn. Finally, the flourish of a pen and stuffing of handwritten invoices into leather-bound order books. The two drivers backed *Cèpes de Bretagne* and *Funghi Porcini di Bosco* up to each other. We loaded the rejected cèpes into one, the porcini into the other. They drove off in opposite directions.

Honshimeji and Beef Stir-Fry

SERVES 2

There's nothing like a quick-cooking stir-fry to show off honshimeji's snappy texture and mild flavor. Fragrant strips of meat are coated with a ginger-scented sauce, spicy enough to coat all manner of fresh vegetables—not just the mushrooms suggested here. For mushroom variety, try substituting oysters, blewits, bluefoot, shiitakes, or wood ears for the honshimeji. If you're feeling up for something different, ostrich meat can be used instead of beef with succulent results.

8 ounces trimmed lean beef tenderloin
    or pork tenderloin, cut into
    2 × ½ × ½ -inch strips

2 tablespoons Mushroom Soy Sauce
    (page 255) or good quality soy sauce

2 teaspoons rice wine vinegar or
    white wine vinegar

2 teaspoons hoisin sauce

1/2 teaspoon Chinese chili paste
    (optional)

2 tablespoons peanut or vegetable oil

8 ounces honshimeji mushrooms,
    cleaned

2 scallions (white and green parts),
    trimmed and thinly sliced

1 tablespoon minced peeled fresh
    ginger

1 clove garlic, minced

1 teaspoon cornstarch

3 cups pea shoots, or mung bean
    sprouts, or radish sprouts

1 package (3.5 ounces) enoki
    mushrooms, trimmed
    and pulled apart into
    clusters of 3 to 5
    mushrooms

1. Pat the meat strips dry with paper towels. Stir the soy sauce, vinegar, hoisin, and chili paste together in a small bowl until the hoisin is dissolved. Set aside.

2. Heat the oil in a wok or large, nonstick skillet over high heat until the oil is rippling. Slip the meat strips into the hot oil and stir-fry until lightly browned, about 2 minutes. Add the honshimeji mushrooms, scallions, ginger, and garlic and continue stir-frying until the mushrooms are wilted and the ginger is fragrant, about 2 minutes. Add the soy sauce mixture and heat to a boil. Boil 30 seconds.

3. Stir 2 tablespoons water and the cornstarch in a small bowl until dissolved. Stir the cornstarch mixture into the wok and heat until boiling and thickened, about 15 seconds. Remove the wok from the heat.

4. Spoon the contents of the wok into the center of a small platter or 2 serving plates, leaving a little of the sauce in the wok. Add the pea shoots and enoki mushrooms to the wok, still off the heat, and toss to coat lightly. Arrange the shoots mixture in a ring around the meat and mushrooms. Serve at once.

Short Ribs with Mushrooms and Winter Greens

The flavors in this stew pot are intense, the meat meltingly tender, and the sauce—with its wine-coated mushroom nuggets— irresistibly mouth-filling. The do-ahead factor makes it a best bet for winter entertaining.

SERVES 4

20 small (about 12 ounces) white or
    pearl onions
1 bunch (about 1 pound) of swiss chard,
    ruby chard, or kale
8 pieces (2 × 2-inches each) short ribs of
    beef about 3½ pounds (see Note)
Kosher or sea salt and freshly ground
    black pepper
2 tablespoons vegetable oil
8 ounces small button mushrooms
3 medium (about 1 pound) portobellos,
    trimmed and cleaned, caps cut
    into 8 wedges each
3 cups Rich Meat Stock (page 282) or
    canned beef broth
1 cup dry red wine
1 cup canned diced tomatoes or
    chopped drained canned plum
    tomatoes

1. Heat a medium-size saucepan of water to a boil over medium-high heat. Trim the root ends from the onions, leaving the core intact. Drop the onions into the boiling water. Bring back to a boil and cook the onions 2 minutes. Drain and run under cold water until they are cool enough to handle. Slip the skins off the onions, leaving the onions whole.

2. Remove any wilted or damaged leaves from the greens. Pull the leaves from the stems. Trim the stems and cut them crosswise into 1-inch pieces. Cut the leaves crosswise into 2-inch pieces. Wash and dry the stems and leaves separately and set aside. (If making the stew in advance, store the leaves in zipper-top bags in the refrigerator box up to 2 days.)

3. Rub the short ribs generously with salt and pepper.

Heat the oil in a heavy large pot or Dutch oven over medium-high heat. Add the short ribs and cook, turning as necessary, until they are well browned on all sides, about 10 minutes. If the bits that stick to the pot start to burn, reduce the heat to medium. Remove the short ribs.

4. Add the button mushrooms, portobello wedges, onions, and stems from the greens to the pot. Pour in the stock, wine, and tomatoes. Tuck the ribs into the mixture. Heat the liquid to a boil, reduce the heat, and simmer, uncovered, until the beef is tender, about 2½ hours. About halfway through, add salt and pepper to taste, keeping in mind the liquid will be further reduced and the seasoning will be intensified. (The short ribs may be prepared to this point up to 2 days in advance. Cool completely, then refrigerate until needed. Bring the stew to a simmer and simmer 10 minutes before continuing.)

5. Remove the short ribs from the pot. Heat the liquid to a boil over medium-high heat. Stir in the leaves from the greens and boil until tender, about 8 minutes. Check the seasoning, adding salt and pepper if necessary. Divide the contents of the pot among 4 shallow serving bowls and top each with 2 short rib pieces.

Note: The whole cut known as beef short ribs usually contain 5 bones and weighs about 4½ pounds. The bones range in size; the longer bones are meatier than the short bones. If buying your short ribs from a butcher ask for the 2-inch pieces to be cut from the meatiest pieces of the longer bones. There may be an extra charge for this, but it's worth it. If buying your short ribs at a grocery store, look for solid, meaty, cube-like pieces that weigh about 8 ounces each.

Red-Cooked Oxtail Stew with Matsutakes

SERVES 4

Oxtail is an underutilized cut that yields a meat so tender, babies could chew it. It readily absorbs flavors as it stews, which makes it an ideal candidate for red cooking. This is a style of Chinese slow-cooking that tenderizes and gives a rich and pronounced flavor to tougher cuts. Red-cooked dishes are usually flavored with rice wine, star anise, and rock sugar and often feature one vegetable. Here I have substituted dark brown sugar for rock sugar and have included two vegetables—carrots and turnips—to deepen the sweet and pungent flavors of the dish. Plus I've chosen matsutakes, the subtle, pine-tinged mushroom that adds sweet flavor and full-bodied texture to any stew. If matsutakes are unavailable, make this dish with bluefoot, St-Georges, or oyster mushrooms. Serve with rice, preferably Asian short-grained rice, found in Asian or Indian markets.

2 whole (about 3½ pounds total) oxtails

5 scallions (white and green parts), trimmed

4 large matsutake mushrooms, cleaned and stemmed

3 tablespoons vegetable oil

10 cloves garlic

6 slices (¼ inch) unpeeled fresh ginger

¼ cup Chinese rice wine, mirin (Japanese rice wine for cooking), or dry sherry

2 cups Rich Meat Stock (page 282) or Rich Chicken Stock (page 281)

2 tablespoons Mushroom Soy Sauce (page 255) or good-quality soy sauce

1 tablespoon dark brown sugar

1 tablespoon rice wine vinegar or white wine vinegar

1 star anise

3 medium (about 1 pound) white turnips, peeled and cut into 1½-inch cubes

5 medium (about 10 ounces) carrots, cut on the diagonal into 1-inch lengths

1. Trim as much fat and tough membrane from the outside of the oxtails as possible.

2. Cut the scallions into white and green parts. Cut the matsutake caps in half, then slice the halves ½-inch thick. Set aside separately.

3. Heat the oil in a heavy 4- to 5-quart pot over medium heat. Add the oxtail pieces, working in batches if they do not fit in a single layer, and sauté, turning often, until they are well browned on all sides, about 12 minutes. Adjust the heat as necessary so the oxtails brown without burning the bits that stick to the pan. Remove the oxtails to a plate.

4. Whack the garlic, ginger, and scallion whites with the flat side of a cleaver or the bottom of a small, heavy saucepan. Add to the pot and stir 1 minute. Add the rice wine and heat to a boil. Stir in the stock, soy sauce, brown sugar, vinegar, and star anise and heat to a boil. Return the oxtails to the pot. Reduce the heat and simmer, covered, 1¼ hours.

5. Remove the oxtails from the pot. Strain the cooking liquid and return it and the oxtails to the pot.

6. Add the turnips, carrots, and matsutake to the pot. Heat to a boil over medium-high heat. Reduce the heat and simmer, uncovered until the meat and vegetables are tender and the sauce is thickened enough to coat the meat and vegetables, about 30 minutes.

Veal Shanks with Yellowfoots and Green Olives

SERVES 4

This big hunk of meat with its tangy accessories was inspired by Tom Valenti, whose Neanderthal veal shank made headlines back when he was chef at Alison on Dominick on the fringe of Tribeca in New York City. When Thierry and I prepare our own version of veal shanks, we make sure they are generously heaped with flavorful yellowfoot mushrooms. Prepared this way, the meat falls off the bone with the mere nudge of a fork. If yellowfoot are not available, use chanterelles, hedgehogs, or black trumpets.

4 large (about 1 pound each)
    veal shanks
Kosher or sea salt and freshly ground
    black pepper
3 tablespoons extra virgin olive oil
1 large orange, scrubbed
1 pound yellowfoot mushrooms,
    trimmed and cleaned
2 large (about 12 ounces) red onions,
    coarsely chopped
1 tablespoon coarsely chopped garlic
2 large (about 1½ pounds) ripe tomatoes,
    peeled, seeded, and coarsely
    chopped, or 1½ cups coarsely
    chopped drained canned
    plum tomatoes

1 large sprig of fresh rosemary
2 sprigs of fresh thyme
3 bay leaves
30 small (about ¼ pound) green olives,
    such as picholine or Spanish,
    pitted
½ cup chopped fresh flat-leaf parsley

1. Rub the veal shanks generously with salt and pepper. Let stand at room temperature at least 1 hour.

2. Heat the oil in a 4- to 5-quart heavy pot over medium heat. Add the veal shanks. Cook, turning as necessary, until lightly browned on all sides, about 10 minutes. The heat should be high enough to cause a lively sizzle without the meat or pan burning.

3. Using a vegetable peeler, remove the zest (the orange part of the skin, without the white underneath) from the orange in several large strips. Place the zest in a bowl and squeeze the juice from the orange over it. Set aside. Cut any mushrooms longer than 2½ inches lengthwise in half; leave smaller mushrooms in 1 piece. Set aside.

4. Remove the shanks from the pan. Add the onions and garlic and cook, stirring often, until light golden brown, about 10 minutes. Add the orange zest and juice, tomatoes, rosemary, thyme, and bay leaves. Bring to a boil. Tuck the shanks into the tomato mixture.

Reduce the heat, cover and simmer 1½ hours. Check every so often, adding a small amount of hot water if the contents of the pot begin to stick, turning the shanks 2 or 3 times, and making sure that the liquid is at a bare simmer.

5. Add the mushrooms and olives. Continue cooking the shanks, turning several times, until tender, about 30 minutes.

6. Transfer the shanks to a serving platter. Discard the orange zest, bay leaves, rosemary, and thyme sprigs. Stir in the parsley and increase the heat to high. Boil, stirring, until slightly reduced and thickened, about 5 minutes.

7. Spoon the sauce over the shanks and serve immediately.

Sautéed Sweetbreads with Chanterelles

*J*ust wait till you try these nut-crusted nuggets of sweetbread, bathed in a tingly mustard-wine sauce. The apricot undertones of the mushrooms marry perfectly with the rich-tasting pecans and the unassertive flavor of the sweetbreads.

Sweetbreads are more common on restaurant menus than on home cooks' shopping lists. To save time and effort, I've eliminated the usual soaking and weighting steps without affecting the taste and texture. You will probably need to order sweetbreads a day or two ahead from the butcher. Scalloped potatoes and green beans sautéed with garlic complete the meal.

MAKES 4 MAIN COURSE SERVINGS OR 6 FIRST COURSE SERVINGS

1¼ pounds sweetbreads, preferably fresh

1 large leek, white part only

½ cup pecan halves, toasted (see box, this
   page)

¼ cup all-purpose flour

2 teaspoons Cèpe Powder (optional,
   page 285)

2 tablespoons unsalted butter

2 tablespoons olive oil

8 ounces chanterelles, cleaned, caps
   cut into ½-inch strips

⅔ cup dry white wine or Champagne

½ cup Light Chicken Stock (page 280) or
   canned low-sodium chicken broth

2 to 3 teaspoons Dijon or grainy mustard

2 tablespoons chopped fresh flat-leaf
   parsley

To Toast Pecans

Preheat the oven to 350°F. Spread the pecans on a baking sheet and toast until golden brown, about 8 minutes. Cool completely before chopping.

1. Heat a large saucepan of water to a boil. Plunge the sweetbreads into the water and keep them submerged just until the water returns to a boil. Drain the sweetbreads immediately and rinse under cold water. Carefully peel the membrane from all surfaces of the sweetbreads. As you peel, the sweetbreads will break into smaller pieces. That is fine, however, do not let the pieces get smaller than 1 to 2 inches. If necessary, repeat the blanching and rinsing with the smaller pieces to remove stubborn pieces of membranes. Set aside.

2. Trim the root end of the leek. Cut the leek in half lengthwise then crosswise into 2-inch lengths. Cut the leek pieces lengthwise into very thin strips. You should have about 2 cups. Clean and dry them as directed on page 79. Set aside.

3. Combine half the pecans, the flour, and the cèpe powder in a food processor and process until the nuts are very finely chopped. Spread out the flour mixture on a plate. Slice the remaining pecans thin crosswise and set aside.

4. Pat the sweetbreads dry. Roll them in the nut flour until completely coated. Heat the butter and 1 tablespoon of the oil in a medium-size, heavy skillet over medium-high heat until the butter is very light brown. Add the sweetbreads and cook, turning as necessary, until well browned on all sides and the fat is absorbed, about 4 minutes. Add the remaining 1 tablespoon olive oil. Add the leek and chanterelles and cook until the leek is wilted, about 3 minutes. Add the white wine. Boil until the wine is almost completely evaporated, 3 to 4 minutes. Add the stock and mustard. Heat to a boil, scraping the bottom of the skillet. Reduce the heat and simmer until there is just enough lightly thickened sauce to coat the sweetbreads and vegetables and the sweetbreads are very tender, about 10 minutes. Stir in the sliced pecans and the parsley. Serve hot.

Pork with Black Trumpets

*I*ntensely flavored wild mushrooms like black trumpets can easily move in and take over a meat like pork. With this one-skillet dish the flavors mingle, yet stay separate. The rich sauce shouldn't be wasted—make a side dish of creamy Old-World Polenta (page 203) or mashed potatoes to soak it up.

SERVES 2

2 large loin pork chops (10 ounces each),
    about ¾ inch thick
2 teaspoons fresh thyme leaves or
    1 teaspoon dried thyme
Kosher or sea salt and freshly ground
    black pepper
White cornmeal or all-purpose flour
1½ tablespoons olive oil
4 scallions, trimmed and thinly
    sliced, white and green parts
    separate
6 ounces black trumpet or
    yellowfoot mushrooms, cleaned
    and trimmed
¼ cup Madeira
½ cup Rich Chicken Stock (page 281)
    or canned low-sodium chicken
    broth

1. Pat the pork chops dry with paper towels. Sprinkle both sides of the chops generously with thyme, salt, and pepper. Coat both sides of the chops with the cornmeal.

2. Heat the oil in a large, heavy skillet over medium heat. Place the chops in the skillet and cook, turning only once, until the chops are well browned and just a trace of pink remains near the bone, about 12 minutes. Transfer the chops to paper towels to drain.

3. Pour off all but a thin layer of oil from the pan. Add the scallion whites and mushrooms and cook until the mushrooms are wilted, about 3 minutes. Carefully pour the Madeira into the pan and boil until almost dry, 1 to 2 minutes. Add the stock and heat to boiling. Tuck the pork chops into the mushroom mixture, increase the heat to high, and boil 4 minutes, turning the chops once.

4. Transfer the chops to 2 serving plates and continue boiling until just enough liquid remains to coat the mushrooms, about 2 minutes. Remove the skillet from the heat, add salt and pepper to taste, and spoon the mushrooms around the chops. Serve hot.

Pork Chops with Cauliflower Mushrooms, Kumquats, and Ginger

SERVES 2

Pork and fruit are such a natural combination that I'm always seeking new fruits to try. Tiny, oval kumquats, found in markets during the winter, provide just the right tangy, citrusy notes to pull a pork chop out of flavor limbo. Add a touch of sweet balsamic vinegar and the perfume of cauliflower mushrooms, and you've got another pork hit. Serve it with mashed potatoes.

2 tablespoons peanut oil

4 ounces cauliflower mushrooms, trimmed, cleaned, and cut into 1-inch dice

7 kumquats, halved and seeds removed

1 scallion (white and most of green parts), trimmed and cut into ½-inch pieces

3 thin slices peeled fresh ginger

1 clove garlic, coarsely chopped

1 tablespoon Mushroom Soy Sauce (page 255)

3 tablespoons pine nuts, toasted (see box, page 125)

2 center-cut boneless pork chops (6 to 8 ounces each)

Kosher or sea salt and freshly ground black pepper

2 tablespoons balsamic vinegar

½ cup Light Chicken Stock (page 280) or canned low-sodium chicken broth

1. Preheat the oven to 350°F.

2. Heat 1 tablespoon of the oil in a medium-size sauté pan over medium-high heat to very hot. Sauté the cauliflower mushrooms, just until they give off some liquid, 1 minute. Add the kumquats, scallion, ginger, and garlic. Cook over medium heat until the liquid evaporates, about 3 minutes. Add the soy sauce and cook 30 seconds. Transfer to an ovenproof baking dish just large enough to hold the chops and mushrooms and stir in the pine nuts.

3. Heat the remaining 1 tablespoon of oil in the same sauté pan over high heat. Sprinkle the pork chops with salt and pepper. Place them in the pan and cook until both sides are browned, about 2 minutes. Set the chops on top of the kumquat mixture.

4. Pour the balsamic vinegar into the pan and scrape up the stuck bits over medium heat. Stir in the stock and boil for 30 seconds. Pour the sauce over the chops.

5. Bake until the pork is no longer pink in the center, 30 minutes. Serve immediately.

Mustard-Coated Lamb Chops Roasted over Wild Oysters

I love putting luscious pan juices to good use. Since lamb has such an assertive flavor, I decided to match it with relatively mild yet fleshy oyster mushrooms. The juices from the roasting lamb chops drench the mushrooms as they roast. Mmmm! Choose a roasting pan that holds the mushrooms in a single layer rather than piled on top of one another or with space between them.
Couscous (page 31) makes a delicious side dish.

2 double (about 8 ounces each)
    loin lamb chops
Seasoning Salt (page 253)
    or kosher or sea salt and
    freshly ground black pepper
2 tablespoons Dijon or grainy mustard
1 tablespoon finely chopped fresh
    rosemary
2 tablespoons olive oil, plus more
    for oiling the pan
2 tablespoons dry red wine
12 ounces large wild oyster mushrooms,
    cleaned, trimmed, and cut into
    1-inch strips, or cultivated
    oyster mushrooms, hard center
    removed and separated into
    individual mushrooms
¼ cup Rich Chicken Stock (page 281),
    Light Chicken Stock (page 280),
    or canned low-sodium
    chicken broth

1. Preheat the oven to 425°F.
2. Rub the lamb chops generously on all sides with salt and pepper. Stir the mustard and rosemary in a small bowl until blended.

Rub about half of the mixture onto the lamb chops. Place the remaining mixture in a large bowl and beat in the olive oil and wine. Add the mushrooms, sprinkle with ¼ teaspoon salt and ¼ teaspoon pepper, and toss to coat. (The chops may be prepared to this point up to 8 hours in advance. Cover and refrigerate the lamb chops and the mushrooms separately and bring them to room temperature before continuing.)

3. Lightly oil a 12 × 8-inch flameproof roasting pan. Arrange the mushrooms in an even layer over the bottom of the pan. Fit a roasting rack over the mushrooms and arrange the chops, without touching each other, on the rack.

4. Roast the lamb chops to medium-rare (an instant-read thermometer inserted into the thickest part of the chop will register 130°F) and the mushrooms well browned and tender, 20 minutes.

Check the mushrooms halfway through cooking. If they are cooking unevenly, remove the rack and stir well. Add 2 minutes to the cooking time if you need to stir the mushrooms.

5. Transfer the chops to 2 serving plates. Place the roasting pan over medium-high heat and pour in the stock. Cook, scraping the pan with a wooden spoon, until the liquid in the pan is reduced enough to lightly coat the mushrooms, 1 to 2 minutes. Check the seasoning, add salt and pepper if necessary, and spoon the mushrooms next to the lamb chops. Serve hot.

Boneless Leg of Lamb with Middle Eastern Stuffing

Seasoning lamb with brewed coffee is a trick we pinched from traditional Middle Eastern cooking. It is almost impossible to identify the secret ingredient, which adds deep flavor without imposing its own distinctive characteristics. The mushroom stuffing is a little crumbly, so if some of it falls from the lamb while slicing and serving it don't worry. Any little bits of mushrooms mix in fine with the pan sauce on the plate.

1 tablespoon coriander seed

1 tablespoon mustard seed

2 teaspoons cumin seed

Piece (½ inch) of cinnamon stick

2 bay leaves

3 tablespoons olive oil

Kosher or sea salt and
   freshly ground
   black pepper

1 pound cremini mushrooms,
   trimmed, cleaned, and coarsely
   chopped

8 ounces oyster mushrooms, trimmed,
   cleaned, and coarsely chopped

⅓ cup (about 1 ounce) pine nuts,
   toasted (facing page)

1 boneless leg of lamb (about
   4 pounds), rolled and tied
   (see Note)

½ cup fairly strong freshly
   brewed coffee

1 cup red wine

1½ cups Rich Meat Stock (page 282),
   Rich Chicken Stock (page 281),
   or canned low-sodium chicken broth

1. Combine the coriander, mustard, cumin, cinnamon stick, and bay leaves in a dry skillet. Place over medium heat and toast until the spices are fragrant and the seeds are lightly browned, about 4 minutes. Cool completely.

2. Grind the spices in an electric spice mill to a coarse powder consistency. Transfer half of the spice mixture to a small bowl. Stir in 1 tablespoon of the olive oil, 1½ teaspoons salt, and ½ teaspoon pepper. Stir to make a smooth paste. Set aside.

3. Heat the remaining 2 tablespoons oil in a large skillet over medium-high heat. Add the mushrooms and toss well. Cook, stirring often, until the mushrooms begin to give up their liquid, about 4 minutes. Increase the heat to high. Cook, stirring often, until the liquid is evaporated and the mushrooms begin to sizzle, about 5 minutes. Sprinkle the mushrooms with the remaining spice mix and salt and pepper to taste. Cook until lightly browned, about 3 minutes. Remove from the heat and cool completely. Stir in the pine nuts. Set aside.

4. Preheat the oven to 425°F.

5. Using your hands or a serving spoon, work the mushroom mixture into the center of the lamb roast, stuffing it evenly along its entire length. Place the roast, smooth side up, in a flameproof roasting pan. Rub the oil-spice mixture evenly over the surface of the lamb.

6. Roast the lamb until an instant-read thermometer inserted into the thickest part of the roast registers 125°F, about 1¼ hours. This will produce a roast that is medium-rare in the thickest parts and more well done toward the thinner parts and ends. Transfer the roast to a carving board and let it stand 10 minutes.

7. Pour the coffee and wine into the roasting pan and place the pan over medium heat on the stovetop. Scrape up the brown bits that stick to the pan and boil until the liquid is reduced to about ¾ cup, 5 minutes. Add the stock and continue boiling until the liquid is reduced by half, 6 minutes. Season to taste with salt and pepper. Pour the sauce into a gravy boat or pitcher.

8. Cut off the strings from the roast. Slice the lamb about ½ inch thick, transferring the slices to a platter or serving plates with a metal spatula to keep them neat and to prevent the mushroom filling from falling out. Pass the pan juices separately.

Note: A boned, rolled, and tied

To Toast Pine Nuts

Heat a dry medium-size sauté pan over medium-low heat. Add the pine nuts and toast, shaking the pan often, until golden brown, about 6 minutes. Cool and set aside.

lamb roast of this size will come from a whole (bone-in) leg of lamb that weighs about 7 pounds. If you have a cooperative butcher, you might ask him to fill the roast with the mushroom mixture before tying it. If not, you will be able to work the stuffing ino the center of a tied roast as described in step 5.

Medallions of Venison with Black Trumpets and Chanterelles

SERVES 4

Venison's assertive, gamey flavor stands up to the heady perfume of black trumpets. The soaking liquid, blended with red wine and accented with thyme, gives the sauce an extra boost. If fresh black trumpets are available, by all means use them instead of the dried. The sauce can be made entirely in advance, but the venison should be cooked just before serving—it can become tough when reheated.

1 ounce (about 1⅓ cups) dried black
    trumpet mushrooms or 4 ounces
    fresh black trumpets
2 tablespoons unsalted butter
8 ounces fresh chanterelles, cleaned
    and sliced ½ inch thick
4 shallots, minced
1 tablespoon fresh thyme leaves
1 cup Rich Meat Stock (page 282),
    if using fresh mushrooms
1 cup dry red wine
½ cup Demi-Glace (see box,
    page 282)
8 medallions (3 ounces each) venison
    (see Note)

Kosher or sea salt or Seasoning Salt
    (page 253) and cracked or
    very coarsely ground
    black peppercorns
2 tablespoons olive oil

1. Place the dried black trumpets in a small bowl and add hot water to cover. Soak until soft, about 30 minutes. Drain the mushrooms, straining the liquid through a coffee filter or a sieve lined with a double layer of cheesecloth, reserving the strained mushroom liquid. Tear the mushroom stems open and rinse the mushrooms well. (If using fresh black trumpets, clean and trim the mushrooms and split in half lengthwise.)

2. Melt the butter in a large skillet over medium-high heat just until it begins to brown. Add the chanterelles and sauté, stirring occasionally, until wilted and lightly browned, about 4 minutes. Add the black trumpets and toss to coat with butter. Add the shallots and thyme. Reduce the heat to medium-low and cook, stirring occasionally, until the shallots are tender, about 8 minutes.

3. Increase the heat to high. Add the wine and boil until almost entirely evaporated, about 4 minutes. Add the strained soaking liquid (if using fresh black trumpets, add 1 cup stock instead) and the Demi-Glace. Boil until the sauce is thickened and reduced to about ½ cup, about 4 minutes. There should be enough sauce to generously coat the mushrooms. (The sauce may be prepared to this point up to 2 days in advance. Refrigerate the sauce and heat just to simmering before continuing. Add a little water or stock, if necessary, to return the sauce to its original consistency.)

4. Pat the venison dry with paper towels. Season both sides generously with salt and pepper. Heat the oil in a heavy, large skillet over medium-high heat. Add the medallions. Cook, turning only once, until the outside is seared and crusty and the venison is cooked to medium, about 8 minutes.

5. Spoon the mushroom mixture onto 4 serving plates. Top each portion with 2 medallions. Serve at once.

Note: If you cannot buy or order medallions, it is easy to cut your own. Start with 4 saddle chops of venison, each about 12 ounces and about ¾ inch thick. With a small sharp knife, cut the meat away from the T-shaped bone to end up with two nearly round medallions, each about 3 ounces.

Cowboy Stew

Buffalo meat has a sweet beefy flavor that is more concentrated than beef because the meat is so compact. Fried-chicken or shiitake mushrooms can stand up to it. The meat is very lean, so keep your chunks large, and test along the way. Here, the potato acts as a

SERVES 4

thickener; if the meat is done before the stew has thickened, lift it out with a slotted spoon, then return it to the pot five minutes before serving. Beef also works well, so if your butcher or specialty grocer does not carry buffalo, use stewing beef. This stew goes well with Mushroom Cornmeal Muffins (page 247).

2½ pounds buffalo stew meat or beef
    stewing meat cut into 1½-inch cubes
½ cup finely diced slab bacon
3 tablespoons olive oil, or more
    as needed
1 medium red onion, cut into 1½-inch
    pieces
2 cloves garlic, diced
½ red bell pepper, stemmed, seeded, and
    cut into 1½-inch cubes
½ teaspoon cayenne
6 tablespoons all-purpose flour
Seasoning Salt (page 253) and freshly
    ground black pepper

½ cup strong freshly brewed coffee
1 medium potato, cut into 1½-inch
    cubes
2 cups Rich Meat Stock (page 282)
1 teaspoon dried thyme leaves
2 bay leaves
2 tablespoons tomato paste
8 ounces fried-chicken mushrooms,
    shiitakes, or cèpes, cut into 1½-inch
    pieces or left whole if small
1 tablespoon chopped fresh flat-leaf
    parsley

1. If the buffalo was frozen, save the liquid that accumulates as it defrosts. It can be added to the stew as a thickener near the end of cooking.

2. Cook the bacon in a large, deep, heavy-bottomed pot over high heat until crisp. Transfer to a large bowl. Add 1 tablespoon of the olive oil to the remaining fat in the pot. Sauté the onion, garlic, and bell pepper over medium heat until translucent, about 4 minutes. Sprinkle the cayenne over the vegetables and cook 30 seconds more. Remove the vegetables and add them to the bacon.

3. Season the flour with ½ tea-spoon seasoning salt and 1 tea-spoon pepper and dredge the meat with it. Heat 1 tablespoon olive oil in the same pot, over high heat. Sear the buffalo or beef in a single layer, cooking in batches if necessary, 3 minutes per batch. Add each seared batch to the vegetables. Since bison is so lean, each batch will require a tablespoon or so of olive oil. After

Buffalo Roadhouse

*O*ur friend Hisa Ota quit being a New York architect when he bought the American Dream. His buffalo ranch, Great Sand Dunes Inn and Country Club in Mosca, Colorado, is stamped with as many architectural details as buffalo hoofprints. In the restaurant's dining room, sitting next to dusty-chaps cowboys, we had our initiation into buffalo. The stew was so tender we thought it couldn't get any better. But the tenderloin out-wows any other cut of buffalo meat. It's a real treat.

the last batch, deglaze the pan with coffee, loosening up all the stuck bits of meat.

4. Place the cooked vegetables, potato, stock, thyme, and bay leaves in the pot. Stir to blend over medium heat, then stir in the tomato paste. Reduce the heat and simmer, uncovered, 1 hour, skimming once or twice. (Beef will take longer. Check the beef by cutting into a piece of meat at 1½ hours. It is done when the meat is tender and cuts apart easily.)

5. Sauté the mushrooms in 1 tablespoon olive oil in a large sauté pan over high heat, about 3 minutes. Reduce the heat to medium, cooking until mushrooms give up their liquid, about 4 minutes more. Season to taste with seasoning salt and pepper.

6. About 15 minutes before the stew is done, add the mushrooms and defrosting juices, if saved, to the pot. The stew is done when the sauce has thickened slightly. Adjust the seasoning and stir parsley into the stew. Serve.

Poultry: Mushrooms' Feathered Friends

Because I often decide what's for dinner at the last minute, and since chicken goes with so many flavors, it has become our default meal. Whole birds, legs, breasts, and shredded meat offer endless possibilities. Exotic mushrooms add juiciness, contrasting texture, woodsy or fruity flavors, and a range of sauce possibilities to this once-lowly bird. Feel Polynesian? Mexican? Russian? Make it happen with chicken! Go Thai with coconut milk infused with aromatic black trumpets. Think Provence with chicken taking on the assertive lemon, fennel, and saffron. Get Southern with irresistibly crunchy drumsticks dipped in shiitake gravy. Today pheasant, squab, and duck are more readily available than ever. We coax their assertive flavors gently to the fore with help from their seasonal companions, wild mushrooms.

Roast Chicken with Chanterelle and Apricot Stuffing

SERVES 4

What a cornucopia of delicious ingredients! Our mushroom-loving friend Joe Dizney is always dreaming up dishes involving chanterelles and corn, and this is his best one yet. The apricot flavors intensify the mushroom's fruity nuances and the butter and sausage add a savory richness.

This stuffing calls for corn bread, for which there are as many recipes as there are Southern cooks. Use your favorite recipe or try a prepared mix. The stuffing (there's about 10 cups) can be used with a goose, turkey, or other bird.

9 tablespoons unsalted butter

3 shallots, minced

3 cloves garlic, minced

1½ pounds fresh chanterelles, trimmed, cleaned, and coarsely sliced

½ cup minced dried apricots (2 ounces)

Pinch of grated nutmeg

½ cup plus 2 tablespoons apricot brandy or Light Chicken Stock or canned low-sodium chicken broth

1 teaspoon fresh lemon juice

Kosher or sea salt and freshly ground black pepper

1 cup diced onion

8 ounces pork sausage, defrosted if frozen, such as Jimmy Dean's

3 ribs celery, diced

5 to 6 cups crumbled corn bread

1½ cups pecans, coarsely chopped

1½ cups julienned dried apricots (8 ounces)

4 scallions (green parts only), sliced ¼ inch thick

½ small bunch chopped fresh flat-leaf parsley

1¼ cups Light Chicken Stock (page 280) or canned low-sodium chicken broth

1 small (4 to 5 pounds) roasting chicken

2 teaspoons olive oil, or more for basting

1. Melt 4 tablespoons of the butter in a large skillet over medium heat. Add the shallots and one-third of the garlic and sauté until just wilted, 1 minute. Add 1 pound of the chanterelles and the minced dried apricots. Stir to coat with the butter. Add the nutmeg and ¼ cup of the brandy. Cover the pan and increase the heat to medium-high. Cook until the mushrooms have re-leased their liquid, about 7 minutes.

2. Uncover the pan, turn the heat to high, and continue cooking until most of the liquid has evaporated, 2 to 3 minutes. Stir in the lemon juice, season to taste with salt and pepper, and transfer the mushroom mixture to a small bowl.

3. In the same skillet, melt 4 tablespoons butter over medium heat. Add the remaining garlic and the onion and sauté until wilted, 2 minutes. Add the sausage and fry, breaking up with a spoon, until it is no longer pink. Add the celery and continue cooking for 3 minutes more.

4. Combine the crumbled corn bread, mushrooms, and sausage in a large bowl. Stir in the pecans, the julienned dried apricots, scallions, parsley, and ¼ cup brandy. Season to taste. You should have about 10 cups stuffing. (The stuffing may be made up to 2 days in advance. Cover and refrigerate. Bring to room temperature before continuing.)

5. Stir in 1 cup stock.

6. Preheat the oven to 450°F.

7. Rub the outside of the chicken with the olive oil. Season liberally, both inside and out, with salt and pepper. Stuff the chicken, close the openings, and truss the chicken (see Note).

8. Roast the chicken for 15 minutes, then baste it with its own juices or a little olive oil. Reduce the heat to 350°F and continue roasting, for about 2 hours. Exact timing depends upon the size of the chicken and the reliability of the oven temperature. It's a good idea to allow an extra 30 minutes. The chicken is done when a fork pierced into the leg near the joint releases clear liquid.

9. Remove the chicken from the roasting pan. Pour off the fat. Pour the remaining 2 tablespoons of apricot brandy into the pan over high heat. Stir, scraping up the stuck bits of meat. Set aside.

10. Melt the remaining 1 tablespoon butter in a medium-size sauté pan over medium-high heat. Add the remaining ½ pound of chanterelles and sauté until most of the liquid has evaporated, about 4 minutes. Add the defatted pan drippings and remaining ¼ cup stock to the sauté pan. Reduce the heat and simmer until slightly thickened, 2 to 3 minutes. Season to taste, and serve in a gravy boat.

11. Remove the stuffing from the chicken. Carve the chicken and serve the sauce and stuffing on the side.

Notes: Extra stuffing can be baked in a casserole dish, covered with aluminum foil. Bake until warmed through, about 30 minutes. Check halfway through; if it appears dry, add some stock, wine, or pan drippings.

Although you can use a needle and thread to truss a chicken after it's been stuffed, I like to use a metal or wooden skewer instead. Pull together the excess skin from both sides of the opening, overlapping it, if possible. Lace a skewer through the skin, as if you were sewing. The opening should be nice and secure.

Mushroom Fried Chicken with Shiitake Pan Juices

SERVES 2 TO 4

*O*nce you've tasted this tender fried chicken with its untraditional shiitake gravy, you will undoubtedly develop a lifelong craving for it. Crunchy outside and super-moist inside, the chicken begs for the smooth sauce studded with soft shiitake slices.

Note that the chicken needs to be marinated for two days in advance of serving.

1 chicken (about 3 pounds), cut into
    8 pieces
1½ cups buttermilk
2 teaspoons kosher or sea salt
¼ teaspoon cayenne
⅔ cup fine yellow or white cornmeal
3 tablespoons Cèpe Powder
    (optional, page 285)
1½ cups vegetable oil, or as needed
8 ounces shiitakes, stemmed, cleaned,
    and sliced ¼ inch thick
1 cup Light Chicken Stock
    (page 280) or canned low-
    sodium chicken broth
¼ teaspoon Worcestershire sauce
Freshly ground black pepper
1 tablespoon chopped fresh flat-leaf
    parsley

1. Trim skin and excess fat from the chicken pieces. Stir the buttermilk, salt, and cayenne together in a bowl large enough to hold the chicken. Add the chicken pieces and turn to coat. Cover and refrigerate for 2 days, turning several times.

2. Stir the cornmeal and Cèpe Powder if using, in a shallow bowl until blended. Remove the chicken pieces from the marinade, one at a time. Let the excess marinade drip off, then roll the pieces in the cornmeal mixture until coated. Transfer the pieces to a wire cooling rack to set the coating. Let the pieces dry 5 minutes. Strain the cornmeal mixture and return it to the bowl. Roll the chicken pieces one more time in the mixture and return them to the rack for 5 minutes more.

3. Preheat the oven to 375°F.

4. Pour oil to a depth of 1 inch in a large (12-inch), heavy skillet, preferably cast-iron. Heat over medium heat until a small corner of a chicken piece gives off a lively sizzle. Place as many chicken pieces as fit without touching in the skillet. Fry the pieces, turning as necessary, until golden brown on all sides, 8 to 10 minutes. Regulate the heat during cooking so that the chicken gives off a steady but not violent stream of bubbles.

5. Transfer the fried chicken

pieces to paper towels to drain and repeat with the remaining chicken. Transfer all the chicken to a baking sheet. Bake the chicken until no trace of pink remains near the bone, about 12 minutes.

6. Carefully pour off all but 2 tablespoons of the drippings in the pan. It is okay for some browned cornmeal to remain in the drippings. Return the pan to medium heat, add the shiitakes, and stir until wilted, about 2 minutes. Add the stock and Worcestershire sauce. Heat to a boil and boil until reduced to ⅓ cup,

4 minutes. Season to taste with salt and pepper and stir in the parsley. Serve the chicken hot, passing the sauce separately.

Pan Gravy

To make a pan gravy, add 1 tablespoon all-purpose flour to the pan after cooking the mushrooms in step 6. Cook for 1 minute, then add the stock. Heat to a boil, stir in ¼ cup milk, butter-milk or heavy (or whipping) cream, and boil just until the sauce is thickened, about 3 minutes.

Thai Chicken with Black Trumpets in Coconut Milk

SERVES 4

There are times when sweet laced with hot and edged in ginger, really hits the spot. In warm countries like Thailand, coconut is used to temper the piquancy of ginger and chiles. We've added black trumpet to round out the medley of sweet and hot. The chicken tastes delicious over jasmine or long-grain rice, which sops up the sauce. If fresh black trumpets are not in season, use reconstituted dried ones.

This dish was inspired by one we enjoyed at the Franklin Station Café, which was, for all intents and purposes, Aux Delices' lunchroom. If you ever called us and ended up on hold for a while, chances are someone had to run to the café to get us. Between Mei's Malaysian stews, Marc's mushroom tart, and glasses of the tart house lemonade, the tiny, fresh-focused café boosted our spirits and refreshed our palates.

2½ cups milk

1⅓ cups (about 4 ounces) sweetened
shredded coconut

4 medium (about 1½ pounds total)
boneless, skinless chicken breasts

Kosher or sea salt and freshly ground
black pepper

All-purpose flour

3 tablespoons vegetable oil

6 slices (about ¼ inch thick) peeled
fresh ginger, finely chopped

3 cloves garlic, finely chopped

1 jalapeño, stemmed and thinly sliced,
(optional)

12 ounces black trumpet mushrooms,
cleaned

2 medium carrots, cut into
2 × ⅛ × ⅛-inch strips

1 red onion, thinly sliced

1 red bell pepper, stemmed and
cut into ¼-inch strips

6 scallions, trimmed and thinly sliced,
green and white parts separate

1 cup fresh cilantro leaves

2 tablespoons fresh lime juice

An old French saying: **Une année de guêpe est une année de cèpes.** *(When the wasps come out in full force, look for an abundant cèpe harvest.)*

1. Preheat the oven to 350°F.

2. Combine the milk and 1 cup of the coconut in a blender. Blend on low speed until the coconut is finely chopped. Heat the mixture in a small saucepan over medium heat just until bubbles form around the edges. Let stand until cooled to room temperature. Strain the mixture, pressing well on the coconut to extract as much of the milk as possible.

3. Toast the remaining ⅓ cup coconut on a baking sheet in the oven until golden brown, about 7 minutes. Stir the coconut once or twice so it browns evenly. Set aside.

4. Pat the chicken breasts dry with paper towels. Sprinkle with salt and pepper, then coat lightly with flour. Heat 2 tablespoons of the oil in a large, heavy skillet over medium heat until rippling. Add the chicken breasts and cook, turning once, until golden brown on both sides, about 3 minutes per side. They will still be pink in the center of the thickest part. Set aside on paper towels to drain.

5. Add the remaining 1 tablespoon oil to the skillet. Add the ginger, garlic, and jalapeño, if using, and stir until the garlic is fragrant, about 1 minute. Stir in the mushrooms. Cook until wilted, about 3 minutes. Stir in the carrots, onion, red pepper, and scallion whites. Cook until the pepper is wilted, about 4 minutes. Sprinkle 1 tablespoon flour over the vegetables and stir 2 minutes. Pour in the strained coconut milk and bring to a boil, stirring constantly. Tuck the chicken breasts into the vegetables. Reduce the heat, cover the skillet, and simmer until no trace of pink remains in the center of the chicken breasts, about 6 minutes.

6. Remove the chicken to 4 serving plates. Add the cilantro leaves, lime juice, scallion greens, and salt and pepper to taste to the sauce in the skillet. Bring to a boil and spoon some of the sauce and vegetables over each chicken breast. Sprinkle with the toasted coconut and serve.

Chicken with Sautéed Cèpes

*A*s unremarkable as chicken can be, this quick-cooked cutlet makes the perfect showcase for the rich indulgence of cèpes. The sautéed cèpes are a simple and delicious side dish on their own. If cèpes are not available, use this recipe as a guideline for sautéing just about any wild or cultivated mushroom.

SERVES 2

PAILLARDS
2 medium (about 6-ounces each) boneless, skinless chicken breasts
2 teaspoons extra virgin olive oil
1 teaspoon finely chopped fresh rosemary
Kosher or sea salt or Seasoning Salt (page 253) and freshly ground black pepper

SAUTEED CEPES
1 tablespoon olive oil
1 tablespoon unsalted butter
1 large shallot, minced
12 ounces fresh cèpes, cleaned and sliced ¼ inch thick
1 teaspoon chopped fresh tarragon or thyme
¼ cup Rich Chicken Stock (page 281), Light Chicken Stock (page 280), or canned low-sodium chicken broth
2 tablespoons Demi-Glace (see box, page 282) or heavy (or whipping) cream (optional)

GARNISH
Additional chopped fresh herbs (optional)

1. To prepare the paillards, place the chicken breasts, smooth side down, on the work surface. Open out the fillet (the long, thin piece that runs the length of the breast) without detaching it, to make a chicken breast of larger area and almost even thickness. Place a breast between 2 large sheets of plastic wrap. Using a meat mallet or small, heavy saucepan, pound the chicken breast to an even ½ inch thickness. Repeat with the other chicken breast.

2. Stir the olive oil and the rosemary together in a small bowl. Rub the mixture into both sides of both of the chicken breasts. Sprinkle with salt and pepper to taste. (The breasts may be prepared to this point up to 1 day in advance. Wrap tightly in plastic wrap and refrigerate. Bring them to room temperature before continuing.)

3. To prepare the cèpes, heat the olive oil and the butter in a large skillet over medium-high heat until foaming. Add the shallot and stir until it begins to brown, about 1 minute. Add the cèpes and tarragon. When the cèpes have absorbed the oil and butter, about 2 minutes, reduce the heat to medium. Sauté the cèpes, stirring often, until they have shrunk and are firm-tender and lightly browned, about 8 minutes. Pour in the stock and bring to a boil. Boil, scraping the brown bits that stick to the skillet, until the stock is almost completely evaporated. Add the Demi-Glace or cream, if using, and bring to a boil. Season to taste with salt and pepper. (The cèpes may be prepared completely in advance up to 2 days before serving. Reheat in a skillet over low heat, adding chicken stock or water as necessary to return to the original consistency.)

4. Preheat a grill to very hot (see Note). Reheat the cèpes, if necessary, remove from the heat, and cover the skillet to keep them warm. When the charcoal fire is ready, place the paillards on the grill. Cook without moving until the underside is well marked, about 1 minute. Give the paillard a quarter turn and let it cook another minute until marked in a diamond pattern. Flip the paillards and cook them just long enough to remove any trace of pink, about 1 minute or less. Transfer to 2 serving plates with the diamond pattern facing up. Spoon half of the cèpes over each and sprinkle with chopped herbs if you like. Serve immediately.

Note: The paillards may also be prepared indoors in a grill pan. Preheat the oven to 200°F. Heat the

Chicken to the Rescue

Growing up, five of us children (the sixth one neatly arrived as the first left for college) packed around the dinner table every night. We each approached this family time differently: to garner praise for an exceptional report card; to air a complaint against a sibling; to ask permission for a sleepover, the car, a year abroad. There was safety in numbers, so as we tore away at roast chicken and quickly emptied the bowls of green beans, rice, and salad, important business got taken care of.

Even though we devoured our food like farmhands, we never really thought about my mother's Herculean effort to produce three meals a day for seven people. Breakfast left the kitchen a mess for mom to tidy after driving whichever of us had missed the bus to school. Brown lunch bags were lined up like ducks in a row, full of nutritional things we'd barter for sweets or ditch in favor of cafeteria french fries. It's no wonder, with days like this, that chicken appeared so frequently on our table—it's predictable, filling, and full of good things. It's soul food.

pan over medium-high heat until very hot, about 10 minutes. Cook the paillards, one at a time, as described in step 4; they will take about the same amount of time. Transfer the first to a serving plate and keep it warm in the oven while cooking the second.

Boneless Chicken Breasts with Mousserons and Enoki

SERVES 2

This French bistro favorite gets its meat and its sauce from the same few-minute sizzle. A mushroomy punch, spiked with cognac and livened with parsley, takes chicken out of the ordinary. If mousserons are not available, use dried mousserons or fresh shiitakes, porcini, or cremini, diced fine.

2 large (about 8 ounces each) boneless chicken breasts, with skin

Kosher or sea salt or Seasoning Salt (page 253) and freshly ground black pepper

1 tablespoon olive or vegetable oil

4 scallions, trimmed and thinly sliced, green and white parts separated

8 ounces fresh mousserons, cleaned, or 1 ounce (1 cup) dried mousserons (see Note)

2 tablespoons Cognac or ¼ cup dry red or white wine

1 cup Rich Chicken Stock (page 281), or Light Chicken Stock (page 280), or canned low-sodium chicken stock

1 package (3.5 ounces) enoki mushrooms, trimmed and broken into 5- to 6-mushroom clumps

2 tablespoons chopped fresh flat-leaf parsley

1. Sprinkle both sides of the chicken breasts with salt and pepper. Heat the oil in a large, heavy skillet, preferably nonstick, over medium heat. Add the chicken breasts, skin side down, and cook until the skin is deep golden brown and crisp, about 6 minutes. Turn the chicken breasts over, reduce the heat to medium-low, and continue cooking until no trace of pink remains in the thickest part of the chicken, about 6 minutes.

2. Remove the chicken breasts. Add the scallion whites and mousserons. Cook until the mousserons are wilted, about 3 minutes. Add the Cognac and cook until evaporated. Add the stock and boil until the sauce is reduced to about ¼ cup, about 4 minutes. Add the enoki, parsley, and scallion greens and stir to mix. Return the chicken breasts to the skillet, skin side up. Reduce the heat and simmer 2 minutes.

3. Serve hot, spooning half of the mushroom mixture and sauce onto each of 2 plates and topping it with a chicken breast.

Note: To use dried mousseron mushrooms, heat the stock to a simmer and pour it over the dried mousseron mushrooms in a heat-proof bowl. Let stand until softened, about 10 minutes. Drain the mushrooms, squeezing lightly to remove as much liquid as possible. Rinse the mushrooms well under cool water and drain well. Strain the soaking liquid through a coffee filter or a sieve lined with a double layer of cheesecloth and set aside. Continue with step 1 and step 2, substituting the soaked mousserons for the fresh and the strained soaking liquid for the stock.

Mediterranean-Style Chicken

SERVES 4

Orange, fennel, and saffron infuse this cooked-in-a-packet meal with provençale flavor. The honshimeji add a toothsome texture to the vegetable mix. Have each person open his own packet and breathe in the aroma before turning it onto the plate. Serve over freshly cooked rice.

2 ounces (about 2 cups) dried wood ear mushrooms
4 boneless, skinless chicken breasts, medium (about 6 ounces each)
¼ cup sesame seeds
2 teaspoons canola oil or vegetable oil
1 to 2 large juice oranges
4 scallions, trimmed and thinly sliced, green and white parts separate
¼ cup good-quality Gewürztraminer or other white wine
2 tablespoons unsalted butter
¼ teaspoon saffron threads
1 small (about 8 ounces) fennel bulb

1 medium red bell pepper, stemmed, seeded, and cut into 2 × ¼-inch strips (about 1½ cups)
4 ounces honshimeji mushrooms, trimmed and cut in half
½ cup very thinly shredded fresh basil (optional)
4 cups cooked jasmine rice

1. Soak the wood ears in enough hot water to cover until they are softened, about 10 minutes. Drain, discarding the soaking liquid. Cut out and discard the central core from each mushroom. Cut the wood ears into 1-inch strips.

2. Pat the chicken breasts dry with paper towels and sprinkle generously with salt and pepper. Coat both sides of the chicken breasts with an even layer of sesame seeds.

3. Heat the oil in a medium-size skillet, preferably nonstick, over medium heat. Add the chicken breasts and cook, turning once, until the sesame seeds are deep golden brown, about 3 minutes per side. The chicken will be quite pink in the center. Set aside.

4. Remove 2 teaspoons of grated zest from the orange. Squeeze ½ cup juice from the orange. Combine the scallion whites, wine, butter, saffron, and orange juice in a small saucepan. Heat to a boil over medium-high heat and boil until the liquid is syrupy and reduced to ¼ cup, about 5 minutes. Remove from the heat, stir in the zest, and cool completely.

5. Place the rack in the lowest position of the oven and preheat the oven to 400°F.

6. Trim the fennel bulb by cutting off the stalks. Cut the bulb lengthwise into quarters and peel off any thick, tough outer layers. Cut the quarters into ¼-inch-wide slices. Toss the fennel slices, red pepper, honshimeji, basil (if using), wood ear mushrooms, and orange juice together in a small bowl until the vegetables are coated with liquid.

7. Cut 4 pieces of parchment paper or aluminum foil into 14 × 12-inch rectangles. Crease the rectangles crosswise. Make a small mound of the vegetables above the crease of each rectangle. Top each with a chicken breast, running parallel to the crease. Top the chicken breasts with the remaining vegetable mixture. Fold the parchment or foil over to cover the chicken and vegetables. Make several very small folds in the top and both open ends to completely seal the packets. Arrange the packets in a single layer on a baking sheet. (The packets may be made up to 1 day in advance. Cook them directly from the refrigerator, increasing the time to 20 minutes.)

8. Bake for 12 minutes. The packets should be puffed slightly, and in the case of parchment, lightly browned. The chicken should be cooked through and the vegetables crisp-tender. To serve the chicken, place a mound of rice onto 4 individual plates. Open the packets (these are steamy hot; keep your face averted) and push the chicken and vegetables out over rice.

Variation: To substitute fish for chicken, choose a thick steak such as cod or swordfish. Follow the recipe for chicken, skipping step 2 and place steaks in packets up to 1 hour before baking.

Happy Turkey Scaloppine

SERVES 4

The day Chris prepared this spring-like dish of turkey cutlets, I was not in a good mood. One bite changed my outlook. The garnish of spring peas and plain old goodness of the morels did the trick and now Happy Turkey is my family's pick-me-up dinner.

1 ounce (about 1½ cups) small dried morels
    or ¼ pound fresh morels
1½ cups Light Chicken Stock (page 280)
    or canned low-sodium chicken broth
1 pound turkey cutlets, cut into 8 pieces
Kosher or sea salt or Seasoning Salt (page
    253) and freshly ground black pepper
All-purpose flour
2 tablespoons unsalted butter
1 tablespoon olive oil
1 cup very thin matchsticks of carrot
1 cup frozen baby peas, defrosted and
        drained, or 1 cup lightly cooked
           fresh peas

2 tablespoons Mushroom-Infused Sherry
    (page 255), dry sherry, or dry white wine
2 tablespoons fresh flat-leaf parsley
2 tablespoons chopped fresh chives
1 teaspoon chopped fresh tarragon

1. If using dried morels, bring the stock to a boil in a small saucepan. Pour the stock over the mushrooms in a heatproof bowl. Let stand until the mushrooms are softened, about 20 minutes. Drain the mushrooms, straining the soaking liquid through a coffee filter or a sieve lined with a double thickness of cheesecloth. Press on the mushrooms to remove as much liquid as possible. Rinse the mushrooms to remove as much grit as possible, then drain thoroughly. Set the mushrooms and liquid aside separately.

2. Place the turkey cutlets between 2 pieces of plastic wrap. Pound lightly with a meat mallet or the bottom of a small, heavy saucepan to an even ½ inch thickness. Sprinkle both sides lightly with salt and pepper. Coat both sides lightly with flour.

3. Melt 1 tablespoon of the butter and the oil in a large, heavy skillet over medium-high heat until the butter just begins to brown, 1 to 2 minutes. Add as many of the cutlets as will fit without touching. Cook just until lightly golden brown on the underside, about 1½ minutes. Turn and cook the second side just until golden brown, no more than 1 minute. Quickly remove the cutlets from the skillet to prevent overcooking and repeat with the remaining pieces if necessary.

4. Add the morels, carrot, and peas to the pan. Increase the heat to high and cook until any liquid has evaporated, about 2 minutes. Pour in the mushroom soaking liquid or stock and sherry and add the remaining 1 tablespoon butter, the parsley, chives, and tarragon. Bring to a boil. Tuck the cutlets into the liquid. Boil until the liquid is reduced to make just enough sauce to lightly coat the turkey and vegetables, about 2 minutes. Taste and adjust the seasoning with salt and pepper if necessary. Transfer the cutlets to 4 serving plates and top each portion with some of the vegetable mix and sauce. Serve immediately.

The Confit Test

Confit de Canard was my initiation ritual into my husband's family. Basically, the test went like this: If I could manage to eat two meals of confit per day, I was in like a shot. Or so it seemed. You see, one day while visiting Thierry's food-is-love aunt in the Dordogne in France, I unknowingly entered the meal-a-thon. We sat down at noon to the hostess's truffle-engorged pâté de foie gras, heaping thick wedges of it on toasted rustic bread. Then the crudités—celery root rémoulade, shredded carrots in vinaigrette, hard-boiled eggs—came out, and I thought, oh, good, vegetables, what a nice finish to a lunch.

But something was distracting the hostess in the kitchen, and popping noises and poultry aromas wafted our way. I was already stuffed, unaware that an entrée was yet to come. It turned out to be confit de canard, a fixture in every Dordogne kitchen. Not only was it irresistibly crackling, salty, and gamey, but after one taste, its tenderness convinced me to accept the obligatory second helping.

Along with the trimmings (potato cubes browned in the same pan of duck fat, and haricots verts sautéed in chunks of butter and garlic) this made for a filling feast. It would have been a perfect meal to complete the day, except for just one thing—an evening meal, especially prepared for us at a local restaurant, was just four hours away! Luckily my soon-to-be relatives ignored my weakened appetite during the later meal—and I was in!

Most Dordogne housewives put up their own confit, and Thierry and I always have a half-dozen unlabeled cans of it in the cellar. The duck legs, which are cast-offs from the bird that produces foie gras, are salted, then slowly simmered in another by-product, duck fat. Because of the birds' slothful lifestyle, the leg meat is not tough. Thus preserved and canned, duck legs make a handy meal. We used to fry them in their unctuous fat, but now, in the interest of living longer, we simmer away the fat and just use the meat.

Duck and Shiitake Tortillas

SERVES 4

Spunky, gamey, and down-to-earth, these tortillas are not your typical drive-through fare. Confit, or preserved duck legs are a bit of a splurge, so feel free to use cooked turkey leg meat instead. Serve the tortillas with all the garnishes as part of a multicourse fiesta, or plain as the appetizer for a hearty, winter meal.

4 preserved (about 1¾ pounds) duck legs
    (see Mail-Order Sources, page 324),
    or 3 turkey drumsticks
    (about 2 pounds)
8 ounces lager beer
½ cup Basic Tomato Sauce
    (page 284) or canned tomato
    purée
1 tablespoon chopped fresh
    oregano or 1 teaspoon dried
    oregano
1½ teaspoons kosher or sea salt
1 teaspoon adobo sauce from
    canned chipotles
1 teaspoon ground cumin
1 pound shiitakes, preferably Oakwoods,
    cleaned, stems removed, caps cut into
    ¼-inch slices
8 flour tortillas (9 inches)

GARNISH
4 cups mesclun, or
    other baby greens,
    or shredded romaine lettuce (optional)
Sour cream (optional)
2 cups Portobello and Basil Salsa
    (page 259, optional)

1. Preheat the oven to 400°F. (If using turkey legs, preheat the oven to 350°F.)

2. Place the duck legs, skin side up, in a small roasting pan and roast until the meat is very tender and the skin is deep golden brown, about 30 minutes. (If using turkey legs, roast until the meat pulls away easily from the bone, about 50 minutes.) Transfer to a wire rack until cool enough to handle. Reduce the oven temperature to 300°F.

3. Pull the skin from the duck and using a small knife, scrape excess fat from the skin. Cut the skin into ¼-inch strips. (If using turkey, discard the skin.) Pour off the fat from the roasting pan, place the duck skin in the pan, and return to the oven. Roast, stirring once or

The Oakwood shiitake, with its plump, soft cap, is a chef's dream. Its lower water content yields a shiitake bursting with earthy notes. The Oakwoods give up hardly any liquid, so if you plan to sauté them, begin over high heat, then add 1 or 2 tablespoons of stock after 1 minute. The standard shiitake has a thinner cap and yields less cooked mushroom.

twice, until crisp, about 6 minutes. Remove with a slotted spoon and drain on paper towels.

4. Remove the duck meat from the bones and shred it coarsely with your fingers, discarding any excess fat. You should have about 2 cups of meat, whether using duck or turkey.

5. Heat the beer, tomato sauce, oregano, salt, adobo sauce, and cumin to a simmer in a heavy 4-quart pot over low heat. Add the shiitakes and stir until they are wilted and have absorbed the liquid, 5 minutes. Cover the pot and simmer, stirring occasionally, until the mushrooms are tender and begin to exude a little liquid, about 20 minutes. (The filling may be prepared to this point up to 1 day in advance. Refrigerate the mushrooms and duck meat and leave the duck skin cracklings at room temperature. Preheat the oven to 300°F before continuing. Heat the mushrooms to a simmer in a small saucepan over low heat.)

6. Stack the tortillas on a baking sheet, wrap the duck confit meat in aluminum foil, and place alongside the tortillas. Bake until warmed through, about 8 minutes for the tortillas and a few minutes longer for the duck. Place the tortillas in a napkin-lined basket. Place the mushrooms, duck meat and cracklings, and other garnishes, if using, in serving bowls in the center of the table and let guests assemble and roll their own tortillas.

Duck, Hedgehog, and Black Trumpet Sausage

*F*rying sausages sends a sweet-savory message into the air, and with wild mushrooms as the surprise ingredient, guests will be impatient to get to the table. These are terrific brunch sausages, but make a good side dish for any time of day. There is a lot of room for play here: You can make the sausages all chicken or all duck, or a combination of the two. Also, fatback will give you a rich and mellow flavor, slab bacon a heartier, smoky flavor. They taste great with pan-fried potatoes.

MAKES ABOUT 8 PATTIES OR 6-INCH LINKS, SERVES 4

1½ pounds boneless, skinless duck or
    chicken thighs or a combination
    of the two (see Note)
4 ounces fatback without skin or slab
    bacon
2 tablespoons Cognac or Mushroom-
    Infused Sherry (page 255)
2 teaspoons minced garlic
1 teaspoon kosher or sea salt, or more to
    taste
1 teaspoon dry mustard
¼ teaspoon freshly ground black pepper,
    or more to taste
⅛ teaspoon ground cloves
⅛ teaspoon grated or ground nutmeg
½ cup (about ½ ounce) dried black
    trumpet mushrooms
2 tablespoons olive oil
2 ounces fresh hedgehog mushrooms,
    cleaned and cut into ¼-inch dice
5 to 6 feet sausage casings (optional)

1. Look over the thighs, trimming any small pieces of bone and removing, if possible, the tendons. Don't worry about trimming the fat. Cut the meat and fatback into 2-inch cubes and place them in a mixing bowl. Sprinkle the Cognac, garlic, salt, mustard, pepper, cloves, and nutmeg over the mixture and toss to coat. Cover and refrigerate at least 6 hours or up to 2 days, stirring occasionally.

2. Place the dried black trumpet mushrooms in a heatproof bowl and pour enough hot water over to cover. Let stand until softened, about 30 minutes. Drain the mushrooms. Tear them lengthwise in half. Rinse the pieces thoroughly, dry well, and finely chop.

3. Heat the olive oil in a large skillet over medium heat. Add the black trumpet and hedgehog mushrooms. Cover the skillet and cook until the hedgehogs have released their liquid, about 4 minutes. Increase the heat to medium-high, uncover the skillet, and cook until the liquid is evaporated, about 5 minutes. Season the mushrooms with salt and pepper to taste and cool completely.

4. Grind the duck mixture through the fine disk of an electric or hand-operated meat grinder. If you don't have a meat grinder, chill the sausage ingredients thoroughly. Place them, in batches, in a food processor and pulse until the meat is coarsely chopped. Transfer the mixture to a bowl and stir in the mushrooms. Test the seasoning of the sausage by broiling or pan-frying a small amount of the sausage. Form patties or links with the mixture.

5. To make sausage patties, divide the sausage mixture into 8 equal portions. Form each into an oval or round patty, about ½ inch thick. (The patties may be prepared to this point up to 1 day in advance. Refrigerate, wrapped in plastic wrap. For longer storage, freeze, well wrapped, until ready to use. Thaw before cooking.)

Broil the patties about 4 inches from the heat or cook them in a large, heavy skillet over medium heat, until well browned on the outside and no trace of pink remains in the center, about 8 minutes.

6. To make sausage links, swish the casings in a bowl of cold water to rinse them. Fit one end of the length of casings over the mouth of a faucet. Run cold water slowly until the casing is untwisted, then increase the water pressure slightly until the casing is inflated. Check for holes: Tiny holes—the size of a pin prick—don't present a problem, but larger holes and tears will lead to trouble later. If necessary choose another length of casing.

Stuff the sausage mixture into the casings using the same grinder used to prepare the sausage mixture. Attach the sausage funnel, but not the cutting blade and disk. (Follow manufacturer's instructions for specific directions.) Be sure not to overfill the casings or they will burst during cooking. Twist the sausage at 4-inch intervals to make links. Refrigerate until needed. (The sausages may be prepared to this point up to 1 day in advance. Refrigerate wrapped in plastic wrap. For longer storage, freeze, well wrapped, until ready to use. Thaw before cooking.)

Pierce each link several times with a fork before cooking. The sausages can be broiled about 4 inches from the heat, grilled over a medium charcoal fire, or roasted in a baking pan at 400°F. Cook the sausages, turning as necessary, until brown on all sides and no trace of pink remains in the center, about 8 minutes, or slightly longer for roasted sausages.

Note: Duck thighs are available at some butchers and through Mail-Order Sources (see page 324). Ask your butcher to bone them for you. Boneless chicken thighs are available in most supermarkets. In either case, trim them as described in step 1. Sausage casings are available at some butchers.

Tame Duck Salmis

*I*n classic French cooking, a salmis is made with a wild game bird that has been partially roasted, cut into pieces, then simmered in a complicated sauce, often enriched with the puréed liver and lots of butter. This version achieves the rich feeling of the original, but with much less effort and fewer calories—puréed mushroom stems and vegetables thicken the sauce. Although we have reduced the amount of work that goes into making a salmis, this dish still requires some time and effort. But because the duck must be cooked ahead and rewarmed

SERVES 4

in the sauce—and because it is so delicious—the salmis makes a great do-ahead company dish.

DUCK

1 boneless (about 1¼ pounds) duck breast

1 tablespoon finely chopped fresh
    rosemary or tarragon

Kosher or sea salt or Seasoning Salt
    (page 253) and coarsely ground
    black pepper

SAUCE

12 ounces wine cap or
    shiitake mushrooms

1 carrot, trimmed and finely diced

1 onion, finely diced

2 cloves garlic, finely chopped

½ cup red wine

2 cups Rich Chicken Stock (page 281) or
    Rich Meat Stock (page 282)

3 bay leaves

1 tablespoon unsalted butter

2 tablespoons Cognac

1. Pat the duck breast dry with paper towels. Gently score the skin with cuts about 1 inch apart that don't touch the duck meat. Rub both sides of the duck breast generously with the rosemary and salt and pepper. Cover the duck and refrigerate at least 6 hours or up to 2 days. Bring the duck to room temperature before continuing.

2. To prepare the sauce, remove the stems from the mushrooms and trim them well. Finely dice and set aside. Slice the mushroom caps about ¼ inch thick and set aside separately.

3. Place the duck, skin side down, in a cold, heavy skillet large enough to hold it comfortably. Place the skillet over medium-low heat. Cook the duck, moving it around in the pan occasionally, until the skin is well-browned and crisp and has rendered much of its fat, about 20 minutes. Pour or spoon off the fat occasionally. Turn the duck breast and cook until the underside is browned, about 12 minutes. Remove to paper towels and cool to room temperature.

4. Pour off all but 1 tablespoon of fat from the pan. Add the carrot, onion, garlic, and reserved mushroom stems. Cook, stirring occasionally, until golden brown. Add the wine and boil until almost completely evaporated, scraping the bottom continuously. Add the stock and bay leaves. Boil until reduced by one half. From the start of the step, this should all take 10 minutes. Cool slightly, then purée the sauce thoroughly in a blender or food processor. Pass the purée through a fine sieve and return it to the skillet.

5. Melt the butter in a separate skillet over medium-high heat until lightly browned. Add the reserved mushroom caps and cook until wilted, about 3 minutes. Remove the pan from the heat, pour in the Cognac, and return the pan to the heat. Cook until all the liquid in the pan is evaporated, 1 minute. Scrape the mushrooms into the sauce and season the sauce, if necessary, with salt and pepper.

6. When the duck is cool, slice it on the bias into ½-inch slices. You should have about 14 slices. Arrange the slices slightly overlapping in the pan containing the sauce. Spoon a little sauce over the duck. (The duck can be prepared to this point up to 1 day in advance. Cover the skillet and refrigerate. Bring to room temperature before continuing.)

7. Rewarm the skillet over low heat until the sauce is bubbling around the edges and the duck is warmed through, about 8 minutes. The duck should be cooked to medium. Serve, spooning some of the sauce over each portion of duck.

Roasted Squab with Black Truffles

*U*nadorned crisp roasted, gamey squab are delicious; infused with the heady aroma of knock-your-socks-off black truffle, these little birds are sensational. This makes a wonderfully impressive holiday dish, and is sure to win over any truffle doubters. Soak up the sauce with mashed potatoes or Celery Root and Potato Purée (page 173). Black truffle trimmings or leftovers can be frozen for Truffle Butter (page 256).

SERVES 2

2 squabs (about 10 ounces each)

1 ounce black truffle, sliced very thin
    or 1 tablespoon black truffle oil
    and 2 tablespoons truffle juice

1 tablespoon olive oil

1½ teaspoons kosher or sea salt, or
    more if necessary

¼ teaspoon freshly ground black
    pepper, or more if necessary

¼ cup Port or Madeira

½ cup Demi-Glace (see box, page 282)

1. About 30 minutes before cooking, remove the squabs from the refrigerator. Trim any excess fat from the birds. With a scissors or small knife cut off the wing tips and, if necessary, the neck and feet. (Save these for broth made with the roasted carcasses or add them to the roasting pan with the squab.) Gently slip 1 or 2 fingers between the skin and the breast meat to make a little pocket. Place 2 or 3 truffle slices between the skin and meat of each breast half.

(If using truffle oil, rub it between the skin and meat.)

2. Place the rack in the center of the oven and preheat the oven to 450°F.

3. Mix the olive oil, salt, and pepper into a paste on a small plate. Rub the paste all over the inside and outside of the squabs with your hands. Place the squabs in a flameproof roasting pan just large enough to hold them side by side without touching. Let stand until they come completely to room temperature.

4. Roast the squabs until the juice runs clear, not pink, when you poke a thin knife inside the thigh where it joins the body, about 17 minutes. Transfer to a plate.

5. Tilt the roasting pan to collect any juices in one corner. Spoon off and discard the fat from the juices. Place the pan over medium heat and bring the juices to a boil. Remove from the heat, pour in the Port, and return it to the heat. Boil, scraping the bottom of the pan with a wooden spoon, until the liquid is reduced by half, about 3 minutes. Stir in the Demi-Glace and remaining truffles (if using truffle juice, add it now) and boil until reduced again by half, about 4 minutes. Pour in any juices that have collected on the plate and place the squabs on 2 serving plates. Season the sauce with salt and pepper, if necessary, and pour over the birds.
Serve hot.

Stuffed Pheasant to Serve When You Can't Get to Europe in the Fall

SERVES 2

*I*f you've never diverged from roast chicken or turkey for celebratory dinners, this sumptuous bird may well change your mind. It's stuffed with a generous helping of French ingredients: Port-soaked prunes and woodsy cèpes. If fresh cèpes are not available, substitute shiitakes.

¾ cup Port

3 pitted prunes

1½ cups Light Chicken Stock (page 280),
    or Rich Chicken Stock (page 281),
    or low-sodium canned
    chicken broth

1 ounce (about 1 cup) dried cèpes

2 sprigs of fresh rosemary

1 pheasant (about 2½ pounds), with
    giblets

2 chicken livers (about 4 ounces)

Kosher or sea salt or Seasoning Salt
    (page 253) and freshly ground
    black pepper

1 slice of prosciutto (½ ounce), cut
    into very thin strips

2 tablespoons unsalted butter, plus
    more for buttering

1 tablespoon olive oil

3 tablespoons minced shallot (1 large)

6 ounces cèpe stems or whole cèpes,
    trimmed and chopped, or 8 ounces
    shiitakes, stemmed and
    chopped

2 slices dry white bread, cut into
    ½-inch cubes

1 strip bacon, cut crosswise into
    thirds

1. Pour the Port over the prunes in a small bowl. Let soak at room temperature until completely softened, about 2 hours. Drain and reserve the Port. Coarsely chop the prunes.

2. Heat the stock to a simmer and pour it over the dried cèpes in a heatproof bowl. Let stand until softened, about 15 minutes. Drain the liquid through a coffee filter or sieve lined with a double layer of cheesecloth and set aside. Rinse the mushrooms well under cold water, drain thoroughly, and finely chop.

3. Remove and finely chop enough rosemary from the end of the sprigs to measure 2 teaspoons. Set the sprigs and the chopped rosemary aside.

4. Remove the giblets from inside the pheasant. Combine the pheasant liver with the chicken livers. If necessary, cut off any of the neck bone that extends from the bird and the feet with a heavy knife. Rinse inside the bird with cool water and pat dry with paper towels. (The pheasant may be refrigerated up to 1 day.) If you are preparing the pheasant now, sprinkle it inside and out with salt and pepper and set it aside at room temperature.

5. Pat the chicken livers and pheasant liver dry and sprinkle with salt and pepper. Heat the prosciutto, butter, and olive oil in a large skillet over medium-high heat until the butter is melted and foaming. Add the livers to the pan and sauté, turning as necessary, until the livers are seared on all sides, but still pink in the center, about 3 minutes. Remove the livers from the pan and reduce the heat to medium.

6. Add the shallot to the skillet and sauté until wilted, about 3 minutes. Stir in the cèpe stems (or shiitake caps) and the chopped rosemary. Sauté until the cèpes begin to sizzle, about 2 minutes. Pour in half of the strained mushroom soaking broth and bring to a boil. Boil until reduced by half to about ⅔ cup, about 6 minutes.

7. Pour the contents of the skillet over the bread in a large bowl. Coarsely chop the livers and add them and the chopped prunes to the bowl. Toss well until the liquid is absorbed and the ingredients are evenly mixed. (The stuffing may be made up to 4 hours in advance. Cover and refrigerate. Bring to room temperature before continuing.)

8. Bring the stuffing and the pheasant to room temperature and sprinkle the pheasant inside and out with salt and pepper.

9. Place the rack in the center of the oven and preheat the oven to 400°F.

10. For a moister stuffing, fill the cavity of the pheasant with the stuffing. For a less moist stuffing, lightly butter two 2-quart baking dishes. Divide the stuffing between the 2 dishes.

11. Place the pheasant into the smallest roasting pan in which it fits comfortably (about 12 × 10 inches). Lay the bacon pieces diagonally across the breast to cover most of the white meat. Roast until the leg wiggles easily where it is attached to the backbone, or an instant-read thermometer inserted into the thickest part of the leg registers 160°F, about 30 minutes for an unstuffed bird and 35 minutes for a stuffed bird. (If baking the stuffing in baking dishes, place them in the oven after the bird has roasted for 10 minutes.)

12. Transfer the pheasant to a large plate and cover loosely with aluminum foil to keep it warm. Pour the reserved port into the roasting pan and scrape with a wooden spoon to loosen any browned bits. Pour the liquid into a small saucepan. Add the remaining mushroom-soaking broth, the chopped dried cèpes, and the rosemary sprigs. Boil until the sauce is reduced by half.

13. Carve the pheasant by removing the legs by bending them away from the body and cutting around the joint that attaches them to the backbone. Keep them warm. Slice the breast meat parallel to the breast bone, including some of the skin with each slice. If the pheasant was stuffed, scoop out the stuffing and place it off to one side of a heated plate. If the stuffing was baked separately in baking dishes, unmold them directly onto the plate. Arrange the sliced breast meat and the legs next to the stuffing. Pour some of the sauce over the meat and pass the remaining sauce separately.

The Last Mushroom House on the Left

Kennett Square, Pennsylvania, is the self-proclaimed Mushroom Capital of the World. In this dreary town between Philadelphia and the Amish country, even overhead clouds remind you of mushrooms. The honkytonk souvenir shop and its adjunct mushroom museum may hold your attention for fifteen minutes or so. Yet this is the spot to buy mushrooms at their dewy freshest.

Our first farm visit in 1987 was an eye-opener. The undecorous aluminum-roofed bunkers were dark, warm, and nose-wrinklingly odorous. Humidity dripped from ceilings onto compact sawdust bundles. Workers with coal-miners' helmets fussed over sprouting shiitakes. Rusty bins contained the Secret Growing Ingredient, which, at the time, nobody was willing to divulge. (Now, of course, everyone knows why mushroom farms are minutes away from horse farms and racetracks.) It was exciting to witness the emergence of fruit from this mundane medium, which seemed so at odds with the elegant mushroom dishes created by New York City's talented chefs.

Exotic—the term applied to nonwhite, cultivated—mushrooms are produced in various ways. Oyster mushrooms sprout from sawdust logs dangling from ceilings like boxers' punching bags. White trumpet mushrooms begin life in glass bottles that line shelves in high-security rooms pumped full of recycled air. Outdoor farms, which produce much more slowly, comprise actual tree trunks sprouting plump shiitakes. Beds of earthy compost sit on damp wood bunks in the dark, hosting experimental crops of not-yet-perfected varieties. Over the years farmers have tried growing hen of the woods, yellow oyster, wine cap, and honshimeji, some mimicking nature, others pure fantasy. A short distance away at the University of Pennsylvania is the nation's mushroom spawn bank—repository for the definitive equivalent of seeds for each cultivated mushroom.

Despite its damp, dank growing rooms and unlovely parking lots full of 18-wheelers with cabs popped open, Kennett Square is undeniably a hotbed of mushroom cultivation. Ten years ago, its portobellos went begging, with excess crops stuffed into storage freezers and mushroom dryers. Now, of course, portobellos have become so mainstream, that entire farms have abandoned buttons for the higher profit brought by these magical disks.

You may not be able to get a good cup of coffee in Kennett Square, but you can bring home a basketful of fresh, moist, shiitake, portobello, and creminis redolent of yeasty earthiness. It's definitely "worth a detour."

Quail with a Mushroom Ragout

SERVES 4 AS A
FIRST COURSE,
2 AS A MAIN
COURSE

Quail's mild gaminess holds up to the strongest wild mushrooms you can find. A ragout of black trumpets, yellowfoot, and hedgehogs is terrific for all game and could include such other autumn mushrooms as chanterelles and wine caps.

4 quails (about 4 ounces each)

2 tablespoons olive oil

1 teaspoon kosher or sea salt

¼ teaspoon freshly ground black pepper

3 tablespoons finely chopped shallots

4 ounces hedgehog mushrooms, cleaned, stem ends trimmed, sliced ¼ inch thick

4 ounces black trumpet mushrooms, cleaned, stem ends trimmed, sliced ¼ inch thick

4 ounces yellowfoot mushrooms, cleaned, stem ends trimmed, sliced ¼ inch thick

2 tablespoons Cognac or bourbon

1 cup Quail Stock (see box, this page) or Rich Chicken Stock (page 281)

2 tablespoons chopped fresh flat-leaf parsley

12 to 16 whole fresh tarragon leaves

Quail Stock

Combine the backbones, necks, wing tips, feet, and giblets (not including the liver) from the quails in a small saucepan with enough chicken stock to cover by 2 inches. Heat to a boil, then reduce the heat and simmer, covered, 1 hour, skimming once or twice. Strain the stock and return it to the saucepan. Boil the stock until reduced to 1 cup.

1. Using kitchen scissors, cut the backbones out of the quail. Cut off the wing tips and, if necessary, the neck bones. Reserve the backbones, wing tips, and necks along with the giblets for stock or discard them. Lay the quails, skin side down, on a work surface, gently open them up, and scrape the bone sides clean with a small knife. Take a careful look at the quail. If there are any feathers, pull them out gently. Rub the quails and a 13 × 9-inch roasting pan with 1 tablespoon of the oil. Sprinkle the quails with the salt and pepper. Place them, skin side up, in the roasting pan.

2. Place the rack in the top position of the oven and preheat the oven to 450°F.

3. Heat the remaining 1 tablespoon oil in a large (12-inch) skillet over medium-high heat. Add the shallot and stir just until wilted, about 1 minute. Stir in the hedgehogs and cook until softened, about 3 minutes. Add the black trumpet and yellowfoot mushrooms in batches to the skillet, stirring each batch until wilted before adding another. Cook until the mushrooms are tender, about 4 minutes. Season

with salt and pepper. (The recipe can be prepared to this point up to 1 day in advance. Bring the quails and mushrooms to room temperature before continuing.)

4. Roast the quail for 8 minutes. Turn and roast until the skin is well browned and no trace of pink remains near the knee joint, about 4 minutes more. Remove the quails and keep warm.

5. Place the roasting pan on the stovetop over medium heat. Pour in the Cognac and stock. Heat to a boil, scraping the bottom of the pan. Boil until reduced by about half, 3 minutes. Pour the contents of the roasting pan into the skillet with the mushrooms. Add the parsley and tarragon and heat to a boil. Boil, stirring, until the mushrooms are heated through. Divide the mushrooms among 4 plates and top each with a quail, skin side up.

Seafood and Fish

Although it may not seem obvious, delicate, sweet fish paired with strong-flavored mushrooms is a match made in heaven. Whether the fish or seafood is soft and tender or pleasantly chewy, mushroom juices mingle happily with their saline counterparts. There is a mushroom that brings out the best in just about every fish or sea creature we eat. Braised monkfish and cèpes blend flavors, producing a brilliant argument for surf and turf. Other combinations, such as scallops with chanterelles, pair off with complementary textures. Musky black truffles exude their expensive perfume just enough to jolt but not overpower lobster. Even a mere hint of mushroom is enough to nudge a dish into the "gourmet" category. When creating your own recipes, remember to coordinate the cooking times of the fish and mushroom. Sometimes mushrooms need to be poached or sautéed before being combined with the fish. If so, just reheat them, uncovered, over medium-high heat at the last minute.

Thai Scallops with Blewits and Mustard Greens

SERVES 4

These scallops in a spicy broth will tingle your palate. The greens and bell pepper are nicely balanced by the sweet scallops and mild blewits. For a more assertive flavor and crunch, season and broil the scallops, then place them in the serving bowls right on top of the vibrant mustard greens. If blewits are unavailable, bluefoot or oyster mushrooms offer similar texture and taste.

Stems from 1 small bunch cilantro,
    washed
2 serrano chilies or 1 jalapeño,
    thinly sliced
1 stalk of lemon grass, cut into
    3-inch lengths
1 cup unpeeled ¼-inch-thick slices of
    fresh ginger (2-ounce piece)
1 bunch (about 1½ pounds) mustard
    greens
2 tablespoons vegetable oil
1 clove garlic, sliced
8 ounces blewit mushrooms, trimmed
    and cleaned, caps sliced ½ inch thick
1 small red bell pepper, stemmed,
    seeded, and cut into ¼-inch strips
1 pound (about 20) sea scallops
Kosher or sea salt (optional)

1. Combine 4 cups of water, the cilantro stems, and chilies in a medium-size saucepan. With the side of a heavy cleaver or the bottom of a small heavy saucepan, whack the lemon grass and ginger slices on a hard surface to bruise them. Add them to the saucepan. Bring to a boil, then reduce the heat and simmer, covered, for 45 minutes. Strain, reserving the broth and discarding the solids.

2. Trim off and discard any wilted or yellow mustard leaves. Remove the stems. Coarsely chop the mustard greens, then wash and dry them, preferably in a salad spinner.

3. Heat the oil in a heavy 4-quart pot over medium heat. Add the garlic and cook until fragrant, about 30 seconds. Add the mushrooms and cook, stirring, until they change color, about 1 minute. Pour in the reserved broth and bring to a boil. Reduce the heat and simmer, covered, until the mushrooms are tender, about 10 minutes. (The recipe may be prepared to this point up to 1 day in advance. Refrigerate until needed.)

4. If necessary, reheat the mushroom broth to a simmer. Stir in the red pepper. Add the mustard greens, a large handful at a time, waiting until the greens wilt before adding another handful. Simmer, uncovered, until the mustard greens are bright green, about 3 minutes. Stir in the scallops and continue simmering until the scallops are firm and cooked through and the mustard greens are tender, about 4 minutes. Check the seasoning, adding salt if necessary. Divide the broth, vegetables, and scallops among 4 warmed shallow bowls.

Variation: Broiled Scallops with Mustard Greens and Blewits in Thai Broth

Prepare the broth, greens, and mushrooms as in steps 1, 2, and 3. Preheat the broiler. Mix 1 teaspoon sesame seeds, ¼ teaspoon onion powder, pinch of crushed red pepper, pinch of garlic powder, 1 teaspoon black sesame or poppy seeds, and 1 teaspoon pink and/or freeze-dried green peppercorn together in a small bowl. Add 2 teaspoons sesame oil and the scallops and toss until coated. Arrange the scallops in a single layer on a broiler pan. Add all the greens to the broth as in step 4. Broil the scallops until golden brown and firm to the touch, about 3 minutes. Remove them from the broiler. Continue cooking the mustard greens until tender. Check the seasoning of the broth, adding salt if necessary. Ladle the broth and vegetables into 4 warm shallow bowls and top each serving with some of the broiled scallops.

Bay Scallops with Sorrel and Chanterelles

This is a six-minute quickie that delivers the wonderful flavor so prevalent in butter-basted French dishes. It makes a great appetizer. The flavor and dense texture of tiny western European *girolles*, chanterelles no bigger than an earplug, offer the perfect contrast to bay scallops.

SERVES 2

16 small (½ inch-long) chanterelles, or as available, cleaned
1½ tablespoons unsalted butter
4 teaspoons finely diced shallot
4 ounces bay scallops
2 tablespoons diced seeded tomato

20 leaves (2 ounces) sorrel, washed and stems trimmed off
Kosher or sea salt and freshly ground black pepper, to taste
1 tablespoon finely chopped fresh chervil

1. If using larger chanterelles, trim the stems close to the caps and quarter the mushrooms so you have uniform, ½-inch-size pieces. Slice the scallops horizontally into thirds.

2. Melt the butter in a medium-size skillet, preferably nonstick, over medium heat. Sauté the chanterelles and shallot until glossed with butter, 3 minutes. Reduce the heat if the ingredients start sticking to the pan. Add the scallops and cook for 30 seconds. Add the tomato and sorrel. Stir frequently to break down the sorrel; it will melt into a sauce. Turn off the heat as soon as it is melted, about 2 minutes. Season to taste with salt and pepper.

3. Transfer to 2 salad plates. Sprinkle with chervil and serve warm.

Clam Nage with Straw and Enoki Mushrooms

SERVES 2

The mingling of seafood and vegetables in a tangy broth opens up the senses and restores the soul. To turn this broth into an Asian-style soup/meal, serve it over jasmine rice.

4 cups Light Chicken Stock (page 280)
    or canned low-sodium
    chicken broth
1 stalk of lemon grass, white part only,
    coarsely chopped and tied in a
    cheesecloth bundle
¼ teaspoon crushed red pepper
1 large shallot, thinly sliced
2 scallions (white parts only), cut on the
    diagonal into 1-inch pieces
1¼ pounds (12 to 18) littleneck clams
1 small (about 8 ounces) head of
    bok choy

4 ounces straw, honshimeji, or shiitake
    mushrooms
1½ ounces enoki
½ ripe tomato
Kosher or sea salt
2 tablespoons fresh cilantro leaves

1. Bring the stock, lemon grass, red pepper, shallot, and scallions to a boil in a large nonreactive pot. Reduce the heat and simmer, skimming any foam from the surface, for 30 minutes.

2. Scrub the clams under cold running water. Rinse the bok choy, shake dry, and trim off the white ends. Slice crosswise into ¼-inch-wide ribbons. Leave straw mushrooms or honshimeji whole but stem, then slice shiitake caps, if using, ¼-inch thick. Trim the stem ends off the enoki and separate the clusters. Core the tomato, remove the seeds, and cut the pulp into ¼-inch strips.

3. Remove the lemon grass bundle from the broth. Bring broth back to a boil. Add the clams and straw mushrooms cover, and reduce the heat to medium. Steam the clams until they open, about 3 minutes. Stir often to give all the clams a chance to open. Any that do not open should be discarded.

4. Stir in the bok choy, and cook over medium heat, stirring, for 1 minute. Stir in the enoki, and cook for 1 minute. Add the tomato strips. Season to taste with salt, top with the cilantro leaves, and serve.

Variation: To serve over jasmine rice, spoon about 1 cup cooked jasmine rice into each of 2 bowls. Transfer the soup solids with a slotted spoon, top each serving with cilantro leaves, and spoon the broth over all.

Mushroom–Stuffed Calamari

SERVES 4

Sweet, toothsome calamari (squid) beg to be stuffed and swaddled in sauce. This moist, rice-based filling is studded with surprises. Earthy cremini mushrooms—shiitakes, portobellos, or cèpes would work equally well—are brightened with parsley and citrus. To add another dimension, serve alongside Old-World Polenta (page 203).

12 medium squid (about 3½ pounds), about
    5 inches long (not including tentacles)
½ cup long-grain rice
2 tablespoons olive oil
1 leek (white part only), cleaned
    (see box, page 79) and finely diced
8 ounces cremini, trimmed, cleaned,
    and finely diced
⅓ cup chopped fresh flat-leaf parsley

2 teaspoons fresh lemon juice
2 teaspoons grated orange zest
1 teaspoon kosher or sea salt
¼ teaspoon freshly ground black pepper
2 cups Dried Mushroom Tomato Sauce
    (page 285; see Note) or Basic Tomato
    Sauce (page 284)
6 ounces fresh spinach, stemmed and
    washed (optional)

1. To clean the squid, grasp the squid firmly, one hand on the body sac, one hand on the tentacles. Pull them apart gently but firmly, removing as much of the viscera with the tentacles as possible. Set the tentacles aside. Rub off the thin mottled skin from the bodies. Remove the long, clear quill from the bodies. Rinse inside the bodies with plenty of cold water to remove sand and ink. Set the bodies aside. Cut off the tentacles just below the eyes, leaving the tentacles in 1 piece.

2. Bring a large pot of water to a boil over medium-high heat. Add the tentacles and cook just until they turn opaque white, about 2 minutes. Drain well and cool completely. Finely chop the tentacles.

3. Bring 1½ cups of salted water to a boil in a small saucepan. Add the rice and cook for 12 minutes. The rice will still be quite firm. Drain and rinse briefly under cold water.

4. Heat the olive oil in a large, heavy skillet over medium heat. Add the leek and cook until wilted, about 2 minutes. Add the cremini and stir until tender and well browned, about 5 minutes. Add the chopped tentacles and stir until the liquid is evaporated, about 3 minutes. Remove the skillet from the heat and stir in the parsley, lemon juice, orange zest, salt, pepper, and rice until blended.

5. Spread about ½ cup of the tomato sauce over the bottom of a 13 × 9-inch baking dish.

6. To stuff the squid, using a teaspoon, fill the bodies of the squid with the rice mixture, using about 4 tablespoons for a 5-inch squid and filling the squid only loosely. The squid will shrink during cooking and will burst if overfilled.

7. Arrange the squid, side by side, on top of the tomato sauce. It will be a tight fit. Spoon the remaining sauce over the squid. Cover the pan tightly with aluminum foil. (The squid can be prepared to this point up to 1 day in advance. Refrigerate. Bring to room temperature before continuing.)

8. Preheat the oven to 350°F.

9. Bake for 30 minutes. Remove the foil, turn the squid over and continue baking, uncovered, until the squid are very tender and the sauce is thick enough to lightly coat the squid, about 20 minutes. If using the spinach, transfer the squid to serving plates, arranging the squid off to the side of the plate. Stir the spinach into the hot tomato sauce until wilted but still bright green. Arrange the spinach next to the squid and spoon some of the sauce over the spinach and squid.

Note: Dried Chilean Porcini are the perfect mushroom for preparing the Dried Mushroom Tomato Sauce for this recipe. Their smoky, earthy flavor marries well with the squid.

Shrimp Chiles Relleños

This smoky filling is yet another reason to love chili peppers. With a tasty tomato sauce and bubbling cheese crust, they make a perfect football-weather meal. If chicken of the woods are not available, use any firm mushroom—bluefoot, portobello, or shiitake. Delicious accompaniments are boiled rice and, of course, *cerveza Mexicano.*

8 ounces medium (about 25 per pound)
    shrimp, peeled and deveined
1 tablespoon vegetable oil
1 tablespoon unsalted butter
1 medium onion, diced
2 teaspoons minced garlic
8 ounces chicken of the woods or
    wine caps, cleaned and
    coarsely chopped
1 cup fresh or frozen corn kernels
8 ounces queso blanco or mild
    feta cheese, crumbled or grated
    coarsely
2 tablespoons chopped fresh cilantro
2 tablespoons fresh lime juice
8 large (5 inches) poblano chilies,
    roasted, seeded, and peeled
    (see box, this page)
2½ cups Basic Tomato Sauce
    (page 284), made with cilantro
    instead of parsley, or other light
    tomato sauce

1. Cut the shrimp crosswise into thirds. Set aside.

2. Heat the oil and the butter in a large skillet over medium heat until the butter is foaming. Add the onion and garlic and cook until the onion is wilted, about 4 minutes. Stir in the mushrooms. Cover the skillet

To Roast Peppers

To roast in the oven, place the oven rack in the upper third of the oven and preheat the oven to 425°F. Rub all sides of the peppers, including grooves very lightly with vegetable or olive oil. Place the peppers in a single layer on a large baking sheet or roasting pan with low sides. Place in the oven and roast, turning a few times with tongs, until they are well browned and even charred in places, 15 to 20 minutes. Transfer the peppers to a heatproof bowl and cover the bowl with plastic wrap. Let cool completely. Cut in half lengthwise and drain the liquid. Scrape out the seeds and membranes, turn the peppers over, and scrape off the skin. Pat the peppers dry before using.

If using the broiler, preheat it, brush the peppers lightly with oil, and place them in a small, low-sided pan. Broil, turning the peppers as the skin blackens, about 12 minutes. Cool and peel as per above.

Peppers can also be roasted over an open flame. If using an outdoor grill, heat the grill to very hot. Otherwise, turn a gas flame to medium-high. Place the oiled pepper on the grill or on the trivet, and watching all the while, cook until the pepper blisters. Cook, using a long-handled fork, to turn the pepper as it blackens, about 10 minutes. Pay close attention, keeping anything flammable—such as potholders, kitchen towels, and clothes—away from the flame. Cool and peel as per above.

and cook until the mushrooms begin to give off liquid, about 2 minutes. Uncover the skillet, increase the heat to high, and cook, stirring, until the liquid is evaporated and the mushrooms are lightly browned, about 3 minutes. Add the shrimp and toss until they turn bright pink and firm, about 30 minutes. Transfer the mixture to a bowl and cool to room temperature.

3. Stir the corn, half of the queso blanco, the cilantro, and lime juice into the mushroom mixture. Divide the filling among the chilies, filling them amply without over-stuffing. Close the chilies so the slits are barely visible. Pour half of the tomato sauce over the bottom of an 8-inch square baking dish in which the chilies fit snugly with crowding. Arrange the stuffed chilies side by side and pour the remaining sauce over. (The chilies can be prepared to this point up to 2 days in advance. Cover and refrigerate. Bring to room temperature before continuing.)

4. Preheat the oven to 350°F.

5. Sprinkle the remaining queso blanco over the chilies. Bake until the sauce in the center of the casserole is bubbling and the cheese is golden brown, about 45 minutes. Let stand 5 minutes before serving.

Chili Tip

Wear rubber gloves when handling chilies. Just one rub of the eye with chili-touched fingers can start a long, painful burn. Wash your hands thoroughly with soap and water afterwards.

Crawfish Tails with Mousserons in Leek-Infused Cream

**SERVES 4
AS A FIRST
COURSE OR
2 AS A MAIN
COURSE**

This simple dish, rich with cream and heady with fresh tarragon, makes a wonderful first course. Served over rice pilaf or buttered noodles, it serves as an elegant main course. It is also a wonderful pasta sauce, this recipe makes enough for one pound of linguine or spaghettini and will serve six. The tiny, feather-light mousserons add an earthy contrast to the crawfish; morels or shiitakes may be substituted. If you can't get crawfish, substitute one pound of small shrimp.

2 medium leeks (white and light
green parts), trimmed
3 cups Light Chicken Stock (page 280) or
canned low-sodium chicken broth
12 ounces mousserons, thoroughly cleaned
½ cup heavy (or whipping) cream
1 tablespoon Mushroom-Infused Sherry
(page 255) or Cognac
1 pound shelled cooked crawfish tails
(see Note)
8 whole crawfish (optional)
25 to 30 fresh tarragon leaves
2 teaspoons minced fresh chives
2 tablespoons finely shredded fresh
flat-leaf parsley leaves
1 teaspoon kosher or sea salt
¼ teaspoon freshly ground black pepper

1. Cut the leeks lengthwise in half, then crosswise into 2-inch lengths. Cut the pieces lengthwise into ¼-inch-thick strips. Place the strips in a large bowl of cool water and wash as described on page 79.

2. Combine the leeks and chicken stock in a large deep skillet.

Bring to a boil over medium heat, reduce the heat, and simmer until the leeks are wilted, about 4 minutes. Add the mousserons, cream, and sherry. Simmer until the mousserons and leeks are tender, 10 minutes.

3. Bring back to a boil, add the crawfish, tarragon, chives, and parsley and boil until the crawfish are heated through and the sauce is reduced enough to lightly coat the vegetables, about 3 minutes. If using raw small shrimp, they will be cooked in about 2 minutes. Season with salt and pepper.

Note: Cooked crawfish tail meat is available frozen. Defrost the crawfish slowly in the refrigerator for best results and cook it only briefly, as described above. If you are boiling live, whole crawfish, you will need about 3½ pounds of whole crawfish to yield 1 pound tail meat. Either way, the finished dish can be garnished with 2 or 3 cooked whole crawfish.

Truffled Lobster with Cilantro Butter

Talk about two of the most costly ingredients you can find! The sweet lobster and earthy truffle are extraordinary foods turned into a love sonnet. Because the recipe takes just minutes to prepare, it is a hot contender for a Valentine's Day feast. It could be served with fresh fettuccine (page 224), a green salad, and Pears Poached in Five-Flavor

SERVES 2

Syrup (page 265). If you prefer, use tarragon or parsley instead of cilantro.

Kosher or sea salt

2 small lobsters (about 1½ pounds each)

6 tablespoons (¾ stick) unsalted butter,
    at room temperature

¾ cup fresh cilantro leaves

¼ teaspoon fresh lemon juice

½ ounce fresh black winter truffle

1. Preheat the broiler.

2. Bring a large pot of water and 1 teaspoon salt to a boil. Plunge the lobsters into it, and boil for 3 minutes. Remove and slice each one lengthwise to separate the halves. The meat will not be fully cooked, but will have pulled away slightly from the shell.

3. Place the butter, cilantro, lemon juice, and a pinch of salt in a mini food processor. Pulse to blend. (The cilantro butter can also be mixed in a deep, small bowl, using the back of a spoon to blend.)

4. Thinly slice the truffle. Tuck the slices between the lobster shell and the meat, all along the length of the body. Spread the cilantro butter on top of the lobster meat. It will be messy.

5. Place the lobsters side by side in a roasting pan that fits under the broiler. Broil the lobsters until the meat turns opaque and the top is crisp, about 4 minutes. Serve hot.

Seven Seas

SERVES 8

Even though Aux Delices des Bois left Tribeca, Thierry and I still love Zutto, the sushi bar that was near our warehouse. It dates back to when Tribeca's cast-iron canopies cast their shadows on silent streets at night. Its metal loading dock held two tables, the precursor to the neighborhood's current profusion of loading-dock cafés. One evening the sushi chef, Albert Tse, made us this special dish, using a fish from each of seven seas. Kind of like a Japanese version of the ancient French dish Coquilles St-Jacques, it combines fin fish and aromatic oyster mushrooms with the scallops and sharpens the flavor with rice wine vinegar, soy sauce, and seaweed. If scallop shells aren't handy, use any ovenproof baking dish.

Chive Tip

Chives make an easy garnish—just take the scissors and snip, snip, snip right over the plate.

12 ounces mixed seafood, such as
    firm fish fillets (salmon,
    kingfish, or halibut), fish
    steaks (tuna or swordfish), sea
    scallops, and peeled and
    deveined shrimp, skin, bones,
    and shells removed
4 ounces oyster mushrooms,
    trimmed and cut into
    ¼-inch dice
2 teaspoons rice wine vinegar or other
    mild white wine vinegar
2¼ teaspoons Mushroom Soy Sauce
    (page 255) or good-quality
    soy sauce
2¼ teaspoons fresh lemon juice
4½ tablespoons mayonnaise
1 tablespoon chopped fresh chives

1. Cut the seafood into ¼-inch
dice. (If the seafood is very fresh,
this can be done up to 1 day in
advance and refrigerated.)

2. Preheat the oven to 350°F.

3. Add the mushrooms to the
seafood and toss to mix well. Combine the mayonnaise, vinegar, soy
sauce, and lemon juice in a small
bowl. Set aside about 3 tablespoons
of the mayonnaise mixture and toss
the rest with the seafood mixture,
using a slotted spoon to thoroughly
combine.

4. Divide the mixture among 8
large scallop shells or 4-inch shallow
gratin dishes. Top each with 1 teaspoonful of the reserved mayonnaise
mixture. (The seafood may be prepared to this point up to 1 day in
advance. Refrigerate, wrapped in
plastic.) Bake until a fork inserted in
the center comes out warm, about
12 minutes.

5. Sprinkle chives over the top
and serve warm.

Roasted Salmon with Wild Mushroom Pan Sauce

SERVES 8

Traditional roasted salmon gets a jolt from fresh spring ramps, a
healthy dose of mushrooms, and a range of herbal notes. Serve it
to your best friends or your boss and his wife without a worry in the
world. Keep an eye on the cooking times. Ramps are available only in the
spring, but you can substitute thinly sliced leeks sliced into 3-inch
lengths.

1 whole side (about 3½ pounds) of
  salmon, skin removed and
  trimmed (see Note)
2 tablespoons olive oil
2 tablespoons mixed chopped herbs,
  such as tarragon, rosemary, and
  chervil
1 tablespoon kosher or sea salt or
  Seasoning Salt (page 253)
½ teaspoon freshly ground
  black pepper
1 pound ramps, washed and trimmed
  (see box, page 77)
1 pound cremini, porcini, or
      other firm mushrooms, or a
      mix of more than 1 kind,
      cleaned and sliced
      ¼ inch thick
      6 cups (tightly packed)
  washed and trimmed chard,
  spinach, escarole, or a mix
  of some of the above
1 large ripe tomato, cored, seeded,
  and diced
½ cup dry white wine
1 package (3.5 ounces) enoki
  mushrooms, trimmed

1. Place the rack in the center of the oven and preheat the oven to 450°F.

2. Place the salmon in a lightly oiled flameproof roasting pan that is large enough for the fish to be flat. Rub the top side of the salmon with the remaining oil, herbs, salt, and pepper. Roast the salmon for 8 minutes.

3. Place the ramps on both sides of the salmon and turn them to coat lightly with oil. Continue roasting until the thickest part of the salmon is springy to the touch, about 8 minutes more. (The thinner tail end will be flaky and fully cooked, the thicker end will be cooked to medium.)

4. Using 2 large spatulas, transfer the salmon and ramps to a serving platter, placing the ramps on top of the salmon. Cover with aluminum foil.

5. Pour off all but 2 tablespoons of the pan drippings. Add the mushrooms to the pan. Return to the oven for 5 minutes, stirring once or twice. Remove and place on the stove top. Add the greens, tomato, and wine and cook over medium heat. Stir until the greens are wilted, about 3 minutes. Remove from the heat and stir in the enoki. Surround the salmon with the mushroom mix.

6. To serve, arrange some of the greens on each plate and top them with the salmon and ramps.

Note: Have your fish seller trim the membrane and any bones from along the belly. The pin bones (thin bones which run perpendicular from the skin through the thickest part of the fillet) can be removed with a tweezers or needlenose pliers. After skinning and trimming, the fillet should be about 1½ inches at its thickest point. If more or less than this, adjust the cooking in step 2 accordingly.

Monkfish Braised with Cabbage and Mushrooms

*B*raising encourages flavors to mingle and produces a succulent fish. This hearty recipe is so intensely mushroomy and autumnal, you could easily replace the fish with poultry or game. It's one of those "Wow!" dishes you'll want to make over and over.

SERVES 2

2 tablespoons olive oil, or more
    as necessary
12 cloves garlic
1 filleted (about 1½ pounds) monkfish tail
    (see Note)
1½ teaspoons Cèpe Powder
    (page 285)
Kosher or sea salt and freshly ground
    black pepper
All-purpose flour
2 cups diced (½ inch) Savoy or
    Napa cabbage leaves
4 ounces wild oyster mushrooms,
    cleaned, trimmed, and cut
    into 1½ × ½-inch strips
4 ounces black trumpet or yellowfoot
    mushrooms, cleaned and cut into
    1½-inch lengths
4 ounces small shiitakes, cleaned,
    stemmed, and caps cut
    in half
1 cup Light Chicken Broth
    (page 280) or canned
    low-sodium chicken broth,
    or more as necessary
½ cup fresh chervil leaves or ¼ cup
    chopped fresh flat-leaf
    parsley

1. Heat the oil in a very small saucepan or skillet over medium-low heat. Add the garlic and fry, turning the cloves as necessary, until they are pale golden brown and tender, about 10 minutes. Transfer to a small bowl with a slotted spoon and set aside. Pour the oil into a large (about 12-inch) deep skillet and set aside.

2. Sprinkle the monkfish generously with salt and pepper, then pat the cèpe powder into all sides of the fillets. Place the flour in a shallow bowl and roll the monkfish in it until well coated on all sides. Tap off excess flour and let stand for a few minutes. A cooling rack is perfect for this as it lets air circulate and prevents the flour from getting damp.

3. Heat the reserved oil used for frying the garlic cloves over medium-high heat. Add the monkfish. Turn gently—a pair of tongs or 2 metal spatulas work well— until well browned on all sides. Transfer to a plate.

4. Add the cabbage, increase the heat to high, and stir until wilted and lightly browned, about 4 minutes. Remove the cabbage, add a thin layer of oil to the pan if necessary, and stir in the mushrooms. Sprinkle with salt and pepper and cook, stirring constantly, until wilted, about 3 minutes. Add the broth and cabbage and bring to a boil. Reduce the heat to a simmer and tuck the monkfish into the mushroom mixture.

5. Cover the pan and simmer for 20 minutes, turning the fillets once. Add the garlic and chervil, cover, and continue cooking until tender, about 5 minutes.

6. To serve either season the mushroom-cabbage mixture, spoon it into shallow bowls, and top with the monkfish, or transfer the monkfish to a serving plate, increase the heat to high, boil the mushroom mixture until just enough liquid remains to coat the vegetables, then season to taste and serve with the fish fillets.

Note: Ask your fish seller to remove the 2 side fillets from the central bone of the monkfish tail and trim the outer membrane, or do it yourself at home. With a small, sharp knife cut down through the meat to the center bone. Starting at the tail end and working along the length of the bone, cut along the bone on both sides of the bone to separate the meat, leaving as little meat on the bone as possible. Free the 2 fillets from the tail. With the same small knife, carefully cut away the gray membrane from the fillets. You should have 2 equal monkfish fillets, each about 7 ounces and free of membrane.

Striped Sea Bass with Morel Cream

SERVES 4

*F*irm and tasty, sea bass needs nearly nothing to make it delicious. However, morels and a herbaceous chive oil turn sea bass into something very special. If you double the amount of chive oil, you'll have enough left to make mashed potatoes, sliced fresh tomatoes, and beef tenderloin much more than ordinary.

1 bunch chives, thinly sliced

¼ cup plus 1 tablespoon olive oil

4 (6 ounces each) striped sea bass
     or black bass fillets, with or
     without skin

1 tablespoon finely chopped fresh
     tarragon

Kosher or sea salt or Seasoning Salt
     (page 253) and freshly ground
     black pepper

2 tablespoons unsalted butter

1 large shallot, chopped

12 ounces small morels, trimmed
     and cleaned

¼ cup dry white wine

1 cup light cream or half-and-half

3 tablespoons chives, reserved from
     chive oil (see step 1)

¼ cup Light Chicken Stock (page 280)
     or canned low-sodium
     chicken broth

1. Set aside 3 tablespoons of the chives. Combine the remaining chives and the ¼ cup olive oil in a blender. Blend until the oil is bright green and the chives are puréed. Strain through a very fine sieve or a sieve lined with a double layer of cheesecloth. Set the chive oil aside (see Note).

2. Rub both sides of the bass fillets with the tarragon and salt and pepper. Arrange the fillets on a non-stick or foil-lined baking sheet. (If using the foil-lined baking sheet, brush the foil lightly with olive oil.) Drizzle the fish with the reamaining 1 tablespoon of oil. Cover and refrigerate until needed.

3. Preheat the oven to 400°F.

4. Melt the butter in a large, heavy skillet over medium heat until foaming. Add the shallot and cook until wilted, about 3 minutes. Add the morels and sauté until lightly browned, about 4 minutes. Increase the heat to high and pour in the wine. Boil until almost entirely evaporated. Pour in the cream and stock. Boil until the sauce is reduced to about ½ cup and thickened enough to lightly coat a spoon, about 8 minutes. Stir in the reserved chives. (The sauce may be prepared up to 1 day in advance. Cool completely and cover before refrigerating and heat to simmering before continuing.)

5. Bake the fillets until just a trace of opaqueness remains in the center, about 6 minutes.

6. Transfer the fillets to 4 serving plates, skin side up if you've left the skin on. Spoon the sauce and mushrooms over the fish. Drizzle the fish with the chive oil. Serve immediately.

Note: The chive oil can be stored in a tightly covered glass jar in the refrigerator for up to 3 days.

Seared Snapper in Chilean Porcini Broth

SERVES 4

The smoky, herbal notes in this sauce are terrific with the white meat of snapper. Dress it up with Celery Root and Potato Purée (recipe follows) or serve it over rice.

5 tablespoons olive oil
4 teaspoons minced shallot
2 teaspoons minced garlic
4 ounces medium shiitakes,
    cleaned
3 ounces button mushrooms,
    cleaned and thinly sliced
1 ounce (about 1 cup) dried porcini
    mushrooms, preferably Chilean
½ cup dry white wine
2 cups Light Chicken Stock
    (page 280) or 1 cup Rich
    Chicken Stock (page 281)
    and 1 cup water
10 sprigs (2 inches) of fresh thyme
1 bay leaf
1 teaspoon whole black peppercorns
6 to 8 tablespoons (¾ to 1 stick)
    unsalted butter, cut into
    ¼-inch slices
1 teaspoon chopped fresh flat-leaf
    parsley
1 teaspoon chopped fresh tarragon
1 teaspoon chopped fresh chervil
Kosher or sea salt and freshly
    ground black pepper
4 fillets (6 ounces each) of red or
    pink snapper, skinless
Additional chopped fresh herbs,
    for garnish (optional)

1. Pour 1 tablespoon of the oil into a medium-size saucepan over low heat. Add the shallot and garlic. Cover and cook, stirring occasionally, until tender, about 3 minutes. Cut the stems from the shiitakes, set them aside, and slice the caps ½ inch thick.

2. Add the shiitake stems, button mushrooms, and dried porcini to the pan. Cover and cook until the mushrooms have rendered their liquid, about 5 minutes. Uncover the pan, increase the heat to medium, and boil until the liquid is evaporated. Add the wine and boil until reduced by half, about 5 minutes.

3. Add the stock and boil until reduced by half, about 15 minutes.

4. Add the thyme, bay leaf, and peppercorns. Reduce the heat and simmer until the liquid part of the sauce is reduced to 1 cup, about 45 minutes. Strain the broth through a sieve lined with a double layer of cheesecloth into a clean medium-size saucepan. Squeeze the mushrooms in the strainer to extract as much liquid as possible. (The broth may be prepared to this point up to

2 days in advance. Refrigerate until needed.)

5. Heat 2 tablespoons of the remaining oil in a medium-size skillet over medium heat. Add the sliced shiitake caps and sauté until tender, about 5 minutes. Remove from the heat and set aside. (The mushrooms may be sautéed up to 1 day in advance. Refrigerate until needed.)

6. Heat the strained broth over medium-low heat to a gentle boil. Whisk the butter into the sauce one slice at a time, waiting for each to melt halfway before adding the next. Add the chopped herbs, salt and pepper to taste, and the shiitake caps. Cover the pan and keep the sauce warm over very low heat.

7. Pat the snapper fillets dry and sprinkle both sides with salt and pepper. Heat the remaining 2 tablespoons of oil in a large skillet, preferably nonstick, over medium-high heat. Add the fillets and cook, turning once, until lightly browned with just a trace of opaqueness remaining in the thickest part, about 4 minutes. Place the fillets in the center of 4 shallow serving bowls and pour the broth around them. Sprinkle the fillets with additional chopped herbs if desired.

Note: If using the Celery Root and Potato Purée, place a rounded large spoonful in the empty serving bowl and lean the fillet against it before pouring the broth into the bowl.

Celery Root and Potato Purée

···

$\mathcal{F}$reshly made mashed potatoes are hard to improve upon, but if you're looking for a bit of a change of pace, wait until you try this. It not only accompanies the snapper recipe above, but everything from roast pork loin to your favorite meat loaf.

1 pound celery root, trimmed, peeled, and
     cut into 2-inch chunks
1 pound russet potatoes, peeled and cut
     into 2-inch chunks
4 tablespoons (½ stick) unsalted
     butter, melted
½ cup milk, or as needed
Kosher or seat salt and freshly ground
     black pepper, to taste

1. Bring a large pot of salted water to a boil over high heat. Add the celery root and boil for 10 minutes. Add the potatoes and continue boiling until the vegetables are tender, 15 minutes more.

2. Drain the vegetables and mash them with a potato masher or pass them through a food mill fitted with the fine disk. Stir in the butter, milk, and salt and pepper.

SERVES 4

Sole Bonne Femme

The term *bonne femme* is a chauvinist allusion to the French house-wife, but the dishes bearing this description are nonetheless rich but the dishes bearing this description are nonetheless rich, creamy, and chock full of our favorite ingredient, mushrooms. French classical cooking is easier to defend if you've got lots of time to putter in the kitchen. This sole recipe toes the classical line in its lavish use of butter and cream, but we've simplified it, and given it a bolder taste. The sauce goes equally well with chicken breast.

8 ounces yellowfoot mushrooms,
    trimmed and cleaned
1 cup Light Chicken Stock (page 280)
    or canned low-sodium
    chicken broth
⅓ cup dry white wine
2 large shallots, finely chopped
¼ cup heavy (or whipping) cream
2 tablespoons chopped fresh
    flat-leaf parsley
2 teaspoons tomato paste
Kosher or sea salt and freshly ground
    black pepper
8 small fillets sole (3 to 4 ounces each),
    such as grey sole or lemon sole
3 tablespoons minced fresh chives

1. Pick the nicest 8 mushrooms and set them aside. Finely chop the remaining mushrooms. (You should have about 2 cups chopped.)

2. Combine the stock, wine, shallots, and chopped mushrooms in a small saucepan over high heat and bring to a boil. Reduce the heat to medium and continue boiling until the liquid is reduced to 1 cup (just barely enough to cover the mushrooms), about 10 minutes. Transfer half of the mushroom mixture to a blender and blend until smooth. Return the mixture to the saucepan. Add the cream, parsley, and tomato paste. Stir until the tomato paste is dissolved. Heat to a boil and boil for 1 minute. Add salt and pepper to taste. (The sauce may be prepared up to 2 days in advance. Cover and refrigerate the sauce until needed.)

3. Preheat the oven to 375°F.

4. Fold the fillets crosswise in half with the pointy, thinner half of the fillet on top. Arrange pairs of the fillets so that one slightly over-laps the other, then arrange the pairs, side by side, in a baking dish in which they fit comfortably. (An 8-inch square dish works well.) Sprinkle with salt and pepper. Spoon the sauce over the fillets, covering them completely. Arrange two of the reserved mushrooms over each pair of fillets. Cover the dish tightly with aluminum foil.

5. Bake until the sauce is bubbling and the fillets are cooked through at their thickest part, about 25 minutes. Carefully transfer each pair of fillets to one of 4 serving plates. Taste the sauce in the baking dish, adjust the seasoning if necessary and divide the sauce among the sole.

6. Sprinkle each serving with chives and serve immediately.

Seared Cod with Porcini à la Grecque

Tom Colicchio is the founding chef of New York's bustling Gramercy Tavern. An avid fly-fisherman, he and my husband Thierry escape to the Catskills to cast from floating canoes, to Yellowstone to capture late-fall fishing, and to the Bahamas to maneuver the saltwater flats. Both live strictly by the catch-and-release credo, yet when Tom gets his hands on a pristine specimen from the fishmonger, this is the kind of magic he works with it.

SERVES 4

PORCINI A LA GRECQUE

7 tablespoons extra virgin olive oil

3 tablespoons finely chopped carrot

3 tablespoons finely chopped celery

3 tablespoons finely chopped onion

3 tablespoons finely chopped cleaned leek
    (see box, page 79)

Kosher or sea salt

8 ounces porcini, trimmed and thinly
    sliced

¼ cup Mushroom Jus (page 254)

2 tablespoons white wine vinegar

2 tablespoons chopped fresh
    flat-leaf parsley

1 tablespoon chopped fresh mint

2 teaspoons chopped fresh tarragon

1 teaspoon ground coriander

Freshly ground black pepper

COD

4 fillets (6- to 8-ounces cod each),
    about 1 inch thick

Kosher or sea salt and freshly ground
    black pepper

1 tablespoon vegetable oil

2 tablespoons unsalted butter, at room
    temperature, or as needed

1 teaspoon fresh chopped thyme

1 tablespoon Cèpe Powder
    (page 285)

1. To prepare the porcini à la grecque, heat 1 tablespoon of the olive oil in a small saucepan over low heat. Add the carrot, celery, onion, and leek and season lightly with salt. Cover and cook, stirring occasionally, until the vegetables are tender, about 4 minutes. Remove and let cool.

2. Heat 3 tablespoons of the remaining olive oil in a heavy wide skillet over medium-high heat. Add the porcini and sauté, stirring, until softened and slippery, about 5 minutes. Add the stock, vinegar, parsley, mint, tarragon, coriander, and remaining 3 tablespoons olive oil. Bring to a boil, reduce the heat, and simmer, covered, until tender, about 8 minutes. Season with salt and

pepper to taste.

3. Remove the mushrooms from the heat, stir in the vegetables, and cool to room temperature. Let stand at least 2 to 3 hours before continuing. (The mushrooms may be prepared to this point up to 3 days in advance. Store, covered, in the refrigerator and bring to room temperature before continuing.)

4. Rewarm the mushrooms over low heat. Drain the mushrooms in a sieve placed over a bowl, pressing lightly to drain well. Transfer the

Marché aux Truffes

The Marché aux Truffes (Truffle Market) in Perigueux, a principal city in the truffle-producing region of Perigord, is best visited on a sunny January Saturday. Scores of bright-colored umbrellas and tents spread over the city's hilltop, cobblestoned place. At this weekly market, local vendors hawk everything from dandelion greens to fresh foie gras to homemade walnut preserves. During the winter's truffle-producing season, which goes from about November to February, the market's duck farmers share their tent with a dozen or so regional truffle vendors.

Truffle hunters man their stands dressed in sports jackets and baggy pants, with tweed casquettes, or caps, pulled low over thick eyebrows. On the oilcloth-covered tables sit

cigar boxes and plastic soup bowls full of truffles. Given the high price of truffles here, sellers must be honest and buyers must be scrupulous. Truffles are sold by weight and by the piece. Each truffle has been brushed to expose the holes and cracks that less trustworthy truffiers pack with dirt to add weight and disguise flaws. The vendors' scales are typically digital, to avoid conflicts about a truffle's weight with the region's sharp housewives. The sellers diligently record sales in grid-marked cahiers, or notebooks.

The truffle merchants talk business—not at all frankly—behind the local syndicat's, or trade union's, common table. Never ready to admit something has brought them good luck, they grouse and discourse on mushroom liquid to a blender and blend at low speed until frothy and emulsified. Season the mushroom liquid to taste with salt and pepper. Set the mushrooms and the liquid aside separately.

5. To prepare the cod, pat dry with paper towels and season both sides fillets generously with salt and pepper. Heat the vegetable oil in a large skillet, preferably nonstick over medium-high heat. Add the cod fillets and cook until the underside is a deep golden brown, about 4 minutes. Flip the fillets, reduce the heat to medium-low, and add the butter and thyme. Sprinkle the cèpe powder over the cod fillets and cook them, basting occasionally with the butter in the pan, until they are barely opaque in the thickest part, about 4 minutes.

6. Place the cod fillets, cèpe powder side up, on 4 serving plates. Arrange the mushrooms in small clusters around the fish. Drizzle the mushroom liquid over the entire plate and serve at once.

better years. By noon one sunny Saturday, they had collectively unloaded thirteen kilos of truffles (almost 30 pounds). Evidently, that was enough, for they, along with every fresh duck, live rabbit, and walnut oil vendor had cleared out by lunchtime.

For those who miss the chance to buy a truffle here, there are other vendors down the hill in a small courtyard ringed by boutiques. This unofficial—and less trustworthy—market belongs to the aproned housewives with colorful scarves, reasonable shoes, and ragged ski jackets. Under beach umbrellas, truffles sit unceremoniously in foil-lined bread baskets. Thrifty housewives pick over the smaller truffles, which they will penuriously divide among the family's home-made pâtés. Truffle scraps will be carefully scraped into eggs for a special omelet. Shopping with my mother-in-law, I learned little tricks, such as to inspect for insect holes packed with fresh dirt; how to tell if less expensive summer truffles are masquerading as their winter counterparts, and how to glean whether the truffles are from the regions considered superior, such as Le Lot and Provence, as touted. Asked if her basket of wares might not be from Spain, a bundled-up old veteran wagged all ten fingers in unison, with the characteristic non, non, non that curtails further discussion.

Truffles that don't make it into customers' hands on market day are too perishable to hold until the following week (a truffle loses its aroma quickly, and may have been unearthed a week earlier). They may be frozen, but are frequently recycled into the land. This is man's way of helping nature along (and investing in next year's profits!).

Little Meals
For Brunch or
Lunch

When a Sunday brunch or special luncheon calls, I rely on dishes like the ones in this chapter. Combined with a simple green salad, they satisfy the stomach and the soul. Hearty do-aheads like stuffed tomatoes wait to be reheated while I work up an autumn-size appetite at the football stadium or take in a matinee. After a long drive—or when leaping across time zones—a one-course meal like a pot pie or stir-fry both restores and focuses blurry-eyed travelers. The flourish required for serving egg dishes heightens the excitement of a party feast. Just make sure your guests are seated and the candles are lit before parading the mystery scrambled eggs or soufflé to the table. Of course, all these recipes can serve as parts of larger repasts; it just depends on how hungry you expect to be!

Scrambled Eggs with Black Truffles

SERVES 6 AS AN APPETIZER OR 2 AS A MAIN COURSE

Jean-Louis Dumonet, chef/owner of Trois Jean, at one time a boutique restaurant in Manhattan, blew away my conception of how truffles should be served with this dish. Regardless of how else you try truffles, serve this recipe to someone you love. The keys to its success are a five-day truffle-egg infusion, and the bain-marie (water bath) cooking process. This recipe is easily doubled. A green salad and mushroom hash (see page 185) as side dishes will transport you to a bistro in the cobblestoned alleys of Starlat in the Dordogne region of France.

6 large eggs

1 ounce black winter truffle

4 tablespoons (½ stick) salted butter,
     plus more to butter the pan

1 tablespoon canned truffle juice

¼ teaspoon kosher salt or sea salt

⅛ teaspoon freshly ground black pepper

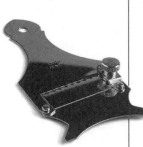

1. Four days before you plan to make this dish, place the eggs in their shells and the truffle in a glass jar. Close the jar and refrigerate it.

2. About 45 minutes before serving, bring the butter and eggs to room temperature. Slice the truffle as thin as possible. Stack the slices and slice into 1/16-inch matchsticks. Cut them in half crosswise.

3. About twenty minutes before serving, lightly butter the sides and bottom of the top pot of a double boiler. Place enough water in the bottom pot of the double boiler so that the bottom of the saucepan barely touches the water. Bring the water to a boil, then reduce the heat

and let simmer.

4. Break the eggs into a medium-size mixing bowl. Add the truffle, 3 tablespoons of the butter, the truffle juice, and the salt and pepper. Whisk to combine. Pour the eggs into the buttered saucepan and place it over the pot of simmering water. Use a wooden spatula to stir the egg mixture. Scrape around the bottom and sides of the pan almost constantly to mix the cooked part of the eggs back into the uncooked part. When done, the eggs should be still wet but nicely curded and a little shiny. You shouldn't see wet streaks of uncooked egg. This will take 10 to 15 minutes, longer if you double the recipe. Taste and adjust the seasoning if necessary.

5. Serve the eggs immediately in 2 soup plates. Top each with half the remaining butter. If serving as an appetizer, divide the eggs among 6 ramekins and top each with ½ teaspoon of the remaining butter.

A Truffle Mass

*I*was with my husband, Thierry, and his parents, and we had caught wind of a Truffle Mass—an annual event—through a truffle grower we had met. It occurs on the feast day of St. Anthony of the Desert, who was chosen by truffle hunters as a patron saint because of his special concern for pigs. The bite in the January air, with the sun coming up strong over the mountains, held promise for the day. A Truffle Mass, after all, is not your ordinary, hometown church service.

The small, ancient village of Lalbenque is home to the Fédération de la Région de Trufficulture du Midi-Pyrénées. This truffle fraternity is one of those tradition-laden specialty food clubs that permeate the world of gastronomy. The "brothers" adopt special robes (rarely do the ceremonial robes come in women's sizes), lapel pins, and dramatically staged, exclusive ceremonies to celebrate the truffle, or a regional wine like pineaud, or even the two-toed, red-capped chicken.

The truffiers, or truffle hunters, are no exception. In their voluminous black capes, three-cornered hats and yellow sashes, they preen like Oxford professors at commencement exercises. Meeting on the steps of the village church, the truffiers compare lapel pins and greet neighbors. The townspeople turn out to help celebrate the harvest, although anyone can attend the Mass and feast that follows at a local bistro.

The mass takes place in a medieval church. Prayers of thanksgiving for the truffle harvest are woven into the usual service, as are requests for continued bounty. Celebrated with intermittent electrical outtages, the mass serves as a church fundraiser. Instead of money, the truffiers place foil-wrapped truffles in the leaf-lined collection basket. The black diamonds will be sold at auction to keep the electricity on.

After mass, we all walked over to the Hôtel du Lion d'Or, a linoleum-decked and garishly lit bistro. It's obvious that deals are done here, among walls filled with photos of handshakes and truffle dogs, truffle trophies, and framed, handwritten odes to the black diamond. Live fanfare erupted at the appearance of the mayor and other luminaries of Lalbenque's truffle trade. Loosened by water glasses of the local wine, the truffiers slipped out of their respectable robes. Bustling waitresses dodged the din of story-telling and wagers to deliver enormous plats du jour, omelettes au diamant noir (eggs with black truffles). For some this was just a festive Sunday lunch. But for us, the creamy unctuousness of eggs tumbled with a torrent of truffles was heaven. More black than yellow, the omelet's curds softened the crunch of truffle slivers. The flavors lingered on throughout the day, as we retraced the winding route back to reality.

SERVES 6 AS A
FIRST COURSE
OR 2 AS A
MAIN COURSE.

Double Mushroom Soufflé

The soufflé of your dreams could involve crab or corn or goat cheese, but mine, way up there in that lofty space called heaven, is flavored with wild, woodsy mushrooms. In fact, this is it. Use a pound of any variety of mushrooms you like; they all make a terrific-tasting soufflé.

A soufflé is not the culinary time bomb it has been made out to be. Handled properly, a soufflé has little chance of deflating before you serve it. Just resist opening the oven door to check on its progress until about five minutes before the end of the suggested cooking time. If you have an oven light use it to see how things are going in there. When you do open the oven to check it, leave the oven door open for as short a time as possible and close it very gently. Once baked, the soufflé can stay put in the turned-off oven with the door wide open for three to four minutes. After that it will deflate.

5 tablespoons unsalted butter

8 ounces hen of the woods mushrooms, cleaned, trimmed, and finely chopped

8 ounces chanterelles or chicken of the woods mushrooms, cleaned, trimmed, and finely chopped

3 tablespoons all-purpose flour

1 tablespoon Cèpe Powder (optional; page 285)

2 cups milk, hot

4 large egg yolks, at room temperature

5 large egg whites, at room temperature

¾ cup finely grated Parmesan cheese

¼ teaspoon freshly grated nutmeg or 2 teaspoons finely chopped fresh tarragon

1. Melt 4 tablespoons of the butter in a medium-size saucepan over medium-low heat. Add the mushrooms and cook, stirring, until they begin to give off liquid, about 4 minutes. Increase the heat to high and cook, stirring, until all the liquid is evaporated, about 4 minutes.

2. Reduce the heat to medium and stir in the flour and cèpe powder. Cook, stirring constantly with a wooden spoon, for 2 minutes. Add the hot milk slowly, stirring constantly. The mixture will be very thick when you start adding the liquid and will thin out as you go. Keep stirring, scraping the bottom and corners of the pan to prevent lumps. Heat the sauce to a simmer and simmer, stirring, for 2 minutes. Transfer the mixture to a large bowl.

3. Beat in the egg yolks one at a time, then stir in ¼ cup of the cheese. Cool the mixture to tepid. Stir in the nutmeg.

4. Preheat the oven to 400°F. Generously butter a 6-cup soufflé dish with the remaining 1 tablespoon butter. Sprinkle the inside evenly with ¼ cup of the cheese and set aside.

5. Beat the egg whites in a clean large bowl until firm but not brittle. With a whisk or one of the beaters, gently fold about one fourth of the whites into the mushroom mixture. Using a wide rubber spatula, fold in the remaining whites. Work from the bottom of the bowl, scraping the bottom and sides, and bringing the mixture up over the whites. Don't overmix—it's better to have a few streaks of egg whites in the batter than a deflated batter that won't rise properly. Transfer the batter to the prepared dish. Sprinkle the top with the remaining cheese.

6. Bake the soufflé until it has risen about 3 inches over the rim of the dish, is deep golden brown, and wiggles only very slightly when you tap the dish gently, about 30 minutes. Gently remove the soufflé from the oven and serve it immediately with a large spoon, including some of the outer crust and softer interior with each serving.

Note: The recipe can be prepared as individual soufflés. Butter six 1-cup soufflé dishes and sprinkle them with cheese. Divide the soufflé mixture among the prepared dishes. Place the dishes on a baking sheet. Sprinkle with cheese, then place them in the oven. Bake for about 20 minutes. Serve at once.

Copper Bowl Chemistry

My dad, a research chemist, was so intrigued by my purchase of an enormous copper bowl for beating egg whites that he did what he does best: he researched it. It turns out that the albumen in egg whites forms a bond with copper, especially when aided by a tiny hit of acid such as lemon juice or vinegar. Before using the bowl for egg whites, toss some sea salt or kosher salt into it, then add a tablespoon or two of vinegar or lemon juice. With an abrasive sponge, scrub, scrub, scrub. Then rinse the bowl in very hot water and turn upside down to dry (no towel). It's ready. Repeat each time you use the bowl for beating egg whites.

Blewit and Crab Rolls

Anyone who's eaten seven lobster rolls in as many days along Maine's meandering coast will appreciate the passion with which we approached this sandwich style. Crossed with classic club ingredients, an intriguing mushroom, and the perfect bread, this sandwich is made for lunch on the lawn. Poaching the blewits renders their juices, which

SERVES 4

mingle with the crab and bread. We make the sandwich a day ahead to give flavors time to mellow. The blewits can be served separately as part of an antipasto platter.

CRAB SALAD

8 ounces lump, backfin, or other
    crabmeat
2 ribs celery, finely diced
⅓ cup mayonnaise, prepared or homemade
1 ripe plum tomato, cored and finely diced
1 tablespoon Dijon mustard
1 tablespoon fresh lemon juice
2 teaspoons finely chopped fresh tarragon

POACHED BLEWITS

1 large sprig of tarragon
1 large sprig of rosemary
3 slices of lemon
3 bay leaves
8 ounces large blewit or bluefoot mushrooms,
    cleaned and trimmed

TO ASSEMBLE:

1 center-cut (8 × 4 × 2½ inches) piece of
    firm-textured bread (see Note)
8 strips of bacon, cooked crisp and
    drained
4 large red lettuce leaves, rinsed and
    well dried

1. To make the crab salad, pick over the crabmeat to remove any shell or cartilage. Stir together the celery, mayonnaise, tomato, mustard, lemon juice, and chopped tarragon in a bowl until blended. Stir in the crabmeat. Cover and refrigerate.

2. To poach the mushrooms, combine 3 cups of water, the sprigs of tarragon and rosemary, the bay leaves, and lemon slices in a medium-size saucepan and bring to a simmer. Add the mushrooms. Cover and simmer until the mushrooms are tender and a pale violet color, about 12 minutes. Cool completely in the broth. (The sandwich may be prepared to this point up to 1 day in advance. Cover and refrigerate the crab salad and the mushrooms in their liquid separately.)

3. To assemble the sandwich, remove the blewits from the broth and drain thoroughly. Using a sharp bread knife, cut the bread into 3 even horizontal layers. Work carefully, holding the knife blade parallel to the cutting surface the whole time. Spread the crab salad evenly over the bottom slice of bread. Top with the middle slice. Arrange the blewits over the bread and top with the remaining slice. Wrap the sandwich very securely in plastic wrap, stretching the plastic slightly as you wrap the sandwich to create a tight bundle. Refrigerate from 4 to 24 hours.

4. About 1 hour before serving, unwrap the sandwich and remove the top slice of bread. Arrange the bacon, then the red lettuce leaves over the blewits. Replace the top bread slice and let the sandwich stand at room temperature for 1 hour. (If you plan to transport the sandwich, rewrap it securely at this point.) Just before serving, cut the sandwich crosswise into 4 pieces.

Note: Use the center cut, so it will be of even thickness, from a loaf about 13 or more inches long. The bread should be firm but not springy or dense and the crust should be crackly but not overly chewy or the bread will be difficult to cut and the sandwich will be difficult to eat. If you cannot find such bread, make 4 club-style sandwiches using 12 slices of seven-grain or dense whole wheat bread. Toast the bread and skip the step in which the sandwich—without the bacon and lettuce—is refrigerated. Just before serving, layer the ingredients into the sandwiches as described in Step 3. Press firmly, then cut the sandwiches into 4 triangles. Long wooden picks inserted into the sandwiches before cutting will help them stay together. A simpler version of the sandwich may be made by layering all the ingredients in a large roll with a chewy consistency, like a Portuguese, kaiser, or hero roll.

Scrambled Eggs with Lobster Mushroom Hash

SERVES 4

What better brunch meal than eggs and lobster (mushrooms, that is!)? This loose hash, full of mild-flavored chunks of lobster mushrooms, is a perfect foil to scrambled eggs. The purpose of the optional cream is to help the hash hold together.

4 tablespoons (½ stick) unsalted butter

½ cup diced onion

12 ounces large lobster mushrooms, cleaned and diced ½ inch (about 2¾ cups)

1½ cups cooked, peeled, diced (½ inch) russet potato (see Note)

2 tablespoons finely chopped fresh flat-leaf parsley

2 teaspoons finely chopped fresh tarragon or thyme

Kosher or sea salt and freshly ground black pepper

3 tablespoons heavy (or whipping) cream (optional)

8 large eggs

½ cup finely chopped chives

1. Melt 3 tablespoons of the butter in a medium-size (8-inch) heavy nonstick or cast-iron skillet over medium heat until it begins to foam. Add the onion and cook, stirring often, until it begins to brown, about 6 minutes. Add the mushrooms and potato. Cook over medium heat until the mushrooms are softened, about 5 minutes. Stir in the parsley and tarragon. Continue cooking, stirring frequently, until the hash is well browned and the mushrooms are very tender, about 20 minutes. Scrape the bits that stick to the pan back into the hash. Add salt and pepper to taste. Stir in the cream, if using. Press the hash into an even layer in the skillet. Lower the heat to medium-low and continue cooking until the underside of the hash is crisp, about 5 minutes.

2. Meanwhile, beat the eggs, chives, and 2 tablespoons water in a bowl until thoroughly blended. Spoon the hash out onto a serving plate and keep it warm. If using a cast-iron pan, wipe it out thoroughly. Add the remaining 1 tablespoon butter to the skillet. Pour in the eggs and cook over medium heat, stirring constantly, to the desired consistency. Remove the pan from the heat and season with salt and pepper to taste. Spoon the eggs next to the hash. Serve immediately.

Note: A leftover baked russet potato works perfectly in this recipe. If starting from scratch, simmer a scrubbed potato (about 8 ounces) in salted water to cover until tender, about 35 minutes. Drain the potato and cool it completely before peeling and dicing.

Corn and Hedgehog Tamales

These hot, cornbready bundles are stuffed with a combination of richly mellow, pungent, and raging flavors. I discovered what they were and how delicious they could be when the Mexican waiter at our local Greek diner offered to trade his tamales for our huitlacoche (weet-la-coach-aye) mushrooms. Being unable to wrest his wife's recipe from him, I worked out this one and it's a good thing, because while figuring it out on my own, I discovered that there are endless possibilities for fillings. Give yourself a couple of hours to prepare these the first time; by all means, do them ahead. Substitute chanterelles, cèpes (boletes), huitlacoche, or black trumpet mushrooms for the hedgehogs with equally *splendido* results.

Serve the tamales with salsa, chips, and avocado slices drizzled with lime juice.

TAMALES

1 ear of fresh corn or ¾ cup frozen
    corn kernels

1 teaspoon white truffle oil (optional)

20 dried corn husks (see Note)

2 tablespoons olive oil, or more if needed

2 cloves garlic

MUSHROOM FILLING

12 ounces hedgehog mushrooms, cleaned
    and sliced ¼ inch thick

⅓ cup Light Chicken Stock (page 280)

Sea salt and freshly ground black pepper

3 tablespoons roughly chopped fresh
    cilantro

MASA

1 cup coarse masa harina (see Note)

1 teaspoon Cèpe Powder (optional,
    page 285

⅔ cup mushroom soaking liquid
    saved from another recipe or
    Mushroom Jus (page 254)

12 tablespoons (1½ sticks) salted butter,
    at room temperature

1 teaspoon baking powder

½ teaspoon kosher or sea salt

1 tablespoon finely chopped chipotle
    in adobo sauce

1. Preheat the grill to hot or preheat the oven to 450°F.

2. Peel back the husk of the corn and remove the silk. Brush the corn with the white truffle oil, if using, and sprinkle with salt. Replace the husk. Grill the corn away from flame until a fork slips in easily, about 15 minutes. Or place the corn on the oven rack and bake for 10 to 15 minutes. When the corn is cool enough to handle, set it on its base to steady it, and use a sharp knife to cut downwards to free the kernels from the cob. You should have ½ to ¾ cup. Or mix the frozen corn kernels with the truffle oil as a small ovenproof bowl and warm in a 450°F oven for 5 minutes.

3. Meanwhile, soak the dried corn husks in warm water, weighted down with a plate and heavy object, until softened, about 20 minutes.

4. Heat the olive oil in a small sauté pan over medium heat. Cook the garlic until soft, about 6 minutes, shaking the pan occasionally. Peel the garlic, mash it with a fork, and set aside.

5. To make the mushroom filling, pour the garlic oil plus enough olive oil to total 2 tablespoons into a medium-size sauté pan. Heat to medium-high, add the hedgehogs, and sauté until their liquid is released, about 2 minutes. Reduce the heat to medium and poor in the stock. Boil until the stock is absorbed by the mushrooms, about 6 minutes. Season with salt and freshly ground pepper. Stir in 2 tablespoons of the cilantro. Set aside.

6. To make the masa, mix the masa harina and cèpe powder in a medium-size bowl. Stir in the soaking liquid or Mushroom Jus with a wooden spoon until the dough gathers into a ball. Using your hands, knead the masa until it no longer sticks to your fingers, about 5 minutes. Set aside.

7. Blend the softened butter,

baking powder, and salt in a large bowl, preferably a mixer bowl. Beat at high speed until the mixture resembles buttercream frosting, with a shiny glow and spreadable consistency, 4 minutes. Spoon 2 tablespoons of the masa into the bowl and blend in with the mixer. Continue adding masa, little by little, until it is fully incorporated into the butter, about 10 minutes. Wipe down the sides of the bowl occasionally. The resulting dough will be light, fluffy, and easy to spread. Finally, mix in the chipotle pepper, the corn kernels, the garlic and the remaining 1 tablespoon cilantro.

8. Shake the water off the 16 largest corn husks. Rip long shreds from the smaller ones to make 2 ties per tamale. Lay 1 husk flat and spoon 2 tablespoons of masa on it in a square shape. Leave at least a ½-inch border on all sides. Spoon 1 tablespoon of mushroom filling in the center of the masa square. Top with 1 tablespoon of masa to completely cover the mushroom filling.

9. Tuck the long sides of the husk over the filling to completely enclose it and place on a work surface, seam side down. Tie both ends of the husk with strips of shredded husk. Repeat with the remaining filling and husks. Set the tamales, seam side down, in a flat steamer basket, such as a rice steamer, couscous pot, or ordinary steam basket, set over boiling water. You may improvise with a metal colander; the tamales will bend but will still be delicious. Cover and steam the tamales for 1 hour over barely boiling water. Check the water level every 15 minutes, and replace as it evaporates. Gently open a tamale to test for doneness (it can be rewrapped); they are done when the masa has a moist, yet crumbly texture.

10. To serve, arrange the tamales in a starburst pattern on a festive plate. Untie the ends, then unroll the wrapping to expose the filling. The filling is steamy hot, so don't lean your face over them as you unwrap.

Note: Dried corn husks are available in Hispanic markets and in most large supermarkets. Masa harina is available in Hispanic markets, as well, and on the flour shelf of most large supermarkets.

Festive Tamales

Biting into the my first tamale—the subtle wave of heat, burst of smoky corn, and the surprise of mushrooms—was no less thrilling to me than my very first oyster. I had never fancied myself a Mexican cook, but after tasting my first tamale, I spent hours poring over cookbooks and tracking down authentic ingredients. Tamales have become a party dish for when we invite the hordes, and I've packaged and frozen tamales as gifts to friends whose palates enjoy a spicy burst. Just about anything can be used as ties, to help set the party mood. My favorite tie is brightly colored pipe cleaners, which twist on and off easily and add to the piñata-and-colada fiesta mood. They fade a bit, but are safe—they don't come in contact with the filling.

The Only Portobello Guide You'll Ever Need

As with a good steak, I dream about portobello possibilities: salad with portobello juice dripping down my chin; a portobello sandwich with melting blue cheese; portobello marinade seeping into nutty couscous. This meaty, juicy mushroom jolts my senses alive. And I am far from alone. Below I have outlined some of my favorite ideas, but go ahead and improvise. The forgiving portobello can be overcooked or undercooked, held in the fridge for a week before and a week after cooking, and eaten hot or at room temperature.

The gills of portobellos lend an inky color to dishes they are stewed or sautéed in. To avoid the black color and to have elegantly thin slices, take this tip from Tom Colicchio, chef/co-owner of the Gramercy Tavern. Holding each mushroom horizontally, he slices off and discards the gills. Then he punches out circles of the denuded cap with a biscuit cutter. They are now ready to be grilled or otherwise prepared.

The portobello stem has a fibrous texture that makes it unsuitable for sautés. But save the stems for a soup base; just dice and sauté them with any other mushroom trimmings you may have. Add water, bring to a boil, skim, and simmer until you have a rich, dark, tasty broth. Strain out the mushrooms, add a handful of julienned vegetables, and call it soup.

PORTOBELLO STRUDEL: Trim edges of 3 grilled portobellos to make triangles. Layer the triangles with thin slices of mozzarella, roasted red pepper, and basil. Bake at 350°F to melt the cheese and warm through, about 12 minutes. Slice in half to serve 2 as a first course.

PORTOBELLO SANDWICH: Spread toasted brioche with garlic mayonnaise, a grilled portobello cap, and a few leaves of arugula.

PORTOBELLO GRAIN SALAD: Toss hot sautéed or grilled portobello slices into a cooked grain, such as quinoa or couscous. Dress with balsamic vinegar, extra virgin olive oil, and lots of chopped fresh herbs, such as mint, basil, chives, and chervil.

PORTOBELLO FAJITA: Slice a grilled portobello. Toss with hot red pepper sauce, chopped fresh cilantro, and sliced tomato. Wrap a soft flour tortilla around all and eat.

PORTOBELLO TACOS: Dice 1 grilled portobello, 1 small tomato, and 3 scallions. Mix with 2 tablespoons homemade or store-bought salsa, 1 tablespoon minced cilantro, and 1 teaspoon minced jalapeño. Divide between crisped tortillas, top with shredded Cheddar cheese, and broil to melt the cheese, 1 minute. Serves 2 as a snack.

SERVES 4

Huitlacoche with Summer Tomatoes

Corny, spicy, and overflowing with juicy goodness, these stuffed tomatoes make a **terrific** meatless summer meal. Stuff them ahead of time and bake just before serving. For a firmer stuffing, add half a cup of cooked rice to the mix. Since huitlacoche (weet-la-coach-aye) is almost never available fresh and seldom frozen, rely on the canned variety, which is available in some Hispanic markets, or substitute shiitake mushrooms—they lack corn flavor, but add their own earth notes.

4 large (about 2 pounds), **washed** tomatoes

Kosher or sea salt

1 tablespoon olive oil

1 medium onion, chopped

1 strip (1 × ¼ inch) of fresh red chili, minced

2 cloves garlic, crushed

8 ounces fresh or canned huitlacoche, not thawed if frozen

4 ounces oyster or button mushrooms

¼ cup Rich Meat Stock (page 282) or canned beef broth

½ teaspoon adobo sauce from canned chilpotle peppers, or 3 drops hot red pepper sauce

½ teaspoon chopped fresh thyme

½ cup fresh chopped cilantro

Freshly ground black pepper

¼ cup coarse bread crumbs

1. Using a paring knife, cut a little "hat" from the top of each tomato. Angle the knife down, cutting about 1 inch of tomato around the core. Trim some flesh off the underside of the hat so that it will sit flat over the stuffing. Using a soup spoon, scoop out the flesh from the inside of the tomato, leaving ¼-inch-thick walls. Drain the flesh in a colander, reserving the juice for another use. Chop the flesh and set aside.

2. Sprinkle the insides of the tomatoes and hats with salt. Turn the tomatoes upside down on a cake rack for about 15 minutes.

3. Preheat the oven to 350°F.

Summer Tomatoes

When it comes to fresh tomatoes, the Farges family's fervor is hard to beat. We buy fresh summer tomatoes whenever we can get our hands on them. As soon as July hits, we're out in the rust-bucket Bronco, cruising rural byways for signs announcing "Local Tomatoes." We've found shoeless boys peddling them on upturned buckets and a gas station with an overflowing crate marked "1 pound free with fill-up." Buying a potty chair at an unfinished-wood furniture store, I picked up a lunchbag full of tomatoes on the counter. Those tomatoes are long gone, but the child's hand-colored bag now evokes lingering memories: three red tomatoes with a balloon reading "Eat us."

4. In a large sauté pan, heat the olive oil over medium heat. Sauté the onion, red chili, and garlic until the onion is soft and translucent, 3 to 5 minutes. Add the huitlacoche, increase the heat to high, and cook until the liquid is released, about 2 minutes. Stir in the mushrooms and cook 1 minute more. Add the stock, *adobo* sauce, thyme, and tomato flesh. Bring to a boil and cook until thickened, about 7 minutes. Season with salt and pepper to taste. Stir in the cilantro.

5. Fill the tomatoes with the stuffing. It will be a little soupy. Top with the bread crumbs, then set the reserved hats on top. Set them in a roasting pan or baking dish in which they fit snugly.

6. Bake until the tomatoes give off some juices and the bread crumbs take on a golden cast, about 15 minutes. Serve immediately.

Woodsy Mushroom Pot Pie

SERVES 6

This dish's dramatic presentation and splendidly aromatic effect make it perfect for a dinner party. The wilder you go with mushroom varieties—hedgehog, black trumpet, and chanterelle are exceptionally tasty—the more you will be transported to a woodsy glen in autumn.

1 pound assorted mushrooms, cleaned

4 tablespoons chopped fresh thyme leaves

4 teaspoons chopped fresh rosemary leaves

1 clove garlic, sliced thin

1 tablespoon tamari soy sauce

2 teaspoons balsamic vinegar

12 ounces (10 to 16) thin to medium
    asparagus spears

2 tablespoons unsalted butter

3 tablespoons all-purpose flour

¼ cup heavy (or whipping)
    cream

2 tablespoons
    chopped
    fresh flat-leaf
    parsley

PASTRY

All-purpose flour, for sprinkling on
    the work surface

1 egg, beaten well with a few drops
    of water

1 sheet (8 ounces; half a package),
    frozen puff pastry, thawed in the
    refrigerator

1. Cut away any tough stems and hard parts from the mushrooms, reserving the stems and hard parts. (If they do not have tough stems or hard parts, cut off about ¾ cup of stems for the broth.) Wash well and place in a food processor. Add 3 teaspoons of the thyme, 3 teaspoons of the rosemary, and the garlic. Process until finely chopped.

2. Transfer the stem mixture to a small saucepan and add 2 cups of water, the soy sauce, and vinegar. Bring to a boil. Scrape down the sides of the pan and reduce the heat to a simmer. Cover and cook over very low heat for 15 minutes.

3. Cut the mushrooms into chunks or slice longer mushrooms lengthwise and set aside. Cut off and discard about a third of the bottom of the asparagus stalks. Cut off the asparagus tips, then cut the remaining stalk diagonally into ¾-inch lengths. Set aside.

4. Strain the mushroom stem liquid into a bowl, pressing down on the mushroom mixture to extract as much liquid as possible. Discard the solids. Cover to keep warm. (You may prepare the pot pie to this point up to 2 days in advance. Reheat the mushroom broth to a simmer before continuing.)

5. Make a light brown roux by melting the butter in a heavy, medium-size saucepan over medium heat until foaming. Stir in the flour and whisk until smooth. Reduce the heat to low and cook, stirring frequently, until the roux is tan, without letting it stick or burn, about 4 minutes. Slowly pour the mushroom broth into the roux, whisking constantly to prevent lumps. When all the broth is added, increase the heat to medium and continue whisking, paying special attention to the corners, until the mixture

comes to a boil. Reduce the heat and simmer, uncovered, for 10 minutes, stirring several times.

6. Add the mushrooms to the sauce and stir to coat. The mixture will look dry, but the mushrooms will give up a lot of liquid as they cook. Simmer, stirring occasionally without letting the sauce boil or stick, for 10 minutes. Stir in the cream, chopped parsley, and remaining thyme and rosemary. Simmer for 3 minutes. Remove from the heat and stir in the asparagus. Cool to room temperature. (The filling can be made to this point up to 1 day in advance. Cover and store in the refrigerator. Before continuing, warm the mushrooms gently over very low heat, adding water a few drops at a time, if necessary, to restore the filling to its original consistency. Heat just to room temperature, without letting the mixture simmer or boil.)

7. Divide the filling among six 5- to 6-ounce ramekins or custard dishes about 3½ × 2 inches.

8. Preheat the oven to 400°F.

9. To prepare the pastry, roll out the puff pastry on a lightly floured work surface to ⅛ inch thick. Add flour as necessary to prevent sticking during the rolling. Measure the diameter of the ramekins and cut 6 circles ½ inch wider than the diameter. Brush the edges with the beaten egg and cover the dishes with the pastry, egg side down. Press the pastry firmly against the sides of the dish. The pastry should be taut across the top of the dish and firmly attached to the dish all the way around. Brush the pastry tops with the remaining beaten egg. Arrange the potpies on a baking sheet and refrigerate for 5 to 10 minutes.

10. Bake until the pastry rises into a dome shape and is well browned, about 20 minutes. Serve at once with a spoon and knife.

My Hero

I've served variations on this hero many times, but this one offers just the right combination of meaty mushroom, sweet mayonnaise, creamy cheese, and crunchy lettuce. Grilling the split roll adds a smokey note to the sandwich. Serve it with big napkins!

SERVES 2

1 recipe Roasted or Grilled Portobello
     Caps (recipe follows)
½ cup coarsely chopped roasted red bell
     peppers, freshly made (see box, page
     163) or bottled
¼ cup prepared mayonnaise
2 hero or club rolls
4 ounces Brie or fresh mozzarella,
     sliced ¼ inch thick, at room
     temperature
2 cups shredded mixed lettuce, any
     combination of romaine, radicchio,
     Bibb, or iceberg

1. Stir the peppers and mayonnaise together in a small bowl. Open the rolls without completely splitting them in half. Spread the mayonnaise mixture evenly over both halves of both rolls. Arrange the cheese to cover half of each roll.

2. Slice the mushrooms and arrange them to cover the cheese.

Arrange the lettuce over the mushrooms, close the sandwich, and serve.

Roasted or Grilled Portobello Caps

*O*nce you've roasted or grilled a portobello mushroom cap, the door is open to endless possibilities. Here are the basic techniques and a few suggestions to get you started. While hot, spread the mushrooms with feta or goat cheese and bits of reconstituted sun-dried tomatoes. Slice into wedges and serve on crusty bread.

MAKES 4 GRILLED OR ROASTED MUSHROOMS

4 medium (about 1 pound) portobello
mushrooms, with caps about
3½ inches across

2 tablespoons extra virgin olive oil,
or as needed

1 teaspoon Seasoning Salt (page 253) or
kosher or sea salt

¼ teaspoon freshly ground black
pepper

1 tablespoon balsamic vinegar,
fresh lemon juice, or soy sauce
(optional)

TO ROAST THE MUSHROOM CAPS:

Preheat the oven to 400°F. Remove
the stems from the mushrooms and
wipe the caps clean. Lightly oil a
baking pan with some of the olive
oil. Rub the remaining oil into the
tops of the caps. Sprinkle the mushrooms with salt and pepper. Place
the caps, gill side up, on the baking
pan. Roast for 10 minutes. Turn and
roast until the mushrooms are tender
and well browned, about 15 minutes.
Remove the pan from the oven
and sprinkle the mushrooms with
vinegar, if desired. Let cool for
2 to 3 minutes before serving.

TO GRILL THE MUSHROOM CAPS:

Preheat a grill to hot. Rub the oil into
all sides of the mushroom caps. (You
may need a little more than 2 tablespoons oil for this.) Sprinkle the
mushrooms with salt and pepper.
Place the mushrooms, gill side up,
near the coolest part of the fire.
Grill the caps until well marked and
brown, about 8 minutes. Turn the
caps and continue grilling until the
mushrooms are tender, about 10
minutes. Move the caps occasionally
during grilling to prevent overbrown-
ing. Remove the caps to a platter
and sprinkle with vinegar, if
desired.

TO STORE COOKED PORTOBELLOS:

Cool the caps to room temperature
and wrap in plastic wrap, then
wrap in aluminum foil. Refrigerate
for up to 1 week.

Grilled Portobellos and Polenta

SERVES 4

Creamy, corny polenta cries out for bright, take-notice flavors. This
one gets a jolt from vinegar-laced portobellos. I think of it as comfort
food for grown-ups, and sometimes serve it with just a green salad and
a glass of red wine.

1 recipe Roasted or Grilled Portobello
    Caps (page 193)

Grated Parmesan cheese

2 tablespoons chopped fresh flat-leaf
    parsley or other herbs

1 recipe Old-World Polenta (page 203)

Slice the mushrooms 1 inch thick. Stir the cheese and parsley into the polenta. Spoon the polenta onto service plates and arrange the mushroom slices overlapping the polenta. Serve immediately.

Cèpe-ly Gulyas

This recipe title is a play on the name of the classical Hungarian dish Szekely Gulyas, an Old World stew of pork and sauerkraut seasoned with caraway and paprika. Here, I've kept the spice notes, replaced the pork with meaty cèpes, and eliminated the sauerkraut. This New World stew is richly delicious served over buttered egg noodles or as a side dish with roasted pork or chicken.

Cèpes are a splurge, and the *bouchons* even more so, but they are worth it. They are the juiciest of mushrooms, and all that great juice goes right into the stew. Though cèpes are popular in Eastern Europe, most American recipes associate cèpes or porcini with French and Italian dishes, so the spice notes will be a surprise hit at the table. If you cannot find cèpes, substitute whole small cremini.

If you would like to prepare a fully vegetarian version of this dish, substitute 2 tablespoons vegetable oil for the bacon and Mushroom Jus (page 254) for the chicken stock.

1 piece (2 ounces) slab bacon, rind
    discarded; cut into ¼-inch dice

1 medium onion, chopped

2 cloves garlic, chopped fine

2 teaspoons good-quality Hungarian
    paprika, either sweet or hot, or a mix
    of the two

1 pound (about 18 pieces) fresh small cèpes,
    called *bouchons*, trimmed and cleaned,
    or 1 pound frozen whole cèpes (see
    Note)

1 cup Rich Chicken Stock (page 281) or
    canned low-sodium chicken broth

2 medium (about 10 ounces) red potatoes,
    peeled and cut into 2-inch cubes

2 cups coarsely chopped canned tomatoes
    with their liquid

¼ teaspoon caraway seeds

Kosher or sea salt and freshly ground
    black pepper

1. Place the bacon in a large,

deep, heavy skillet. Place the skillet over medium heat and cook until the bacon has rendered its fat and is brown and crisp, about 10 minutes. Turn the bacon pieces occasionally. Remove the bacon from the skillet and set aside.

2. Add the onion, garlic, and paprika to the pan. Cook over medium-low heat, stirring often, until the onion and garlic are lightly browned, about 5 minutes. Increase the heat to medium-high and add the mushrooms. (If they are frozen they will sputter quite a bit until the water on the surface evaporates.) Cook until the mushrooms begin to give off their liquid, about 3 minutes. Add the stock, potatoes, tomatoes, and caraway seeds. Bring to a boil,

then reduce the heat to a simmer. Season lightly with salt and pepper. Cover and simmer, stirring occasionally, until the potatoes are tender, about 20 minutes.

3. Remove the cover, add the bacon, and increase the heat to medium-high. Boil, stirring often, until the liquid is reduced enough to lightly coat the vegetables, about 5 minutes. Season to taste with salt and pepper and serve hot.

Note: If you cannot find bouchons, you may substitute large mushrooms, trimmed and cut into quarters. If using frozen whole mushrooms, do not defrost them first, or they will lose much of their flavorful juice in the process.

Daube de Champignons

SERVES 6

Traditionally a French *daube* is a stew made with meat—usually beef—or poultry in a narrow-mouthed crock called a *daubierè*. The *daube* bakes for hours in the oven or on the hearth. Sometimes the meat is browned first, but often it is simply layered with bacon or pork fat, vegetables, and herbs. In this mushroom version, firm-textured hedgehog mushrooms are seasoned with fresh herbs and aromatic vegetables and slowly baked, uncovered, until meltingly tender. The mushrooms brown and the liquid takes on a mahogany color and ultra-rich flavor.

Other firm mushrooms, such as cèpe and chicken of the woods, would also work. Serve this dish as a light meal with a green salad and lightly toasted French bread or simply over buttered noodles. It also makes a lovely side dish to serve with roast squab or veal.

1 piece (2 ounces) slab bacon with rind
2 sprigs of thyme
2 sprigs of tarragon
2 bay leaves
2 tablespoons olive oil
2 ribs celery, trimmed and sliced ¼ inch thick
1 medium onion, cut into 1-inch cubes
2 medium carrots, cut into 2-inch lengths
2 cups Rich Meat Stock (page 282), Rich Chicken Stock (page 281), or water
2 pounds hedgehog mushrooms, trimmed, larger mushrooms cut in half
Kosher or sea salt and freshly ground black pepper
¼ cup chopped fresh flat-leaf parsley

1. Cut off and reserve the rind from the bacon. Cut the bacon into ¼-inch dice.

2. Bring a small saucepan of water to a boil. Add rind and boil for 3 minutes. Drain. Tie the thyme, tarragon, and bay leaves in a bundle with kitchen twine.

3. Preheat the oven to 325°F.

4. Heat the oil in a heavy 3- to 4-quart heavy ovenproof casserole over medium heat. Add the bacon and cook until it begins to sizzle. Stir in the celery, onion, and carrots and cook until the vegetables are lightly browned, about 10 minutes. Stir in the stock and bring to a boil. Stir in the mushrooms and salt and pepper to taste. Tuck the herb bundle and blanched bacon rind into the vegetables.

5. Place the casserole in the oven and bake, until the vegetables are very tender and the liquid has cooked away to below the level of vegetables, about 1½ hours. Check the casserole as it cooks and stir the browned top layer into the center 3 or 4 times during the cooking process. Remove the herb bundle and bacon rind before serving. (The *daube* may be prepared to this point up to 3 days in advance. Reheat the *daube* to simmering.) Stir in the parsley and serve.

Grains, Beans, Pasta, and Potatoes

*G*rains often put me in mind of this country before farming turned into agribusiness. There's something wholesome and unadulterated about rice and the whole corn family—polenta, grits, hominy. And the same can be said for wild mushrooms, which existed long before the portobello factories revved up their engines.

There are lots of reasons to pair mushrooms with grains, beans, and pasta. These familiar goods are easily stocked in the pantry and make great last-minute meals. Mingling bland but texturally appealing starches with the vivacious character of wild mushrooms brings out the best in both. The range of possibilities is vast, running from utterly simple Fettuccine with Wild Forest Sauce to exotically inclined Dal with Escarole and Cremini or White Bean Purée with White Truffle. And combining legumes with mushrooms produces inviting vegetarian main-dish meals.

Gorgonzola Polenta with Roasted Fried Chickens

SERVES 4

Roasted mushrooms turn homey, by-the-fireside polenta into an elegant first or main course. The polenta can be prepared in advance and reheated in a slow oven. For a change of pace, mash roasted garlic (see box) into the polenta instead of the cheese.

1 pound fried chicken mushrooms, or other
   firm mushrooms like cèpes, shiitakes,
   or chanterelles, or a mix, cleaned
2 tablespoons extra virgin olive oil
1 teaspoon minced fresh tarragon or sage
¾ teaspoon kosher or sea salt or Seasoning
   Salt (page 253)
Freshly ground black pepper
3½ cups Gorgonzola Polenta (page 203)
⅓ cup Rich Chicken Stock (page 281), Light
   Chicken Stock (page 280) or canned
   low-sodium chicken broth

1. Preheat the oven to 425°F.

2. Trim off any tough stems from the mushrooms. Slice into 2-inch strips. Combine the olive oil, tarragon, and salt in a medium bowl. Add the mushrooms, sprinkle with freshly ground pepper, and toss until coated with the seasoning mixture.

3. Spread the mushrooms in a single layer in a flameproof roasting pan. Roast, stirring from time to time, until well browned and tender, about 15 minutes.

4. Place the roasting pan with the mushrooms still in it over medium heat on the stove top and stir in the stock. Continue stirring, scraping up the little brown bits that stick to the pan, until the stock is almost completely evaporated, about 1 minute. Divide the polenta among 4 warm shallow serving bowls, keeping it as much as possible to one side of the bowl. Spoon the mushrooms and juices alongside the polenta. Serve at once.

Roasted Garlic

I like to roast garlic on the grill as the coals begin to fade, but it can just as easily be done in the oven. First preheat the grill to hot (if using the oven, preheat to 350°F). Drizzle a dozen garlic cloves, still in their skins, with olive oil and sea or kosher salt, then bundle them in aluminum foil. Place the packet directly on the dying coals (or in a baking pan in the oven), and roast, turning occasionally, about 30 minutes. Check for doneness by inserting a knife into a clove. Cool to room temperature. Store in the refrigerator, wrapped in foil, for about 1 week.

To use, slip the cloves out of their skins and mash with a fork. Add to vinaigrettes, spread on chicken breasts, mash into potatoes, and melt into tomato sauce.

How to Clean and Cut Selected Mushrooms for a Ragout

Enoki Mushrooms: Trim the root ends, leaving just enough of the root attached to hold the mushrooms together. Break the mushrooms into small clumps of 4 to 5 mushrooms each.

Hen of the Woods: Plunge the mushrooms in a large bowl of cool water. Shake them to remove excess water, then roll them gently in a clean, dry kitchen towel to dry. Slice the mushrooms through the center into ¼-inch strips.

Lobster Mushrooms: Trim the tough stem end of the mushrooms. Wipe the mushroom clean with a dry paper towel. Cut the mushrooms into ¼-inch strips. If the strips are longer than 3 inches, cut them lengthwise in half.

Mousserons: Roll the mushrooms in a clean, dry kitchen towel to remove as much dirt as possible. If they are still not clean, plunge them into a large bowl of cool water, swish gently, then drain. Pat dry with the kitchen towel.

Portobellos: Wipe the caps with a dry paper towel. Cut off the stem flush with the bottom of the cap. You may reserve the stems for another use. Slice the caps ¼ inch wide, then cut the strips into ¼-inch dice.

Shiitakes: Wipe the mushroom caps clean with a dry paper towel. Trim off the stems flush with the caps. You may reserve the stems for another use, like Mushroom Jus (page 254) or Wild Mushroom Stock (page 73). Slice the caps ¼ inch wide. If the caps are larger than 3 inches, cut them in half before slicing.

Polenta with a Wild Mushroom Ragout

A mushroom ragout is a mixture of mushrooms that are first sautéed, then simmered with a little liquid. It is one of the best ways to savor wild and exotic mushrooms. By varying the mushrooms, the flavoring ingredients, the liquid they are simmered in, and the fat

**MAKES ABOUT
3 CUPS,
SERVES 4**

they are sautéed in, you can create endless variations. A ragout can stand on its own as a first course, or be teamed with any number of partners. Here I've paired it with polenta to serve as a hearty main course.

1½ pounds mixed exotic mushrooms, preferably at least one of each type (see Note)

3 to 4 tablespoons unsalted butter, olive oil, vegetable oil, or rendered chicken fat (see box, page 280), or a mixture

¼ cup finely chopped shallot or leek white

2 tablespoons Cognac, brandy, Port, Armagnac, Calvados, or bourbon or ¼ cup dry red or dry white wine

⅓ cup Rich Chicken Stock (page 281) Rich Meat Stock (page 282), or 3 tablespoons Demi-Glace (see box, page 282)

2 teaspoons chopped fresh tarragon, thyme, flat-leaf parsley, or chervil

1 teaspoon kosher or sea salt or Seasoning Salt (page 253)

Freshly ground black pepper

3 tablespoons heavy (or whipping) cream (optional)

1 recipe Old-World Polenta (recipe follows)

1. Clean all the mushrooms. Cut them according to the guide on page 201.

2. Melt the butter in a large, heavy skillet over medium heat. Add the shallot and cook until wilted but not brown, about 4 minutes. Add the firm mushrooms and cook until softened, about 4 minutes. Stir in the medium-textured mushrooms. Cook until all the mushrooms are soft and they begin to give off liquid, about 3 minutes. Stir in the delicate mushrooms.

3. Remove the pan from the heat. Add the Cognac and ignite the mixture with a long kitchen match (see box, facing page). When the flames die down, return the pan to high heat and boil until the liquid is evaporated, about 15 seconds. Add the stock, herbs, salt, and pepper to taste. Stir in the cream, if using, and heat to a boil. Boil until the liquid is thickened enough to lightly coat the mushrooms, about 2 minutes. Adjust the salt and pepper, if desired. Serve hot over polenta.

Note: Select mushrooms from each of the following groups.

• Firm mushrooms, such as portobello, cremini, shiitake, hedgehog, morel, cèpe, matsutake, wine cap, or lobster mushrooms

• Medium-textured mushrooms, such as chanterelle, mousseron, lactaire, hen of the woods, charbonnièr, puffball, or cauliflower mushrooms

• Delicate mushrooms, such as black trumpet, honshimeji, yellowfoot, oyster, or enoki mushrooms

Old-World Polenta

There are times when only a homey dish like polenta will do. Made like a porridge, with coarsely ground cornmeal, it is honest, creamy, and bursting with wholesome goodness. Polenta—with or without the suggested additions—makes the perfect foil for wild mushrooms, especially mixtures of strong-flavored ones. Another way to serve polenta is to pour it into a buttered baking pan, and, when firm, cut into wedges or squares, almost like cornbread.

2 teaspoons kosher or sea salt
½ cup coarse yellow cornmeal
   (see Note)
Freshly ground black pepper
1 to 2 tablespoons unsalted butter
   (optional)

1. Heat 2½ cups of water and the salt in a 2-quart saucepan over high heat. Reduce the heat to a simmer and very gradually pour the cornmeal into the water, stirring constantly. It should take about 3 minutes to add all the cornmeal. Continue stirring until the mixture is the consistency of oatmeal and the individual grains of cornmeal are tender, about 4 minutes. Remove from the heat and stir in pepper to taste and butter, if using. The polenta can be covered and held off the heat for about 10 minutes before serving. Stir 1 or 2 tablespoons hot water into the polenta before serving.

Note: Coarse cornmeal has the consistency of fine grains of sand and is available in health food stores and Latino and Italian groceries. Fine cornmeal used for baking will make an acceptable but less interesting substitute.

**ABOUT 3½ CUPS
SERVES 4**

A Note About Adding Flammable Liquids to a Pan

When flambéing anything in a skillet, it's very important to follow some basic rules:

1. **Clear the surrounding area of flammable items, such as hanging dish towels.**

2. **Remove or tuck in flapping sleeves and tie back loose hair.**

3. **Have a fire extinguisher or sand nearby.**

4. **Remove the pan from the stove, holding the pan at arm's length, as you add the alcohol or ignite its contents.**

Variations: **Gorgonzola Polenta:** Remove the rind from 2 ounces Gorgonzola cheese, preferably dolce latte, and cut the cheese into thin slices. Add the cheese to the polenta in place of, or in addition to, the butter. Polenta that has both Gorgonzola and butter added will be slightly runnier than polenta with just one of the two.

Parmesan Polenta: Stir 3 tablespoons freshly-grated Parmesan cheese into the polenta along with, or in place of, the butter.

Herb Polenta: Add 1 to 3 teaspoons of finely chopped fresh rosemary, sage, or thyme, or a combination, to the polenta about halfway through the cooking. If you like it creamier, stir in 2 tablespoons light or heavy cream as well.

Polenta-Stuffed Morels

SERVES 6 AS
A SIDE DISH

The most luscious thing about this corn and mushroom duo is how the soft, grainy filling is barely contained by the earthy, toothsome morel walls. Stuffing morels is easy when you have the drive-through size. The gigantic ones are usually available as morel season is winding down, around the Fourth of July (although it can continue until Labor Day in exceptional years!). Dried morels, reconstituted, make a fine substitute.

1 cup Light Chicken Stock (page 280) or canned low-sodium chicken broth

3 tablespoons unsalted butter

24 large morels (about 1 pound), cleaned and trimmed, or 2 to 3 ounces dried morels, soaked in warm water for 30 minutes, drained and trimmed

¼ cup coarse yellow cornmeal

½ teaspoon salt

¼ cup grated Parmesan cheese

1 tablespoon chopped fresh chives or fresh flat-leaf parsley

Freshly ground black pepper

¼ cup chopped shallots

1. Place the stock and 1 tablespoon of the butter in a large skillet over medium heat. Bring to a simmer, then add the mushrooms and simmer, turning them in the liquid once or twice, until softened but not tender, about 5 minutes (add 5 minutes more if using dried morels). Using a slotted spoon, transfer the mushrooms to a platter to cool. Set aside the cooking liquid.

2. Meanwhile, stir 1 cup of water, the cornmeal, and salt in a small, heavy saucepan until smooth. Place the saucepan over low heat and heat to a simmer, stirring constantly. Stir until the polenta is thickened and the cornmeal is tender but still slightly grainy, about 10

minutes. Remove the polenta from the heat and stir in the cheese, chives, and pepper to taste. Let cool to tepid, about 5 minutes, stirring often.

3. Transfer the polenta to a pastry bag fitted with a narrow, plain tip. Or spoon the polenta into 1 corner of a 1-quart, heavy sealable plastic bag. With a scissors, snip off about ⅛ inch of the corner of the bag where the polenta is.

4. Preheat the oven to 325°F.

5. Insert the pastry tip or the tip of the bag as far as possible into a mushroom. Squeeze the polenta slowly from the pastry bag to fill the whole mushroom evenly with polenta. Repeat with the remaining mushrooms. Arrange the mushrooms in a single layer in a 9-inch square baking dish, or other dish in which they fit comfortably in a single layer. Add any liquid that has accumulated on the mushroom platter to the reserved mushroom cooking liquid.

6. Melt the remaining 2 tablespoons butter in a small skillet over medium heat until foaming. Stir in the shallots and cook until wilted, about 2 minutes. Add the reserved cooking liquid to the skillet and heat to a boil. Pour the liquid over the mushrooms and cover the dish tightly with aluminum foil. (The mushrooms may be prepared to this point up to 1 day in advance. Refrigerate the mushrooms and bring them to room temperature 30 minutes before continuing.)

7. Bake the mushrooms until the liquid in the baking dish is simmering and the mushrooms and filling are heated through, about 20 minutes. Serve the mushrooms very hot, spooning some of the liquid in the pan over them.

Hominy with Huitlacoche

Hominy has a chickpea-like crunch, that blends beautifully with the huitlacoche's corny flavor, and the manchego's tang. This terrific side dish was created by Patricia Williams, a Native American, who left her imprint on several well-known New York restaurants. Serve it with Mushroom Fried Chicken (page 134) or as a main-dish brunch treat. If huitlacoches (weet-la-coach-ayes) are unavailable, substitute hedgehogs or creminis.

SERVES 6 AS A SIDE DISH

4 tablespoons (½ stick) unsalted
    butter
4 tablespoons chopped shallots
2 tablespoons chopped garlic
1 can (29 ounces) hominy, rinsed and
    drained
1 cup dry white wine
2 cups Light Chicken Stock (page 280) or
    canned low-sodium chicken broth
8 ounces huitlacoche
3 tablespoons grated manchego cheese or
    Parmesan cheese
¼ cup chopped fresh cilantro
Kosher or sea salt and freshly ground
    black pepper

1. Melt 2 tablespoons of the butter in a large, heavy skillet over medium heat until foaming. Add the shallots and cook until translucent but not browned, about 3 minutes.

Add the garlic and continue cooking 2 minutes.

2. Add the hominy and stir until coated with butter and shallots. Pour in the wine. Cook until it is nearly all absorbed, about 15 minutes. Add the stock and cook at a simmer until 2 tablespoons liquid remain, about 30 minutes.

3. Melt 1 tablespoon of the butter in a medium-size skillet over medium heat until foaming. Cook the huitlacoche with its juices until no liquid remains in the pan, about 4 minutes. Add the huitlacoche to the hominy, cover, and cook for 2 minutes. Remove the skillet from the heat. Stir in the remaining 1 tablespoon butter, cheese, cilantro, and salt and pepper to taste. Serve hot.

Whole Grain Timbales with Wild Mushrooms

*SERVES 5 AS A
FIRST COURSE*

I love the presentation of these tasty, good-for-you timbales. With a portobello cap—or, if you overturn the timale, a portobello base—and a ring of greens, you will be tempted by more than the aroma and the enticing bits of mushroom. You can serve the timbales as a first course, but they also make a great light meal with the addition of a salad of mesclun or mâche. If you have colorful or decorated ramekins, don't bother unmolding the timbales.

⅓ cup wheat berries

⅓ cup pearl barley

About 2 tablespoons olive oil

Kosher or sea salt

⅓ cup kasha

4 ounces yellowfoot mushrooms,
   cleaned and cut into ¾-inch
   pieces

4 ounces black trumpet mushrooms,
   cleaned and cut into ¾-inch
   pieces

Freshly ground pepper

1 leek (white part only), cleaned
   (see box, page 79)

2 tablespoons Garlic Mayonnaise
   (page 28)

2 tablespoons finely chopped chives

2 tablespoons finely chopped
   fresh parsley

5 Roasted Portobello Caps
   (page 193)

1. Place the wheat berries and barley in separate medium-size bowls, add water to cover by 1 inch in each bowl, and soak for at least 3 hours or for as long as overnight.

2. Brush the insides of five 3½-inch (4-ounce) ramekins with **just** enough olive oil to coat.

3. Bring a large pot of salted water to a boil. Add the kasha and boil gently for 3 minutes. Drain the wheat berries, add them to the pot, and continue cooking 4 minutes. Drain the barley, add it to the pot, and cook another 8 minutes. All the grains should be tender, not mushy. Drain and place in a medium-size bowl.

4. Preheat the oven to 325°F.

5. Slice the leek into matchsticks. Line up the matchsticks and cut them into 1-inch lengths.

6. Heat 1 tablespoon olive oil in a medium-size sauté pan over medium high. Sauté the mushrooms until they give up their liquid, about 6 minutes. Season to taste with salt and pepper and mix them into the grains.

7. In the same sauté pan, heat 1 teaspoon olive oil over medium heat. Add the leeks and sauté, stirring, until translucent yet still soft, about 3 minutes.

8. Stir the mayonnaise, chives, and parsley into the grain-mushroom mixture. It should be a bit stiff. Spoon the mixture into the ramekins, filling up to the top. Top each ramekin with a few strands of cooked leek.

9. Place the ramekins in a roasting pan. Place the pan in the oven. Pour hot water into the pan to reach halfway up the side of the ramekins.

10. Bake the timbales for 30 to 35 minutes. Timbales are done when the leeks are crispy and the grain mixture begins to pull away from the sides of the ramekins.

11. About 10 minutes before the end of cooking, set a portobello cap, gill side down, on top of each ramekin to heat through. Serve the grain timbales in the ramekins or reverse onto a plate, then quickly turn right side up onto a salad plate.

Cabbage Rolls Stuffed with Winter Mushrooms and Kasha

These wholesome, enticing rolls enfold wild mushrooms, spinach, and nutty kasha bathed in a surprise tomato sauce. While the cabbage preparation requires patience, it pays off in flavor. If you would like a completely vegetarian dish, replace the chicken broth with water. The rolls are best when allowed to sit, at least briefly, for a short period after the initial baking.

Kosher or sea salt

1 medium (about 2½ pounds) head of Savoy
     cabbage

2 tablespoons olive oil

1 tablespoon unsalted butter

1 pound winter mushrooms, such as black
     trumpets, yellowfoots, or hedgehogs,
     cleaned and coarsely chopped

½ cup (packed) steamed spinach (about
     8 ounces fresh spinach leaves), coarsely
     chopped or ½ cup frozen chopped
     spinach, thawed and squeezed dry

¾ cup kasha (buckwheat groats)

1 large egg white

1 medium onion, finely diced

1½ cups Light Chicken Stock (page 280) or
     water

½ cup walnuts, coarsely chopped

Freshly ground black pepper

3 cups Sweet-and-Sour Tomato Sauce
     (page 285)

1. Bring a large pot of salted water to a boil over high heat.

2. Using a paring knife, cut the core from the cabbage, remove any wilted or yellow leaves. Carefully remove 20 of the largest outermost leaves, working slowly to keep the leaves intact. Cut away the thickest part (the lower third) of the central rib from each leaf. This will leave a roughly circular leaf with a V-shaped notch. Add half of the leaves to the boiling water, press gently with a spoon to submerge them, and cook until wilted and barely tender but not mushy, about 4 minutes. Place a colander in a bowl and using a wire skimmer or slotted spoon, carefully lift out the cabbage leaves and place in the colander. Let the water return to a boil and repeat with the remaining cabbage leaves.

3. Rinse the cabbage leaves under cold lightly running water until cool enough to handle, then drain them as thoroughly as possible. Spread out on kitchen towels to drain.

4. Heat 1 tablespoon of the oil and the butter in a large (12-inch) skillet over medium-high heat until the butter is bubbling. Add the mushrooms a handful at a time, stirring each until wilted enough to make room for more. Cook, stirring, until all the mushrooms are tender, about 5 minutes. Season to taste with salt. Transfer the mushrooms to a large bowl, add the spinach, and set them aside.

5. Combine the kasha and egg white in a small bowl and stir until the kasha is coated. Heat the remaining 1 tablespoon oil in the skillet over medium heat and add the onion. Cook, stirring, until wilted and just beginning to brown, about 5 minutes. Stir in the kasha and cook until the grains swell slightly and separate. Pour in the stock and heat to boiling. Lower the heat, cover, and simmer until the kasha is tender and the liquid is absorbed, about 20 minutes. Add the cooked kasha and walnuts to the mushroom mixture and stir to mix. Season with salt and pepper.

6. Stir ½ cup of water into the tomato sauce. Spread 1 cup of the tomato sauce over the bottom of an 11 × 9-inch baking dish.

7. Carefully remove one of the leaves from the towels to the work surface. If it tears don't fret. Place the leaf outer side down and with the V-shaped notch toward you. Gently spread the leaf out to its full size, including the folds that will have occurred along the leaf's edge. Overlap the 2 edges of the cut made by removing the rib to make a rough circle that forms a shallow cup. Place about ½ cup of the kasha filling in the center of the leaf about one third up from the bottom. Fold the bottom of the leaf over the filling, then fold both sides over the filling. Roll the filling away from you to form a neat cabbage roll. Make sure the filling is completely enclosed and the roll is neat and compact, or the rolls will fall apart when baked and served. If you cannot easily lift and move the roll without its flopping about use a toothpick pushed through the roll to hold it together. Place the roll, folded side underneath, in the prepared baking dish.

Continue with the remaining leaves and filling, placing the rolls side by side in the baking dish. You should have from 16 to 20 rolls. Pour the remaining sauce over the rolls and shake the dish a little to distribute the sauce evenly. Cover the dish with aluminum foil. (The cabbage may be prepared to this point up to 2 days in advance. Refrigerate the dish and bring it to room temperature at least 1 hour before baking.)

8. Preheat the oven to 350°F.

9. Bake the cabbage rolls 30 minutes. If you are serving the dish at once, remove the foil and continue baking until the sauce around the center rolls is bubbling and the edges of the casserole are browned, about 20 minutes. (If you are making the cabbage rolls in advance, cool the cabbage to room temperature, cover the dish tightly with aluminum foil, and refrigerate for up to 2 days. To reheat, let the

covered dish of cabbage rolls stand at room temperature about 1½ hours. Place the covered dish in a 325°F oven for 30 minutes. Remove the foil and check the cabbage. If the sauce is too thick, pour about ¼ cup of water over the rolls and shake the pan gently to mix. Continue baking, uncovered, until the cabbage rolls are heated through.)

10. Serve hot, removing the toothpicks, if used, first.

Many Fragrant Vegetables Fried Rice

SERVES 6 AS A
SIDE DISH OR 3
AS A MAIN
COURSE

*I*f you're like me, there are many nights when only Chinese food will do, delivered in tidy white boxes and accompanied by a zillion accoutrements. You probably also wonder what to do with all the leftover rice. Use it to create Vegetable Fried Rice, which tastes much better made at home. One of the nicest things about homemade Chinese is getting to inhale the aroma of fresh vegetables, aromatic mushrooms, and soy sauce as they meld in the wok.

If your wok, like most home woks, doesn't get blazing hot, spread the rice mixture along its sides to help it brown and sizzle.

4 tablespoons vegetable oil

3 scallions (both white and green parts), trimmed and thinly sliced

2 tablespoons chopped peeled ginger

3 cloves garlic, minced

8 ounces assorted mushrooms, such as black trumpet, lobster, and bluefoot mushrooms, cleaned, trimmed, and sliced very thin

¼ cup Light Chicken Stock (page 280) or canned low-sodium chicken broth

3 tablespoons Mushroom Soy Sauce (page 255) or good-quality soy sauce

1 tablespoon oyster sauce or hoisin sauce (optional)

1 cup fresh bean sprouts

1 small onion, finely diced

½ cup thinly diced Chinese long beans or green beans, halved lengthwise before dicing

3 cups cooked long-grain or brown rice (1 cup raw)

½ cup chopped cooked broccoli rabe or broccoli stems

¼ cup finely chopped blanched fresh spinach (about ½ small bunch spinach before blanching)

1. Place a wok over high heat and add 2 tablespoons of the vegetable oil. Swirl the wok to coat the sides with oil. Add the scallions, ginger, and garlic and swish them around in the oil until the ginger is fragrant, about 30 seconds. Add the mushrooms and stir-fry until coated with the ginger mixture and softened, about 2 minutes. Add the stock, 1 tablespoon of the soy sauce, and the oyster sauce, and toss until there is just enough sauce to coat the mushrooms generously, about 3 minutes. Remove from the heat and spoon the mushrooms into a small bowl.

2. Wipe the wok clean. Then return it to high heat, and add the remaining 2 tablespoons oil. Add the bean sprouts, onion, and beans and stir-fry until the onions are wilted and the beans are bright green, about 3 minutes. Add the rice, broccoli, and spinach and stir-fry until all the ingredients are evenly distributed and the rice begins to sizzle, about 2 minutes. (If the rice doesn't show much sizzle, spread it in an even layer about half way up the sides of the wok. Leave it there, without stirring, until it starts to sizzle.) Add the remaining 2 tablespoons soy sauce and stir-fry until it is evenly distributed. Add the mushrooms and toss until warmed through. Remove from the heat and transfer the rice to a serving platter. Serve immediately.

Down-Home Dirty Rice with Mousserons

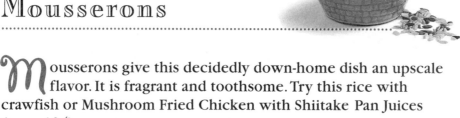

Mousserons give this decidedly down-home dish an upscale flavor. It is fragrant and toothsome. Try this rice with crawfish or Mushroom Fried Chicken with Shiitake Pan Juices (page 134).

SERVES 6

4 cups Light Chicken Stock (page 280), canned low-sodium chicken broth, or water

Necks, giblets, and livers from 2 chickens or 1 turkey

2 tablespoons unsalted butter

½ cup finely chopped celery

½ cup finely chopped red bell pepper

½ cup finely chopped onion

8 ounces mousserons, cleaned

1½ cups long-grain rice

Kosher or sea salt

⅓ cup chopped scallion

2 tablespoons chopped fresh flat-leaf parsley

Hot pepper sauce (optional)

1. Heat the stock in a medium-size saucepan over low heat. Add the chicken necks, gizzards, and hearts, cover, and simmer until the meat pulls easily from the neck, about 40 minutes. Drain, reserving the cooking liquid. You should have about 4 cups. Keep the cooking liquid warm. Pull the meat from the chicken necks and finely chop the giblets and livers.

2. Coarsely chop the chicken livers. Melt the butter in a medium-size saucepan over medium heat until foaming. Add the celery, pepper, onion, and livers and sauté, stirring occasionally, until the onion is wilted, about 6 minutes. Add the mushrooms, increase the heat to high, and cook until the vegetables begin to brown, about 5 minutes. Add the rice and stir until coated with butter. Add the reserved cooking liquid and bring to a boil. Season lightly with salt. Stir the rice, reduce the heat, cover, and simmer.

3. Cover without stirring until the rice is tender and most of the liquid is absorbed, about 15 minutes. Remove from the heat, stir in the scallion, parsley, salt to taste, and hot pepper sauce if desired. Let stand 3 to 5 minutes before serving.

Lidia Bastianich's Risotto with St-Georges Mushrooms

SERVES 6 AS A FIRST COURSE

Risotto is a dish that some chefs take to ethereal heights, far outshining its humble country origins. Lidia Bastianich, chef and owner of Felidia restaurant in Manhattan, is one of these chefs. In spring, she makes it with St-Georges mushrooms, which add a discreetly earthy note. It is delicious with more St-Georges shaved raw over the top. Cèpes make an outstanding substitute, and can be used raw as a garnish. Any other exotic mushroom must be cooked first.

8 ounces St-Georges mushrooms, cleaned and stem ends trimmed
2 tablespoons plus 2 teaspoons unsalted butter
Kosher or sea salt and freshly ground black pepper
3 tablespoons extra virgin olive oil
¾ cup finely chopped onion
2 tablespoons minced shallot
2 cups Arborio or Carnaroli rice
⅓ cup dry white wine
5½ to 6 cups Light Chicken Stock (page 280) or canned low-sodium chicken broth, kept hot
2 tablespoons chopped fresh flat-leaf parsley
⅓ cup freshly grated Parmigiano-Reggiano cheese or other Parmesan cheese

1. Set aside 3 to 4 of the firmest and prettiest mushrooms. Slice the remaining mushrooms ½-inch thick.

2. Melt 2 tablespoons of the butter in a large skillet over medium heat until foaming. Add the sliced mushrooms and cook, stirring, until they begin to give up liquid, about 3 minutes. Increase the heat to medium-high and continue cooking, stirring occasionally, until the liquid is evaporated and the mushrooms begin to brown, about 8 minutes. Season to taste with salt and pepper and set aside.

3. Heat the olive oil in a wide, heavy, 4-quart flameproof casserole over medium heat. Add the onion and shallot and cook, stirring often, until light golden brown, about 8 minutes. Add the rice and stir until the edges turn translucent, 1 to 2 minutes. Add the wine and stir until completely evaporated. Add about ½ cup of the hot stock. Stir until all the stock has been absorbed. Continue adding stock in small batches, enough to completely moisten the rice each time, and stirring until it has been absorbed, until the rice is tender but still firm, about 18 minutes from the time the wine was added.

4. About 10 minutes into the cooking time add the sautéed mushrooms. Adjust the heat so the rice cooks at a very gentle simmer throughout and season the rice from time to time with salt.

5. Stir in the chopped parsley and remove the casserole from the heat. Stir in the remaining 2 teaspoons butter until melted. Stir in about half of the cheese, check the seasoning, and serve immediately, ladled into warm, shallow bowls. If you have a truffle shaver, use it to slice the reserved mushrooms over the risotto at the table. If not, slice the mushrooms as thin as possible at the last minute with a mandoline or very sharp knife. Pass the remaining cheese separately.

Risotto with Corn and Chanterelles

**SERVES 4 AS A
FIRST COURSE**

I made this immensely satisfying risotto with chanterelles found near our house in upstate New York. They were so dewy, fresh, and perfumed, I could hardly wait to get them into the skillet! To intensify the corn flavor, replace the chanterelles with huitlacoche.

3 cups Light Chicken Stock (page 280) or
    canned low-sodium chicken broth
2 tablespoons unsalted butter
1 onion, finely chopped
1 cup Arborio rice
½ cup white wine
Kosher or sea salt and freshly ground
    black pepper
1 tablespoon olive oil
8 ounces chanterelles, trimmed, cleaned,
    and sliced ¼ inch thick
2 shallots, finely minced
2 teaspoons minced garlic
1 ear of corn, cooked and kernels removed,
    or ¾ cup defrosted frozen corn
½ cup milk
2 tablespoons chopped fresh herbs, such as
    chervil, chives, and parsley

1. Place the stock in a medium-size saucepan and heat to a simmer over medium heat. Reduce the heat and keep warm.

2. Melt 1 tablespoon of the butter in a large, heavy saucepan over medium heat until foaming. Add the onion and sauté until wilted but not browned, 2 minutes. Stir in the rice to coat with butter. Pour in the wine and cook 1 minute.

3. Reduce the heat to low and stir in 1 ladleful of stock at a time. As soon as each addition is absorbed by the rice, add another ladleful. Cook, stirring, until just just ½ cup stock remains and the rice is tender but still firm, about 20 minutes. Season to taste with salt and pepper. Turn off the heat and cover.

4. Heat the remaining 1 tablespoon butter and the olive oil in a medium-size sauté pan over medium-high heat. Add the mushrooms and sauté until they give up their liquid, about 2 minutes. Add the shallots and garlic and reduce the heat to medium. Continue cooking until the shallots are soft and translucent, 1 to 2 minutes. Season to taste with salt and pepper.

5. About 2 minutes before serving, add the corn and milk to the mushrooms. Swirl it around until the milk is hot. Remove from the heat, and stir in 1 tablespoon of the herbs.

6. Warm the remaining chicken stock and stir it into the risotto. Ladle the risotto into soup plates. Top with the chanterelles and garnish with the remaining fresh herbs.

Mushroom Chili

MAKES 8 CUPS, SERVES 4 AS A MAIN COURSE

Rich, chunky, and tongue-tingling spicy, this chili is guaranteed to carry the crowd through overtime at any Super Bowl party. Don't be put off by the long ingredient list—once the beans have soaked overnight, this chili is quickly prepared. It can be doubled and is even better when made a day or two in advance and reheated. Serve over brown or white rice with baked tortilla chips and garnish with your favorite fixings.

1 cup dried calypso beans or black beans, soaked (see box, this page), or 3 cups drained canned black beans

3 tablespoons vegetable oil

1 large onion, diced

4 large cloves garlic, minced

1 large jalapeño, seeds removed, minced

2 medium (about 12 ounces total) portobello mushrooms, stemmed, cleaned and diced ½ inch

3 large (about 12 ounces total) oyster or chicken of the woods mushrooms, trimmed and cut into ½-inch dice

2 teaspoons chili powder

2 teaspoons ground coriander

1 teaspoon ground cumin

2 cups canned diced plum tomatoes or canned whole plum tomatoes with their liquid, finely diced

2 tablespoons chopped fresh oregano

1½ teaspoons kosher or sea salt

2 tablespoons fresh lime juice or cider vinegar, or more to taste

2 tablespoons chopped fresh cilantro, or more to taste

½ teaspoon hot red pepper sauce, or more to taste

Sour cream (optional)

Grated Cheddar cheese (optional)

1. If using dried beans, place them in a medium-size saucepan with cold water to cover by 4 inches. Heat to a boil. Reduce the heat to a simmer and cook the beans, uncovered, until tender, about 45 minutes. Drain the beans, reserving the cooking liquid.

2. Heat the oil in a 4-quart pot over medium heat. Add the onion, garlic, and jalapeño. Sauté, stirring occasionally, until the onion is wilted, about 4 minutes. Add the

To Soak Beans

Rinse and pick over the beans and place them in a medium-size bowl. Pour in enough cold water to cover by 4 inches. Soak the beans at cool room temperature for 8 hours or overnight in the refrigerator. Drain and rinse the beans and continue with the recipe.

For a quick soak, rinse and pick over the beans and place them in a large pot. Add cold water to cover by 4 to 6 inches, bring to a boil, and boil for 1 minute. Remove from the heat and let stand, covered, for 1 hour. Drain and rinse the beans and continue with the recipe.

portobellos, oyster mushrooms, chili powder, coriander, and cumin. Sauté until the mushrooms have absorbed the oil and begin to shrink, about 4 minutes. Add the tomatoes, oregano, and salt. Heat to a boil, then lower the heat to a simmer. Cover the pot and cook until the portobellos are very soft, about 20 minutes.

3. Add the beans and enough of the reserved cooking liquid to cover the mushroom mixture (about 1 cup). Simmer for 10 minutes.

4. Stir in the lime juice, cilantro, and hot pepper sauce. Taste and adjust the seasoning, adding more lime juice, cilantro, pepper sauce, or salt to taste. Serve hot, passing sour cream and grated Cheddar cheese, if desired.

Roasted Portobello Caps with Warm Bean Filling

SERVES 4

The anchovy and herbs justly impose themselves on this creamy filling of beans, tomato, and yellow pepper. Small, firm portobello or large cremini caps are a perfect container for this Tuscan filling.

½ cup dried baby lima beans, white beans or flageolets, picked over and soaked (page 215) or 1½ cups canned small white (Great Northern) beans, rinsed and drained

4 small (about 12 ounces) portobellos, with caps about 3½ inches across, trimmed and cleaned

5 tablespoons extra virgin olive oil

Kosher or sea salt and freshly ground black pepper

1 tablespoon fresh lemon juice

1 teaspoon Dijon mustard

1 teaspoon anchovy paste or minced canned anchovies

6 to 8 fresh sage leaves, finely chopped, or 2 teaspoons crumbled dried sage

½ teaspoon fresh thyme leaves or dried thyme, crumbled

1 medium-size ripe tomato or 2 large ripe plum tomatoes, cored and cut into ¼-inch dice (about ¾ cup)

1 large yellow bell pepper, roasted (see box, page 163) peeled, stemmed, seeded, and cut into ¼-inch dice or ⅔ cup diced drained canned roasted red pepper

⅓ cup thinly sliced scallion greens or chopped fresh parsley

1. Drain and rinse the beans. Place them in a small saucepan of simmering water and cook until tender, from 30 minutes to 1 hour, depending on the type of bean. Add hot water, if necessary, to keep the beans well submerged. Warm the canned beans if using.

2. Preheat the oven to 400°F.

3. Cut the stems of the portobellos flush with the caps. Clean and trim the stems. Brush a baking sheet with 1 tablespoon of the oil. Place the mushroom caps, gill side down, on the baking sheet. Brush the mushroom caps and stems with 2 tablespoons of the oil and sprinkle with salt and pepper. Roast until the edges of the caps are sizzling and browned, about 15 minutes. Turn the mushroom caps over and continue roasting until a fork slips easily into the cap, about 5 minutes. Remove the caps and let cool to room temperature. Remove and finely dice the mushroom stems.

4. Beat the remaining 2 tablespoons olive oil, the lemon juice, mustard, anchovy, sage, and thyme in a small bowl until blended. Add the tomato, pepper, scallion greens, and diced mushroom stems. Toss to coat. Drain the beans and add them to the bowl. Toss well. Place the mushroom caps, gill side up, on serving plates and spoon the white bean salad into the caps. Serve warm.

A Bean Is a Bean

At Aux Delices, we carried a few varieties of limited-edition dried beans. They had cute names and came with little histories. We began to wonder when we saw similar-looking beans, such as black-and-white mottled calypso, called by different names for half the price. Taste tests showed the difference between these heirloom beans and their disinherited cousins to be negligible.

Matsutakes Simmered with Chinese Black Beans

SERVES 2

You wouldn't think that a simple mushroom could radiate so much flavor throughout a simmered dish. But the matsutake does, and when combined with Asian flavors, it is at its most flavorful. This little plate could be served as tapas, over rice as a vegetarian dinner, or as a nest for grilled filet mignon, pork chops, or chicken breasts. If you can't get matsutake, use honshimeji mushrooms.

2 large (about 8 ounces each) matsutake
 mushrooms, cleaned, or 12 ounces
 small matsutakes

½ cup Light Chicken Stock (page 280) or
 canned low-sodium chicken broth

2 tablespoons Mushroom Soy Sauce
 (page 255) or good-quality soy sauce

2 tablespoons Chinese rice wine, mirin
 (Japanese seasoned wine), or sherry

2 teaspoons minced peeled fresh ginger

1½ teaspoons Asian sesame oil

2 scallions, trimmed and thinly sliced, white
 and green parts separate

1½ teaspoons fermented Chinese black
 beans (see Note)

2 tablespoons cold water

1 teaspoon cornstarch

1. Trim and discard the stems from the matsutakes. Cut the caps in half, then cut them crosswise into ½-inch slices. (If using small matsutakes, simply trim the tough parts of the stems.)

2. Combine the stock, soy sauce, rice wine, ginger, sesame oil, and scallion whites in a medium-size saucepan. Heat to a boil over medium-high heat. Add the mushrooms. Reduce the heat and simmer, uncovered, until the mushrooms are tender, about 15 minutes. Stir often.

3. Add the black beans and scallion greens. Stir 2 tablespoons cold water and the cornstarch together in a small bowl until the cornstarch is dissolved. Stir into the mushroom mixture. Reheat to a simmer, then simmer until the sauce is opaque and thickened, about 30 seconds. Serve hot.

Note: Salted black beans, sometimes labeled fermented black beans, are small black soy beans that are fermented slowly over a period of several months. They are available, usually in small plastic bags or cans, in Chinese and some Asian groceries. The beans should feel soft and supple through the bag. If possible, avoid black beans that are seasoned, usually with ginger or five-spice powder. Those seasonings can always be added fresh to the dish if you like.

Dal with Escarole and Cremini

SERVES 4 TO 6

This thick, rich mixture is based on the Indian bean dish called dal. In India, dal can be served as a main course, a porridgey soup—great on a blustery day—or, most frequently, a side dish. The pungent spices find an earthy partner in cremini. Left to simmer, the porridge thickens up. Use thickened dal as a bed for grilled chicken breast, a light meal with a salad alongside, or as a room-temperature side dish.

1 pound (about 2 cups) yellow split peas

6 cups Light Chicken Stock (page 280), canned low-sodium chicken broth, or water

2 teaspoons kosher or sea salt or Seasoning Salt (page 253), or more as needed

1 small (about ¾ pound) head of escarole

7 tablespoons olive oil

1 pound cremini, shiitakes, or portobellos, or a mix of the three, trimmed and sliced

4 cloves garlic, thinly sliced

2 teaspoons fennel seeds (optional)

1 teaspoon anise seeds

¼ teaspoon crushed red pepper flakes

1 tablespoon fresh lemon juice

1. Pick over the split peas and, if necessary, remove any stones or other grit. Rinse the peas under cold running water and drain thoroughly. Heat the stock and salt to a boil in a medium-size, heavy-bottomed saucepan and stir in the peas. Bring back to a boil, reduce the heat, and simmer, uncovered, until very tender, about 40 minutes. Stir often, especially toward the end of cooking, to prevent sticking.

2. Remove any wilted or bruised outer leaves from the escarole. Cut off and discard the leaf tips. Cut the escarole lengthwise in half, then cut out the core. Cut the escarole cross-wise into 2-inch pieces. Wash well, changing the water if necessary, until all grit is removed. Drain and dry well, preferably in a salad spinner.

3. Heat 2 tablespoons of the oil in a large (12-inch) skillet over medium heat. Stir in the mush-rooms, increase the heat to high, and toss to coat with oil. Sauté until lightly browned, about 5 minutes. Transfer the mushrooms to a bowl and keep them warm. Add 1 tablespoon of the remaining oil and the garlic to the skillet. Cook just until fragrant, about 10 seconds. Stir in the escarole, in batches if necessary, and cook until wilted. Remove the skillet from the heat and stir the escarole into the peas. Simmer 3 minutes.

4. Heat the remaining 4 table-spoons oil in a small skillet over medium heat. Stir in the fennel, anise, and red pepper flakes. Heat just until the seeds sizzle and become fragrant, about 30 seconds. Remove the seasoned oil from the heat.

5. Stir the lemon juice into the dal. Taste and add salt if necessary. Serve hot, topped with mushrooms and drizzled with some seasoned oil.

Note: The dal can be reheated. You will need to stir in water until the dal is the consistency you like, less water for a thick side dish, more for a soup. Adjust the seasoning before serving.

White Bean Purée with White Truffle

**MAKES 1 CUP,
SERVES 4 AS
AN APPETIZER**

When beans began entering our culinary vocabulary in the Sixties, they were banished to the same chapter as that vegetarian bellwether, brown rice. Luckily, the lowly pod has bootstrapped its way into major restaurants. This white bean purée is as versatile as the Little Black Dress. Spread a few creamy spoonfuls under a veal chop or fish steak, stuff into a hollowed-out tomato or cremini, or simply adorn little toasts.

⅓ cup dried white beans, picked over and
    soaked (see box, page 215)
2 teaspoons olive oil
1 teaspoon plus 1 tablespoon white
    truffle oil
2 cloves garlic, minced
¼ ounce white truffle, thinly sliced
    (optional)

¼ teaspoon kosher or sea salt
¼ teaspoon freshly ground black pepper
Toast (optional)
1 teaspoon finely chopped fresh herbs,
    such as parsley or chives

1. Rinse and drain the beans. Place in a heavy saucepan, add enough cold water to cover by about 2 inches, and bring to a boil over high heat. Skim the foam from the surface, reduce the heat, and simmer, stirring from time to time, until they are tender and easily break when pinched between 2 fingers, 1 to 1½ hours.

2. Heat the olive oil and 1 teaspoon white truffle oil in a very small sauté pan. Over medium heat, add the garlic and sauté until soft

Squirrel Food

White truffles are so rare and expensive, that it's a good idea to keep an eye on the ones you've purchased. David Michael Cane, a food radio show host, has a story we all should heed. When in St. Louis on food business, he was put in charge of a bundle of white truffles nestled in newspaper. Their powerful aroma was perfuming his hotel room, so he took them out to the balcony. He ducked into the room to get some reading material. Upon returning, the bundle was gone! He went absolutely mad with confusion, doubt, fear, and rage. Then a slight noise attracted his attention to the neighboring balcony, where a squirrel was licking its chops. To this day, he swears that squirrel winked at him.

but not burned, about 4 minutes. Set aside.

3. Drain the beans, reserving the cooking liquid.

4. Place the beans in a food processor with 2 tablespoons of the cooking liquid, the white truffle (if using), the remaining 1 tablespoon white truffle oil, the garlic with its oil, salt, and pepper and purée until a bit thicker than mashed potatoes.

Set aside some cooking liquid to thin out the purée just before serving. (Covered, the purée will keep 3 days in the refrigerator.)

5. Bring the purée to room temperature. Adjust the consistency by adding cooking liquid. Spoon the purée onto toast, if desired, or onto a plate. Garnish with chopped fresh herbs.

Pasta with Hedgehog and Oyster Mushrooms

*D*on't be daunted by the long ingredient list; this main-dish pasta is meant to accommodate whatever is fresh and available at your local market. Feel free to experiment with different mushrooms, to substitute ham for poultry, and Middle Eastern couscous for orzo. As is, this one-pot meal bursts with a variety of flavors and textures.

SERVES 6

2 tablespoons olive oil

1 medium onion, diced

2 cloves garlic, thinly sliced

8 ounces oyster mushrooms, cleaned and torn into ½-inch strips

8 ounces hedgehog mushrooms, trimmed, cleaned, and sliced ½ inch thick

4 cups Light Chicken Stock (page 280), canned low-sodium chicken broth, or water

12 ounces tender, young green beans, trimmed and cut into ½-inch lengths

1½ cups canned diced tomatoes, with their liquid

1 small zucchini or yellow squash, trimmed and cut into ¼-inch dice

1 cup diced smoked turkey, smoked chicken, smoked turkey sausage, or roasted turkey or chicken

Kosher or sea salt and freshly ground black pepper

1½ cups toasted orzo (see Note)

2 teaspoons fresh lemon juice

2 tablespoons chopped fresh flat-leaf parsley

Freshly grated Parmesan cheese (optional)

1. Heat the olive oil in a heavy 4-quart pot over medium heat. Add the onion and garlic and cook, stirring occasionally, until they begin to brown, about 5 minutes. Stir in the oyster and hedgehog mushrooms. Cook until they wilt and begin to give off their liquid, about 4 minutes. Increase the heat to medium-high and continue cooking until the liquid is evaporated and the mushrooms begin to brown, about 4 minutes.

2. Add the stock, green beans, tomatoes, zucchini, and smoked turkey or chicken and heat to a boil. Add salt and pepper to taste. Stir in the orzo and bring back to a boil. Reduce the heat and simmer, stirring constantly for 1 minute. (The orzo will stick quite a bit at first, then less as you continue stirring.) Cover the pot and cook, stirring very often and scraping the bottom and sides of the pot, until the orzo is tender, about 15 minutes. The mixture should be creamy and dense, like risotto or oatmeal.

3. Stir in the lemon juice and parsley. Season to taste, if necessary, with salt and pepper. Cover the pot and let stand 3 minutes. Serve very hot, passing grated cheese if desired.

Note: To toast the orzo, place it in a large skillet over medium-low heat and toss frequently, until uniformly golden brown. Cool completely. If you like the taste of toasted orzo, you can toast the whole box at once, cool it completely, and store it in an airtight container.

Fettuccine with Shiitakes

**SERVES 2 AS A
MAIN COURSE,
4 AS A FIRST
COURSE**

Mario Batali is a feisty, ponytailed redhead whose motto could be "the pasta course waits for nobody." Mario hosted one of the first TVFN cooking shows, "Molto Mario," where he entertained viewers with real-people cooking peppered with unintentionally hilarious asides. Po, his tiny converted diner in Greenwich Village, bustles with the exuberance of an Italian fishing village. Now his second New York success, the restaurant Babbo, is opened and thriving as well as a third, Lupa. When I'm desperate for dinner, this soothing, simple, and easy-to-shop-for recipe of his invariably comes to the rescue.

5 tablespoons extra virgin olive oil

2 cloves garlic, thinly sliced

8 ounces shiitakes, stemmed, cleaned, and cut in half

1 cup Light Chicken Stock (page 280) or canned low-sodium chicken broth

2 ounces Cinzano or sweet red vermouth

8 ounces fresh fettuccine

1 bunch of arugula, cleaned and chopped (1 cup)

1. Heat 3 tablespoons of the olive oil in a large sauté pan over medium heat. Sauté the garlic until soft but not burned. Add the shiitakes and cook until they give up their liquid, 2 to 3 minutes.

2. Pour in the stock and Cinzano. Bring to a boil and boil until reduced by half, about 5 minutes. The sauce should just coat the mushrooms.

3. Bring a large pot of salted water to a boil. Drop in the fettuccine and bring back to a boil. Taste, and drain when it is slightly al dente but no longer crunchy, about 1 minute.

4. Over high heat, toss the arugula into the shiitake sauce until it just wilts. Pour the sauce over the drained pasta and drizzle with the remaining 2 tablespoons olive oil. Serve hot.

Fettuccine with Wild Forest Sauce

SERVES 6

$\mathcal{W}$ hen it all comes down to essence, this is it: your basic pasta with wild mushrooms, brightened with fresh herbs (and smoothed out with cream, if desired). You may substitute dried for fresh fettuccine (about one pound). The sauce may be made ahead.

1 pound Fresh Homemade Pasta (recipe follows)

3 cups Light Chicken Stock (page 280) or canned low-sodium chicken broth

About 3 cups (3 ounces) mixed dried mushrooms, such as porcini, morels, and shiitakes

3 tablespoons unsalted butter

2 shallots, finely chopped

2 cloves garlic, minced

¼ cup heavy (or whipping) cream (optional)

1 bunch of fresh chives, cut on the bias into ½ inch lengths (about ¾ cup)

½ cup finely shredded fresh basil leaves

¼ cup chopped fresh flat-leaf parsley

Kosher or sea salt and freshly ground black pepper

½ cup freshly grated Parmesan cheese, plus more for passing

1. Prepare the pasta dough and cut it into ½-inch-wide noodles according to the directions in the following recipe.

2. Bring the stock to a boil in a small saucepan and pour it over the mushroom mix in a large heatproof bowl. Let stand until the mushrooms are softened, about 20 minutes. Drain through a sieve lined with cheesecloth or a paper towel into a bowl. Press gently on the mushrooms to extract as much liquid as possible. Rinse well and chop the mushrooms coarsely, removing any tough bits as you go. Set the mushrooms and soaking liquid aside separately.

3. Melt the butter in large skillet over medium-high heat until foaming. Add the shallots and garlic and cook, stirring often, until golden brown, about 4 minutes. Add the chopped mushrooms and cook, stirring constantly, until any liquid is evaporated and the mushrooms are sizzling, about 5 minutes. Add the soaking liquid, reduce the heat, and simmer until just enough liquid remains to coat the mushrooms, about 10 minutes.

4. Stir in the cream (if using), the chives, basil, and parsley. Bring to a boil and boil 2 minutes. Season to taste with salt and pepper and keep warm. (The sauce may be made up to 2 days in advance and refrigerated. Gently warm in a small saucepan before using.)

5. Cook the fettuccine in a large pot of boiling salted water until al dente (tender but firm), 1 to 3 minutes. Measure and reserve about 1 cup of the pasta cooking liquid and drain the pasta throughly in a colander. Return the pasta to the pot and stir in the mushroom sauce. Add enough of the reserved cooking liquid to make a creamy sauce that coats the pasta well. Season to taste with salt and pepper. Stir in ½ cup of the grated cheese and transfer the pasta to 6 warm, shallow bowls. Pass additional grated cheese separately.

Fresh Homemade Pasta

This recipe can be used for pappardelle, fettuccine, angel hair, ravioli—any shape or kind of pasta you desire. It makes about 1 pound.

2 cups all-purpose flour, or as needed
3 large eggs
3 teaspoons olive oil

1. Set aside 2 tablespoons of the flour, then combine the rest with the eggs and oil in a food processor. Process until the mixture forms a soft but not sticky ball around the blade and spins with the blade. If necessary, add some or all of the remaining flour. Transfer the mixture to a lightly floured surface.

2. Knead the dough until it is smooth and very elastic, adding small amounts of flour to the surface as necessary. The dough is ready when it doesn't need flour to keep from sticking to your hands and it springs back to its original shape when stretched. Let the pasta rest under an overturned bowl 20 to 30 minutes before continuing.

3. Divide the dough into 6 even pieces if you're working with a pasta machine or 4 even pieces if you're working with a rolling pin. Work with 1 ball at a time, keeping the others under the bowl. Roll out each portion of the dough to about ⅟₁₆ inch thick. (You should be able to read a newspaper through it. If it gets to a point where it snaps when stretched, let the dough rest under a lightly floured kitchen towel for 5 minutes before continuing.)

4. Hang the sheets of pasta over a rack or between the backs of two chairs. Let rest 10 minutes, or until they are no longer so wet that the dough sticks to the knife when cut, but not so dry that it cracks. Cut the pasta sheets with a knife or pizza cutter according to the directions in the recipe. (The noodles can be made up to 4 hours in advance. Store at room temperature in single layers between lightly floured kitchen towels. Cover the top noodle with a floured towel.) Or, the pasta can be left to dry, and then stored in airtight containers for 13 days.

Pappardelle with Rabbit and Wild Mushrooms

With its heady mix of dried and fresh wild mushrooms, this hearty stew is a perfect marriage of deep flavor and tenderness. It's worthy of your most robust aged Bordeaux. If desired, substitute chicken legs for the rabbit, adjusting cooking time as necessary.

Homemade pappardelle may be prepared four hours in advance, then cooked at the last minute.

SERVES 6

RABBIT SAUCE

2 hind legs (about 1½ pounds) of rabbit
(see Note)

Kosher or sea salt or Seasoning Salt
(page 253) and freshly ground
black pepper

1 tablespoon olive oil

1 medium onion, finely chopped

1 rib celery, trimmed and finely
chopped

1 medium carrot, finely chopped

10 cloves garlic, thinly sliced

½ cup dry red wine

1 cup Rich Chicken Stock (page 281),
Rich Meat Stock (page 282), or
canned low-sodium chicken
broth or canned meat broth

2 bay leaves

1 tablespoon finely chopped fresh
rosemary

6 dried juniper berries

1 ounce (about 1½ cups) dried
chanterelles

1 cup boiling water

2 tablespoons unsalted butter

8 ounces fresh chanterelles,
hedgehog, black trumpet, and/or
yellowfoot mushrooms, cleaned
and sliced ¼ inch thick

TO FINISH

1 recipe Fresh Homemade Pasta
(page 224), or 1 pound
store-bought fresh pappardelle
or dried fettuccine

¼ cup chopped fresh flat-leaf
parsley

2 tablespoons unsalted butter

⅓ cup freshly grated Parmesan cheese,
preferably Parmigiano-Reggiano,
plus more to pass

1. To make the rabbit sauce, pat the rabbit legs dry and rub them on all sides with salt and pepper. Heat the oil in a heavy, large skillet over medium heat. Add the rabbit legs and cook, turning, until golden brown on all sides, about 12 minutes. Cover the pan if necessary to reduce splattering.

2. Remove the rabbit and add the onion, celery, carrot, and garlic to the skillet. Sauté, stirring frequently, until browned, about 5 minutes. Pour in the wine and boil until reduced by half, about 2 minutes. Add the stock, bay leaves, rosemary, and juniper. Reduce the heat, cover, and simmer until the rabbit is very tender, about 50 minutes.

3. Cover the dried chanterelles with the boiling water and soak until softened, about 15 minutes. Drain the mushrooms, reserving the liquid. Strain the mushroom liquid through a coffee filter or sieve lined with a double layer of cheesecloth. Rinse the mushrooms thoroughly and, if necessary, cut them into ½-inch-wide strips.

4. Remove the rabbit from the sauce and set aside to cool. Add the soaked mushrooms and the strained soaking liquid to the skillet and heat the sauce to a boil. Boil until the sauce is reduced by one third, about 15 minutes.

5. Remove the rabbit meat from the bone and shred it into ½-inch-wide pieces no longer than 2 inches. Discard any pieces of fat and gristle. Add the shredded rabbit to the sauce.

6. Melt the butter in a large skillet over medium-high heat just until it begins to brown. Add the fresh mushrooms and sauté, stirring, until wilted and lightly browned, about 3 minutes. Add the mushrooms to the sauce and simmer over low heat 5 minutes. (The sauce may be prepared to this point up to 2 days in advance. Refrigerate and heat to simmering before continuing.)

7. To finish, cut the homemade pasta into 5 × 1½ inch ribbons. Cook the pasta in a large pot of boiling salted water just until tender, 30 to 60 seconds, depending on how long the pasta has been standing. (Fresh store-bought pappardelle should take about the same amount of time; cook dried fettuccine according to package directions.) Stir constantly and gently. Set aside about ½ cup of the pasta cooking liquid and drain the pasta in a colander. Return the pasta to the pot over low heat and add the sauce, parsley, and butter. Stir until the butter is melted and the sauce coats the pasta. If necessary, add enough of the reserved pasta cooking liquid to make a sauce that lightly coats the pasta. Stir in the cheese and serve, passing more cheese if you like.

Note: Rabbit is sold at some supermarkets and butcher shops and through mail order (see page 324).

Gnocchi with Honey Mushrooms and Tomatoes

SERVES 2 AS A MAIN COURSE

The ephemeral honey mushroom debuts in gourmet stores in the hottest part of August, offering itself to autumn-hungry gourmands. Here's what I cooked up one oppressively sultry night after a long, hot, perspiring—but inspiring—subway ride home. If you're not lucky enough to catch the honey mushroom, try this recipe with honshimeji or oyster mushrooms.

Kosher or sea salt

1 tablespoon unsalted butter

8 ounces honey mushrooms trimmed
    and cleaned

½ cup Rich Chicken Stock (page 281),
    or canned low-sodium chicken broth

Freshly ground black pepper

8 ounces gnocchi (see Note)

1 teaspoon Truffle Butter (page 256) or
    salted butter

2 tablespoons cored, seeded, and diced
    tomato

1 cup trimmed washed watercress

2 tablespoons chopped fresh herbs
    such as chives, chervil, and
    parsley

¼ cup freshly grated Parmesan cheese
    (optional)

1. Bring a medium-size pot of salted water to the boil.

2. Melt the butter in a large sauté pan over medium heat until foaming. Add the mushrooms, and cook for 4 minutes, or until wilted.

Over high heat, add the stock and boil until it coats the mushrooms, 2 to 3 minutes. Season to taste with salt and pepper.

3. Drop the gnocchi into the boiling water. When they float to the surface, boil 30 seconds more. Drain. Place in a shallow pasta bowl and toss with the Truffle Butter.

4. Add the tomato, watercress, and herbs to the mushrooms. Cook over medium heat, stirring constantly, until the watercress softens, about 1 minute. Pour this sauce over the gnocchi and toss. Adjust the seasoning as necessary. Sprinkle with grated cheese, if using.

Note: Gnocchi are little dumpling-like balls of pasta made with potato mixed into the dough. They are available fresh in Italian markets, as well as gourmet stores and some supermarkets. Look for them in the refrigerator section.

Wild Mushroom Manicotti with Thyme Jus

**MAKES 14 TO
16 MANICOTTI,
SERVES 6**

This recipe can be made with a svelte thyme broth or with a robust tomato sauce. In both, the filling is the same, a smooth, creamy mushroom mélange. The tomato version was the brainchild of our good friend Steven Raichlen. The manicotti and sauces can be made a day ahead and held separately in the refrigerator.

Kosher or sea salt

1 package (8 ounces) manicotti

1 tablespoon olive oil

1 pound of earthy mushrooms, such as
shiitakes, cremini, portobellos, or
fried-chicken mushrooms, cleaned,
trimmed, and sliced ¼-inch thick

1 onion, finely chopped

1 clove garlic, minced

½ teaspoon Seasoning Salt (page 253) or
kosher or sea salt

½ teaspoon freshly ground black pepper

2¼ cups Light Chicken Stock (page 280) or
canned low-sodium chicken broth

1 shallot, finely chopped

2 teaspoons fresh thyme or 1 teaspoon dried
thyme leaves (not powder)

1 large egg, beaten

15 ounces ricotta cheese

½ cup freshly grated Parmesan cheese

Butter, for dish

2 tablespoons chopped fresh chives

1. Bring a large pot of salted
water to a boil. Add the manicotti
and cook according to package
directions. Drain the pasta, then lay
the noodles flat in a large baking
dish so they don't touch. Cover
with plastic wrap, pressing down
lightly to remove any air.

2. Heat the olive oil in a large
sauté pan over high heat. Add the
mushrooms and cook until they
give up some liquid, about 1 minute.
Reduce the heat to medium and
cook until the mushrooms start to
wilt. Add the onion, garlic, ¼ teaspoon Seasoning Salt, and ¼ teaspoon
pepper, and sauté another 3 minutes.
Pour in ¼ cup of the stock and cook

over medium heat until stock is absorbed, about 4 minutes. Set aside
to cool for 15 minutes.

3. Place the remaining 2 cups
stock, the shallot, and thyme in a
medium-size saucepan. Bring to a
boil, reduce the heat, and simmer
10 minutes. (Thyme broth may be
prepared 1 day in advance and kept
in the refrigerator.)

4. Stir together the egg, ricotta,
Parmesan, and remaining salt and
pepper in a mixing bowl. Stir in the
mushrooms and mix thoroughly.

5. Preheat the oven to 350°F.
Butter the bottom and sides of an
11 × 8-inch casserole dish.

6. Using a teaspoon, gently stuff
the manicotti. Place the stuffed manicotti in the casserole dish. Pour the
thyme broth over all. Bake, uncovered, until bubbly, about 30 minutes.

7. Transfer the manicotti to
serving plates. Spoon thyme
broth over each portion and
sprinkle with chopped chives.

Variation: Wild Mushroom Manicotti with Tomato Sauce

Omit step 3. Prepare 1 recipe of
Basic Tomato Sauce (page 284),
adding 1 teaspoon dried oregano
and 1 bay leaf to the tomatoes
before simmering. Instead of
buttering the casserole dish, spoon a
layer of tomato sauce on the bottom.
Lay the manicotti over it, then pour
the rest of the sauce over. Sprinkle ½
cup of Parmesan over the top. Bake
as in step 6. Replace the chive
garnish with chopped parsley.

Hen of the Woods Ravioli

Nothing makes the palate stand up to attention like a garlicky, aromatic surprise package. If possible, take advantage of a fading charcoal fire to cook the ramps in advance. The rest of filling takes just minutes. Use store-bought fresh pasta sheets or Homemade Fresh Pasta (page 224).

3 medium ramps, trimmed or 1 medium
    leek, white and light green parts only
    (see box, page 79)
Olive oil
Kosher or sea salt and freshly ground
    black pepper
3 tablespoons finely diced slab bacon
    or smoked ham
4 ounces hen of the woods, cleaned
    and finely chopped

2 tablespoons heavy (or whipping)
    cream
2 tablespoons chopped fresh chervil or
    parsley
1 large egg
12 sheets of fresh pasta, about 7 × 4½
    inches, homemade (page 224) or
    store-bought (usually labeled
    lasagne sheets)
⅔ cup Light Chicken Stock (page 280)
    or canned low-sodium chicken
    broth
2 tablespoons unsalted butter
½ cup freshly grated Parmesan cheese

Monster Hens

Nothing stops a wild hen of the woods. Left to flourish, it embraces branches, whole living plants, and anything else that gets in its way. One of our more productive mushroom pickers always hauled his weekend harvest up and down New York's inhospitable subway stairs in a clunker of a shopping cart. One haul netted a 42-pound hen of the woods. At that size, there is a lot of woody, undesirable stem. To trim this monster, I took a big knife and hacked away. Embedded in the massive, calloused stem, among the miniature ferns, was a blue plastic doll!

1. Preheat a grill to low, or preheat the broiler.

2. Brush the ramps with the olive oil and sprinkle them with salt and pepper. Grill the ramps, turning often, until lightly charred and tender, about 8 minutes or broil the ramps indoors about 3 inches from the heat. Thinly slice the ramp greens and finely chop the whites. Set aside separately.

3. Place the bacon in a large skillet over medium heat. Stir until it begins to brown. Stir in the mushrooms and ramp whites. Cook until the mushrooms absorb the bacon

Ravioli Tips

To prevent ravioli from bursting, follow these easy steps.

- **Cool the filling completely before filling the pasta.**

- **When sealing the ravioli, use the tines of a fork to crimp the edges shut.**

- **Let the ravioli stand for 10 minutes before cooking to assure the egg-wash seal.**

- **Add olive oil and salt to the water.**

- **Once the water boils, reduce it to a gentle boil for cooking.**

- **Slip the ravioli into the water with a slotted spoon. Immerse it and let the ravioli float off.**

- **Stir the ravioli gently to keep them apart.**

- **Cook the ravioli in batches; if they are crowded they may stick to each other.**

- **Ravioli are done when the pasta no longer has dark spots, except where it billows over the filling.**

- **Slip the ravioli into a colander one or two at a time, using a slotted spoon.**

- **As soon as the ravioli are drained, transfer to individual plates for saucing.**

fat, about 2 minutes. Reduce the heat to low and cook, stirring occasionally, until the mushrooms are tender, about 10 minutes. Add the cream and chervil. Stir until the mushrooms absorb the cream, 1 to 2 minutes. Cool the mushroom filling.

4. Using the egg and pasta sheets, make the ravioli as described in the box on page 232.

5. Add 1 tablespoon olive oil to a large pot of salted water and bring to a boil over high heat. Add the ravioli, bring back to a boil, reduce the heat, and simmer about 4 minutes. Stir gently and frequently to prevent sticking. Using a slotted spoon, carefully transfer the ravioli to a colander.

6. Heat the stock and butter in a large, heavy skillet over medium heat until boiling. Add the ravioli and ramp greens. Swirl the skillet to prevent the ravioli from sticking and simmer until the ravioli are heated through, about 2 minutes. Transfer to 4 shallow serving bowls and sprinkle generously with the Parmesan cheese.

Ravioli Stuffed with Squash, Hazelnuts, and Chanterelles in Sage Butter

MAKES 60
RAVIOLI,
SERVES 10 AS A
FIRST COURSE,
6 AS A MAIN
COURSE

Ravioli always make a wonderful surprise package, but what a surprise these ravioli deliver! The nutty, sweet filling, with its counterpoint of sage butter, could almost be served for dessert. Fall mushrooms and fall squash seem destined to go together.

1 medium (2 pounds) acorn squash or
    similar hard squash
¼ cup hazelnuts, toasted and peeled
    (see box, page 41)
12 fresh sage leaves
4 ounces chanterelles, cleaned, and
    trimmed, cut into ¼-inch dice

6 tablespoons (¾ stick) unsalted
    butter
2 tablespoons finely chopped shallot
Seasoning Salt (page 253) or kosher or
    sea salt and freshly ground
    black pepper
⅓ cup plus 3 tablespoons Light Chicken
    Stock (page 280) or canned
    low-sodium chicken stock
1 large egg
20 sheets of fresh pasta, about
    7 × 4½ inches, homemade (page 224)
    or store-bought (usually labeled
    lasagna sheets)
1 tablespoon olive oil

1. Preheat the oven to 350°F.

2. Cut the squash in half and discard the seeds. Place the halves, cut side down, in a small baking dish. Bake until the flesh is soft, easily pierced with a fork, about 30 to 45 minutes.

3. Place the hazelnuts in a food processor and pulse until crushed but not gluey. Set aside. Chop 8 of the sage leaves into ¼-inch pieces. Leave 4 leaves whole. Set aside.

To Make Ravioli

Beat the egg well with a few drops of water. Arrange 2 pasta sheets side by side. Brush 1 sheet with the beaten egg mixture. Place 6 level teaspoons of filling on top of the brushed pasta, leaving ½ inch from the edges of the pasta sheet and about 2 inches between mounds. Cover with the second pasta sheet. Starting at one of the short edges, press the top sheet against the bottom, working around the filling to seal it in. Cut the filled sheets evenly between the filling into 6 square ravioli. Press the edges of each ravioli with a fork to securely seal in the filling. Repeat with the remaining pasta sheets and filling. Let stand for at least 10 minutes before cooking. (The ravioli may be prepared to this point up to 1 day in advance. Store them in the refrigerator in a single layer on a tray covered with plastic wrap.)

4. Melt 2 tablespoons of the butter until foaming in a large sauté pan over high heat. Sauté the chanterelles until they give up some liquid, about 1 minute, then reduce the heat to medium. Add the shallot and cook until wilted, 2 minutes. Season with salt and pepper to taste. Add ⅓ cup stock and simmer until the stock is absorbed, 1 to 2 minutes.

5. When the squash is soft, discard the seeds and scoop out the flesh. You should have about 2½ cups. Place the squash and 3 tablespoons stock in a medium-size bowl. Mash roughly with a fork until few lumps remain. Fold in the crushed hazelnuts and chanterelles. Season the filling with salt and pepper. Keep in mind that it's better to overseason, as intensity is lost while cooking.

6. Using the egg and pasta sheets, make the ravioli as described in the box on the facing page, using 1 teaspoon filling per ravioli, topping each with a piece of chopped sage leaf before closing.

7. Add 1 tablespoon olive oil to a large pot of salted water and bring to a boil over high heat. Add the ravioli, bring back to a boil, reduce the heat, and simmer about 4 minutes. Stir gently and frequently to prevent sticking. Using a slotted spoon, carefully transfer the ravioli to a colander.

8. For the sauce, melt the remaining 4 tablespoons butter until foaming but not brown. Add the whole sage leaves to the butter and cook over low heat until crisp, about 3 seconds.

9. To serve, divide the ravioli among shallow bowls, drizzle the butter over the ravioli, and garnish the plates with the sage leaves.

Un-Ravioli

When I returned from a year at the cooking school La Varenne in Paris, my enthusiasm for ravioli was at an all-time high. In my first New York apartment on a dishrag-wringing August day, I discovered that my roommate's friends had been invited to sample the fruits of my French cooking school education. Out came the never-used Imperia pasta machine, the eggs, flour, Parmesan. Bent over an unstable work table, I rolled until the pasta sheets came smooth, and stretched strips like Ace bandages throughout the hopelessly humid living room. Into the little pillows went shiitake mushrooms, which I'd just discovered for $21 a pound. I sealed them, got the water underway with a touch of olive oil and salt, and seated the guests. Up to the surface floated little bits of pasta, garlic, and mushrooms—the ravioli had burst! (See the box on page 231 to avoid repeating my disaster.) We called it a wash and went on to the tarte tatin.

Eco-Musée de la Truffe

They say there's a museum for everything, and the intriguing little French Eco-Musée de la Truffe is proof. This oddity feels perfectly at home in Sorges, a village in the truffle-centric Dordogne region. There, bus shelters sport mushroom ads and **Interdit Ramassages de Champignons** (No Mushroom Foraging) signs sprout from fields like so many toadstools.

Housed in a round stone building typical of the region, the museum follows truffles from Cleopatra's days to modern hunting methods, such as the geiger counter. Handwritten signage, papier-mâché dioramas, and unwieldy scrapbooks detail the role of southwestern France in truffle culture. This is a good place to immerse yourself in newspaper clippings about truffle dog competitions and truffle chicanery (and there has been plenty of that!). The museum also organizes truffle forays and sells antique-style pig postcards.

The exhibits explain the symbiotic relationship between a host tree and its complex bundle of mycelium (the embryo, so to speak, of the truffle). The relationship begins tentatively in April, as tree roots absorb the mycelium's minerals. After a summer blossom hastened by warm rains, the truffle gains weight and momentum by keeping its minerals and taking sugars from the tree. Bold growth ripens the truffle until mid-November, when it can be harvested. But those who can wait until January are rewarded with the knock-your-socks-off aroma of a robust, fully ripened truffle.

In Cubjac, a small Dordogne village, the annual **Concours des Chiens Truffiers** (Truffle Dog Competition) puts the test to truffle dogs' noses. The dogs are raised for robustness, solid paws and nails, and a truly chic look when dressed in a red bandana. One also supposes a natural or learned love of truffles. They are rigorously trained by their masters to unearth these black diamonds. We haven't asked what the prize is—perhaps a few truffle biscuits.

Truffled Baked Potato

SERVES 1

That two ingredients as basic as truffles and potatoes can produce such intense flavor is truly remarkable. This recipe came from Victoria Vesell, a long-time Aux Delices des Bois customer. The heavenly aromas released by the truffles are folded into a steaming hot baked potato. This is a good way to use up leftover truffle shavings, and it works just as well with white truffles as black (replace black truffle butter and oil with white truffle butter and oil). If you can't get one of the three truffle ingredients, increase the other two, tasting as you go along.

1 large (8 ounces) russet potato, scrubbed

1 tablespoon heavy (or whipping) cream

2 teaspoons black truffle oil

½ ounce black truffle, thinly sliced (optional)

¼ teaspoon kosher or sea salt

¼ teaspoon freshly ground black pepper

1. Preheat the oven to 400°F.

2. Prick the potato with a fork in a few places. Bake until a fork slips in and out easily, about 50 minutes. Remove the potato but leave the oven on. Slice the potato lengthwise, in half. Scoop out the flesh, leaving about ⅛ inch of potato attached to the skin, and transfer to a small bowl. Using a fork, mix the flesh well with the remaining ingredients, then stuff potato back into its skin.

3. Return the potato halves to the oven. Bake until warmed through, about 7 minutes. Serve hot.

Gratin of Porcini, Jerusalem Artichokes, and Potatoes

This unusual gratin gets an extra helping of earthiness with dried porcini. The vegetables will be slightly runny, and taste especially good when served with a rare sliced steak. For a firmer texture, stir the topping into the vegetables before serving.

SERVES 4

1 cup (1 ounce) dried porcini mushrooms

1 cup Light Chicken Stock (page 280) or canned low-sodium chicken broth, or as needed

1 pound Jerusalem artichokes (Sunchokes), scrubbed

8 ounces red-skinned new potatoes, scrubbed

⅓ cup heavy (or whipping) cream

1½ teaspoons kosher or sea salt

¼ teaspoon freshly ground black pepper

4 saltine crackers, crumbled very fine, or ⅓ cup fine dry bread crumbs

1 tablespoon Parmesan cheese

1. Place the mushrooms in a heatproof bowl. Heat the stock just

to a boil, then pour it over the mushrooms. Let stand until softened, about 20 minutes.

2. Meanwhile, peel the Jerusalem artichokes with a paring knife, removing as much of the skin as you can. Slice the Jerusalem artichokes ¼ inch thick and drop into a bowl of cold water. If the potatoes are more than 2 inches across at their widest point, cut them in half; if not leave them whole. Slice the potatoes ¼ inch thick and add them to the Jerusalem artichokes.

3. Preheat the oven to 350°F.

4. Drain the mushrooms, re-serving the soaking liquid. Rinse the mushrooms and coarsely chop them. Strain the reserved liquid through a coffee filter or paper towel into a bowl. Add the cream, salt, and pepper. Drain the Jerusalem artichokes and potatoes and add them with the chopped mushrooms to the liquid in the bowl. Stir well and pour into a 4-cup baking dish. Cover with alu-minum foil and bake for 20 minutes.

5. Uncover and bake for 35 min-utes more. Stir together the cracker crumbs and cheese and sprinkle over the top. Bake until the topping is light golden brown and the Jeru-salem artichokes are tender, about 10 minutes.

6. Let stand for about 10 minutes before serving.

Parsnip Purée with Port-Glazed Mushrooms

SERVES 6

*F*or a dressed-up alternative to mashed potatoes, try this sweet-tangy purée topped with port-roasted mushrooms. It makes a wonderful side at a wintry get-together that features a perfectly cooked rib roast or porterhouse steak. It also sets off a roast chicken or one of the more intriguing game birds. And although it is probably pretty obvious, the holiday turkey and ham paired with Parsnip Purée are naturals.

1 pound parsnips, peeled and cut into
   1-inch lengths
Kosher or sea salt
1 large (about 8 ounces) russet potato,
   peeled and cut into 1-inch cubes
8 ounces honshimeji mushrooms,
   trimmed and cut in half
8 ounces oyster mushrooms, trimmed
   and cut into ½-inch strips
2 tablespoons olive oil
Freshly ground black pepper
¼ cup good-quality Port
¼ cup Rich Meat Stock (page 282) or
   canned low-sodium chicken
   broth
1 tablespoon black truffle oil
   (optional)
2 tablespoons unsalted butter
2 tablespoons milk

1. Place the oven rack in the lowest position and preheat the oven to 400°F.

2. Cook the parsnips in a large pot of boiling salted water for 10 minutes. Add the potato and continue cooking until both vegetables are tender, about 20 minutes.

3. Toss the honshimeji and oyster mushrooms with the olive oil and a pinch of salt and pinch of pepper in a bowl until the mushrooms are coated with oil. Spread the mushrooms out in an even layer in a baking pan. Roast until lightly browned, about 12 minutes, tossing once or twice. Pour the Port and stock into the roasting pan, return the pan to the oven, and cook, stirring once or twice, until most of the liquid is evaporated, about 5 minutes. Remove the pan, drizzle the truffle oil (if using) over the mushrooms, and toss well.

4. Drain the parsnips and potatoes. Pass them through a food mill fitted with the fine disk into a mixing bowl. Or mash the vegetables with a potato masher. Beat in the butter, milk, and salt and pepper to taste.

5. Transfer the vegetable mixture to an oval 10-inch (or similar size) baking dish. The vegetable mixture should fill the dish about halfway. Spoon the mushrooms and their liquid in an even layer over the vegetable mixture. Cover the dish with aluminum foil. (The casserole may be assembled up to 1 day in advance and refrigerated. To serve the casserole, bring it to room temperature, then bake at 400°F for 20 minutes, covered, and 10 minutes, uncovered.)

6. Bake the casserole 15 minutes. Remove the aluminum foil and continue baking until the mushroom layer is a rich brown and glazed, about 10 minutes. Serve immediately.

Mushroomy Breads

*I*n our household, a meal doesn't appear on the table without some sort of bread. My husband, Thierry, diehard Frenchman that he is, will go to any length to assure it is on the table. Once, when we were at a beach house in Brittany, we realized just before lunch that there was no bread. Thierry hopped on a bike, scoured the surrounding villages for an open *boulangerie,* and triumphantly returned with several bedraggled baguettes just as the meal was winding down. Since then, we have added crackers and cocktail toasts to our pantry, along the lines of emergency long-life milk, *just in case.*

The truth be told, mushrooms don't work miracles with a baguette. Yet they transform savory crackers, biscuits, and focaccia dough into something this side of sublime. The crisp, soft, and chewy breads in this chapter add an intriguing mushroom flavor to menus. These simple recipes can either complete a meal or turn snacking into a mini-feast. Several call for cèpe powder. If you can't find it locally, you can mail-order it (see page 324), or you can make your own (page 285).

Porcini-Dust Twists

These crisp, mushroomy twists take all of ten minutes to prepare. They make an excellent emergency hors d'oeuvre and are delicious served alongside soup.

8 ounces (½ package), frozen puff pastry
  thawed ahead of time in the
  refrigerator
Flour, for rolling dough
2 teaspoons Cèpe Powder (page 285)
1 large egg, beaten with a fork

1. Preheat the oven to 400°F.

2. Carefully unfold the pastry. Roll it out on a lightly floured surface to a 14 × 10-inch rectangle. Sprinkle the cèpe powder over the pastry.

3. Cut the pastry into 7 × ¾-inch strips. Twist each strip loosely as you lay it on an ungreased baking sheet. Leave about 1 inch between twists. Brush the twists with the egg and refrigerate for 10 minutes.

4. Bake until golden brown and crisp, 10 to 12 minutes. Transfer to a cooling rack. (The twists may be made ahead and stored for 2 or 3 days in an airtight container. If they get soft, heat in a 350°F oven for about 4 minutes.)

Variation: **Palmiers:** Dust the rectangle with cèpe powder and lay it out so the long part is parallel to the counter edge. Starting with the near edge, roll lengthwise to the center. Then roll the far edge to the center. Holding the rolls together with 1 hand, use a sharp knife to slice ¼-inch-thick pieces. Lay them on their sides on the baking sheet. Brush with egg, chill, and bake as directed.

Mushroom Croutons

Tossed with butter, tarragon, and cèpe powder, these croutons add crunch to salads and soups. With Parmesan-dusted crackers going for over twenty dollars a pound at New York gourmet emporiums, this recipe is a real bargain.

4 cups bread cubes (½ inch) made from
    day-old dense bread
2 teaspoons Cèpe Powder (page 285)
1 teaspoon kosher or sea salt or Seasoning
    Salt (page 253)
1 teaspoon dried tarragon
1 tablespoon unsalted butter, melted,
    or olive oil
3 tablespoons very finely grated Parmesan
    cheese (optional)

1. Preheat the oven to 350°F.

2. Place the bread cubes in a large bowl. Sprinkle with the cèpe powder, salt, and tarragon and toss to coat. Drizzle the butter around the sides of the bowl. Toss again until evenly coated with butter and seasonings. If you like, sprinkle the grated cheese over the croutons and toss again.

3. Spread out in an even layer on a baking sheet. (If you have an all-metal wok, use it to bake the croutons in a single layer; they will be easier to stir.) Bake until golden brown, about 12 minutes. Toss the croutons and redistribute them from time to time during baking. Cool completely before using. (The croutons may be stored up to 2 days in an airtight container.)

Mushroom Sesame Crackers

These crisp, light little crackers bring an exciting dimension to snacks and hors d'oeuvres. The nonfat milk keeps the fat content low, resulting in an airy, crisp cracker. Just spread with goat cheese or another topping, and sprinkle with fresh herbs.

1½ cups pastry flour
¼ cup cornstarch
2 tablespoons Cèpe Powder (page 285)
1½ teaspoons kosher or sea salt
½ teaspoon baking powder
¼ cup sesame seeds
¼ cup vegetable oil
¼ cup nonfat or low-fat milk
Milk, for brushing the tops (optional)
½ cup water, or as needed
Kosher or sea salt, sesame seeds, or freshly
    grated Parmesan cheese (optional)

1. Preheat the oven to 400°F.

2. Sift the pastry flour, cornstarch, cèpe powder, salt, and baking powder into a large mixing bowl. Stir in the sesame seeds and make a well in the center of the dry ingredients. Pour the vegetable oil and ¼ cup milk into the well and using a fork, gradually stir the dry ingredients into the well to form a coarse dough. Gradually add enough of the water, mixing constantly, to form a smooth

**MAKES ABOUT
10 DOZEN
2-INCH SQUARE
CRACKERS OR
5 DOZEN
3-INCH ROUND
CRACKERS**

and soft dough. When the dough becomes too stiff to mix with the fork, start mixing it with 1 hand while you add water with the other. Turn the dough out of the bowl and knead it a few times, just until the dough is very smooth and no streaks of flour or cèpe powder remain. Cover the dough loosely with a kitchen towel and let it rest 10 minutes.

3. Divide the dough in half. Roll 1 half out on a floured surface to about ⅛ inch thick. Reflour the surface if necessary to prevent sticking. Let the dough rest 5 minutes. Cut the dough into 2-inch squares, 3-inch rounds or any other desired shape. Gather up any dough scraps, reroll and cut

them as described above.

4. Transfer the crackers with a thin metal spatula to ungreased baking sheets. Prick the entire surface of each cracker with a fork at ¼-inch intervals. If desired, brush the crackers very lightly with milk and sprinkle them with either salt, sesame seeds, or Parmesan cheese.

5. Bake until the crackers are light golden brown underneath and crisp, about 12 minutes. Transfer the crackers to wire racks to cool completely. (The crackers may be stored up to 1 week in airtight containers. If necessary, recrisp on a baking sheet in a 250°F oven for 4 to 6 minutes.)

Winter Pizza with Black Trumpet Mushrooms, Tomato-Sage Salsa, and Fontina

MAKES 4 PIZZAS

Pizza makes a wonderful way to showcase these wild winter mushrooms. Although tomatoes are not at their best when black trumpets are available, the more fully flavored tomatoes on the vine are sold in most supermarkets during the colder months.

12 ounces black trumpet or yellowfoot
  mushrooms or a mix, cleaned
2 tablespoons olive oil
Kosher or sea salt and freshly ground
  black pepper
2 small cloves garlic, minced

10 small fresh sage leaves, finely chopped
2 large (about 6 ounces each) ripe tomatoes,
  cored, seeded, and cut into ¼-inch dice
4 Cornmeal Pizza Crusts (recipe follows)
About 2¼ cups shredded imported fontina
  cheese (about 8 ounces)

1. Coarsely chop the mushrooms. Heat 1 tablespoon of the oil in a large skillet over medium heat and add the mushrooms. Sprinkle with salt and pepper and cook, stirring, until tender, about 6 minutes. Transfer to a bowl and set aside.

2. Clean the skillet, dry it well, and add the remaining 1 tablespoon oil. Heat it over medium heat, add the garlic and sage, and remove from the heat. Place the tomatoes in small bowl and scrape the garlic-sage mixture over the tomatoes, making sure to get every drop. Add salt and pepper to taste. Let the tomato mixture stand about 15 minutes, tossing once or twice.

3. Preheat the oven to 450°F.

4. Top the pizza crusts with the mushroom mixture, dividing it evenly and leaving about ½-inch border around the edges. Sprinkle the tomato-sage mixture, then the grated cheese over the mushrooms.

5. Bake until the underside is well browned and the topping is bubbling, about 15 to 20 minutes. Rotate the pans from rack to rack and side to side about halfway through the baking.

Cornmeal Pizza Crusts

....

This is my favorite recipe for pizza crust. I love its cornmeal crunch, its thinness without being model-starvation-thin, and its bashful yeasty flavor. Top it with just about anything and your pizza's sure to be a hit. This recipe makes four 8-inch crusts.

1 cup warm water
1 tablespoon plus 2 teaspoons olive oil
1 envelope dry yeast
½ teaspoon sugar
2½ cups all-purpose flour, plus more
    for kneading
⅓ cup fine yellow cornmeal, plus more
    for the baking sheets
1½ teaspoons kosher or sea salt

1. Stir together the water, 1 tablespoon of the olive oil, the yeast, and sugar in a medium-size bowl until the yeast is dissolved. Let stand in a warm place for 5 minutes. It should look slightly foamy. If not, let it stand 5 minutes more.

2. Add 2½ cups flour, ⅓ cup cornmeal, and the salt. Stir vigorously, scraping down the sides of the bowl, until the mixture forms a stiff dough.

3. Turn the dough out onto a floured surface and knead it by folding the dough in half toward you then pushing the dough firmly away from you with the heels of your hands. Knead, sprinkling the surface and the dough with flour when the dough begins to stick to your hand, until the dough is no longer sticky but is very elastic. You'll know the dough is ready when you can knead it for half a minute or so without adding flour.

4. Wash out the bowl, dry it well, and pour the remaining 2 teaspoons oil into the bottom. Place the dough in the bowl and turn to coat it with oil. Cover the bowl with a kitchen towel and place it in the warmest part of the kitchen until doubled in size, about 1 hour.

5. Turn the dough out onto a lightly floured surface and punch it down until deflated. Cut the dough into 4 equal pieces, shape each into a round and let rest 15 minutes. The dough can be frozen at this point for up to 1 month. Place each in a doubled zipper-top bag before placing in the freezer. Bring to room temperature before rolling the dough. Sprinkle two 18 × 12-inch baking sheets with cornmeal.

6. Roll or stretch each circle of dough out to an even 8-inch circle, about ¼ inch thick. If you find the dough becoming very elastic and difficult to roll, cover it and let it rest a little before trying again. Transfer the circles to the prepared baking sheets and let rest in a warm place about 20 minutes.

7. Top and bake as directed in the Winter Pizza recipe, page 243, steps 3 to 5.

A Non-Pizza Palate

We had invited some chefs and their kids for Sunday lunch, and I figured they would prefer pizza to grown-up food. As we took the pizza out of the oven, four-year-old François, the child of Philippe and Susan Boulot, burst out crying. Turns out, he didn't like pizza. With parents who would sooner make passion fruit ice cream than run to the deli for a pint of Häagen-Dazs, it's not surprising François craved the finer things in life. So he had a bowl of bouillabaisse with the adults, and I learned to never underestimate a child's taste!

Mini Focaccia with Three Toppings

MAKES 8 MINI
FOCACCIA

Practically speaking, these out-of-hand meals belong in lunch boxes, picnic baskets, and in the freezer for last-minute meals. But it would be a shame not to savor them at their best—fresh, warm, and yeasty, just out of the oven. Serve as a prelude to an Italian meal, or as the star of a focaccia-and-salad lunch or dinner. I've suggested three of my favorite toppings, but if you're considering focaccia as perfect for a children's party (they are), slather them with tomato sauce and mozzarella cheese and bake as described in Winter Pizza on page 243, steps 3 and 5.

4 recipe Cornmeal Pizza Crusts (page 243)
2 teaspoons Cèpe Powder (optional;
    page 285)
Cornmeal for dusting
Topping for focaccia (optional; recipes
    follow)
2 tablespoons olive oil
1 tablespoon chopped fresh flat-leaf
    parsley or other herb
Kosher or seat salt (optional)

1. Prepare the dough for the pizza through step 4, adding the cèpe powder (if using), along with the flour in step 2. Sprinkle the baking sheets lightly with cornmeal and set aside. Prepare one of the toppings, if using, for focaccia while the dough is rising.

2. Transfer the risen dough to the work surface. Punch down the dough until deflated. Divide the dough into 8 equal pieces. Stretch each piece of dough with your fingers into a 3½-inch-wide circle or a 4½ × 2½ inch oval. It doesn't matter if the shapes are a little uneven, but they should be of even thickness. Transfer the dough to the prepared baking sheets. Press the surface of each firmly with your fingertips to make several deep indentations. Brush the tops with the olive oil.

3. Preheat the oven to 450°F.

4. Sprinkle the focaccia with parsley and salt or the prepared topping and bake as described in step 5 on page 243.

Grilled Portobello Mushroom Topping

The dough enfolds the porto-bellos and traps the juices as it bakes . . . mmm! Since the portobellos can be prepared a few days in advance, this version is good for entertaining.

2 small Roasted or Grilled Portobello
    Mushrooms Caps (page 193)
½ cup freshly grated Parmesan or
    Romano cheese

1. Prepare the Mini Focaccia as described on this page through step 2.

2. Cut the portobello mushroom caps in half, then crosswise into ¼-inch strips. Arrange the strips over the tops of the dough, pressing lightly onto the surface. Sprinkle the cheese over the mushrooms.

3. Cover the dough, let the focaccias rise, and bake as described in Winter Pizza, steps 3 and 5 on page 243.

Black and White and Red All Over

a tangle of delicate mushrooms set atop juicy tomato rounds tastes every bit as delicious as it looks. I've chosen two mushrooms that I'd like you to try, but if you have trouble finding either of them, substitute cremini.

2 tablespoons olive oil
4 ounces black trumpet mushrooms,
    cleaned and torn into ½-inch-wide
    strips
4 ounces oyster mushrooms, cleaned and
    torn into ½-inch-wide strips
Kosher or sea salt and freshly ground
    black pepper
2 large (about 6 ounces) ripe plum
    tomatoes, cored and
    thinly sliced
½ cup shredded imported Fontina
    cheese

1. Prepare the Mini Focaccia as described on page 245 through step 2.

2. Heat the oil in a large skillet over medium-high heat. Add the mushrooms and toss to coat with oil. Sprinkle with salt and pepper. Reduce the heat to medium-low, cover, and cook until the mushrooms begin to release their liquid, about 4 minutes. Uncover the skillet, increase the heat to medium, and cook until the liquid is evaporated, about 4 minutes. Cool the mushrooms completely.

3. Top the dough with the tomato slices, and divide the mushroom mixture over the tomato slices. Press the tomatoes and mushrooms lightly onto the surface. Sprinkle the cheese over the top.

4. Cover the dough, let the focaccias rise, and bake as described in Winter Pizza, steps 3 and 5 on page 243.

Provençale Onion-Anchovy Topping

S weet, salty, and pungent notes add up to irresistible taste in this simple topping recipe that I borrowed from southern France.

1 tablespoon extra virgin olive oil
2 to 3 anchovy fillets
1 large onion, thinly sliced
Freshly ground black pepper

1. Prepare the Mini Focaccia as described on page 245 through step 2.

2. Heat the oil in a medium-size skillet over medium-low heat. Add the anchovies and cook, stirring, until they dissolve. Add the onion and cook, stirring occasionally, until golden brown and tender, about 12 minutes. Season to taste with pepper and cool.

3. Divide the mixture among the focaccia, pressing lightly onto the surface. Cover the dough, let the focaccias rise, and bake as described in steps 3 and 5 on page 243.

Mushroom Cornmeal Muffins

MAKES SIX
2¾-INCH MUFFINS

These muffins have a big flavor that can handle *huevos rancheros* as well as Mushroom Chili (page 215). Of course, they are equally delicious served warm with butter or Mushroom Sour Cream (page 258). The muffins are best when made fresh—no more than six hours before eating them.

Vegetable cooking spray or butter, for greasing the muffin pan

1½ cups all-purpose flour

½ cup yellow or white cornmeal

2 tablespoons Cèpe Powder (page 285)

2½ teaspoons baking powder

1 teaspoon kosher or sea salt

¼ freshly ground black pepper

1 cup milk, or as needed

¼ cup Basic Duxelles or 4 frozen duxelles cubes, thawed (page 283)

2 tablespoons thinly sliced fresh chives or chopped fresh flat-leaf parsley

7 tablespoons unsalted butter, melted

2 tablespoons freshly grated Parmesan cheese or finely shredded gruyère cheese

1. Place the rack in the upper third of the oven and preheat the oven to 400°F. Lightly grease a 6-muffin tin (with cups that measure 2¾ × 1¼ inches) with vegetable cooking spray or butter.

2. Sift the flour, cornmeal, cèpe powder, baking powder, salt, and

pepper into a medium-size bowl. Make a well in the center of the mixture and add the milk, duxelles, and chives. Add 6 tablespoons of the butter. Toss with a fork just until the liquid is absorbed and no streaks of white remain. A few lumps may remain. Overmixing will result in tough muffins.

3. Divide the mixture among the prepared muffin cups, mounding them slightly in the center. Brush the top of each muffin with the remaining 1 tablespoon melted butter. Sprinkle with cheese.

4. Bake until golden brown and risen over the top of the pan by about 1 inch, about 22 minutes. Cool in the pan 5 to 10 minutes before serving.

Oven-Fresh Mushroom Biscuits

MAKES 8
BISCUITS,
SERVES 4

These flaky biscuits carry a pat of butter as far as it would ever hope to go. Serve them warm to sop up sauces, stews, and Mushroom and Ham Gravy (page 258).

⅓ (½ ounce) cup dried black trumpet
    mushrooms
Vegetable cooking spray or butter, for
    greasing baking sheet
½ cup quick-cooking oats
1½ cups all-purpose flour
2 teaspoons Cèpe Powder
    (page 285)
1 tablespoon baking powder
1½ teaspoons kosher or sea salt
6 tablespoons vegetable shortening,
    lard, or butter, or a mixture,
    cut into very small pieces,
    very cold
⅔ to ¾ cup milk

1. Place the mushrooms in a small bowl and add hot water to cover. Soak until soft, about 30 minutes. Drain the mushrooms, strain the soaking liquid through cheesecloth, and reserve ¼ cup. Pull the mushrooms lengthwise in half and rinse under cool water to remove any grit. Drain well and pat dry with paper towels. Finely chop the mushrooms and set aside.

2. Preheat the oven to 375°F. Lightly grease a baking sheet with vegetable cooking spray or butter.

3. Grind the oats in a food processor to the consistency of fine meal, about 1 minute. Combine the oats, mushrooms, flour, cèpe powder, baking powder, and salt in a large bowl and stir to mix. Rub the shortening very quickly into the flour mixture with your fingertips, until the pieces are the size and shape of small corn flakes. Refrigerate the mixture about 10 minutes.

4. Sprinkle enough of the milk over the flour mixture, while tossing lightly with a fork, to make a moist dough that holds together easily. Turn the contents of the bowl out onto a well-floured surface and with floured hands and a few quick pushes, pat the dough into an 8 × 4-inch rectangle. Cut the dough into eight 2-inch squares. Transfer the biscuits to the baking sheet with a metal spatula and bake until doubled in height and light golden brown on top, about 25 minutes. Remove and cool the biscuits 10 minutes before serving.

Mushroom Condiments

Sauces and sauce finishers such as Truffle Cream and Roasted Shiitake Ketchup add the sometimes invisible flourish that makes a dish stand out from the crowd. Most of these recipes infuse basic ingredients—water, dairy products, soy sauce—with heady mushroom flavors. They are added to sauces and or dished out in dollops. Some are steeped before using and can remain in the pantry for several months. The Seasoning Salt, which I consider essential in any frequent-sauté kitchen, doesn't contain mushrooms but rather adds an herbal dimension to sautés. The Portobello and Basil Salsa and Mushroom and Ham Gravy are great brunch condiments; set them out with platters of eggs and baskets of Mushroom Cornmeal Muffins and Mushroom Biscuits.

Roasted Shiitake Ketchup

There's something so robust, so spicy, so saucy about this ketchup that we use it on everything. Think burgers and fries, of course, but also fried fish, ham, corn, and fried chicken.

3 tablespoons vegetable oil

3 medium onions, sliced ¼ inch thick

1 pound ripe plum tomatoes, cored and
    cut lengthwise in half

8 ounces shiitakes, cleaned and stemmed

1 cup boiling water

½ ounce (about ½ cup) dried porcini,
    preferably Chilean

1 cup canned crushed tomatoes or
    1 cup finely chopped drained
    canned tomatoes

1 jalapeño seeded, stemmed, and minced

2 tablespoons balsamic vinegar

2 tablespoons sugar

2 teaspoons mustard powder

2 teaspoons kosher or sea salt

2 teaspoons soy sauce

1 teaspoon Worcestershire sauce

¼ teaspoon freshly ground black pepper

1. Preheat the oven to 400°F. Line a baking sheet with aluminum foil and brush the foil lightly with oil.

2. Arrange the onion slices in a single layer on the baking sheet and brush with oil. Roast, turning the slices and moving them to different places on the pan, until the onions are deep brown on both sides, about 25 minutes. Remove the onions as they reach doneness. Cool to room temperature.

3. Brush the foil with a little more of the oil. Arrange the tomatoes, cut side down, on half of the pan and the shiitake mushroom caps, gill side down, on the other side of the pan. Brush the tomatoes and mushrooms with oil. Roast until the tomatoes are very soft and the skins are shriveled and the mushrooms are wrinkled but firm, 15 minutes. Remove from the oven and cool to room temperature.

4. Meanwhile, place the dried porcini in a small bowl and pour the boiling water over them. Let stand until the mushrooms are softened, about 15 minutes. Drain the mushrooms, straining the soaking liquid through a coffee filter or a sieve lined with a double thickness of cheesecloth. Set the soaking liquid aside. Rinse the porcini thoroughly and drain well. Put them in a bowl.

5. Lift the shiitakes off the baking sheet and add them to the porcini. Scrape the tomatoes and any juices on the baking sheet into a food processor. Add the roasted onions. Process, stopping once or twice to scrape down the sides of the workbowl, until the vegetables are finely chopped. Add the crushed tomatoes, jalapeño, vinegar, sugar, mustard, salt, soy sauce, Worcestershire, and pepper. Process until smooth. Transfer the mixture to a 3- to 4-quart heavy saucepan. Stir in the mushroom soaking liquid.

6. Place the shiitakes and porcini in the food processor and process until very finely chopped, scraping the sides of the workbowl if necessary, to chop them evenly. Add to the tomato mixture. Heat the mixture to a boil over medium-high heat. Reduce the heat to a bare simmer—1 or 2 bubbles rising to the surface at a time. Simmer, stirring often, until the mixture is thick enough to mound high on a spoon, about 1 hour. Carefully watch the ketchup and don't let it stick to the pot as it thickens. Cool to room temperature. Check the seasoning. (The ketchup can be stored in a tightly covered contained in the refrigerator for up to 3 weeks.)

Seasoning Salt

This invaluable seasoning stands next to our stove for tossing into mushrooms, vegetables, soups, and stews. It keeps indefinitely.

Use a 3-cup glass or ceramic container that is about as tall as it is high for this. A liter French preserving jar—the kind with the rubber gasket around the top—that measures about 3½ inches high and across the neck, is perfect.

You'll need to start the salt one to three weeks before using.

2⅔ cups kosher or sea salt, or as needed
2 tablespoons fresh thyme leaves
¼ cup (loosely packed) fresh rosemary
   leaves
20 fresh sage leaves

1. Pour ⅔ cup of the salt in an even layer over the bottom of a very clean and very dry container. Spread the thyme leaves in an even layer over the salt. Spread another ⅔ cup salt over the thyme and top it with the rosemary leaves. Spread ⅔ cup salt over the rosemary and top it with the sage leaves. Top with the remaining salt.

2. Place the container in a cool dry spot. Let stand until the herbs are completely dry, 1 to 3 weeks, depending on the humidity. Check the herbs by brushing aside the top layer of salt and pulling out a sage leaf. If it crumbles easily the herbs are ready. If not, return the sage leaf and cover the herbs completely with salt.

3. When the herbs are dry, the salt may be a little moist. To dry out the salt for storage and to intensify the herb flavor, transfer the contents of the jar to a large, clean skillet, preferably stainless steel or nonstick. (Cast-iron may turn the salt dark.) Place the skillet over low heat and stir the salt until is dry and very warm to the touch. Cool the salt completely. Rub the dried salt between your palms to crumble the herbs before storing in an airtight container. For a finer consistency, pulse the salt in a food processor until the herbs are fine.

Mushroom Jus

**MAKES ABOUT
1 CUP**

This rich, concentrated mushroom essence imparts a wild, woodsy flavor to soup, sauces, and just about any other dish. Only a teaspoonful is needed. To make a flavorful jus, save up mushroom trimmings and stems in the freezer until you have enough for this recipe.

Farmer Ray

Farmer Ray has broad hands creased with good soil, a peppered beard made for tugging, and a Santa Claus twinkle in his friendly eyes. From his second-career farm in upstate New York, he used to bring us bushel baskets overflowing with Jerusalem artichokes, lavender, rhubarb, and all manner of exotic squash, which were later turned into dinner or sold to our more adventurous chef-customers.

Before his return to the land, Ray worked at Bouley, a Tribeca restaurant, since closed. I once asked Ray what they could possibly be doing with all the button mushrooms they ordered—thirty pounds a pop, three times a week. In response, he brought me a jar of what looked like flat Coke and tasted like essence of mushroom—Mushroom Jus. This is his recipe.

5 pounds mushrooms, including white
   button mushrooms, cremini, oyster
   mushrooms, and trimmings from any
   wild mushrooms

1. Place mushrooms and ½ cup water in a stockpot. Bring to a boil over high heat and skim the foam from the surface. Reduce the heat and simmer, uncovered, for about 5 hours, skimming and stirring from time to time. Strain the mushrooms through a sieve, pushing to release the juices. Discard the mushrooms. Let cool.

2. Store tightly covered in the refrigerator for 3 months or freeze in ice-cube trays (see page 284, step 3 for directions), then transfer to sealable freezer storage bags.

Mushroom Soy Sauce

oy sauce and mushrooms are wonderful together, so it's no surprise that this little condiment tastes so good. It actually gets better over time; keep it for six months in a tightly-covered jar in the refrigerator. Splash it into stir-fries, vinaigrettes, and grilling marinades.

You'll need to start the sauce two to three weeks before using.

1 ounce (about 12 medium) dried shiitake
    mushrooms
1 bottle (10-ounce) good-quality soy sauce
    or tamari sauce

1. Place the mushrooms in a clean heatproof jar with a tight-fitting lid. A 1-pint canning jar works well. Heat the soy sauce and ⅓ cup water in a small saucepan over medium heat just to a boil. Pour the liquid over the mushrooms. Let stand until cool. Cover the jar and steep the mushrooms in the soy mixture in a cool place until the soy sauce develops a pronounced mushroom flavor, 2 to 3 weeks.

2. Strain the liquid through a fine sieve into clean jar with a tight fitting lid. Press on the mushrooms to extract as much liquid as possible. Store in the refrigerator for up to 6 months.

Note: The mushrooms can be re-used to season soups and sauces. Rinse them briefly and use sparingly as they can be very salty.

Mushroom-Infused Sherry

his homemade condiment imparts a mysterious sweet and woodsy flavor to anything that needs a jolt. Use it to deglaze pans, jazz up sautés, and drizzle into bean soups, stews, and stir-fries. Dried Chilean porcini will give the sherry a more pronounced, smoky flavor. Good-quality dried cèpes will produce a mellower result. The mushrooms will probably throw off sediment, so let the bottle stand upright before you pour. Start infusing one week before using.

½ cup (about ½ ounce) dried porcini
    mushrooms, preferably Chilean
2 cups good-quality dry sherry

1. Choose the cleanest mushrooms possible and brush them as thoroughly as possible to remove grit and sand. Place the mushrooms in a clean 2- to 3-cup jar with a tight-fitting lid. Pour the sherry over them and shake a few times to moisten the mushrooms. Let stand upright and undisturbed in a cool, dark place until the color is notably darker, about 1 week.

2. You may use the sherry at this point. Spoon the sherry off the top. Replace the quantity of sherry you spoon off with fresh sherry. Or, let stand for 2 to 3 weeks more and strain the sherry through a coffee filter, discarding the mushrooms.

Truffle Butter

MAKES ½ CUP

My son Julien helped make this when he was three years old. If he could read directions, he could have done it all by himself! For flavor-per-ounce, this has to be the truffle's shining moment. Let little pats melt over a fish fillet or lobster, grilled veal chops, or a nice steak. Swirl into warmed Mushroom Jus (page 254) to make a fettuccine sauce. Brush over toast and float on top of soup.

½ ounce fresh white or black truffle
8 tablespoons (1 stick) salted butter, at
    room temperature

1. Place the truffle in a food processor. Pulse until the truffle is about the size of grains of rice. Add the butter and pulse just to mix. Transfer to a small bowl and refrigerate.

2. When the truffle butter has firmed up enough to handle, about 20 minutes, roll the butter into a log. Wrap in plastic wrap, then aluminum foil, and place in a sealable freezer storage bag. Store in the freezer for up to 6 months.

3. To use, slice what you need from the log. Use the butter frozen.

Truffle Cream

The ethereal flavor of Truffle Cream transforms mashed potatoes into an edible cloud, and veal pan juices into a silky glaze. Drizzle the cream over roast meats, into pasta sauces, and under fish filets. Finish with a sprinkling of chives. One way to lessen the cost of such a rare and expensive ingredient as truffles is to stretch one truffle over several recipes. Bits of truffle can be kept in the freezer in a sealable freezer storage bag and added to whenever you indulge. Truffle pieces are also available canned and in jars, and cost less than fresh ones (see Mail-Order Sources, page 324).

2 tablespoons black truffle shavings

1 cup heavy (or whipping) cream

1. Combine the truffle shavings and cream in a small, heavy saucepan and bring just to a boil over medium heat. Reduce the heat immediately to low, and simmer for 8 minutes.

2. The cream is best used immediately, but it can be stored, tightly covered, in the refrigerator for up to 1 day.

The Truffle Hunter

Out in the woods, truffle hunters revert to the caveman ethic of every man for himself. To begin with, the hunter goes out—often under cover of night—accompanied only by his pig or dog. Once the 500-pound Limosin pig has been coaxed into the back of the car, the truffier ties on the pig's bandana. He takes along a spatula-like piochon to dig with, and an iron-tipped stick to whack the pig on the nose when he gets the truffle. This whack dislodges the truffle from the pig's mouth. Man and pig park far from the actual truffle spot, lumber past Defense de Truffier (No Truffle Hunting) signs, and crisscross the woods in an effort to lose prying competitors. A hunter will recognize a likely truffle spot by the telltale ring of scorched earth encircling oak, chestnut, hazelnut, and pine trees. If the truffle is not ready for harvest, he will surreptitiously indicate the spot with stones and cover it with leaves. This spot becomes his to check, year after year, until he passes it along or until his pig gives out.

Mushroom Sour Cream or Yogurt

MAKES 1 CUP

Whether made with sour cream or yogurt this simple condiment is delicious on baked potatoes, grilled sirloin steak, or pork chops. Stir it into bean soups or chili. The goat cheese variation tastes wonderful on all of the above, and even better on warm focaccia or served with roasted plum tomatoes.

1 cup regular or low-fat sour cream or
    plain yogurt or mild goat cheese
    (see Note)
¼ cup Basic Duxelles (page 283)
¼ teaspoon freshly ground black pepper
Large pinch of grated nutmeg
1 teaspoon honey or brown sugar

Stir all the ingredients together in a small bowl until blended. Store in a covered container in the refrigerator for up to 1 week. Check the seasoning again before using.

Variation: Mushroom Goat Cheese: Bring 1 cup (about ½ pound) mild goat cheese to room temperature. Mix in the ingredients, substituting 1 teaspoon Dijon mustard or grainy mustard for the honey.

Mushroom and Ham Gravy

SERVES 4

Nothing is more luscious over a split, freshly baked Mushroom Biscuit (page 248) than this Southern-style gravy, especially when served piping hot. For a simpler breakfast treat, spoon it over toasted wheat bread or into the middle of a fluffy omelet.

2 tablespoons unsalted butter
1 tablespoon vegetable oil
12 ounces white button mushrooms or
    chanterelles, cleaned, trimmed,
    and cut into ½-inch wedges
8 ounces smoked ham, cut into ½-inch cubes

2 tablespoons all-purpose flour
1½ cups Light Chicken Stock (page 280) or
    canned, low-sodium chicken broth, hot
2 tablespoons chopped fresh flat-leaf parsley
Freshly ground black pepper, to taste
Kosher or sea salt, if necessary

1. Heat the butter and oil in a heavy, skillet, preferably cast-iron, over medium heat until foaming. Add the mushrooms and ham and cook until the liquid given off by the mushrooms has evaporated and the ham and mushrooms begin to sizzle and brown, about 10 minutes.

2. Sprinkle the flour over the ham and mushrooms and cook, stirring, 2 minutes. Add the stock gradually while stirring constantly. Bring to a boil, and reduce the heat, and simmer. Stir in the parsley and pepper to taste. Simmer 3 minutes. Taste the gravy and season with salt, if necessary.

Portobello and Basil Salsa

*I*f you're in the habit of grilling, the portobellos can be grilled one day, and turned into this delicious salsa the next (or the next). Roasted cremini make an equally tasty salsa.

*MAKES ABOUT
6 CUPS*

4 Roasted Portobello Caps (page 193)
½ cup finely diced ripe tomato or sun-dried tomato
½ cup finely diced red onion
1 tablespoon extra virgin olive oil
1 teaspoon balsamic vinegar
½ teaspoon kosher or sea salt, or more if needed
¼ teaspoon freshly ground black pepper, or more if needed
½ cup very finely shredded fresh basil leaves

1. Cut off and discard the gills from the mushrooms. Cut the remaining cap into ¼-inch dice. You should have about 1½ cups. Toss the diced mushrooms with the tomato, onion, oil, vinegar, salt, and pepper. Let stand at room temperature, tossing occasionally, 2 hours. (The mushroom mixture may be refrigerated, covered with plastic wrap, for up to 1 day; bring to room temperature before serving.)

2. Add the basil and toss to mix. Check the seasoning, adding salt and pepper if necessary. Serve within 1 hour after adding the basil.

Sweet Endings

I could have gone whole hog and presented a dazzling array of mushroom sweets—Chilean Porcini Fudge, Chanterelle-Corn Ripple Ice Cream, or Poached Oyster Mushrooms in Lavender Syrup. Fear not—there is only one fungus dessert, and it's not meringue mushrooms. More about it in a minute.

Mushroom meals can be rich and robust or just pleasantly filling. With this in mind, I've chosen desserts that provide a triumphant finish for all kinds of mushroom menus. Hearty, meaty, winter meals taper off best with an exotically spiced rice pudding or one of several fruity confections. Langourous soup and salad lunches work their way up to thick slices of French Country Lemon Tart or Coconut Flan. Finger-licking outdoor summer meals cry out for messy, boisterous desserts, such as an Ice Cream Sundae with Rum-spiked Bananas and Warm Butterscotch Sauce or Plum Tart with Walnut Crust. For those of you who prefer to go straight from appetizer to dessert, there's the ultimate gratification of Fallen Chocolate Soufflé with Dried Cherries.

And now for that one true dessert in keeping with the focus of this book. It is Truffle Ice Cream, guaranteed to blow your budget and blow your guests away. What could be more astonishing than scooping into what appears to be vanilla ice cream and being serenaded with the almost-chocolatey flavor of black truffles? Wait for that super special occasion and treat yourself like royalty. A little scoop is all it takes.

Coffee Granita

SERVES 6

*G*ranita—which comes in many flavors from citrus to melon—is like a snow cone for grown-ups. This one is ultra-refreshing after a summer dinner of solidly seasoned grilled foods. Add Toasted Pine Nut and Chocolate Shortbread Cookies (page 272) to complete the meal.

½ cup sugar

2 cups freshly brewed strong coffee

Juice of 1 lemon, strained

2 tablespoons dark rum

½ cup heavy (or whipping) cream

1. Combine the sugar and ½ cup water in a small saucepan and bring to a boil over medium heat, stirring constantly. Boil 1 minute. Pour the coffee into a medium-size bowl and stir in the sugar syrup. Stir in the lemon juice and rum. Cool to room temperature.

2. Divide the coffee mixture between 2 ice-cube trays and place the trays in the freezer until solid. (The granita may be prepared to this point up to 3 days in advance. Transfer the frozen cubes to a sealable freezer storage bag until needed.)

3. Place 4 to 5 cubes in each of 6 small bowls or stemmed glasses and let stand at room temperature until they can be crushed easily with a fork, 4 to 6 minutes.

4. Meanwhile, whip the cream in a small bowl until it holds soft peaks.

5. Crush the cubes coarsely with a fork until the granita has the texture of a very coarse snow cone. Or, place the cubes, a few at a time in a blender and pulse a few times to crush. Place a dollop of whipped cream over each serving and serve immediately.

Ice Cream Sundae with Rum-Spiked Bananas and Warm Butterscotch Sauce

No matter which component of this gooey dessert strikes you—the plain-vanilla ice cream, the darkly tropical bananas, or the finger-licking butterscotch sauce—it should bring out the kid in you. Creamy butterscotch sauce holds forever in the fridge and you may find yourself warming it up for waffles or sneaking a spoonful as a quick pick-me-up. To turn the sundae into a real taste of the tropics, use coconut ice cream and top with paper umbrellas. Remember to take the ice cream out of the freezer about 15 minutes before assembling the sundaes so that you can scoop it without a struggle.

BUTTERSCOTCH SAUCE

¾ cup sugar

¼ cup light corn syrup

½ cup heavy (or whipping) cream

4 tablespoons (½ stick) unsalted butter,
    cut into pieces

¼ teaspoon kosher or sea salt

DARK BANANAS

3 ripe but firm bananas

1 tablespoon fresh lemon juice

2 tablespoons unsalted butter

2 tablespoons light or dark brown sugar

2 tablespoons dark rum

TO ASSEMBLE

Vanilla ice cream or vanilla frozen yogurt

Whipped cream (optional)

½ cup macadamia nuts, toasted and
    crushed (see box, page 264)

1. To prepare the sauce, combine the sugar and corn syrup in a small, heavy saucepan. Heat over medium heat, stirring often, until the sugar is dissolved. Continue cooking, without stirring but swirling the pan often, until the mixture is a medium-amber color, 350°F on a candy thermometer. Remove the syrup from the heat and quickly pour in the cream. Work carefully and quickly. The mixture will bubble vigorously. Stir until the bubbling subsides. Stir in the butter and salt until incorporated into the sauce. Set aside. (The sauce may be prepared up to 2 weeks in advance and kept covered in the refrigerator. Reheat the sauce in a heavy saucepan over low heat or in a microwave oven at medium power.)

2. When you're ready to assemble the sundaes, if necessary, reheat the butterscotch sauce to a simmer.

3. Meanwhile, prepare the bananas. Cut the bananas lengthwise in half, then crosswise in half and toss the pieces in a bowl with the lemon juice. Melt the butter in a large skillet over medium heat until foaming. Add the banana pieces and toss until coated with butter. Sprinkle the brown sugar over the bananas and toss gently just until the sugar is melted. Pour the rum into the skillet and heat to a boil. Boil until the liquid is smooth and thick, about 1 minute.

4. To assemble, divide the banana pieces and sauce among 4 plates. Arrange 2 scoops of ice cream over the banana pieces. Drizzle the sauce over the ice cream and top with the whipped cream (if using), and the macadamia nuts. Serve immediately.

To Toast Macadamia Nuts

Spread the nuts on a heavy baking sheet and bake in a 350°F oven just until golden brown, about 10 minutes. Remove and let cool completely. Whack the nuts with a meat mallet or small heavy skillet until chunky.

Truffle Ice Cream

**MAKES ABOUT
1½ QUARTS,
SERVES 6 TO 8**

For a truly elegant occasion, where the finale leaves a lasting impression on your guests, nothing quite beats Truffle Ice Cream. So skimp on the hors d'oeuvres and splurge on this surprise ending. Because of its low sugar content, the ice cream will not hold well, and is best served the same day you make it.

2 cups milk
2 cups heavy (or whipping) cream
3 ounces fresh truffle, sliced into
    ¼-inch matchsticks (see Note)
½ vanilla bean, preferably Tahitian
8 large egg yolks
½ cup sugar

1. In a 2-quart, heavy saucepan, heat the milk, cream, truffle, and vanilla bean until just hot to the touch. Remove from the heat, cover, and steep for 1 hour.

2. Strain the mixture, setting aside the vanilla bean and the truffle. Put the truffle pieces in a blender with 1 tablespoon of the milk mixture. Purée until very fine, adding more of the milk mixture if it is too dry. Set aside the truffle purée.

3. Whisk the egg yolks and sugar in a medium-size bowl until well mixed, about 2 minutes.

4. Reheat the milk mixture over low heat, to very warm but not steaming. Whisk a ladleful of the milk mixture into the eggs, whisking vigorously. When it is incorporated, add about half the remaining milk mixture in the same way.

5. Pour the egg mixture into the remaining milk mixture on the stove. Turn the heat up to medium-low. Stir constantly with a wooden spoon, getting the spoon into all the corners and sides. It's important that this cream does not curdle. Continue stirring until the cream thickens a bit, about 10 minutes. Test by coating the spoon, holding it at a 45-degree angle over the pot, then running your finger across it. If the imprint stays for a few seconds before running together, the cream is done.

6. Set the cream aside to cool to room temperature stirring from time to time, about 1 hour. Then, refrigerate it for about 15 minutes.

7. Freeze the cream in an ice-cream maker according to the manufacturer's directions. Mix in the truffle purée and stir well. Freeze until firm.

Note: There are a few ways to substitute for costly, whole French truffles: saved-up trimmings that you've frozen, canned truffle peelings, or a combination of the two. But be sure to use what is commonly known as the French winter truffle (*tuber melanosporum*).

Truffles Start to Finish

We once held a Truffle Dinner at the Mark Hotel in New York. In came a Maître Truffier from France. In came fifteen pounds of truffles. And in came the pastry chef, Susan Boulot, with this ice cream recipe adapted from a distinguished Gascon chef, André Daguin. After truffle salad, truffle this and truffle that, the only dessert that would possibly do was truffle ice cream. It was a huge hit and caught on like mad in New York restaurants.

Pears Poached in Five-Flavor Syrup

The aromatic Chinese seasonings used here work magic with pears. It is simple to turn the poached pears into sorbet; just follow the directions on page 266. We love this sorbet any time, but after a hearty winter ragout it's pure heaven.

SERVES 6

1 lemon, scrubbed

6 whole star anise (available at Asian groceries)

2 whole cinnamon sticks (3 inches each)

6 slices (¼ inch) unpeeled fresh ginger

2 teaspoons Szechuan or black peppercorns

1 bottle (750 ml) Riesling, gewürztraminer, or other fruity white wine

2 cups sugar

6 ripe but firm Comice or Anjou pears

Whipped cream, heavy (or whipping) cream, or vanilla ice cream (optional)

1. Remove the zest (the yellow part only of the peel) from the lemon with a vegetable peeler.

2. Cut a 4-inch square of double-thick cheesecloth. Place the star anise, cinnamon, ginger, and peppercorns in the center of the square and tie the opposite ends of the square together to enclose the spices securely.

3. Combine the wine, 4 cups of water, sugar, and lemon zest in a heavy, deep pot in which the pears fit comfortably. Add the cheesecloth bundle of spices to the liquid. Cut the lemon in half and squeeze the juice into the liquid, reserving the cut halves. Bring the mixture to a boil over high heat and boil, stirring occasionally, 10 minutes.

4. Peel the pears, leaving the stems intact. With an apple corer or small paring knife, remove the core (not the stems) and seeds from the pear without breaking through the sides. To prevent the pears from darkening, rub the outer surface of the pears with the lemon halves as you work.

5. Slip the pears into the poaching liquid. They should be entirely covered by the poaching liquid. If not, add more water. Bring the liquid back to a boil, reduce the heat, and simmer, uncovered, until the pears feel tender when poked with a wooden skewer or cake tester, about 25 minutes. Remove the pot from the heat and cool the pears to room temperature in the liquid. The pears may be served at room temperature or chilled in the cooking liquid and served cold. Either way, serve the pears in shallow bowls, drizzling a little of the poaching liquid over each and accompanying the pears with whipped cream, heavy cream, or vanilla ice cream, if desired.

Note: The poaching liquid may be reused. Strain it through a fine sieve and refrigerate for up to several months in a covered container. Before cooking the next batch of pears, reheat the liquid to simmering and, if necessary, add enough water to cover the pears.

Variation: **Spiced Pear Sorbet:** Cook the spiced pears as described through cooling to room temperature in the poaching liquid in step 3. Measure 1½ cups of the cooking liquid and strain it into a small saucepan. Heat to a boil over high heat and boil until reduced to ¾ cup, 6 to 8 minutes. Remove the stems from the pears and cut them into quarters. Place the pear pieces in a food processor and process until finely chopped. With the motor running, add most of the reduced cooking liquid. Taste the pear mixture and, if necessary, add the remaining liquid. The mixture should be slightly sweeter than you would like; freezing the pear mixture will reduce the sweetness.

Add enough fresh lemon juice to make the mixture quite tart, about 2 tablespoons; again, the level of tartness will be reduced by the freezing process. Pass the mixture through a fine sieve and refrigerate to chill thoroughly. Freeze the pear mixture in an ice-cream maker according to the manufacturer's directions. Store the sorbet in the freezer no longer than 2 days. Let stand at room temperature 5 minutes before serving.

Apricot Compote with Almonds

This compote is so simple, yet it makes a thoughtful finish to an elaborate meal. My brother-in-law Joel brought the recipe from India and made it for a family meal. It can be dressed up with a dollop of mascarpone or vanilla-accented whipped cream.

SERVES 4

2 pounds ripe apricots
3 tablespoons dark brown sugar
1 tablespoon apricot brandy or kirsch
    (optional)
½ cup whole almonds, coarsely chopped

1. Cut the apricots in half and remove the pits.

2. Place the apricots, sugar, and brandy in a nonreactive pot. Cook over low heat, stirring with a wooden spoon, until the apricots are broken down, 30 to 40 minutes. The fruit will be soft and the juice, syrupy thick.

3. Mix the almonds into the compote. Serve warm, spooned into sundae dishes.

Tapioca and Caramelized Tangerine Parfaits

Smooth, light, and bursting with tangerine flavor, this layered dessert is a throwback to the multilayered parfaits that were so popular in the fifties.

2½ cups milk

¾ cup sugar

¼ cup quick-cooking tapioca

1 large egg

2 tablespoons tangerine liqueur or
Grand Marnier

3 tangerines

Whipped cream or candied tangerine
peel (optional; see box,
this page)

1. Combine the milk, ½ cup of the sugar, the tapioca, and egg in a medium-size, heavy saucepan. Whisk until the egg is thoroughly incorporated and let stand 15 minutes.

2. Bring the mixture to a boil, stirring constantly, over medium heat. Remove from the heat and stir until the tapioca stops boiling. Stir in the liqueur, place a piece of plastic wrap directly on the surface, and cool the tapioca to room temperature.

3. Peel the tangerines, removing the peels in as large pieces as possible if you plan to make the candied tangerine peel. Separate the tangerines into segments. Cut just enough of the membrane from each segment to scrape out the seeds; it is important to leave enough membrane intact to hold the segment together. Scrape out the seeds and set the segments aside.

4. Combine the remaining ¼ cup sugar and 2 tablespoons of

To Make Candied Tangerine Peel

Cut enough of the tangerine peel into 2 × ¼ × ¼-inch strips to measure a loosely packed ½ cup. Blanch the peel in a small saucepan of boiling water for 1 minute. Drain. Combine the blanched peel with ¼ cup sugar and 2 tablespoons water in a small heavy saucepan and heat to a boil over medium-high heat. Reduce the heat and simmer until the peel is tender and the syrup is reduced, about 3 minutes. Cool the peel completely in the syrup. Drain the peel thoroughly and dab it dry with paper towels. Toss the peel in a bowl with enough sugar to coat the pieces generously, then arrange them in a single layer on a wire cooling rack with enough space between them to allow them to dry. Let stand in a cool, dry place until they are completely dry and the sugar is crunchy, about 4 hours. If it is very hot or humid, it may be necessary to toss the peels in sugar again to recoat them. Store in the refrigerator in a container with a tight-fitting lid.

water in a medium-size (about 10-inch) heavy skillet over medium heat. Heat to a boil, swirling the skillet constantly to dissolve the sugar. Continue boiling, swirling the pan often, until the water is evaporated and the sugar begins to change color and turn a pale golden brown. (The number and size of the bubbles will increase dramatically when the syrup is about to change color. Pay careful attention: Once the syrup begins to change color, it will begin to darken rapidly.) It should take about 4 minutes from the time the syrup comes to a boil until it begins to change color. Remove the skillet from the heat and continue to swirl very gently. The sugar should continue to darken off the heat. When it reaches a medium-amber color, quickly add the tangerine segments and toss or stir gently in the caramel until coated. Don't worry if the caramel lumps and hardens in places, the lumps will dissolve as the tangerines cool. Set the skillet aside and cool the tangerines to room temperature.

5. Spoon about ⅓ cup of tapioca into each of four 8-ounce parfait, sundae, or tall wine glasses. Divide about half of the tangerines and caramel evenly among the glasses. Repeat with the remaining tapioca and tangerines. Cover each glass with plastic wrap and refrigerate until thoroughly chilled. Serve cold, topped with whipped cream or candied tangerine peels, if you like.

Cardamon-Rum-Spiked Rice Pudding

Redolent of exotic spice and creamy, this rice pudding satisfies longings for comfort food. Since rice pudding is an extremely personal matter, you may garnish this recipe in several different ways. If you don't care for raisins in yours, simply omit them and whisk half the amount of rum into the milk mixture. You may choose to pour cream over the top of warm or chilled pudding, or top it with a dollop of whipped cream or a drizzle of warm Butterscotch Sauce (page 263). Or do nothing at all—except eat it!

SERVES 6

½ cup raisins

¼ cup dark rum

½ teaspoon kosher or sea salt

1½ cups long-grain rice

3 large egg yolks

⅔ cup sugar

1 teaspoon ground cardamom or

    2 teaspoons grated lemon zest

¼ teaspoon ground cinnamon

3½ cups milk

1. Toss the raisins and rum in a small bowl and let stand, tossing occasionally, while preparing the pudding.

2. Heat 3 cups of water and the salt to a boil in a medium-size, heavy saucepan. Stir in the rice and return the water to a boil. Reduce the heat, and simmer the rice, covered, until it is tender and the water is absorbed, about 20 minutes. Transfer the rice to a larger, heavy saucepan and fluff the grains with a fork.

3. Place the egg yolks in a medium-size bowl. Add the sugar, cardamom, and cinnamon and whisk until blended. Whisk the milk into the yolks and beat the mixture until smooth. Add the milk mixture and raisins and rum to the rice in the saucepan. Stir over medium-low heat until slightly thickened, about 10 minutes. (The pudding will thicken further as it cools.) Be sure to cook the rice over gentle heat and to stir continuously. If the mixture gets too hot, the eggs will cook and the pudding will be grainy and not properly thickened. The best way to judge when the pudding is ready is to insert an instant-read thermometer into the center of the pudding. It will register 180°F when the pudding is ready.

4. Transfer the pudding to a serving bowl and stir it until it is no longer steaming. Serve at room temperature or refrigerate until completely chilled.

Coconut Flan

SERVES 8

My mother-in-law was famous for her *genre de,* or sort of, desserts. Not wanting to be bothered by actual recipes, she'd whip up her own approximation of *île flottante* or *crème caramel.* When we asked what was for dessert, the response always began, *genre de.* Here's her *genre de flan à la noix de coco,* which I'd scribbled on the inside cover of a *Paris Match* magazine as she stirred and mixed.

When this flan bakes, the bottom becomes a moist cake, the top a richly flavored mousse.

1 can (14 ounces) sweetened condensed
   milk

1¾ cups milk

3 large eggs, separated

2 cups shredded coconut

½ cup sugar

1. Preheat the oven to 350°F.

2. Whisk together the condensed milk, milk, egg yolks, and shredded coconut in a medium-size bowl.

3. Make the caramel in a small, heavy pot—a copper sugar pot is ideal. Place the sugar and 1 teaspoon of water in the pot and cook over medium heat, swirling the pot almost constantly. The sugar will lump, get yellow, and finally melt. When it is all melted, bubbling, and starts to change color, remove it from the heat, continuing to swirl. When it reaches a caramel color, immediately pour it into a 9 × 5 × 3-inch loaf pan, preferably glass.

4. Beat the egg whites until stiff. Fold them gently into the milk mixture. Turn this mixture into the loaf pan. Place the pan in a roasting pan and put it in the oven. Pour hot water into the roasting pan until it reaches about halfway up the sides of the loaf pan.

5. Bake for 1 hour to 1 hour and 15 minutes. Check doneness by tapping with your finger. It's done when the top barely jiggles any more.

6. Cool the flan completely. To unmold, put about 1 inch of hot water in the sink. Place the pan in hot water just until the flan pulls away from the sides, about 10 seconds. Reverse onto an oblong serving plate.

Mango Cobbler with Crunchy Ginger Topping

*I*n July, when mangoes can go for as low as two for a dollar, this dessert is more than a summer treat—it's a must. Steven Raichlen, who abandoned Boston for the untamed culinary outpost of Miami years ago, inspired this dessert by his total devotion to such tropical foods as mango.

SERVES 6

5 tablespoons unsalted butter, melted

1 package (3 ounces) ladyfingers, to line the
     soufflé dish

½ cup pecans, toasted (see box, page 120)
     and cooled

¼ cup crushed ginger snaps

¼ cup (firmly packed) brown sugar

3 to 4 ripe mangoes, peeled

1 teaspoon finely chopped candied ginger

3 tablespoons granulated sugar

1 tablespoon cornstarch

½ teaspoon grated lime zest

2 teaspoons fresh lime juice

Crème fraîche or ice cream (optional)

1. Preheat the oven to 350°F. Generously butter a 7-inch soufflé dish with 1 tablespoon of the melted butter.

To Peel a Mango

Deeply score the skin lengthwise, then crosswise, in a diamond pattern. Peel off the skin. Holding the mango so the flat part of the pit is perpendicular to the cutting board, cut the flesh off the pit.

2. Dip the top, rounded side of the ladyfingers into 1 tablespoon melted butter. Line the dish with the ladyfingers, buttered side against the side of the dish, tops peeking above the rim.

3. Combine the pecans, ginger snaps, brown sugar, and remaining 4 tablespoons melted butter in a food processor. Pulse just until mixed to a coarse texture. Set aside the topping. (The topping can be stored, covered tightly, for up to 3 weeks in the refrigerator.)

4. Mix the mangoes (you should have 3 cups of mango cubes) with the candied ginger, granulated sugar, cornstarch, lime zest, and lime juice. Pour into the prepared mold. Bake for 20 minutes.

5. Reduce the heat to 325°F. Remove the mold from the oven. Top the fruit with a thick layer of ginger topping. Return to the oven and bake until the topping is nice and crisp, 30 minutes more. Spoon onto plates and serve with crème fraîche or ice cream, if desired.

Toasted Pine Nut and Chocolate Shortbread Cookies

Serve these light and slightly chocolatey wafers with a glass of Port or tumbler of milk. Leave them out for Santa Claus, and you'll probably get a little something extra in your stocking!

2 cups all-purpose flour

¼ teaspoon salt

¼ teaspoon baking powder

1 cup pine nuts, toasted (see box, page 125) and cooled

½ cup sugar

1 cup (2 sticks) unsalted butter

½ cup coarsely grated semisweet chocolate (4 ounces)

2 teaspoons dark rum or 1 teaspoon vanilla extract

1. Stir the flour, salt, and baking powder together in a small bowl. Set aside.

2. Grind the pine nuts and sugar in a food processor until the consistency of very coarse sand. It is fine if a few larger pieces of pine nuts remain; it is better than grinding the pine nuts too fine.

3. Combine the butter and pine nut mixture in the bowl of an electric mixer. Cream at low speed until the sugar is completely incorporated. Stir in the dry ingredients with a sturdy spoon and when they are almost completely incorporated, stir in the chocolate and rum.

4. Form the dough into an 8 × 2-inch cylinder. Wrap the dough in plastic wrap and refrigerate for at least 2 hours. (The dough may be prepared to this point and refrigerated up to 1 week or frozen up to 2 months. Defrost frozen dough thoroughly in the refrigerator, about 12 hours, before continuing.)

5. Preheat the oven to 350°F.

6. Slice the cookie dough into ¼-inch-thick rounds and arrange them, side by side, on ungreased cookie sheets. Bake until the cookies are golden brown around the edges and on the underside, about 12 minutes. Cool completely on the baking sheets then transfer the cookies to serving platters. (The cookies, though fragile, may be stored in an airtight container in a cool spot for a few days.)

French Country Lemon Tart

SERVES 8

There's something about this tart, with its fluted crust and sheer lemon surface, that recalls a sunny café terrace and a lazily-winding river somewhere in the French countryside. It comes from Jean-Jacques Carquillat, whose desserts at the Kingston, New York, restaurant Le Canard Enchaîné bring the words flaky, intense, and buttery to mind all at once.

This recipe makes two tart crusts, one for now and one to freeze. For best results, use a fluted metal tart mold with a removable bottom, and prepare both the pastry and filling the night before baking.

LEMON FILLING

Grated zest of 2 lemons

½ cup fresh lemon juice

2 large eggs

1 large egg yolk

½ cup granulated sugar

½ cup heavy cream

PASTRY

6 tablespoons unsalted butter, cut
    into 1-inch pieces and at room
    temperature

1½ cups confectioners' sugar

6 large egg yolks

2¼ cups all-purpose flour

GARNISH

Whipped cream (optional)

Candied violets (optional)

Mint leaves (optional)

1. To prepare the filling, the night before baking the tart, whisk together the filling ingredients in a medium-size bowl. Cover with plastic wrap and refrigerate.

2. To prepare the pastry, combine the butter and confectioners' sugar in a food processor and pulse to blend. Add the egg yolks and pulse to blend. Add the flour in 3 batches. All the ingredients must be added very quickly, with just a 5-second pulse to blend. (To mix by hand, place the butter pieces in a large mixing bowl and use a wooden spoon to quickly press the confectioners' sugar into it. Stir the egg yolks with a fork and add them to the dough until just blended. Add the flour in 3 batches, stirring just until blended.)

3. Turn the dough out onto a lightly floured surface. Gather the dough into a ball to completely mix in the flour. This is a softer dough than usual pie dough, but if it is too sticky to form into a mass, add a few pinches of flour. Divide the dough in half and freeze 1 ball, wrapped in plastic wrap and then placed in a zipper-top bag. It will keep for up to 1 month. Thaw in the refrigerator before using.

4. Press the other ball of dough into an 9-inch metal tart tin with a removable bottom. It will be thicker than a usual pastry shell, between ¼ and ½ inch thick. Roll a rolling pin over the top to trim off extra dough. Refrigerate, covered with plastic wrap, overnight (see Note).

5. Place aluminum foil on the bottom of the oven to catch spills. Place one oven rack in the center of the oven and one in the lower third. Preheat the oven to 375°F.

6. Bake in the lower part of the oven just until golden, about 15 minutes. It will be puffy and still damp in spots. Press down to release any trapped bubbles. Whisk the filling to blend and pour as much as will fit into the shell. There may be some leftover filling.

7. Bake the tart on the center rack until the crust is firm and nicely browned, about 30 minutes. To test for doneness, jiggle the tart pan. When the filling doesn't jiggle, it is done. Cool the tart completely on a wire rack.

8. Remove the rim of the tart mold. Serve the tart with dollops of whipped cream, and a few candied violets or mint leaves, if desired.

Note: If pressed for time, place the uncooked tart shell in the freezer for 15 minutes instead of refrigerating overnight.

Plum Tart with Walnut Crust

The taste of warm plums oozing sweet, thick juices, is enhanced by this tart's nutty brown crust. Make it as a summer luncheon dessert, accompanied perhaps by a dollop of crème fraîche or vanilla ice cream.

SERVES 8

½ cup walnut halves

1¼ cups flour, plus more for rolling out pastry

5 tablespoons sugar

¼ teaspoon kosher or sea salt

8 tablespoons (1 stick) unsalted butter, cold, cut into 6 to 8 pieces

1 large egg yolk

1 tablespoon ice water, or more as needed

2 tablespoons blueberry, red currant, or apricot jam

2 pounds small ripe plums, cut in half and pitted

Vanilla ice cream or crème fraîche, for serving

1. Place the walnuts, flour, 3 tablespoons of the sugar, and the salt in a food processor and pulse until the walnuts are coarsely ground. Add the butter pieces and pulse until the mixture resembles coarse meal. Add the egg yolk and 1 tablespoon ice water through the feed tube. Pulse just until the dough is moist and holds together when pressed between your fingers. If it is too dry add more water, a few drops at a time. Turn the dough out onto a lightly floured surface.

2. Quickly push the dough away from you with the heel of your hand, a little at a time. This assures that the butter is properly blended into the dough. Gather it up into a flat patty. Put the dough on a dish, cover with plastic wrap, and refrigerate for 15 minutes or as long as overnight.

3. Place an oven rack in the bottom third of the oven. Preheat the oven to 350°F.

4. Roll out the pastry dough on a lightly-floured surface, to a 10-inch round, ¼ inch thick. Loosely wrap the crust around the rolling pin, then unroll it into a 9-inch glass pie pan. Trim the edges with a sharp knife and flute the edges.

5. Prick the crust with a fork. Line it with aluminum foil, then fill with pie weights or dried beans.

Bake in the lower part of the oven until the bottom of the crust is somewhat dry, about 15 minutes. Remove the crust from the oven and remove the pie weights and foil.

6. Melt the jam in a small saucepan over low heat.

7. Arrange the plums, cut side up, in a tight circle. Sprinkle with sugar. Paint the plums with the warm jam.

8. Bake the tart on the center rack until the crust is golden brown and the plums are soft, 20 to 30 minutes. Serve warm with a scoop of vanilla ice cream or dollop of crème fraîche.

Fallen Chocolate Soufflé with Dried Cherries

SERVES 6

*F*rançois Payard's pastry has a magical quality to it. He directed the pastry brigade at one of New York's top restaurants, Daniel, and now has an acclaimed bakery/restaurant called Payard Patisserie. This is his solution for those who yearn for a grown-up brownie with a warm, melting center.

¼ cup dried cherries

Hot water

6 tablespoons (¾ stick) unsalted butter,
    plus more for the ramekins

6 tablespoons plus 2 teaspoons sugar,
    plus more for the ramekins

2 large eggs, separated

4 ounces extra bitter chocolate, cut into
    small pieces

½ teaspoon fresh lemon juice

1 teaspoon all-purpose flour

1. Place the dried cherries in a small heatproof bowl and pour enough hot water over them to cover. Let stand until softened, about 5 minutes. Drain well.

2. Preheat the oven to 400°F. Butter six 8-ounce ramekins or baking dishes. Sprinkle sugar into each ramekin, then roll and tap to form an even layer of sugar over the bottom and sides of the ramekins. Spoon the cherries into the ramekins, dividing them evenly.

3. Beat the egg yolks and 6 tablespoons of the sugar in a medium-size bowl until smooth and creamy.

4. Melt 6 tablespoons butter in a small saucepan over low heat until foamy. Pour the butter over the chocolate in a small bowl and stir until the chocolate is melted. Immediately add the chocolate mixture to the egg yolk mixture and stir until smooth.

5. Beat the egg whites and lemon juice in another bowl until foamy. Add the remaining 2 teaspoons sugar and beat until the egg whites form stiff peaks when the beaters are removed. Sprinkle the flour over the chocolate mixture and add one third of the egg white mixture. Using a rubber spatula, gently fold the egg whites into the chocolate mixture, scraping along the bottom of the bowl and bringing the chocolate mixture up through the center. When just a few streaks of white remain, add the remaining beaten egg whites and fold them into the mixture in the same way. Divide the mixture among the ramekins and place them on a baking sheet.

6. Bake until the soufflés have risen about 1 inch above the rim of the ramekin and the top is firm and cracked in places, about 10 minutes. Serve immediately.

The Basics

*a*s the chefs at La Varenne (the French cooking school in Burgundy) used to say, "Without a good stock you can't have a good sauce." Over the years I've agreed with them hundreds of times—both with my successes and my duds. Chris's stock recipes work perfectly time after time, because they are so elemental. Make them in batches and store in freezer containers, labeled by date.

Of course, I'm as realistic and harried as the next guy about the value of homemade. Many is the night I open a can instead of the freezer without a tinge of guilt at using commercially prepared chicken broth. Another alternative is to poach a chicken in water with an onion, an herb or two, and a few grains of pepper, then reserve the cooking liquid to use as stock. If you do get a chance to make stock yourself, save it for a special dish when that extra depth of flavor will make a noticeable difference.

Duxelles, tomato sauce, and a simple mushroom ragout are three other basics we don't see living without. With additions of this and that, these recipes lift familiar dishes out of the doldrums. Don't hesitate to add your favorite palate pleaser to one or the other—a pinch of curry, a grating of orange zest, a sprinkling of tarragon.

Light Chicken Stock

This is the stock to use for making soups. It is pale in color, yet rich with flavor and gelatin, which will give soups good body. It is so easy to prepare, and makes such a difference to homemade soups, there is really no excuse not to have some in the freezer.

7 to 8 pounds raw chicken backs, necks, and giblets (but not the liver)

2 carrots

1 large yellow onion, unpeeled and quartered

1 head of garlic, separated into unpeeled cloves

1. Pull off as much of the fat and skin from the backs and necks as possible. Combine the chicken, carrots, onion, and garlic in a 5-quart stockpot. Pour in enough cold water to cover the chicken by 1 inch (about 3 quarts). Heat over high heat to a boil. Reduce the heat to medium and boil 5 minutes. Skim all the foam and fat that rise to the surface.

2. Adjust the heat to a bare simmer—1 or 2 bubbles rising to the surface at a time. Simmer until the bones fall apart when poked with a fork, about 8 hours. Check the pot occasionally, skimming the foam and fat as it rises to the surface, and adding water as needed to keep the bones submerged.

3. Ladle the stock through a sieve lined with a double thickness of cheesecloth or a clean kitchen towel into a bowl. Quickly cool to room temperature. Refrigerate, uncovered, until completely chilled and a layer of firm fat forms on top.

4. Remove the fat from the surface. Render the chicken fat, if desired (see box). Warm the stock over low heat and ladle into 1-cup storage containers with tight-fitting lids. Refrigerate for up to 5 days or freeze for up to 3 months. Heat to a boil before using.

How to Render Chicken Fat from Soup

Scrape the fat from the surface of chilled stock as cleanly as possible, with as little of the stock clinging to it as possible. Place the fat in a small saucepan over medium-low heat. Because there is water in the fat, the contents of the pan will come to a boil. Reduce the heat to low and cook the fat, watching closely, until it stops boiling and is a pure, bright yellow color, 5 to 10 minutes. At this point any impurities in the fat will have begun to brown. Remove the pan from the heat and cool the fat completely. Strain the fat through a fine sieve and store it, tightly covered, in the refrigerator for up to 3 months.

Rich Chicken Stock

**MAKES ABOUT
8 CUPS**

*R*oasting the bones before simmering them adds a dark, rich flavor to the stock, making it perfect for sauces and braising. There are no vegetables in this stock because you will probably use it in a reduction sauce and the flavor of the vegetables may become too concentrated during reduction.

7 to 8 pounds raw chicken backs, necks,
and giblets (but not the liver)

1. Preheat the oven to 400°F.

2. Pull off as much of the fat and skin from the backs and necks as possible. Arrange the chicken in an even layer in a roasting pan and roast, turning the pieces once or twice, until well browned, about 30 minutes. Transfer the chicken with tongs or a slotted spoon to a 5-quart stockpot.

3. Pour in enough cold water to cover the chicken by 1 inch (about 3 quarts). Heat over high heat to a boil. Reduce the heat to medium and boil 2 minutes. Skim all the foam and fat that rises to the surface.

4. Adjust the heat to a bare simmer—1 or 2 bubbles rising to the surface at a time. Simmer the stock until the bones fall apart when poked with a fork, 6 to 7 hours. Check the pot occasionally, skimming the foam and fat as it rises to the surface, and adding water as needed to keep the bones submerged.

5. Ladle the stock through a sieve lined with a double thickness of cheesecloth or a clean kitchen towel into a bowl. Quickly cool to room temperature. Refrigerate, uncovered, until completely chilled and a layer of firm fat forms on top.

6. Remove the fat from the surface. Render the chicken fat, if desired (page 280). Warm the stock over low heat and ladle into 1-cup storage containers with tight-fitting lids. Refrigerate the stock for up to 5 days or freeze it for up to 3 months. Heat to a boil before using.

Rich Meat Stock

Plan to make and freeze a few batches of stock in the fall, when cooler weather pulls us indoors. Hearty, meaty stews and more complex recipes usually call for this rich base.

5 to 6 pounds meaty beef or
    veal bones
1 pound beef shin or veal neck

1. Preheat the oven to 450°F.

2. Arrange the bones in a single layer in a roasting pan. Roast until well browned, about 45 minutes, turning once or twice. Transfer to a 6-quart stockpot. Pour in enough water to cover the bones by 1 inch, about 4 quarts. Heat over high heat to a boil. Reduce the heat to medium and boil 2 minutes. Skim all the foam and fat that rises to the surface.

3. Adjust the heat to a bare simmer—1 or 2 bubbles rising to the surface at a time. Simmer until the meat falls apart very easily when poked with a fork, about 10 hours. Check the pot occasionally, skimming the foam and fat as it rises to the surface, and adding water as needed to keep the bones submerged.

4. Ladle the stock through a sieve lined with a double thickness of cheesecloth or a clean kitchen towel into a bowl. Quickly cool to room temperature. Refrigerate, uncovered, until completely chilled and a layer of firm fat forms on top.

5. Remove the fat from the surface and discard. Warm the stock over low heat and ladle into 1-cup storage containers with tight-fitting lids. Refrigerate for up to 5 days or freeze for up to 3 months. Heat the stock to a boil before using.

Demi-Glace

Demi-glace is a very concentrated meat or poultry stock used to enrich sauces for birds, meat, and other dishes. It is rich, potent, and quite unlike anything else. Demi-glace has a special affinity for mushrooms and that is why several of our recipes call for its use.

To make demi-glace, pour either Rich Meat Stock or Rich Chicken Stock (page 281) into a small sauté pan or skillet. Heat to a boil. Reduce the heat, simmer, uncovered, and reduce the stock until it is about one fourth of its original volume and thick enough to lightly coat a spoon. The time will vary, depending on the amount of stock you started with, the size of the pan and how rich the stock was to begin with. Count on about 20 minutes. Don't boil the stock too hard, or it will stick and scorch in places. Store the demi-glace in the freezer for up to 4 months. (If you'd prefer to buy demi-glace, which can be frozen, see Mail-Order Sources, page 324.) One cup of stock makes about ¼ cup of demi-glace.

Basic Duxelles

**MAKES ABOUT
1¼ CUPS**

*D*uxelles is a sauté of chopped mushrooms that is cooked until all the liquid is rendered and evaporated. It is used as a stuffing for everything from ravioli to chicken breasts. My method of making duxelles is a little unorthodox. As much of the mushroom's liquid as possible is drawn out over low heat, then the heat is turned up, the liquid is boiled off, and the mushrooms are allowed to brown in the remaining butter. This produces a more compact duxelles with a more intense flavor than the traditional method. Frozen as described below, in amounts as small as one tablespoon cubes, duxelles are a great boon to last-minute hors d'oeuvres and impromptu pasta dishes.

Part of the joy of duxelles comes from blending different mushroom flavors or celebrating an individual's flavor, so you're invited to mix and match.

12 ounces fresh mushrooms, any of one
    type, or a mix of several, trimmed
    and cleaned (see Note)
2 tablespoons unsalted butter
½ teaspoon kosher or sea salt
Freshly ground black pepper
2 tablespoons chopped fresh flat-leaf
    parsley

1. After cleaning, cut the different mushrooms as follows: For firm, regularly shaped mushrooms like cremini, portobellos, hedgehogs, puffballs, and shiitakes, trim the stems, if any, and thinly slice the caps, no more than ¼ inch thick and 1 inch long. For irregularly shaped mushrooms like hen of the woods and cauliflower, cut into ½-inch slices, then crosswise ½ inch thick. For soft mushrooms like chanterelles, yellowfoot, and black trumpets, cut strips ½ inch long and ½ inch across.

2. Melt the butter in a large, heavy skillet over medium heat until foaming. Stir in the mushrooms, a handful at a time, and cook each batch until the mushrooms wilt enough to show the bottom of the pan. Continue adding mushrooms until all are in the pan. Reduce the heat to low and cook, stirring occasionally, until the mushrooms seem to have given up all their liquid, 5 to 10 minutes, depending on the types of mushrooms. (If in doubt, let the mushrooms stand off the heat for 5 minutes to see if they give up any more liquid.) Turn the heat to high. Stir the mushrooms until the liquid is evaporated and the mushrooms begin to sizzle, about 3 minutes. Transfer the mushrooms to a plate and let cool to room temperature.

3. Place the mushrooms in a food processor and use quick on/off pulses until the mushrooms are finely chopped. Store, covered, for up to 1 week in the refrigerator or freeze for up to 3 months. To freeze cubes, place 1 tablespoon of the duxelles into each compartment of an ice-cube tray. Tamp down the duxelles and freeze with a piece of plastic wrap applied directly to the surface. When solid, transfer the cubes to a sealable plastic container or freezer bag.

Note: If you are using mushrooms where most or all of the stems are discarded, like shiitake, portobello, cremini, or fried chicken mushrooms, weigh them after removing the stems, if possible. Otherwise, add a few ounces to the total.

Variations: **Parmesan Duxelles:** Stir 2 tablespoons grated Parmagiano-Reggiano or other good-quality Parmesan cheese into the duxelles after it has cooled to room temperature.

Creamy Duxelles: Stir 2 tablespoons heavy (or whipping) cream into the duxelles before removing from the heat.

Chunky Duxelles: Cool the sautéed mushrooms to room temperature. Transfer to a cutting board and coarsely chop. Do not use the food processor.

Basic Tomato Sauce

MAKES 3 CUPS

This simple tomato sauce is clean, fresh, and versatile. Because there are few added flavorings, it's the perfect base for building sauces. Freeze it in one- and two-cup containers for maximum flexibility.

2 tablespoons olive oil

1 medium onion, diced

2 small cloves garlic, minced

1 can (28 ounces) plum tomatoes with liquid, finely chopped

1½ teaspoons kosher or sea salt or Seasoning Salt (page 253)

¼ teaspoon freshly ground black pepper

¼ cup finely chopped fresh basil or flat-leaf parsley

1. Heat the oil in a 2-quart, heavy saucepan over medium heat. Add the onion and garlic. Cook, stirring, until the onion is wilted, but not brown, about 5 minutes.

2. Add the tomatoes, salt, and pepper. Bring to a boil, reduce the heat, and simmer, uncovered, 30 minutes. Add the basil and simmer 5 minutes more. Remove from the heat and cool to room temperature. The sauce can be refrigerated, covered, for up to 5 days or frozen in airtight containers for up to 3 months.

Variations: **Sweet-and-Sour Tomato Sauce:** Add 2 tablespoons sugar to the wilted onion and cook, stirring, until dissolved, about 1 minute. Add 2 tablespoons white wine vinegar or cider vinegar with the tomatoes, salt, and pepper. Cook as directed.

Dried Mushroom Tomato Sauce: Place 1 cup dried mushrooms in a small bowl. Add hot water to cover and soak until soft, about 30 minutes. Drain the mushrooms. Strain the soaking liquid through a coffee filter and set aside. Rinse the mushrooms thoroughly to remove all grit. Finely chop the mushrooms. Add the mushrooms and strained soaking liquid to the sauce along with the tomatoes. Simmer an additional 10 minutes (45 minutes in all).

Fresh Mushroom Tomato Sauce: Clean, trim, and finely chop 4 to 8 ounces of full-flavored mushrooms like portobellos, shiitakes, or cremini, or a combination. (Cut off and discard the dark gills from the underside of portobellos or the sauce will turn brown.) Sauté with the onion as directed in step 1.

Cèpe Powder

Mushroom powder gets sprinkled all over everything in our house. It flavors soups, stews, fricassees, and sauces that need an extra jolt. We use it to make tamales, muffins, and pasta dough and sprinkle it on breadsticks. And not only is it versatile, it's easy to make.

1 ounce cèpes or other dried mushrooms

Grind dried mushrooms in a food processor or coffee grinder until finely ground. Store in a tightly closed jar or zipper-lock bag in a cool place, such as the refrigerator or freezer, for up to 6 months.

Note: Since the powder is not commercially treated, it will not totally dissolve in liquid. The little bits that remain on top of a stew can be skimmed off without compromising the flavor.

Mushroom Primer: Tasting Your Way Through Field and Farm

Wild (foraged) mushrooms appear only at certain times of the year; cultivated ones are abundant year round. This handy primer will give you an overview of the mushrooms that are included in this book. It's not meant as a foraging guide, but as a quick ready reference to help you shop for wild mushrooms in an educated way.

If you're interested simply in the availability of a particular mushroom, check the Wild Mushroom Calendar (page 288). If you'd like more information, turn to the individual mushroom's primer page. Besides a photo, I've included what to look for when purchasing the mushroom, and how to clean, store, and prepare it. If you can't find a particular mushroom, I offer up some substitutes that can be readily used in its place. The cooking methods that I suggest here bring out the best characteristics of the variety. And finally, to get you started, I recommend a good, simple recipe to help you discover the flavor and texture of each mushroom.

Enjoy!

Wild Mushroom Calendar

This chart is a guide to the seasonal availability of mushrooms that grow in the wild. Since their appearance really depends upon nature, the season could be longer or shorter, or even skipped, from year to year.

JANUARY

Black Truffle
Black Trumpet
Chanterelle
Fried Chicken
Hedgehog
Pholiote
Yellowfoot

FEBRUARY

Black Truffle
Black Trumpet
Hedgehog
Yellowfoot

MARCH

Black Trumpet
Black Truffle
Morel
Mousseron
Wild Oyster

APRIL

Black Trumpet
Cèpe/Porcini
Coral
Morel
Mousseron
Puffball

MAY

Morel
Mousseron
Puffball
St-Georges
Wild Oyster

JUNE

Black Trumpet
Cèpe/Porcini
Morel
Mousseron
Puffball
St-Georges
Wild Oyster

JULY

Black Trumpet
Cèpe/Porcini
Chanterelle
Chicken of the
  Woods
Lobster
Morel
Mousseron
Ovoli
Summer Truffle
Wild Oyster

AUGUST

Chanterelle
Chicken of the
  Woods
Hedgehog
Honey
Lactaire
Lobster
Ovoli

SEPTEMBER

Chanterelle
Chicken of the
  Woods
Hedgehog
Hen of the Woods
Honey
Lactaire
Lobster
Matsutake
Wine Cap

OCTOBER

Black Trumpet
Blewit
Blue Chanterelle
Cauliflower
Cèpe/Porcini
Chanterelle
Chicken of the
  Woods
Fried Chicken
Hedgehog
Hen of the Woods
Lactaire
Lobster
Matsutake
Mousseron
Parasol
Puffball
White Truffle
Wine Cap
Yellowfoot

NOVEMBER

Black Truffle
Black Trumpet
Blewit
Cauliflower
Cèpe/Porcini
Chanterelle
Charbonnier
Hedgehog
Lactaire
Matsutake
Mousseron
Parasol
Pig Ear
White Truffle
Yellowfoot

DECEMBER

Black Truffle
Black Trumpet
Cauliflower
Cèpe/Porcini
Chanterelle
Hedgehog
Matsutake
White Truffle
Yellowfoot

BLACK TRUMPET

A.K.A. HORN OF PLENTY, BLACK CHANTERELLE

This wickedly black mushroom perfumes any dish with an intense aroma and taste. Loosened from forest floors throughout the United States and Europe, it is fragile, inconsistently sized, and anything but timid. Trumpets have a long, hollow stem that flares out to a fluted shape with ruffled edges. The color varies from mousy brown to purply-gray to jet black. The French call it *trompette de la mort,* or trumpet of death. Look for black trumpets as early as July but count on a consistent supply from November to March. When not available, use yellowfoot, thinly sliced hedgehogs, or dried black trumpets.

SELECT/STORE: Look for dry, intact mushrooms with no damp spots. The cap should hold its trumpet shape without going limp. Trumpets are fragile, so be careful to stow them on top of your groceries. Place in a shallow woven basket and loosely cover with paper towels. Store on a wire shelf in the refrigerator for up to 4 days.

PREPARE: Black trumpets grow in the woods, so to avoid cooking and serving black trumpets with ferns and leaf skeletons, do a quick colander shake (see Cleaning Mushrooms, page 5). Trim the tough stem ends. Pull the mushroom in half lengthwise to brush away the sand in the stem. If cleaning out each stem is too daunting, aim the water nozzle at them, tossing all the while. Dry and cook immediately.

COOK: Sauté. This ragout-type mushroom pairs well with a wetter mushroom such as yellowfoot or chanterelle. Its perfumed flavor brings out the best in scallops, fish, chicken, and game.

BEGINNER RECIPE:
THAI CHICKEN WITH BLACK TRUMPETS IN COCONUT MILK *(page 135)*

BLEWIT

*B*lewits appear briefly in early fall. With a mild, mushroomy aroma, the blewit makes a perfect fish or savory custard partner. Its pale ivory-to-beige flesh is faintly stained purple, as though it had been pickling in grape juice. The gilled cap is supported by a stocky stem. The bluefoot mushroom, cultivated in the United States and in France where it is called *pied bleu,* is a cousin of the blewit, with a firmer, drier texture and equally pleasing aroma. For substitutes, try fleshy wild oyster mushrooms or chicken of the woods. Look for blewits in October and November.

SELECT/STORE: Look for firm, unbroken caps with a nice blue-purple stem. Whether 1 inch or 6 inches in diameter, they are relatively dry. Place in a shallow woven basket and loosely cover with paper towels. Store on a wire shelf in the refrigerator for up to 1 week.

PREPARE: Trim off and reserve stems for Mushroom Jus (page 254). Use a damp paper towel or paring knife to remove any debris that clings to the caps.

COOK: The blewit, sautéed and highly seasoned, adds a crunchy note to eggs. Sauté, add chicken stock, and simmer until the liquid is absorbed. Then fold the mushrooms into an almost-cooked omelet or soft scrambled eggs. Or marinate with Mushroom-Infused Sherry (page 255) and a dash of peanut oil and grill. They are also delicious pickled for a still August afternoon when cooking is the last thing on your mind.

BEGINNER RECIPE:

BLEWIT AND CRAB ROLLS

(page 183)

BLUEFOOT

A.K.A. *PIED BLEU*

*D*ry, velvety, and of a striking blue hue, the bluefoot has gills under a wavy cap and a stem, which is good for dicing into duxelles. It is the cultivated version of the wild blewit and is available year round.

SELECT/STORE: Choose mushrooms with unbroken caps and gills. When brittle or limp, the flavor has mostly dissipated. Place in a shallow woven basket and loosely cover with paper towels. Store on a wire shelf in the refrigerator for up to 1 week.

PREPARE: There is no need to wash bluefoot. Cut off the fibrous stem ends and dice the remainder of the stem for a sauté of mixed mushrooms or for duxelles. Slice the cap ½ inch thick or keep whole to grill.

COOK: Sauté in butter over medium-high heat, then simmer in stock to soften. Marinate the caps and grill around the edges of the fire. Bluefoot can also be pickled, to serve as a salad. Try bluefoot in recipes that call for button mushrooms or use them when blewit are not available.

BEGINNER RECIPE:
GARLIC FLAN AND SAUTEED BLUEFOOTS
(page 52)

CAULIFLOWER MUSHROOM

As fungi goes, this one is atypical in shape. It grows more like a seaweed than a mushroom. Its thick, pale yellow branches can emerge in undulating layers; others form a dense clump. Either way, the cauliflower mushroom offers an assertive perfume unlike any other. It is available between October and December. Otherwise, substitute hen of the woods, lobster, or black trumpet.

SELECT/STORE: Look for mushrooms that are firm, moist, and free of dark spots. Place cauliflower mushrooms in a shallow woven basket and loosely cover with paper towels. Store on a wire shelf in the refrigerator for up to 3 days.

PREPARE: Trim off the root end. If dirt is embedded among the branches, rinse them under running water and shake dry. Cut into bite-size pieces.

COOK: Sauté or roast. Pair the cauliflower mushroom with soft foods like eggs, polenta, mâche salad, and vegetable purées. *Warning:* Avoid cooking cauliflower mushrooms with red wine. This combination very occasionally will cause an upset stomach.

BEGINNER RECIPE:
MACHE WITH CAULIFLOWER MUSHROOMS AND SOFT-COOKED EGG
(page 93)

CÈPE · PORCINI

Somehow, the English-speaking world never got around to deciding on a common name for this succulent, earthy mushroom. Bolete is its correct English name, but outside that region, the terms cèpe and porcini are more often used. I refer to *boletus edulis* as cèpe, because France is my point of reference; others, more familiar with Italy, say porcini. No matter your name of choice, the mushroom has an ivory, bulbous stem and brown, rounded cap. Frozen cèpes are available year round, and produce stellar results in any recipe that requires sautéing or roasting. A reasonable substitute is the shiitake.

The European season for fresh cèpes can begin as early as July, more likely September, and it's often finished in about five weeks. In some years there is also a late spring crop.

SELECT/STORE: In the United States, cèpes are often halved lengthwise right in the forest. If there are holes in the stem and cap, the mushroom is left on the ground. You can check for maggots by squeezing the mushroom gently. If it crumbles, discard it. In a very fresh cèpe, the springy underside of the cap is beige. As the mushroom ages, it darkens to a greenish brown. This discolored part is bitter and should be trimmed off. Place cèpes in a shallow woven basket and loosely cover with paper towels. Store on a wire shelf in the refrigerator for 2 to 3 days.

PREPARE: Use a paring knife to shave clumped dirt off the root end. Scrape off any dirt on the stems—there is a lot of flavor in the outer layer—or brush with an old toothbrush. Trim off any greenish part under the cap. Make ¼-inch slices through the stem and cap.

COOK: Sauté and roast whole cèpes; grill the caps whole. Sauté the stems first, adding the caps about 3 minutes later. The stems are delicious diced into ½-inch pieces and sautéed with same-size cubes of potatoes.

BEGINNER RECIPE:
CHICKEN WITH SAUTEED CEPES
(page 137)

CHANTERELLE

A.K.A. GIROLLE, PFIFFERLING, GOLDEN CHANTERELLE

Chanterelle sports that well-loved pumpkin glow and fruity aroma. Early summer ushers in the first variety: a firm mini that would fit nicely on dollhouse dinnerware. If this eastern European variety delights, the Nova Scotia chanterelle of August thrills. Its pert shape and sweetly fruity aroma make it the darling of top-notch chefs. Following this act in late September, the Pacific Northwest chanterelles suffer in looks, but not in flavor. They are the workhorse that sustains the kitchen through the busy holiday season. In January, the last hurrah kicks in—an unwieldy but welcome California crop. If you really must replace chanterelles with a more available mushroom, use hedgehogs or make a mixture of whatever exotic varieties you find.

SELECT/STORE: Look for firmness, and a bright yellow color. Steer clear of mushrooms that exude liquid when pressed lightly between two fingers. The cap can be curled under, but more often it flutes out in a trumpet shape. Browned and fraying edges indicate drying, which means the flavor has dissipated. Place chanterelles in a shallow woven basket and loosely cover with paper towels. Store on a wire shelf in the refrigerator for up to 1 week. Chanterelles can also be frozen for up to 3 months (see page 9).

PREPARE: Remove the tough stem end of the mushroom. If there is dirt between the gills, wipe it off with a damp paper towel. For large mushrooms, slice across the cap, and chop the stem into small dice. Medium chanterelles can be sliced through the cap and stem. Use tiny ones whole.

COOK: The chanterelle's apricot nuances make it a natural choice for chop and pasta sauces. Chanterelles flaunt their best in the sauté pan, add depth to stews, and make a crunchy side dish when roasted.

BEGINNER RECIPE:
BAY SCALLOPS WITH SORREL AND CHANTERELLES (*page 159*)

CHICKEN OF THE WOODS

A.K.A. CHICKEN, SULFUR SHELF

This summer and early fall wild mushroom fans out from tree trunks like a Japanese fan. Lots of people confuse it with hen of the woods, which is a ruffled, gray-brown mushroom. Chickens, as chefs call them, are dense, firm, and somewhat dry; they range in color from bright yellow to orange. The mushrooms are layered like lettuce leaves, with knobby edges. If you can't get them, use bluefoot, lobster, or oyster mushrooms.

SELECT/STORE: Chickens should be vibrantly colored. The smooth top should yield slightly when pressed. As they dry out, chickens lose that succulence, start to gray, and develop a cheesy white film around the edges. Place them in a shallow woven basket and loosely cover with paper towels. Store on a wire shelf in the refrigerator for up to 4 days.

PREPARE: This is a low-maintenance mushroom. Wipe with a damp towel to remove any dirt. For stews, slice from the stem end out toward the edge, then slice again crosswise. Grill chickens whole.

COOK: Because of their dry, dense texture chickens are best cooked in moist heat. Since the flavor is rightly called chicken-y, they'll sop up a spicy Mexican marinade as well as a cumin cream or Mushroom Soy Sauce (page 255).

BEGINNER RECIPE:
SHRIMP CHILES RELLENOS
(page 163)

CREMINI

Cremini, portobello, and white button mushrooms are botanical triplets. The cremini looks like a button mushroom, just a bit larger and with a dry, brown cap instead of white. Use cremini when you want earthy flavor and a nice crunchy texture. Available year round in just about every metropolis, it's the least expensive of the cultivated exotics.

SELECT/STORE: It's hard to get a bad cremini. Ideally the cap is still attached to the stem with a thin veil. It should be dry, with a matte surface, and an aroma redolent of mushroom. If the cap is wrinkled, the gills are flattened, or the mushroom is squishy, pass it by. Place cremini in a shallow woven basket and loosely cover with paper towels. Store on a wire shelf in the refrigerator for 1 week or even longer.

PREPARE: Some creminis have sandy dirt on the tip of the stem (this helps the mushroom live longer). Trim it off before cooking. Wipe the cap with a damp cloth or plunge the cremini in water and drain quickly. If you don't use the stems (as in a stuffed mushroom recipe), save them in the freezer for your next stock or soup.

COOK: Sauté sliced cremini, roast or grill caps. Creminis add depth to soups and an earthy note to salads and pasta toppings. They seem made to toss with tomatoes, yet their aggressive flavor is tamed by meat, fresh herbs, and cheese.

BEGINNER RECIPE:
SLOW-ROASTED CREMINI WITH BARLEY
(page 96)

ENOKI

Enoki is often found sitting forlornly on the supermarket shelf, its diminutive size and embarrassing plastic shrink-wrap threatening to send it into oblivion. But on the plate, it's a dainty, Q-Tip–shaped reminder of the mushroom kingdom's power. Enoki shows best as a crunchy garnish for soup, salad, or sauced meats. It is cultivated and almost always imported from Japan.

SELECT/STORE: The shrink-wrap should be tight over the cluster. Avoid slimy-looking or droopy packages. Store in the refrigerator for 1 week or longer. When the plastic starts to loosen its grip on the mushrooms, it's time to use up the enoki fast.

PREPARE: Trim the root ends and separate the mushrooms from the clump.

COOK: Sprinkle raw enoki with lemon and salt as an appetizer. Drop into an Asian broth for the last minute of cooking. Ditto for a sauté or stir-fry. Goes especially well with seafood.

BEGINNER RECIPE:
BONELESS CHICKEN BREASTS WITH MOUSSERONS AND ENOKI
(page 139)

FRIED CHICKEN

The cap of this flavorful brownish mushroom can be a little bit clammy. Stems join together in a cluster, although they are often separated before shipping. Fried-chicken mushrooms have a pungent autumn aroma, so they work well in recipes calling for cèpes or shiitakes. They appear in the early fall.

SELECT/STORE: Give the caps a pinch; if they bounce back, the mushrooms are fresh. The caps should be turned under and the gills still erect. Place fried chickens in a woven shallow basket and loosely cover with paper towels. Store on a wire shelf in the refrigerator for up to 1 week.

PREPARE: Pat off any forest cling-ons with a damp paper towel. Trim off most of the hollow stem, which doesn't have much flavor.

COOK: Play on the earthy notes of the fried chicken, pairing it with beef, buffalo, or chicken in rich sauces. Let red wine contribute acidity and add butter to sweeten the deal.

BEGINNER RECIPE:
GORGONZOLA POLENTA WITH ROASTED FRIED CHICKENS (*page 200*)

HEDGEHOG MUSHROOM

A.K.A. SWEET TOOTH, *PIED DE MOUTON*

The slight bitterness of the hedgehog sets it apart from the fruity chanterelle, with which it is often confused because they are both pumpkin colored. You can tell the difference by looking under the cap: Hedgehog caps rest on top of a stem and have tiny teeth under the cap; chanterelles are flute-shaped, with gills under the cap. Hedgehog season begins in late summer and usually runs through January, but sometimes it extends through March. Hedgehogs and chanterelles are often substituted for one another, more for their appearance and texture than for flavor.

SELECT/STORE: Avoid hedgehogs with fraying edges, dark, wet spots, or matted teeth under the cap. Place in a shallow woven basket and loosely cover with paper towels. Store on a wire shelf in the refrigerator for about 1 week.

PREPARE: Trim off most of the stem and cut into uniform pieces. Forget trimming tiny—¾ inch or less—hedgehogs; they look beautiful whole. The stems on small specimens are not too woody to eat.

COOK: "Hedgies" take wonderfully to the sauté pan, as well as to the roasting pan. Their "teeth" break off into the sauce, sparkling like flecks of gold. Hedgehogs have a flavor note best described as tangy, adding a pleasant contrast to pork, corn, and ham.

BEGINNER RECIPE:
HEDGEHOG AND BUTTERMILK SOUP
(page 80)

HEN OF THE WOODS

A.K.A. MAIITAKE

The leafy, layered look goes vertical. The dense layers of this mushroom grow from a central base, spreading out as layers are added. They are enormous; some specimens weigh in at a hefty 25 pounds. This includes a lot of unusable stem, so be sure to calculate recipes by eye instead of heft. Available year round, the cultivated hen of the woods, under human control, grows only big enough to fill a lumberjack's hand. It is more fragile and fragrant than the wild variety. Hen of the woods pop up in forests in October. Both versions vary in color from beige to brown to gray.

SELECT/STORE: Hen of the woods should be firm and fresh-looking with a pleasant perfume. Wet spots and matted or brittle "leaves" are sure signs of a hen past its prime. Place them in a shallow woven basket and loosely cover with paper towels. Store on a wire shelf in the refrigerator for about 1 week.

PREPARE: Plunge the mushrooms into a large bowl of cool water. Shake to remove excess water, then roll them gently in a clean kitchen towel to dry. Cut hens according to the recipe by slicing into strips or by dicing.

COOK: Hens are excellent sautéed or grilled. Simmer in soups or add to ravioli fillings.

BEGINNER RECIPE:
WARM SALAD OF HEN OF THE WOODS WITH BITTER GREENS AND BACON
(page 90)

HONEY MUSHROOM

A.K.A. HONEY CAP

You'll never find this mushroom in your local supermarket, because honey caps don't grace every forest glen. But there are enough to see in specialty markets throughout the country. It looks like a leggy doll with a jaunty cap, and has a flavor slightly reminiscent of a mellow Port. (Sometimes the name *honey* is applied to a different tiny mushroom with a sticky cap, but this variety is rarely cultivated anymore.) Look for honey mushrooms in August and September. Substitute honshimeji, mousseron, pholiote, or shiitake mushrooms cut into ½-inch dice.

SELECT/STORE: Honey mushrooms have long, slender stems that cluster at the root end. The small, caramel-colored caps should be free of blemishes and still turned under. Place them in a shallow woven basket and loosely cover with paper towels. Store on a wire shelf in the refrigerator for up to 5 days.

PREPARE: Although there usually isn't any dirt, if any clings to the cap, wipe it off with a damp paper towel. Trim the stems to 1 inch before cooking. Trim off most of the stem before sautéing.

COOK: The honey is a sauté mushroom, good with butter and a touch of something sweet, such as dates, Port wine, or balsamic vinegar. Keep the caps whole for a nice presentation. The honey mushroom goes well with pork.

BEGINNER RECIPE:
GNOCCHI WITH HONEY MUSHROOMS AND TOMATOES *(page 227)*

HONSHIMEJI

A.K.A. CLAMSHELL, BEECH

This closed-umbrella-shaped mushroom is about 1 inch high, with lots of crunch and a delicate flavor. Cultivated year round by just a few growers, it can be soft beige to snowy white. If you don't see them where you live, substitute canned straw mushrooms or fresh oyster mushrooms. If honshimeji are not available, substitute oyster mushrooms or small chanterelles or hedgehogs.

SELECT/STORE: Honshimeji should be firm and dry. Beware of limpness and wrinkles. Place the mushrooms in a shallow woven basket and loosely cover with paper towels. Store on a wire shelf in the refrigerator for up to 5 days.

PREPARE: Wipe off any debris with damp paper towels. Either leave the mushrooms whole or split them in half lengthwise. The stems are edible.

COOK: Because of the honshimeji's Japanese origins, we lean toward soups and stir-fries. But a quick sauté with a splash of soy sauce makes honshimeji a natural accompaniment to fish.

BEGINNER RECIPE:
HONSHIMEJI UDON BROTH
(page 69)

HUITLACOCHE

A.K.A. CORN SMUT

*F*irst, the pronunciation: weet-la-coach-aye. This jet-black, candy-corn–shaped fungus is a farmer's nightmare turned chef's temptation. It attacks the cobs right in the field, sucking out all that corn flavor, and returning it in the sauté pan. While farmers may feed it to the pigs (imagine corn-flavored bacon!), huitlacoche is nature's gift to cooks. It often comes from Mexico; there it is spread on tortillas and rolled inside tamales. The kernels are the size of lima beans, and melt into a creamy consistency when cooked.

Finding fresh huitlacoche is rare, and depends upon one's access to cornfields. The most reliable source of huitlacoche is canned, which is sold in specialty, south-of-the-border gourmet markets, and by mail order (page 324). There really is no way to replace the flavor, color, and texture of this wondrous fungus. But many recipes are still tasty when another assertive mushroom such as black trumpet, shiitake, or porcini replaces the huitlacoche.

SELECT/STORE: If you find huitlacoche fresh, place it in a shallow woven basket and loosely cover with paper towels. Store in the refrigerator for up to 1 week. Huitlacoche can also be frozen for a year or more (see page 9).

PREPARE: If it is canned, drain the liquid but do not rinse the mushrooms. For fresh huitlacoche, gently wipe off any dirt with damp paper towels. There is no need to chop this fungus.

COOK: To cook huitlacoche, sauté over high heat to quickly render the juices. For flavor companions, think corn and cilantro (Mexican style), grits (Southern style), and tomato (American style). Keep in mind that corn smut turns inky black when cooked, and it will darken soups and sauces.

BEGINNER RECIPE:
HUITLACOCHE WITH SUMMER TOMATOES *(page 190)*

LACTAIRE

A.K.A. MILKY CAP

This unusual-looking mushroom may strike you as beautiful or as bizarre. It has a pumpkin color, run through with green veins, tender flesh, and a stand-up-and-take-notice flavor. Lactaire pop out among late-summer, early-autumn fallen leaves. When not available, substitute bluefoot, blewit, hedgehog, or oyster mushrooms.

SELECT/STORE: Look for mushrooms that are firm and highly colored. Lactaires tend to crumble when worms have gotten into them, so press into the cap and stem with a finger to check for firmness. Place them in a shallow woven basket and loosely cover with paper towels. Store on a wire shelf in the refrigerator for no more than 2 days.

PREPARE: Slice off the stem flush with the cap. Wipe off dirt and other cling-ons with a damp paper towel.

COOK: With their firm texture and tangy bite, lactaires are traditionally pickled, although they make a nice soup garnish when thinly sliced and sautéed in butter.

BEGINNER RECIPE:
PICKLED LACTAIRE

(page 88)

LOBSTER

One look at this knobby, pitted, flame-orange creature explains how it got its name. It does indeed hail from the piney forests of the lobster state, Maine, as well as other forests in the United States from the northeast to the northwest. Its season—midsummer to late fall—follows campers, conveniently situating itself along hiking paths and gravel roads. Out of season, use another bulky, flavorful mushroom, such as portobello or hen of the woods.

SELECT/STORE: This fairly dry mushroom should be devoid of white mold and soggy edges. Its pits are colored from white to black to orange, and its broad stem is orange throughout. Place lobsters in a shallow woven basket and loosely cover with paper towels. Store on a wire shelf in the refrigerator for up to 1 week.

PREPARE: Slice off the stem flush with the cap. Wipe clean with a damp paper towel, and use a toothbrush to remove stubborn dirt from the pits. Slice the cap about ¼ inch thick. Marinades and olive oil tenderize this firm mushroom and give punch to its seafood-like flavor.

COOK: Grilling is the way to go with lobsters. Pair with seafood, polenta, and corn. Use it in soups and stews as a flavor-adder.

BEGINNER RECIPE:
MAINE LOBSTER SALAD (*page 99*)

MATSUTAKE

A.K.A. PINE MUSHROOM

With a reputation for being exorbitantly expensive and for having aphrodisiac properties, this spring mushroom doesn't find its way into every local market. Because it commands a high price in Japan (where they are as rare as truffles), pickers sometimes desert morel hunting when the matsutake appear. In the Idaho hills, where many pine mushrooms grow, clashes have erupted among mushroom pickers competing for the valuable "matsu." This delicate, pine-scented mushroom is exported to Japan, where it is auctioned off for hundreds of dollars a pound. Individual mushrooms are beautifully wrapped and presented as gifts to loved ones and business contacts. If you don't find them in your market, substitute oyster mushrooms.

SELECT/STORE: There are five grades of matsutake. The grades describe the cap's growth from pristine closed-umbrella shape to flat-out open. I think all the grades are tasty, although Grade 5 matsutakes, the fully-open caps, are older and less fresh-tasting. Mushrooms should not be dried out or brittle and should have a pleasing scent reminiscent of pine. Place matsus in a shallow woven basket and loosely cover with paper towels. Store on a wire shelf in the refrigerator for up to 3 days.

PREPARE: Slice off the stem. Wipe any dirt or plant bits off the caps with a damp paper towel. Discard the stems and slice the caps.

COOK: The matsutake's buttery flavor comes out in the sauté pan. They are equally succulent in a Japanese broth flavored with seaweed.

BEGINNER RECIPE:
MATSUTAKE AND SEAWEED SOUP
(page 70)

MOREL

The flavor of the revered morel grips the palate's attention, and its pocked crevices beg for velvety cream sauces. Coloring and shape vary according to the kind of morel that is in season, season being from first thaw to the dog days of summer. One-inch high, gray to black coneheads come first, followed by larger, rounder ones, colored from blond to beige to dark brown. Huge morels, which usually signal the end of the season, can be as big as your palm and are blond. When they go out of season, use dried ones, calculating about 1 ounce of dried for 4 ounces fresh. The dried morels are not only more intensely flavored, they reconstitute to the same springy texture as fresh morels.

SELECT/STORE: Look for dry, unbroken specimens. The aroma should be of freshly-turned soil. White streaks usually mean mold. Place morels in a shallow woven basket loosely covered with paper towels. Store on a wire shelf in the refrigerator for up to 1 week.

PREPARE: Slice off the stem. Slit the caps in half lengthwise and brush out sand with a damp paper towel or brush. They can be rinsed under cool running water and patted dry with paper towels. If the morels are not sandy, use them whole. But keep in mind that all the pieces should be about the same size, no matter how large or small they are to begin with.

COOK: Morels love nothing more than cream. They also go well with corn, peas, chicken, fish, and rich red wine reduction sauces.

BEGINNER RECIPE:
STRIPED SEA BASS WITH MOREL CREAM
(page 170)

MOUSSERON

A.K.A. FAIRY RING

This woodsy, nymph-like mushroom is no bigger than a fingernail. It bears all the goodness of the soil in its tiny beige-brown cap. A pretty variation of this mushroom is the deeply regal violet mousseron; the flavor is the same as the regular mousseron. Mousserons grow in a circle, as though dancing fairies had left behind impressions of their tiny feet. Its season is early spring through mid-summer. The dried mousseron reconstitutes very well, yielding a texture very similar to the fresh mousseron. Similar flavor notes sing out from shiitake mushrooms.

SELECT/STORE: Mousserons should be dry and springy, with a fragrant decaying-leaf scent of the forest floor. Dark, limp, or wrinkled mousserons have hit and passed their prime. Place them in a shallow woven basket loosely covered with paper towels. Store on a wire shelf in the refrigerator for up to 4 days.

PREPARE: Keep the stems intact; there's no need to trim them off. Shake out cling-ons like fern and leaf bits. If the mousserons are not clean, plunge them in a bowl of cool water, swish gently, drain, and roll in a clean kitchen towel.

COOK: With their delicate texture, mousserons seem destined for quick sauté and lightly flavored ragouts. Accent with chervil and tarragon and tuck into crepes or serve alongside a hearty veal chop.

BEGINNER RECIPE:
CRAWFISH TAILS WITH MOUSSERONS IN LEEK-INFUSED CREAM (page 164)

Oyster Mushroom

A.K.A. PLEUROTTE

The white oyster mushroom and its designer-hued cousins, the yellow (or canary), blue, and pink oyster, are flat, shell-shaped mushrooms. Most oysters are cultivated year round and come in a variety of shades, from pearly white to mousy brown. We prefer the ones that grow in clusters, for their smooth exterior, chewy texture, and lack of stem. Wild oysters, which grow on tree trunks in the summer (May, June, and July), are fleshier, often larger—even saucer size—and yield a double dose of that oyster-like flavor. Some farmers cultivate these large fleshy ones and label them Italian oyster mushrooms.

SELECT/STORE: Look for crisp, dewy mushrooms with no wrinkles or dried-out edges. Fresh oysters feel moist and smell like fresh fungi. Stemmed oysters yield less than the clusters. Place them in a shallow woven basket loosely covered with paper towels. Store on a wire shelf in the refrigerator for up to 4 days.

PREPARE: Wild oysters are often so large that any dirt between the gills can be dislodged with a small soft brush. Cultivated oysters are smaller and cleaner, and rarely need to be brushed off. Oyster stems can be trimmed flush with the cap and sent to the stockpot or freezer—they are woody and best not sautéed.

COOK: The oyster's mellow flavor is enriched by fresh herbs, creamy sauces, and briny stocks. Use it also as an inexpensive stretcher in a fricassee or stew calling for a medley of wild mushrooms. Grill or roast the large, fleshy oysters.

BEGINNER RECIPE:
DOUBLE OYSTER GRATIN (page 58)

PARASOL

A.K.A. COULEMELLE

The umbrella-like cap of this mushroom is soft, with little shingles on the outside like a Swiss hut. It has a tall stem, a brown-beige cap, and a nutty-meaty flavor. The parasol is an autumn mushroom, available briefly in October and/or November. When not available, use shiitake mushrooms.

SELECT/STORE: The cap should be soft, full, and free of dark spots. Check that the gills are still dry. This highly perishable mushroom should be wrapped loosely in damp paper towels and stored on a wire shelf in the refrigerator to hold for 1 or 2 days at most.

PREPARE: Parasols are brittle. When young the cap is egg-shaped with edges that almost meet the stem. As the mushroom grows, the cap opens away from the stem into a parasol shape that gives the mushroom its name.

Eventually, the cap opens completely and becomes flat with a slightly raised center. At this point it may split around the edges. Handle them carefully, especially if they are young and the caps are still cup-shaped, the perfect shape for stuffing. Remove the stems, trimming off tough ends and dicing the remaining part for sautés. Brush the caps gently with a soft brush to remove forest cling-ons.

COOK: The fragile caps of parasol mushrooms should be handled delicately. Bread and fry open caps as a pocket for fillings, such as soft goat cheese or fresh tomato salsa. The flat larger caps, when breaded and fried, make a perfect side dish for baked fish fillet, stuffed tomatoes, and omelets.

BEGINNER RECIPE:
HERB-CRUSTED PARASOLS

(page 47)

POMPOM

A.K.A. POMPOM BLANC™

Pompoms are cultivated by just a few farmers in the United States. They are round, soft orbs covered with fine silky "feathers." Cut in half, they show off a creamy white, spongy interior. If you can't find them, a puffball or thick wild oyster will provide similar texture and flavor.

SELECT/STORE: Pompoms, generally around 4 to 6 inches in size, should be mostly ivory color and have a fresh, mushroomy smell. Brown blotches indicate that spoilage is starting. Store them in a shallow woven basket loosely covered with paper towels. Store on a wire shelf in the refrigerator for up to 3 days.

PREPARE: There is nothing to clean or trim.

COOK: Pompom's mild flavor attracts mildly assertive ones. Try it with fish, ham, and cheese. Since it soaks up fat like a sponge, sautés must be done quickly. Grill, roast, or braise in stock or tuck into foil packages with fresh herbs and a splash of white wine and bake.

BEGINNER RECIPE:
POMPOM WITH BRESAOLA
(page 89)

PORTOBELLO

A portobello's hearty flavor and firm texture make it a great meat substitute. As an inexpensive, readily-available, American-cultivated mushroom, it adapts well to our constantly evolving American cuisine. The portobello originated in Pennsylvania's (yes, Pennsylvania!) mushroom-farming corridor. There, Italian immigrant farmers cultivated the brown mushrooms they remembered from the old country. These cremini, it turned out, developed large caps when left to grow a few more days. The farmers gave the large variety its own name, portobello.

SELECT/STORE: Look for smooth caps that are turned under, and dry, unbroken gills. There's usually a little harmless growing medium on the caps and around the stem end. Portobellos have a long shelf life. Place them, uncovered, in a shallow woven basket. Store on a wire shelf in the refrigerator for up to 10 days.

PREPARE: If there is some dirt on the cap, brush it off with a damp paper towel. Cut off the stem flush with the bottom of the cap. Reserve the stems for another use, such as Mushroom Jus (page 254) or Wild Mushroom and Multigrain Soup (page 73). Slice the caps for a sauce (remove the dark gills, which add an inky color to stews or sautés) or roast or grill the caps whole.

COOK: Go easy on the marinade; this thirsty mushroom is like a Turkish towel in a four-star hotel. The more you give it, the more it absorbs. We usually paint the marinade on the top of the cap just before grilling. Portobello sautés equally well.

BEGINNER RECIPE:
ROASTED PORTOBELLO CAPS WITH WARM BEAN FILLING (page 216)

PUFFBALL

This creamy white, round, stemless mushroom grows in fields and backyards. It has a spongy texture like a Nerf ball. When the puffball dries up, it releases a gray puff of smoky dust if stepped on—thus the name. The flavor is mild and reminiscent of a button mushroom. Puffballs appear in markets anywhere from April through June. When not available, use a fleshy mushroom such as wild oyster, portobello, or even the familiar button variety.

SELECT/STORE: Gently push into the puffball; it should resist and spring back. Size is not relevant to flavor; puffballs normally weigh in at about 12 ounces, but we once found a 28-pound specimen! Wimpy, soggy, or discolored puffballs are past their prime. Place them, uncovered, in a shallow woven basket. Store on a wire shelf in the refrigerator for up to 3 days.

PREPARE: Wipe off the surface of the puffball, then slice it thick or thin.

COOK: Puffballs need a little marinade or a spritzing of olive oil. Fresh herbs, such as thyme and oregano, will add extra flavor. Grill or sauté or use instead of tofu in an Asian-style soup or stir-fry.

BEGINNER RECIPE:
MEXICAN PUFFBALL PIZZA
(page 42)

ST-GEORGES

The St-Georges resembles an unevenly shaped white button mushroom, with a fleshy, pale peanut-butter–colored cap and a short stem. This delicately earthy mushroom doesn't create a huge stir, mostly because mushroom pickers are way too hepped up about morels and mousserons in spring to bother harvesting it. However, they are harvested in France and available in markets or by mail order (see page 324) in May and June. If you can't get St-Georges, use matsutake, oyster, bluefoot, or button.

SELECT/STORE: Brush off any dirt clumps with a toothbrush and trim off stem ends. Place the mushrooms in a shallow woven basket loosely covered with paper towels. Store on a wire shelf in the refrigerator for up to 1 week.

PREPARE: Trim off the woody part of the stem; cut the cap into quarters or slice.

COOK: Sauté in olive oil or butter, to eat with fish, roasts, or in risotto. Use the St-Georges as you would a button mushroom or cremini. It can be eaten raw, which suits it for salads or as a last-minute addition to soup.

BEGINNER RECIPE:
LIDIA BASTIANICH'S RISOTTO WITH ST-GEORGES MUSHROOMS
(page 212)

SHIITAKE

This round-capped mushroom has a brown, downturned cap over an ivory, woody stem. It is cultivated outdoors on oak logs or indoors in vast growing rooms. The caps can be ½ inch around or up to 3 inches, dusty beige or deep brown, or anywhere in between. This mushroom is conveniently available almost everywhere, all the time. Shiitakes are gutsy with an earthy flavor and a buttery texture.

There is a variety of shiitake called Oakwood, which delivers a really intense and deep flavor. Its cap resembles sun-dried cracked mud. Since it has a very low moisture content, it gives up little liquid and is even helped by the addition of stock or water while cooking. When a recipe calls for Oakwood, it's in order for the shiitake flavor to contribute to the recipe in a big way. But if you can't get this special kind, just use a regular shiitake.

SELECT/STORE: Look for firm, fragrant, unwrinkled caps. Avoid mushrooms with black or wet spots and an ammonia-like odor. Sometimes the black spots just mean the DNA took a wrong turn; if the mushroom smells fresh, simply cut off the spots. Place shiitakes in a shallow woven basket and loosely cover with paper towels. Store on a wire shelf in the refrigerator for up to 1 week.

PREPARE: Trim off the stem and add it to your trimmings stockpile. Wipe the caps clean with a damp paper towel. Small mushrooms can be used whole; larger ones can be grilled or sliced ¼ inch thick.

COOK: Whole, firm, large caps are great on the grill or roasted. Slice caps into fricassees, broths, stir-fries, and sauces. Shiitakes go equally well with fish, meat, and pasta.

BEGINNER RECIPE:
MUSHROOM FRIED CHICKEN
WITH SHIITAKE PAN JUICES
(page 134)

STRAW MUSHROOM

A.K.A. PADDY STRAW

These plump, bite-size mushrooms add a juicy crunch and somewhat slippery texture to Asian dishes. The beige-brown cap is shaped like a closed umbrella, and is about 1 inch long. The white stem is edible. Straw mushrooms are not available fresh; they come canned in brine. Button or cremini can be substituted.

SELECT/STORE: Find them in Asian markets and in supermarkets. If the whole can is not used, transfer the mushrooms and brine to a plastic container, and store, tightly covered, in the refrigerator for up to 2 days.

PREPARE: Drain the brine and discard. Slice the mushrooms lengthwise if the recipe calls for small pieces.

COOK: The straw mushroom's crunchiness makes it ideal for stir-fries and Asian-style broths. It is already cooked.

BEGINNER RECIPE:
CLAM NAGE WITH STRAW AND ENOKI MUSHROOMS
(page 160)

Truffle, Black

Truffles are used as an aromatic. They are wildly romanticized, perhaps to justify the price. Flavor and cooking style vary with the kind of truffle.

The black winter truffle (*Tuber melanosporum*) is the most flavorful of the black truffles. It is the truffle to use whenever a recipe in this book calls for black truffle. It has a black, bumpy exterior and dark interior with white veins running through it. It is harvested in France in the Perigord and in Provence, as well as in Spain, Italy, and Portugal. This truffle has an earthy aroma and is used to make truffle juice, truffle oil, and truffle butter. Look for it from November through March.

The summer truffle (*Tuber aestivum*) appears from midsummer to mid-December and costs about one third less than the winter truffle. Like its winter cousin, it has a bumpy, brown-black exterior. The interior of a ripened summer truffle is dusky white, whereas the black winter truffle, when totally ripe, is black inside with some

Black Truffle Dividends

- *Black truffle oil is great for basting poultry and drizzling over wild game.*

- *Black truffle juice is used to boost the flavor of sauces and sautés.*

- *Black truffle butter helps bind meat sauces and flavor rice, pasta, and vegetables.*

- *Black truffle paste can be used in pasta doughs, stuffings, and sauces.*

white veins. In November, the two seasons converge; the winter truffle debuts unripe and with a white interior. At this point, unscrupulous vendors try to pass off the summer truffles as winter ones. Since they look alike, your best bet is to buy them from a trusted source. The summer truffle's flavor is pungent and earthy, but much less so than its winter counterpart.

The Chinese truffle (*Tuber indicum*) has the characteristically bumpy surface and dark-brown color of a black truffle. It tends to be small and hard. Its aroma is consistent with the low price it commands. Mixed with black winter truffles, it helps bring down the cost of a truffle dish.

SELECT/STORE: Black truffles should be firm, with a slightly bumpy surface. Sometimes rotting sections have been shaved off, which shouldn't affect the flavor. This actually allows you a peek at the interior. Early on in its season, the winter truffle is white-to-beige inside and tastes less pungent. By January, it is fully ripe and at its best: jet black inside, with a few white veins. The summer truffle, with its black, slightly bumpy exterior, should be firm and have a pleasing aroma.

If you can't use your truffle right away, or if it has come to room temperature during shipping, an ice bath will rejuvenate it. Place in a bowl of icy water to cover, then refrigerate overnight. Drain on paper towels, pat dry, and store in the refrigerator. I keep truffles in a shallow woven basket, loosely covered with paper towels. Sometimes they get tucked among unbroken eggs in a closed jar. The flavor penetrates the shells, so you can have a truffled omelet without slicing into the truffle. The flavor of any of the truffles dissipates rapidly, so use or freeze within a few days.

PREPARE: Occasionally, truffles have some surface dirt. It helps to keep them fresh, so brush it off lightly with a toothbrush just before using. Don't wash or peel truffles. When a recipe calls for truffle peelings, it means leftover pieces or crumbs that you have gathered from various uses and stored in the freezer. Use a truffle shaver (often called a chocolate shaver), a mandoline, or a very sharp knife to make extra thin slices.

COOK: You need heat to release the musky, earthy flavor of the black truffle: Layer potatoes with truffles, scramble slivers with eggs, tuck slices under the skin of a roasting chicken. For a simple sauce, heat Demi-Glace (page 282) or Rich Chicken Stock (page 281) in a small saucepan and swirl sliced truffle in it at a simmer.

BEGINNER RECIPE:
SCRAMBLED EGGS WITH BLACK TRUFFLES (page 180)

TRUFFLE, WHITE

A.K.A. ALBA TRUFFLE

The white truffle comes from the Piedmont region of Italy; it is often called the Alba truffle. It is dirty white with a highly pungent, garlicky aroma. This truffle usually appears in late October and nearly always finishes by New Year's.

SELECT/STORE: Store white truffles loosely covered in a basket, or closed in a jar with whole eggs. The flavor dissipates rapidly, so use it or freeze it within a few days. It has long been recommended to store white truffles in Arborio rice, thereby infusing the rice with the truffle's flavor. Fill a jar halfway with rice, nestle the truffle in it, then cover completely with more rice. Store in the refrigerator, tightly covered, for up to 2 days. Any longer and the rice will draw the moisture out of the truffle, drying it out and robbing it of its flavor.

PREPARE: Dab at any dirt with a damp paper towel. Remove dark or wet spots with a knife. Use a truffle/chocolate shaver, cheese grater, mandoline, or fine, sharp knife to slice the truffle.

COOK: The heady white truffle is best used raw. Shave it over thin-sliced beef, pasta, risotto, and soft lettuces dressed with truffle oil.

BEGINNER RECIPE: WHITE BEAN PUREE WITH WHITE TRUFFLE (page 220)

White Truffle Dividends

- White truffle oil is highly flavored, so use it just a drop at a time. Use it to flavor a vinaigrette (do not replace the recipe's oil with truffle oil, or it will overpower the salad), drizzle it over vegetables or sliced meat, or stir it into risotto, polenta, and pasta.

- White truffle paste helps bind ravioli stuffings and adds kick to sauces.

- White truffle sauce is a mixture of mushrooms and white truffle. Its caviar-like consistency makes it good for sauces and as a spread.

WINE CAP

Wine caps have a thick, ruddy brown cap on a white stem. Available in September and October, they take on the autumnal flavor of the woods in which they are found. When wine caps are not available, substitute shiitake mushrooms.

SELECT/STORE: Wine caps can be enormous or tiny but should smell like a damp forest and have a soft, dry cap. Avoid limp, dark-spotted specimens. Place in a shallow woven basket loosely covered with paper towels. Store on a wire shelf in the refrigerator for up to 4 days.

PREPARE: Trim off the stems and wipe the caps free of debris with a damp paper towel. Slice if sautéing or leave caps whole to grill or roast.

COOK: Sauté, grill, roast, or stew. The woodsy flavor of wine caps asserts itself in any dish, from soup to enchiladas.

BEGINNER RECIPE:
BIG FAT SIRLOIN STEAK WITH RED WINE, MARROW, AND WINE CAP MUSHROOMS
(page 108)

WOOD EAR

A.K.A. TREE EAR

This black mushroom is imported from China and sold dried. (Cloud ear, contrary to what some people think, is a different mushroom.) If you find fresh wood ear, it's probably because it has been reconstituted. The mushroom's chewiness, dark color, and mild flavor make it a great addition to Chinese dishes. The wood ear's unique texture makes it difficult to replace. Substitute other dried Chinese mushrooms, or canned straw mushrooms.

SELECT/STORE: Know that when these babies hit the water, they are going to expand. A pound of dried wood ears will fill a wet bar sink, so one or two pieces are usually sufficient for a recipe. Look for unbroken, brittle mushrooms and store them in a tightly closed glass jar in a cool place for up to 1 year.

PREPARE: Soak in warm water for at least 30 minutes. Trim off the base and slice into ribbons. The soaking liquid is not flavorful, so it's best to discard it.

COOK: Add to stir-fries and wonton stuffings. Chicken and pork are natural wood ear partners.

BEGINNER RECIPE:
GLAZED JADE VEGETABLES WITH WOOD EARS (page 41)

YELLOWFOOT

A.K.A. YELLOWFOOT CHANTERELLE

This fragrant member of the chanterelle family has a delicate, mousy brown, trumpet-shaped cap sitting on a muted gold stem. From France, we get a brown version of the yellowfoot called *chanterelle grise* (which means gray in French, go figure); the two are interchangeable. Look for the yellowfoot and chanterelles grise from early fall to late January. Chanterelle or hedgehog mushrooms could be substituted for yellowfoot.

SELECT/STORE: Yellowfoot have a high water content, so expect them to be a little soggy. However, they should hold their shape, not droop, and should not be slimy. A fresh, fall aroma says "Eat me." Place in a shallow woven basket loosely covered with paper towels. Store on a wire shelf in the refrigerator for up to 3 days.

PREPARE: Trim at the stem end. Occasionally there is a cache of dirt in the hollow of the cap or in the stems. To check, slice open through the cap and stem, and wipe with a damp paper towel or rinse thoroughly.

COOK: Most yellowfoot end up in the sauté pan. There, their juices can happily mingle with fresh herbs and the makings of a wild mushroom sauce. If making a mélange of wild mushrooms, cook firmer ones such as hedgehogs and chanterelles first. My favorite ragout is a mixture of yellowfoot, black trumpet, and hedgehog mushrooms. Yellowfoot go exceedingly well with roasts and chops yet work subtle wonders with fish and starches.

BEGINNER RECIPE:
SOLE BONNE FEMME *(page 174)*

MISCELLANEOUS MUSHROOMS

There are several mushrooms that are appealing to cook but are not readily available due to seasonality or perishability. Instead of introducing them in a big way, they are described briefly below (to whet the appetite). To store, place any of these mushrooms in a shallow woven basket loosely covered with paper towels. Store on a wire shelf in the refrigerator for up to 4 days (unless otherwise noted).

Candy Cap (*Lactarius fragilis*): This little red mushroom has a sweet maple syrup flavor and is as close to dessert as mushrooms get. It has a small cap perched atop a stem, and can be used whole as garnish. The season for this mushroom is winter.

Charbonnier (*Russule charbonnière*): Not particularly intriguing, taste-wise, the charbonnièr still has its followers. Its cap is wavy and tinted gray (thus its name's reference to *charbon,* or coal) to burgundy. The gills are bright white. Available in late summer and early fall, the charbonnièr adds texture to a ragout or sauté of wild mushrooms.

Coral (*Hericium coralloides*): This creamy yellow mushroom looks like its aquatic double, with spindly branches that shoot off from a base. It appears in forests in the summer and early fall. Some varieties of coral mushrooms aren't edible, so only buy them from a sure source. It is best roasted, but can be deep-fried or sautéed as well. Use in recipes calling for cauliflower mushrooms.

Ovolo (*Amanita Caesarea*): This mushroom comes from a family of extremes—Amanita—that produces the most deadly mushrooms and the most delicious. This one is delicious, and its egg shape—*ovoli* in Italian—gives it its name. Ovoli rival the porcini in flavor, and are best sautéed, grilled, or if very small, sliced raw into salad. They are available briefly in summer and should be eaten within 2 days.

Pholiote (*Pholiota mutabilis*): Small-capped and leggy, the pholiote (pronounced full-ee-ote) resembles the honey mushroom in many ways. It is very perishable, so it's best to get it into the sauté pan within a day of purchase. The pholiote's odd name stems from its French provenance. It is cultivated, and may be found through mail-order sources (see page 324) or at specialty markets year round. The season for the wild pholiote is summer.

Pig Ear (*Gomphus clavatus*): The pinkish-brown gills and flesh of the pig ear undoubtedly gave it its cuddly name. The wavy yellow cap is medium tex-tured, and the flavor is mildly earthy. It is in season in early fall, and makes a good addition to a wild mushroom ragout.

Mail-Order Sources

T here is a wonderful bounty of international ingredients readily available to most shoppers these days. When you need something that your local market doesn't stock, the push of a few telephone buttons or computer keys should summon them to you. Here are the mail-order sources that we like for their superb quality and customer service—including our own Marché aux Delices, of course.

FRESH, DRIED, FROZEN, AND POWDERED WILD AND EXOTIC MUSHROOMS; TRUFFLES AND TRUFFLE PRODUCTS; SEA SALT; SPECIALTY PRODUCE SUCH AS WHITE ASPARAGUS

Marché aux Delices
(888) 547-5471
www.auxdelices.com
staff@auxdelices.com

FOIE GRAS, CONFIT DE CANARD, RABBIT, GAME, AUSTRALIAN LAMB, POULTRY, DEMI-GLACE, DUCK FAT, BUFFALO

D'Artagnan
(800) 327-8246
www.dartagnan.com

TRUFFLE TREES

Garland Gourmet Mushrooms
and Truffles
(919) 732-3041

CHILE PEPPERS, CORN HUSKS, MEXICAN INGREDIENTS, AND SOME ASIAN INGREDIENTS

Kitchen/Market
(888) 468-4433

CONDIMENTS, SPICES, NUT AND OTHER FLOURS, SEAWEEDS, AND INGREDIENTS FOR EXOTIC CUISINES

The CMC Company
(800) 262-2780
www.Thecmccompany.com

SPICES, HERBS, ETHNIC CONDIMENTS

Adriana's Caravan
(800) 316-0820
adricara@aol.com
Penzeys Spices
(414) 679-7207
www.penzeys.com

GERMAN-STYLE CHARCUTERIE

Schaller & Weber
(800) 847-4115
(212) 879-3047

CHEESE

Murray's by Mail
(888) 692-4339
www.murrays_cheese@msn.com

KITCHEN EQUIPMENT, SUCH AS OYSTER MITTS

Bridge Kitchenware
(800) 274-3435
www.bridgekitchenware.com

NUTS

A. L. Bazzini Company
(800) 228-0172

SPECIFIC EXOTIC MUSHROOMS SUCH AS POMPOM BLANC™ AND CLAMSHELL™

Gormet Mushrooms, Inc.
(707) 823-1743

Conversion Table

OVEN TEMPERATURES

Fahrenheit	Gas Mark	Celsius
250	½	120
275	1	140
300	2	150
325	3	160
350	4	180
375	5	190
400	6	200
425	7	220
450	8	230
475	9	240
500	10	260

NOTE: Reduce the temperature by 20 C (68°F) for fan-assisted ovens.

APPROXIMATE EQUIVALENTS

1 stick butter = 8 tbs = 4 oz = ½ cup

1 cup all-purpose presifted flour/dried bread crumbs = 5 oz

1 cup granulated sugar = 8 oz

1 cup (packed) brown sugar = 6 oz

1 cup confectioners' sugar = 4½ oz

1 cup honey/syrup = 11 oz

1 cup grated cheese = 4 oz

1 cup dried beans = 6 oz

1 large egg = 2 oz = about ¼ cup

1 egg yolk = about 1 tbl

1 egg white = about 2 tbl

Please note that all the above conversions are approximate, but close enough to be useful when converting from one system to another.

LIQUID CONVERSIONS

US	Imperial	Metric
2 tbs	1 fl oz	30 ml
3 tbs	1½ fl oz	45 ml
¼ cup	2 fl oz	60 ml
⅓ cup	2½ fl oz	75 ml
⅓ cup + 1 tbs	3 fl oz	90 ml
⅓ cup + 2 tbs	3½ fl oz	100 ml
½ cup	4 fl oz	125 ml
⅔ cup	5 fl oz	150 ml
¾ cup	6 fl oz	175 ml
¾ cup + 2 tbs	7 fl oz	200 ml
1 cup	8 fl oz	250 ml
1 cup + 2 tbs	9 fl oz	275 ml
1¼ cups	10 fl oz	300 ml
1⅓ cups	11 fl oz	325 ml
1½ cups	12 fl oz	350 ml
1⅔ cups	13 fl oz	375 ml
1¾ cups	14 fl oz	400 ml
1¾ cups + 2 tbs	15 fl oz	450 ml
1 pint (2 cups)	16 fl oz	500 ml
2½ cups	1 pint	600 ml
3¾ cups	1½ pints	900 ml
4 cups	1¾ pints	1 liter

WEIGHT CONVERSIONS

US/UK	Metric
½ oz	15 g
1 oz	30 g
1½ oz	45 g
2 oz	60 g
2½ oz	75 g
3 oz	90 g
3½ oz	100 g
4 oz	125 g
5 oz	150 g
6 oz	175 g
7 oz	200 g
8 oz	250 g
9 oz	275 g
10 oz	300 g
11 oz	325 g
12 oz	350 g
13 oz	375 g
14 oz	400 g
15 oz	450 g
1 lb	500 g

INDEX